PORTRAITS OF AN ARTIST

A Casebook on James Joyce's A PORTRAIT OF THE ARTIST AS A YOUNG MAN

PORTRAITS OF AN ARTIST

A Casebook on James Joyce's

A PORTRAIT OF THE ARTIST AS A YOUNG MAN

WILLIAM E. MORRIS
CLIFFORD A. NAULT, JR.

OHIO UNIVERSITY

THE ODYSSEY PRESS, INC · *New York*

Preface

James Joyce's *A Portrait of the Artist as a Young Man* is one of those books—one thinks also of *Youth, Huckleberry Finn, Great Expectations,* and *Look Homeward, Angel*—which are best encountered for the first time when one is still relatively young, unformed, and uncorrupted, and this despite inevitable charges that Joyce is obscure, or dreadfully difficult, or perhaps obscene. Whatever troubles adolescence finds in Joyce's novel, they are at least partly the inventions of the sophisticated and mature; college students, these editor-teachers have found, and freshmen above all, provide a nearly ideal public for James Joyce's remarkable first novel, which speaks not only to them and about them, but in large measure speaks for them. Stephen Dedalus is their contemporary, their classmate, and his world opens worlds they willingly enter.

They are special problems, however, which are likely to be overlooked or too facilely resolved by a majority of students if the *Portrait* is simply served up raw. This is true, of course, of any literary work that finds its way into a college syllabus; still, the problems presented by Joyce are of a peculiarly Joycean nature, and of a nature peculiar to the modern novel (as distinct from many older works and contemporary novels which follow the older conventions), and they are not to be waved away by calling them common to a genre. Hence *Portraits of An Artist: A Casebook on James Joyce's "A Portrait of the Artist as a Young Man."* While it goes without saying that first, last and always it is the teacher's function to underscore such problems and translate them into terms his students can grasp, if he is anything like us he is not immune from areas of ignorance, and aids to specific works—such as this one—are always welcome. We have tried to provide not a substitute for teaching but a supplement to it.

The following collection makes no attempt to exhaust the possibly inexhaustible variety of Joyce's novel. Indeed, a casebook many times the length of this one, which included selections from the entire bibliography, could scarcely do that. On the other hand, the collection does provide expert guidance into portions of the Joycean labyrinth, and any number of threads the reader can follow to take him where they will. Rather than an end in itself, the text is intended as no more than a starting point, or, shifting the metaphor, as a skeletal frame upon which the attentive reader can and should construct his own interpretations.

Portraits of An Artist is also designed for use as a controlled-research text for the writing of documented critical papers. Each selection is thus given adequate bibliographical description for such documentation, and page references to the original publications are included. A number of questions for study, discussion, and individual investigation are provided, as are suggested topics for papers of various lengths. These are not meant to be exhaustive, and the most fruitful work will undoubtedly come from lines of interpretation the student discovers for himself.

For those who might find missing some selections they regard as "indispensable," we can only say that length and reprint permissions are battles we had to fight as best we could. We won some skirmishes and lost others. Our apologies, then, beforehand for whatever omissions seem too glaring, and our special thanks to Mr. Marshall Best of the Viking Press and Joyce scholars and permissions editors everywhere for whatever virtues our compilation does contain. For their aid in preparing manuscript, thanks to Misses Christina Wetz and Lucretia Aurand, our undergraduate assistants at Ohio University. We wish also to thank Miss Catherine Nelson and the staff of the Ohio University library, and our wives and children for as much forbearance as they could bear.

W. E. M.
C. A. N. Jr.

A Note on Using the Text

Portraits of An Artist is to be used, of course, in conjunction with James Joyce's first novel, *A Portrait of the Artist as a Young Man.* Two excellent and inexpensive editions of the novel are readily available: *A Portrait of the Artist as a Young Man* (Compass Book C9; New York: The Viking Press, 1956) and *The Portable James Joyce,* edited, with an introduction and notes, by Professor Harry Levin of Harvard (New York: The Viking Press, 1947). The latter volume also includes *Dubliners, Exiles,* Joyce's poems, and passages from *Ulysses* and *Finnegans Wake.*

The selections in *Portraits of An Artist* are reprinted, in whole or in part, precisely as they originally appeared in print (less footnotes in some instances, where the editors did not believe the documentation relevant to the issues at hand; minor changes have also been made in two instances, at the authors' request—we have noted these where they occur). The precise page ending of each page of each source has been marked in the text by the page number in slashes (thus /416/ and /417/ in the case of the Garnett report in Part II) at the end of the last word of the particular page. Article titles in brackets have been supplied by the editors; all other titles are those of the originals. Full bibliographical details for each selection appear at the foot of its first page, as well as in the bibliography. Thus it is possible to cite the original source when discussing or writing about the selections, or when quoting. The forms used are, in the main, those recommended by the Modern Language Association.

Part VII offers suggestions for discussing and/or writing about the novel and the printed interpretations of it. These are divided as follows (1) those dealing specifically with the reprinted selection; (2) those dealing with the reprinted selections in one combination or another; and (3) those dealing with matters embracing the whole of the collection and some matters outside the criticism printed herein. Finally, there is a 100-entry checklist of criticism on the *Portrait* and *Stephen Hero.*

Acknowledgments

We wish to acknowledge with thanks the following permissions to reprint materials in this book:

C. G. Anderson, for "The Sacrificial Butter," *Accent*, XII (Winter 1952), 3-13.

The Western Humanities Review, for James R. Baker, "James Joyce: Esthetic Freedom and Dramatic Art," *Western Humanities Review*, V (Winter 1950-1951), 29-40.

The Johns Hopkins Press, for Elizabeth F. Boyd, "Joyce's Hell-Fire Sermons," *Modern Language Notes*, LXXV (November 1960), 561-571. And for Julian B. Kaye, "Who is Betty Byrne?" *Modern Language Notes*, LXXI (February 1959), 93-95.

The Sewanee Review and Mrs. Irene H. Chayes, for "Joyce's Epiphanies," From *The Sewanee* Review, Summer, 1946. Copyright 1946 by *The University of the South*. And *The Sewanee Review* and Mr. Ellsworth Mason, for "Joyce's Categories," From *The Sewanee Review*, Summer, 1953. Copyright 1953 by *The University of the South*.

The Croessman Collection of James Joyce, Southern Illinois University Library, for the photograph of Clancy, Byrne, and Joyce.

Richard Ellmann, for "A Chronology of the Life of James Joyce," in Stuart Gilbert, ed., *Letters of James Joyce,* Viking Press, 1957.

Oxford University Press, Inc., for the selections from Richard Ellmann, *James Joyce,* Oxford University Press, 1959.

Rudd Fleming and *The University of Kansas City Review*, for "Quidditas in the Tragi-Comedy of Joyce," *UKCR*, XV, 4 (Summer 1949), 288-296.

Yale University Press, for the selection from Melvin Friedman, *Stream of Consciousness: A Study in Literary Method*, Yale University Press, 1955. And for the selection from William T. Noon, S.J., *Joyce and Aquinas*. Yale University Press, 1957.

University of Oklahoma Press, for the selection from William Powell Jones, *James Joyce and the Common Reader*, University of Oklahoma Press, 1955.

The Viking Press, Inc., for James Joyce's limerick for Ezra Pound, from *The Letters of James Joyce*, edited by Stuart Gilbert. By permission of The Viking Press, Inc. And for permission to reprint passages from *A Portrait of the Artist as a Young Man*.

New Directions, for the selections from the introduction and text of James Joyce, *Stephen Hero*, edited by Theodore Spencer, John J. Slocum and

Herbert Cahoon, Copyright © 1944, 1955 by New Directions, Publishers. And for the selection from Harry Levin, *James Joyce: A Critical Introduction,* Copyright © 1941, 1960 by New Directions. Reprinted by permission of New Directions, Publishers.

John V. Kelleher, for "The Perceptions of James Joyce," *The Atlantic Monthly,* CCI (March 1958), 82, 84, 86, 88, 90.

Indiana University Press, for the selection from Hugh Kenner, *Dublin's Joyce,* Indiana University Press, 1956.

The Journal of Aesthetics and Art Criticism, for Shiv K. Kumar, "Bergson and Stephen Dedalus' Aesthetic Theory," *JAAC,* XVI (September 1957), 124-127.

New York University Press, for the selections from Marvin Magalaner and Richard M. Kain, *Joyce: The Man, the Work, the Reputation,* New York University Press, 1956.

Joseph Prescott and The Modern Language Association of America, for "James Joyce: A Study in Words," *PMLA,* LIV (March 1939), 304-307.

Purdue Research Foundation and *Modern Fiction Studies,* for Grant H. Redford, "The Role of Structure in Joyce's 'Portrait,'" *Modern Fiction Studies,* IV (Spring 1958), 21-30.

Oscar A. Silverman and The Libraries of the University of Buffalo, for page six of *James Joyce Epiphanies,* introduction and notes by O. A. Silverman, Lockwood Memorial Library, University of Buffalo, 1956.

Columbia University Press, for the selections from Kevin Sullivan, *Joyce Among the Jesuits,* Columbia University Press, 1958. And for the selection from William York Tindall, *The Literary Symbol,* Columbia University Press, 1955.

Holt, Rinehart and Winston, Inc., for the selection from Dorothy Van Ghent, *THE ENGLISH NOVEL: Form and Function,* Copyright © 1953, by Dorothy Van Ghent. Reprinted by permission of the publishers, Holt, Rinehart and Winston, Inc.

The National Council of Teachers of English, for Eugene M. Waith, "The Calling of Stephen Dedalus," *College English,* XVIII (February 1957), 256-261.

Contents

PART I

SOME PRELIMINARY CONSIDERATIONS

The Joyce Enigma

RICHARD M. KAIN

The discovery of Joyce is an unending quest. Though he may feel bewildered or exasperated by the obscurity of the text, the sensitive reader immediately notes a strange power, akin to that of great poetry. The hypnotic magic of the style and the widening implications of the story suggest the presence of genius. Here is a writer who must be heeded. This awareness deepens with each rereading. Image and symbol haunt the memory; themes provide endless opportunity for speculation. For in the work of Joyce dream opposes reality and the inner life of the mind is juxtaposed against the external world. Man exists in present and past alike, and even as he enacts his own drama he relives that of mythical forebears.

Whatever be the final judgment, this work is obviously the product of a sensibility complex and original. The labyrinth was the author's own symbol of his technical cunning, for it was the creation of the mythological Daedalus, whose name Joyce adopted for his quasi-autobiographical artist. Rather than Shakespeare's figure of art as a mirror held up to nature, or Stendhal's modification of it in his definition of the novel as a mirror that travels along a highway, one may suggest the best image for Joyce's art to be that of a many-faceted prism, catching half-lights and projecting magnified distortions. As the young Stephen Dedalus reflects on the nature of language during one of his meditative rambles in the *Portrait,* he uses prism and mirror as contrasting metaphors, the prism for "a language many-coloured and richly storied" and the mirror for "a lucid supple periodic prose." /3/

Marvin Magalaner and Richard M. Kain, *Joyce: The Man, the Work, the Reputation* (New York: New York University Press, 1956), p. 3.

A Chronology of the Life
of James Joyce

RICHARD ELLMANN

1882   On 2 February James Joyce was born at 41 Brighton Square, Rathgar, Dublin. He was the eldest son of John Stanislaus Joyce, rate collector, and Mary Jane Joyce (*née* Murray). Of the fifteen children in the family, only ten survived infancy; among these Joyce had the closest relationship with his brother Stanislaus, born 17 December 1884.

1888   The Joyce family had moved to Bray, and in September Joyce was sent to Clongowes Wood College (Jesuit), where he remained until June 1891, returning home only for holidays.

1891   Late in 1891 Joyce, fired by the death of Parnell on 6 October, wrote a verse broadside, his first printed work, with the title of *Et Tu, Healy*. It celebrated the dead hero and attacked his chief political enemy. No copy survives.

1893–98   Joyce, withdrawn from Clongowes when the family fortunes began to decline, was sent to Belvedere College, also a Jesuit school, from April 1893. He made a brilliant record, winning several prizes in the intermediate examinations.

1899–1902 Joyce's career at University College, Dublin, was marked by his break with his Catholic background and his emergence as a writer. In May 1899, he refused to join a protest gainst the heresy of Yeats's *Countess Cathleen*. On 20 January 1900 he read a paper on

Stuart Gilbert (ed.), *Letters of James Joyce* (New York: The Viking Press, 1957), pp. 43-50. One date changed at author's request.

'Drama and Life' before the Literary and Historical Society; his essay on 'Ibsen's New Drama' (*When We
Dead Awaken*) was published in the *Fortnightly Review* for April 1900; a pamphlet, 'The Day of the Rabblement', attacking the parochialism of the Irish Literary Theatre, was written on 15 October 1901; an essay
on 'James Clarence Mangan' was published in May
1902. During this period, also, he wrote a play entitled
A Brilliant Career and translated two plays of Hauptmann. /43/

After receiving his degree on 31 October 1902, Joyce
considered attending medical school in Dublin, but decided to study in Paris instead. He planned to be both
doctor and writer. Leaving Dublin in late November,
he stopped briefly in London to see W. B. Yeats, Arthur
Symons, and various editors, then proceeded to Paris.
There he quickly abandoned his medical studies, but
lived the life of a Bohemian student, fascinated by the
scene and usually its hungriest observer. Twenty-three
book reviews by him appeared in a Dublin newspaper
from 11 December 1902 to 19 November 1903.

1903   In April his mother's last illness began; on receipt of
an urgent telegram from his father, Joyce returned to
Dublin. Mary Jane Joyce died on 13 August.

1904   7 January is the date of the first draft of *Stephen
Hero,* a later version of which was published (post-
humously) in 1944.

About March Joyce obtained a position as teacher at
the Clifton School, Dalkey, where he remained until the
end of June. On 16 May he sang at the Feis Ceoil, a
music festival, but failed to win because he could not
read music at sight. About 10 June he met Nora Barnacle, and shortly thereafter, perhaps on 16 June (the day
he later chose as the date for *Ulysses*), fell in love with
her. Opposed to marriage and unable to live openly
with her in Dublin, he decided to return to the Continent. Before leaving he wrote the satirical broadside,
'The Holy Office', distributed not long after his departure on 8 October.

Upon arriving with Nora in Zurich he found that
his expected position as teacher at the Berlitz School
was not available, and proceeded to Pola (now in Yu-
goslavia) to teach English at the Berlitz School there.

During 1904 his first published poems and stories appeared.

1905   In March Joyce was transferred to the Berlitz School in Trieste.

On 27 July his son Giorgio was born.

In September his difficulties with publishers began with the rejection by Grant Richards of *Chamber Music*.

In October Stanislaus Joyce, at his brother's urging, came to live in Trieste.

At the end of November the submission of the manuscript /44/ of *Dubliners* to Grant Richards started a contentious correspondence over the book.

1906   In July Joyce, bored with Trieste, took his wife and son to Rome, where a position in a bank awaited him.

1907   On 17 January 1907 he contracted with Elkin Mathews for the publication of *Chamber Music*.

In March, Rome having proved unsatisfactory, Joyce returned to Trieste, where after a brief spell of teaching at the Berlitz School he found private lessons more profitable.

Early in May *Chamber Music* was published.

On 26 July, St Anne's Day, his daughter Lucia Anna was born.

1909   On 1 August Joyce returned to Ireland for a visit. At the beginning of September, he signed a contract for the publication of *Dubliners* by Maunsel & Co. in Dublin. On 9 September he returned to Trieste, and interested some businessmen there in starting up cinemas in Ireland. With their backing he returned to Dublin on 21 October and opened the Cinematograph Volta on 20 December.

1910   Unwilling to remain as manager, Joyce returned to Trieste in January, and the Volta was soon after sold. In July Maunsel & Co., suddenly fearful because of the candour of *Dubliners*, postponed publication of the book.

1912   From July to September Joyce made his last trip to Ireland, going to Galway as well as Dublin. He was unable to persuade Maunsel & Co. to publish *Dubliners* and the printer broke up the type. Joyce's impressions of Dublin were summarized in the broadside, 'Gas from a Burner', written on his return journey.

1913   Through Yeats's intercession Joyce was brought into communication with Ezra Pound, who interested Miss Dora Marsden, the editor of the *Egoist,* in his work.

1914 A lucky year: in January Grant Richards agreed to publish *Dubliners,* and did so on 15 June. From 2 February 1914 to 1 September 1915 *A Portrait of the Artist as a Young Man* was published (thanks to Miss Dora Marsden and subsequently to Miss Weaver, who was to become his patron) in the *Egoist* (London) in serial form. In March Joyce began work on *Ulysses,* but put it aside for a time to write *Exiles,* finished in 1915.

1915 Although his brother was interned because of the war at /45/ the beginning of 1915, Joyce was left undisturbed in Trieste by the Austrian authorities. At the end of June he was permitted to depart for Switzerland on his word of honour to remain neutral. In August, through the intercession of Pound, Edmund Gosse, and Yeats, he received a gift of money from the Royal Literary Fund.

1916 In September he received a grant from the British Treasury Fund.

On 29 December the *Portrait* was published in New York.

1917 On 12 February the *Portrait* was published in London.

Later this year Joyce received a first gift from Miss Weaver.

During this year Joyce's eye troubles grew worse and made necessary his first eye operation late in the summer. On 12 October he went to Locarno to recover in the milder climate.

1918 In January Joyce returned to Zurich. Here Mrs Harold McCormick gave him a monthly stipend to enable him to write. Temporarily in funds, he organized, with Claud W. Sykes, the English Players, whose first production, Wilde's *Importance of Being Earnest,* took place on 29 April. A quarrel with the leading actor over salary brought about two inconclusive lawsuits, the first in October 1918, the second in February 1919.

In March the *Little Review* (New York) began to publish *Ulysses* in serial form, completing half the book by the end of 1920.

On 25 May *Exiles* was published in England and the United States.

1919   Early in the autumn Mrs McCormick withdrew her
subsidy, and in October Joyce returned with his family
to Trieste. There he taught English at a commercial
school and worked hard at *Ulysses.*

1920   In June Joyce went with his son to Desenzano, Italy,
to meet Ezra Pound, who persuaded him to come to live
in Paris so as to promote the publication of his work.
The same month the Joyce family moved to Paris.

In October the Society for the Suppression of Vice
lodged a complaint against the *Little Review* in New
York for publishing certain passages of *Ulysses.*

1921   The final stages of preparing *Ulysses* for the public:
in /46/ April Joyce agreed to have Sylvia Beach publish
it in Paris. On 7 December Valery Larbaud, who had
read the manuscript, delivered a eulogistic lecture on
Ulysses, which, published in the *Nouvelle Revue Fran-
çaise* in April 1922, set the key for the critical reception.

1922   On 2 February, Joyce's birthday, *Ulysses* was published.

On 1 April Nora Joyce took the two children to Ireland to visit her mother, but was obliged to leave at
once because of the Irish civil war. In May Joyce
planned a trip to London but gave it up because of eye
trouble. He went there, however, in August, returning to
Paris in late September, then in mid-October went to
Nice, intending to winter there. Because of pressure of
affairs he returned to Paris.

1923   On 10 March Joyce wrote a first sketch for a character
in *Finnegans Wake.*

From late June to mid-August, he and his family went
to London, Bognor (on the Sussex coast), and London
again.

1924   Another year of severe eye trouble.

In April 1924 the first fragment of *Finnegans Wake*
was published in the *Transatlantic Review* (Paris).

From July to mid-August the Joyces were at St Malo
and Quimper in Brittany: they returned to Paris at the
beginning of September and late in the month went to
London for about three weeks.

1925   In July the *Criterion* (London) published a second
fragment from *Finnegans Wake.*

Late in July Joyce was at Fécamp; in August at Ar-
cachon, returning to Paris early in September.

On 1 October the *Navire d'Argent* (Paris) published *Anna Livia Plurabelle*.

1926 From late July to September at Ostend and Brussels.

1927 During 1927 Joyce, in a fit of depression over *Finnegans Wake* and his friends' comments on it, considered abandoning the book.

On 2 February an international protest against the piracy of *Ulysses* in the United States was promulgated.

From April 1927 to May 1938 sections of *Finnegans Wake* were published in *transition* (Paris) by Eugene Jolas.

In April Joyce went to London to be guest of honour at a dinner of the P.E.N. Club. He spent May and June at The Hague and Amsterdam. /47/

On 5 July *Pomes Penyeach* was published.

1928 In March Joyce went to Dieppe and Rouen; at the end of April he was in Toulon, returning in May. From July to mid-September he was at Salzburg.

On 20 October *Anna Livia Plurabelle* was published in book form. Mrs Joyce had a serious but successful operation in November, after their return to Paris.

1929 The French translation of *Ulysses* was published in February.

During July and August Joyce spent a few days in London, a month in Torquay, a few days in Bristol.

In August *Tales Told of Shem and Shaun* was published.

1930 In January Joyce began his efforts, which would last into 1934, to promote the career of John Sullivan, Irish-French tenor.

In May and June Dr Alfred Vogt began a series of eye operations on Joyce in Zurich.

In June *Haveth Childers Everywhere* was published.

During July and August Joyce was in London, then for a few days in Oxford, and then in Llandudno (Wales). In September he was briefly at Étretat, where he was involved in a motor accident.

On 10 December Giorgio Joyce and Helen Kastor Fleischmann were married.

1931 In April Joyce spent a few days at Wiesbaden; at the end of the month he gave up his Paris flat, and in May went to London. He took a flat in Kensington and furnished it, intending to set up an English domicile. On

4 July he and Nora Joyce were married at a registry office in London 'for testamentary reasons'. In September they let their London flat and returned to Paris, where they took a furnished flat for the winter.

On 29 December Joyce's father, John Stanislaus Joyce, died in Dublin at the age of 82.

1932   On 15 February a grandson, Stephen James Joyce, was born.

In March Lucia Joyce suffered a mental breakdown, the first serious indication of her schizophrenia. The Joyces had planned to go to London in April, but her violent protests broke off the trip. From July to September they were at Zurich, and made a short visit to see Lucia at Feld- /48/ kirch (Austria), where she was staying with Mrs Eugene Jolas. They then returned to Zurich and after the middle of September went on to Nice, where Lucia joined them.

During this year Paul Léon became Joyce's principal helper.

1933   In May the Joyces went to Zurich. They spent the summer at Evian (on the Lake of Geneva) to take the waters and be near Lucia who was in an institution in the neighbourhood.

On 6 December Judge John M. Woolsey issued his famous decision on *Ulysses*, ruling that it was not pornographic and making possible its American publication.

1934   In February *Ulysses* was published in New York.

During March Joyce went on a motor tour with friends to Grenoble, Zurich, and Monte Carlo. In April he went to consult Dr Vogt in Zurich.

In May 1934 Giorgio Joyce and his family went to the United States, where they remained until November 1935.

In June *The Mime of Mick Nick and the Maggies* was published.

At the end of July Joyce went to Spa, Belgium; in September he travelled to Zurich and Geneva, remaining in Zurich until the end of the year so as to be near Lucia.

1935   At the end of January Joyce returned to Paris from Zurich. In February Lucia went to London, and she spent March to July in Dublin, her mind showing increasing signs of strain. From August to December she stayed with Miss Weaver.

In September Joyce spent some days at Fontainebleau.

1936   On 26 July *A Chaucer A B C*, with initial letters by Lucia Joyce, was published as part of her father's frantic efforts to make her well.

During August and September the Joyces were in Denmark, and also visited Bonn en route.

In December *Collected Poems* was published.

1937   In August the Joyces were in Zurich, in September at Dieppe.

In October *Storiella as She Is Syung*, the last fragment of *Finnegans Wake* to appear separately in book form, was published.

1938   From August to September the Joyces were in Zurich and Lausanne. /49/

1939   On 2 February Joyce exhibited a first bound copy of *Finnegans Wake*, although the book was not officially published in England and America until 4 May.

In July the Joyces were at Étretat, in August at Berne; when war was declared they were in Zurich. Returning to France they stayed at La Baule, to be near Lucia's *maison de santé*, from September to December. In December they went to St Gérand-le-Puy, near Vichy.

1940   On 14 December the Joyces left St Gérand-le-Puy for Zurich, after elaborate negotiations for themselves and prolonged but unsuccessful efforts to enable Lucia, whose *permis de sortir* had expired meanwhile, to accompany them.

1941   Joyce died 13 January, at 2 a.m., in the Schwesterhaus vom Roten Kreuz in Zurich, as a result of a perforated ulcer. /50/

[Themes, Styles, and Episodes]

WILLIAM POWELL JONES

He not only compressed the realistic details of an adolescent's struggles against his environment, but with the compression he changed the aim, symbolized in the new title, to the spiritual evolution of a serious writer who develops a new artistic creed as he revolts against those things in his life that tied him down—his family, his religion, his country, and his fleshly desires. An analysis of *Portrait of the Artist* will show how he does this.

Chapter I.

The *theme* is the importance of childhood and early schooldays at Clongowes Wood in forming the artist. Emphasizing the keen sense impressions of the growing child, the chapter provides background for later attitudes on family, religion, and politics.

The *style* is mostly realistic for the chapter is full of incidents like those in *Dubliners,* moments that reveal the sensitive boy who listens. Yet even here there is a prophecy of the stream-of-conciousness style as the future poet is partially revealed in terms of the thoughts of the boy commenting on what he takes in through the senses. Examples of acute sense impressions are abundant: smells like the odor of his mother and father, the smell of urine on an oilsheet, the smell of peasants ("air and rain and turf and corduroy"), the coid night smell of a chapel, the smell of wine on a priest's breath at first communion; sounds, ugly like the "suck" of dirty water let out of a washbasin, beautiful like the sound of cricket bats ("pick, pack, pock, puck; like drops of water in a fountain falling softly in the brimming bowl"); touch, like that of the cold slime of a ditch or of the prefect's cold /26/ hands on his feverish brow, which reminds him of rats with sleek, slimy coats and black, shin-

William Powell Jones, *James Joyce and the Common Reader* (Norman, Oklahoma: University of Oklahoma Press, 1955) pp. 26-35.

ing eyes; sight, like the earth in geography lessons, a big green ball in maroon clouds, or like the Christmas colors of red holly and green ivy; taste, like that of the turkey and ham and celery and plum pudding of Christmas dinner. The realism is made keener, even in boyhood, by passages dominated by imagination, the stream of consciousness that becomes more prominent as the book progresses. For example, as Stephen lies feverish in bed, a ghost story becomes in his mind a vivid picture of "marshals who had received their death wound on battlefields far away over the sea." In the same infirmary episode he imagines himself being buried—the scene is full of pomp and sadness and beauty, and he wants to cry not for himself but for the beautiful, sad words of an old song. Before Stephen has recovered, he is reminded by the flickering of fire on a wall of waves that in turn call up the sorrowful face of Brother Michael addressing a multitude of people about Parnell, and that reminds him of home.

Episodes (epiphanies):
Miscellaneous impressions of Stephen's early childhood. Various scenes around school culminate in illness at the infirmary (1–26).

Realistic scene of the Christmas party at home, where the impression of prosperity and hospitality is interrupted by a frantic and vociferous quarrel between members of the household over the Church and the Irish patriot Parnell (26–41).

Series of school scenes where Stephen struggles valiantly and with partial success against the bullying of unsympathetic schoolmates and the tyranny of Jesuit discipline. The high points are /27/ two scenes in which Stephen's brutal and unfair treatment by Father Dolan is contrasted with his kindly treatment by the rector, Father Conmee. Father Arnall, gentle though strict, represents the middle ground of futile compassion (41–61).

Chapter II.

The *theme* is Stephen's change and growth through a variety of experiences: from childhood to adolescence, from Blackrock to Dublin, from Clongowes school to Belvedere, from romantic love to purchased sexual solace.

The *style* is similar to that of Chapter I but places growing emphasis on the boy's mental reactions to external happenings.

Episodes:
Nostalgic pictures of Stephen's idyllic life at the early home he is about to leave: walks with Uncle Charles and glimpses of the adult world that seems drawing near, for which he must get ready; reading romances and building from them a dream world of his

own that includes a Mercedes who is not even aware that she is his
love; adventures with a rough boy, Aubrey Mills (compare the boy's
companion of "The Encounter" in *Dubliners*). The key to this
epiphany is in the boy's brooding upon the image of Mercedes,
imagining himself transfigured as they stood alone: "Weakness and
timidity and inexperience would fall from him in that magic moment" (65–71).

Sharply realistic scenes from new life in Dublin and at Belvedere
College accentuate Stephen's disillusionment over the weakness of
his father and the unfriendly school life. The move to Dublin with
its cheerless house sends him embittered around the new city, where
he notes with vague dissatisfaction the vast /28/ variety of the city
that is from now on to be the scene of all his writing—its docks,
carts, and bales of merchandise, even the ill-dressed, bearded po-
liceman. Angry at being young and having to face the squalor of
the new world shaping up, Stephen pretends to chronicle with patience and detachment what he sees. Meanwhile, his love life progresses, for the visionary Mercedes gives way to a real girl; he wants
to kiss her, but instead goes home to write a poem in which he does
kiss her. The boys at school tease him in admiration of his prowess
with the ladies; they admire him for his ability to act and to imitate
the rector, but they do not hesitate to torment him for not confess-
ing that Byron was no good. Stephen feels happy only when he is
far from his schoolmates; he rebels against them and his family.
"Cast down by the dull phenomenon of Dublin," he spends his
spare time reading "subversive writers" who set up a ferment in his
brain. He reflects on doing many decent things, such as taking part
in the Irish national revival or working to restore the family fortunes, but he rejects these phantoms. His rebellion is symbolized at
the end of the episode by his ignoring his admiring family after a
successful theatrical performance and walking at breakneck speed
through the streets until "wounded pride and fallen hope and baffled desire" disappear, and he becomes calm again (71–96).

Vividly realistic scenes of a trip taken by Stephen and his father
to Cork where family property is to be sold at auction. Here the
family tradition of good fellowship and "manliness" is shown in
the pictures of his father's tremendous extrovert masculinity and
his grandfather's reputation with women. The reminder causes a
faint sickness in Stephen as he recalls his own position at school,
"proud and sensitive and suspicious, battling against /29/ the
squalor of his life and against the riot of his mind." The virility of
Simon Dedalus mocks the boy's "bodily weakness and futile enthusiasms." He now knows that he is separated from his father by

"an abyss of fortune or of temperament." After this realization he feels completely lost, with nothing stirring within him but a cold and loveless lust (97–108).

Stephen attempts to find "order and elegance" by spending his prize money on lavish gifts for his family, but when his money has been all spent his futile isolation becomes more apparent than ever. In the final scene of this rebellious and unhappy chapter, Stephen turns to savage physical desire as an outlet. For a moment he appears to have found peace in his surrender to a whore. (108–14).

Chapter III.

The *theme* of this chapter, sin followed by remorse, repentance, and final redemption, is in one frantic and frightening episode.

The *style*, dictated by the boy's mental agony, is dominantly that of the stream of consciousness, made more poignant by the seemingly objective reporting of two sermons that are masterpieces of emotional oratory. This long epiphany, a revelation in almost the religious sense of the word, depicts a crisis in Stephen's life. It begins with avid pursuit of the sensual pleasures to which he has yielded, prowling for a "sudden call to his sin-loving soul" from the soft, perfumed flesh of the whores. The very thought of the religious devotions which he has renounced reminds him of the lewd kisses, and the heavy burden of the sins leads him nearer in his imagination to "the refuge of sinners," the Blessed Virgin /30/ Mary. He attends a Jesuit retreat lasting three days, which is described in great detail. The sermons describe vividly the terrors of the last judgment and the horrible punishment awaiting sinners, even to the rain that, falling noiselessly, will rise until it covers the earth and chokes off all life. The final sermon reiterates the tortures of Hell, physical and spiritual, stretching out into eternity, the mere thought of which makes the brain reel dizzily. The sermon ends with an emotional call to repentence that would do credit to an evangelist. The effect of all this on the sensitive boy's imagination is overwhelming. He kneels beside his bed, trying to find a way back to grace, but in his mind he sees creatures that remind him of his foul sins of lust, "goatish creatures with human faces, horny browed . . . their long swishing tails besmeared with stale shite, thrusting upwards their terrific faces." After long agony and a restless walk through the dark streets, Stephen seeks a chapel where he can confess his sins. He walks home and sits by the fire in the kitchen, "not daring to speak for happiness." The communion breakfast of white pudding, eggs, sausages, and tea symbolizes the simplicity and beauty of life that now lies all before him.

Chapter IV.

The *theme* is that of Stephen's new life of devotion and contemplation followed by rejection of a call to the priesthood in order to take up the more complete life of the priestly writer.

The *style* is almost completely dominated by stream of consciousness, since the motivation for Stephen's decision is entirely in his own mind. This chapter, a masterpiece of interior monologue, is the high point of the book. /31/

Episodes:

In his new life Stephen strives "to undo the sinful past" by constant mortification, disciplining his senses in ways that require ingenuity; for example, the only odor distasteful to him "was a certain stale fishy stink like that of longstanding urine: and whenever it was possible he subjected himself to this unpleasant odor." He becomes very inventive at mortifying the touch, enduring every itch and pain and carrying his arms stiffly at his sides like a runner (170–78).

The director conveys to Stephen a call to the priesthood. At first he is filled with pride and elation, but, as he thinks it over, he is repelled by the passionless chilliness of the ordered life. During his walk home, he notices the disorder, misrule, and confusion that attract him more. This feeling is emphasized by finding his parents are out looking for a new house since they have been evicted again. Struck by the pain and weariness in life that are yet balanced by hope of better things, Stephen knows he has rejected the priesthood. (178–90).

This epiphany is packed with beauty and precision as the new life develops in the artist's mind. His entering the university symbolizes the break with the past and marks "the first noiseless sundering of his life from his mother's." Anticipation of his new adventure fills him with the exaltation of fitful music and triple-branching flames and wild creatures racing. It is then that Stephen realizes that what goes on in the mind is more important than what happens externally, that words mean more than things, that "the contemplation of an inner world of individual emotions" put into words is more pleasing to him than "the reflection of the glowing sensible world through the prism of a language many- /32/ coloured and richly storied." He knows that such a conception of the writer's art will involve daring experimentation, but he takes courage in thinking of Dedalus, the fabulous artificer whose name he bears, a hawk-like man flying with the wings he had invented, above the waves and slowly climbing, "a symbol of the artist forging anew in his workshop out of the sluggish matter of the earth a new soaring impalpable imperishable being."

Stephen then walks along the shore of Dublin's tidal waters, even as he does later in *Ulysses*, fashioning in his mind the subject matter of his new writings. He feels himself near the wild heart of life in the changing waters, the line of seawrack, and the endless drift of seaweed. The human element he recognizes ecstatically in a girl, the embodiment of health and beauty, the purely feminine without shame or wantonness, and in his mind he welcomes her with profane joy as part of the new life. Stephen then finds shelter in a sandy nook, where he falls asleep. A new world appears to him, a world "fantastic, dim, uncertain as under sea, traversed by cloudy shapes and beings," a world he is not fully to explore until many years later in *Finnegans Wake*. He rouses, refreshed and calm, and watches the rim of the young moon embedded in the sand and the tide flowing in fast (190–201).

Chapter V.

The *theme* is the careful development and resolving of all themes in the book as the artist meets conflicting forces, both old (family, religion, politics) and new (aesthetics, science). He resolves to live abroad and write about Ireland.

The *style* is a mixture of realism and stream of consciousness, pointing toward *Ulysses*. Two long realistic episodes describing /33/ university life are separated by a highly imaginative account of the process of poetic creation. At the end is a sort of summary of all themes in diary form.

Episodes:

The artist rejects the miseries of home life, symbolized by his mother's complaints that he has given up religion by going to the university. He finds consolation in such sensual things as dripping trees after rain and in the beauty of certain books, yet the ancient words of Aristotle and Aquinas from his aesthetics classes seem dead. Even the casual words in the streets seem to be sterile; the artist must inject new meaning into them to make them come to life. Long realistic passages reproduce faithfully the conversation of university students and faculty. Stephen has learned to banter with others and to joke in pig Latin. Lengthy discussions of science and aesthetics seem to show the futility of learning (202–54).

A reverie about a girl Stephen has met contrasts with the prosaic real girl as he encounters her in other passages, showing that to the artist the mental image is more important than the deed; "In the virgin womb of the imagination the word was made flesh." The glow of mind is even keener in the darkness before the dull, white light of dawn covers the world. As his imagination glows, the poet becomes overwhelmed with desire, and the dreamer's sexual orgasm becomes linked with the pleasing, warm flow of words: "the liquid letters of speech, symbols of the element of mystery, flowed forth over his brain" (254–63).

Realistic scenes from university life are interspersed with poetic descriptions of Stephen's thoughts. Conversations with fellow-students, especially Cranly, reveal his arguments against /34/ Irish nationalism and the Roman Catholic Church. Cranly tries to get inside Stephen's shell, but the revolt and the loneliness remain to the end. Stephen most fully characterizes himself when he tells Cranly that he will not serve what he no longer believes in, even if it means loneliness and loss of friends, and that he will try to express himself as freely and wholly as he can, using as defense the weapons of silence, exile, and cunning (263–92).

A summary of all themes is given in diary form, concisely though seemingly in no apparent order, as if the artist wished to make certain points quite clear in brief notes that resemble fragments of thought (of the catechism technique in the "Ithaca" episode of *Ulysses,* as shown on page 91 below.) Among others, the following decisions are recorded as if they were a prelude to the opening of *Ulysses:* (1) the break with his family (his mother arguing about religion, his father suggesting membership in a rowing club and the study of law); (2) the break with an unnamed girl he has been seeing; (3) the break with the Church; (4) the break with Ireland, symbolized by final resolve to be an exile; (5) the determination to be a writer, forging in the smithy of his soul the uncreated conscience of his race, symbolized by the allusion to the ancient Dedalus in the final entry: "Old father, old artificer, stand me now and ever in good stead" (292–99). /35/

PART II

IMPACT

[Rejection by a Publisher's Reader]

EDWARD GARNETT

James Joyce's 'Portrait of the Artist as a Young Man' wants going through carefully from start to finish. There are many 'longueurs.' Passages which, though the publisher's reader may find them entertaining, will be tedious to the ordinary man among the reading public. That public will call the book, as it stands at present, realistic, unprepossessing, unattractive. We call it ably written. The picture is 'curious,' it arouses interest and attention. But the author must revise it and let us see it again. It is too discursive, formless, unrestrained, and ugly things, ugly words, are too prominent; indeed at times they seem to be shoved in one's face, on purpose, unnecessarily. The point of view will be voted 'a little sordid.' The picture of life is good; the period well brought to the reader's eye, and the types and characters are well drawn, but it is too 'unconventional.' This would stand against it in normal times. At the present time, though the old conventions are in the background, we can only see a chance for it if it is pulled into shape and made more definite.

In the earlier portion of the MS. as submitted to us, a good deal of pruning can be done. Unless the author will use restraint and proportion he will not /416/ gain readers. His pen and his thoughts seem to have run away with him sometimes.

And at the end of the book there is a complete falling to bits; the pieces of writing and the thoughts are all in pieces and they fall like damp, ineffective rockets.

The author shows us he has art, strength and originality, but this MS. wants time and trouble spent on it, to make it a more finished piece of work, to shape it more carefully as the product of the craftsmanship, mind and imagination of an artist. /417/

Edward Garnett, report to the British publisher, Gerald Duckworth, quoted from a MS copy in the Slocum Collection of the Yale University Library in Richard Ellmann, *James Joyce* (New York: Oxford University Press, 1959), pp. 416-17.

[Early Reviews and Notices]

MARVIN MAGALANER

From its first appearance, the *Portrait* was recognized as a work of genius, the finest of the contemporary confessional novels. The courage of the author, his fresh style, his uncanny psychological insight, his command of dialogue marked him as the most promising novelist of his generation. In view of the timidity of the English printers, it is surprising that Joyce was so widely accepted. The book had appeared in *The Egoist* from February 16, 1914, to September 1, 1915. Miss Harriet Weaver, sponsor of Joyce and an editor of the magazine, told of the difficulties of securing an English printer.[1] The result was that after publication in New York in 1916, American sheets were bound and issued in England in 1917.

Of course there were those who lamented Joyce's addiction to the "revolting by-paths" of naturalism, though conceding his "undoubted power."[2] He seemed "unpleasantly precocious," his work "A Study in Garbage," "A Dyspeptic Portrait," the pageant "of a tortured liver," the coarseness of which mars its "uncommon beauty, descriptive power and insight"; it is "Realism Run to Seed," a "brilliant and nasty variety of pseudo-realism."[3] Yet even these opponents conceded the power and skill of the novelist. Possibly the most characteristic reaction is that of *The Irish Booklover,* which lamented the fact that "a master of a brilliant descriptive style" and one as skilled in dialogue "as any living writer" should so "jar on one's finer feelings:" /102/

Marvin Magalaner and Richard M. Kain, *Joyce: The Man, the Work, the Reputation* (New York: New York University Press, 1956), pp. 102-07, 324-25.
[1] Harriet Weaver, *The Egoist,* III (March 1, 1916), 35.
[2] *The Athenaeum,* February 1917.
[3] *Post* (Birmingham), February 21, 1917; *Everyman,* February 23, 1917; *The Freeman's Journal* (Dublin), April 7, 1917; *The Independent,* May 5, 1917; *Weekly Times* (Manchester), March 3, 1917.

Oh! the pity of it. In writing thus is he just to his fine gifts? Is it even wise, from a worldly point of view . . . ? Above all, is it Art?[4]

Few were as unperceptive as the reviewer for the *Knickerbocker Press,* who "could not tell what he was driving at" and who was so "intensely" bored as to conclude that the book "as a whole means nothing." *The Bellman* mocked it as an example of the confessional novel, wherein the hero, "moody, sensitive, pessimistic and a trifle daft . . . in a vain and tortuous search for the thing he should do, does an amazing number of things . . . he should not do—arguing, from start to finish, on all conceivable subjects." This type of novel is "no better in an Irish guise than it has been in any other."[5] Yes, it can still be as entertaining to quote the more extreme blunders now as it was for *The Egoist* editors in 1917, classifying them under such headings as DRAINS ("we feel he would be really at his best in a treatise on drains") or OPPORTUNITIES OF DUBLIN (Ernest Boyd's complaint that Joyce was blind to the better side of the city). *The Irish Booklover's* questions concerning the advisability of writing esoterically was captioned WISDOM. *The Sphere*—ADVANTAGES OF IRISH EDUCATION—had promised to find half a dozen graduates of Clongowes Wood, including Sir Arthur Conan Doyle, who have become "most conventional citizens of the Empire."[6] It is entertaining, but it perpetuates one of our most sentimental myths—that of the misunderstood genius, mocked in the marketplace.

More frequent was the recognition of genius. The Italian critic Diego Angeli, whose comments Joyce himself translated from *The Egoist,* characterized Joyce as "a new writer with a new form" and with "new aims" that make the work "the first streak of the dawn of a new art."[7] Others noted that his "extraordinary gifts," originality "almost to the extent of appearing foolish," mark Joyce as "amongst the few great masters of analytic reminiscence."[8] His originality is found to be "almost overwhelming"; the work "would give distinction to any list of contemporary fiction in any country"; particular scenes—the Christmas dinner, the sermon—are "comparable with the best in English literature."[9] The *New Statesman* found that "Nobody is surprised to find all writing London talking about this book." Joyce is "already known as a finished artist," and the dia-

[4] *The Irish Booklover,* VIII (1916), 9-10.

[5] *The Bellman,* March 3, 1917.

[6] *The Sphere,* IV, 74.

[7] Diego Angeli, *The Egoist,* February 1918. /324/

[8] Clippings from the *Herald* (Boston); *Cambrian News,* August 16, 1918; and *The Cambridge Review.*

[9] *Eastern Morning News,* February 28, 1917; *Land and Water; New Age,* July 12, 1917.

logue, descriptions, and images make the *Portrait* "the most /103/ exquisite production of the younger school" and, indeed, "the most authentic contribution to English literature" in some time.

Joyce's uncompromising sincerity was almost universally noted. The author W. N. P. Barbellion exclaimed in his diary, "James Joyce is my man . . . a writer who tells the truth about himself." He admired the "candour and verisimilitude" and added, "I wish I could discuss James Joyce with someone." Joyce's "naked truthfulness," "sincere intent" and "unconquered though ingrowing and indeterminate idealism," and "fine Irish veracity" make the work "terribly honest," "one of the most remarkable confessions outside Russian or French literature."[10]

The author's psychological vividness is no less remarkable; indeed, *Medicine and Surgery* found it the most striking of the book's many qualities. For as "a close and searching study of mental processes" it is "of surprising worth," revealing "a man's life such as you know . . . to be true." The author is "not only a writer of the first rank but an analyst of human character whose knife is dexterously handled." The surgical metaphor will recur in reviews of *Ulysses*; it gives rise to a debate that still continues. J. C. Squire rather inconsistently accused him of an olfactory preoccupation—he "can never resist a dunghill"—and yet found his detachment "almost inhuman." A more reasonable resolution of the inconsistency was that of *The Irish Times*, which suspected that "undoubtedly a personal animus" lay "behind the author's ostentatious detachment." The fact that the tone is "so uniformly depressing" makes one doubtful of the book's veracity, but Stephen is a type "unfortunately common to Dublin," and the book's value lies in its "extraordinary power in presenting a real problem." In his taste for the unpleasant, Joyce has an "almost Russian naïveté." Even Zola, with his "keen pig's nose," only registered nasty smells, but Stephen actually liked them, *The Dublin Review* noted.[11] H. G. Wells also found "a cloacal obsession," though it did not prevent him from praising the work. It is Wells's phrase, incidentally, that Joyce answers in *Ulysses*, where Professor MacHugh links Roman and English imperialism in that they bring to every conquered shore sanitary conveniences.[12]

Joyce's break with the church came in for its share of attention. *The Catholic World* found occasion to moralize on the hero's apos-

[10] W. N. P. Barbellion, *A Last Diary* (London: Chatto and Windus, 1920), pp. 35, 92-93, 95; see also *Gazette* (Birmingham), March 29, 1917; *The Nation*, CIV, 403; *The English Review*, XXIV, 478; *The Irish World*, March 15, 1919.

[11] J. C. Squire, *The Dublin Review*, CLXVI, 137; *Irish Times*, April 14, 1917.

[12] H. G. Wells, *New Republic*, X (March 10, 1917), 158.

/104/ tasy, though it granted the book's vividness. The "irresistible effect of sharp, first-hand reality" is acknowledged. The hero himself is an enigma, with the main contrast that of a "manner of self-sufficiency and cold acuteness" joined to a basic "irrationality of motive." Stephen's self-love finally leads to a paradoxical conclusion, causing "this apostle of self to speak of finding freedom when he has left truth at home."[13] The indictment is not so unsympathetic as it might seem. Joyce later called Frank Budgen's attention to his own ironical treatment of Stephen: "Some people . . . forget that it is called *A Portrait of the Artist as a Young Man.*"

Most early readers took Stephen's troubles seriously and identified him with the author as a "man of a soul," possessing, as Ernest Boyd wrote, "an uncontrolled horror and detestation of the circumstances which moulded and governed his life." His idealism is "unconquered though ingrowing and indeterminate"; he is, in the words of the *Manchester Guardian,* a "Sensitivist," who, though helpless, is "keenly concerned for intellectual experience and for a faith" and who is unique among modern heroes in having "a genuine sense of sin." Though supine, Stephen carries within himself the possibility of conquering his weaknesses, in which case a man and an artist would emerge "from the lounger."[14]

Francis Hackett and Ernest Boyd approached the novel from their own experience of Irish life. To Hackett its significance was in disposing of the myth of Irish wit and irresponsibility and in revealing "the inevitable malaise of serious youth" with "tenacious fidelity." Boyd termed it "the chronicle of a soul stifled by material and intellectual squalor" but thought it unfair to the finer aspects of Dublin life. For the problem is basically that of the lower middle-class Catholic:

Culture for him is represented by the pedantries of mediaeval metaphysics, religion by his dread of hell. Left to drift abjectly between these extremes Stephen Dedalus disintegrates . . . .

American readers likewise felt it a valuable portrait of the true Irishman, "proud, critical, idealistic, hating everything English" or, as another reader put it, "strange, proud, imperious, secret, and subtle-minded."[15] Joyce's Dubliners are "people under a blight,"

[13] *The Catholic World,* CV (June 1917), 395-97.
[14] *Guardian* (Manchester), March 3, 1917; *The English Review,* XXIV, 278; *The Nation,* CIV, 403; *New Ireland,* March 3, 1917.
[15] Francis Hackett, *New Republic,* X (1917), 138; Ernest Boyd, *New Ireland,* March 3, 1917; *Evening Post* (Chicago), March 30, 1917; *Literary Review,* December 17, 1921.

having "something of the frowsiness, the shabbiness, the dirtiness of /105/ Dublin"; the same critic had "never seen a religion so unspiritually presented":

The author knows the theology but if there's any soul in it I cannot discover it.[16]

James Gibbons Huneker saw Joyce's affinities with Chekhov, Maupassant, and Huysmans but found him "an Irishman, who sees the shining vision in the sky." Yet he is "too Irish to be liked by the Irish."[17] Though chary of direct expression, Joyce reveals "the greatest contempt for a social organization which permits so much vileness to flourish"; he explains "how we breed and develop our Stephen Dedaluses, providing them with everything they crave, except the means of escape from the slime which envelops them." The book is "redolent of the ooze of our shabby respectability, with its intolerable tolerance" of such conditions. H. G. Wells found it to be "the most living and convincing picture . . . of an Irish Catholic upbringing," whereas Padraic Colum saw more sensitively the essential Catholicism of Joyce's mind:

Even in the way the book is written there is something to make us think of the Church—a sense of secrecy, of words being said in a mysterious language, of solidity breaking into vision.[18]

The newness of the words, the freshness of the style caught the attention of most critics. *The Scotsman* noted Joyce's mastery of hypnotic suggestion, "a rare skill in charging simple forcible language with an uncommon weight of original feeling." Joyce has surpassed *Dubliners* in "the genius which welds naturalism, realism, and the imaginative." The prose has such mastery that "even his most casual descriptions haunt the mind." As a stylist he is almost unequaled, particularly for his sentences "with many facets, tranparent, full of meaning."[19]

Ezra Pound emphasized the authentic economy of Joyce's style, "the nearest thing to Flaubertian prose" in current English, with no padding of "pages of slosh." There is a "curiously seductive interest" in such "clear-cut and definite sentences." Even the seemingly objectionable has its aesthetic purpose:

I have yet to find in Joyce's published works a violent or malodorous

    [16] *Reedy's Mirror*, February 3, 1917.
    [17] James G. Huneker, *Unicorns* (New York: Charles Scribner's Sons, 1917), pp. 187-94.
    [18] Padraic Colum, *Pearson's Magazine*, May 1918.
    [19] *Evening Post* (Chicago), March 30, 1917; *The Freeman's Journal*, April 7, 1917; *Herald* (Glasgow), March 8, 1917.

phrase which does not justify itself not only by its verity but by the /106/ heightening of some opposite effect, by the poignancy which it imparts to some emotion or to some thwarted desire for beauty.[20]

Joyce, "the best prose writer of my decade," joined Wyndham Lewis and Eliot in making "the most important contribution to English literature of the past three years," indeed, as author of one of the few works that show creative invention.[21]

In Mencken's characteristically trenchant words, "a Joyce cult now threatens," following the rage for Dunsany. The Irish have contributed to the stodginess of English literature "a gypsy touch, a rustic wildness, a sort of innocent goatishness." One of the first to remark the music of the Anglo-Irish idiom, Mencken found that any page of Synge or Dunsany shows "how they have retaught the tone-deaf Sassenach how to write *pour le respiration et pour l'oreille*." The magic of their imagination is seen in the contrast between Dunsany, where "A deer cavorts in the forest, a horn winds, it is the springtime of the world," and Phillpotts, who "suggests a cow munching alfalfa in a stall." The *Portrait*, "sure in its effect and original in its method," is "new both in plan and in detail."[22] /107/

[20] Ezra Pound, *The Future*, May 1918.

[21] Margaret Anderson, ed., *"The Little Review" Anthology* (New York: Hermitage House, 1953), reference to CXXXI, 101.

[22] H. L. Mencken, *Smart Set*, LII (August 1917). /325/

PART III

SOME READINGS

[Joyce's *Portrait*]

HARRY LEVIN

The history of the realistic novel shows that fiction tends toward autobiography. The increasing demands for social and psychological detail that are made upon the novelist can only be satisfied out of his own experience. The forces which make him an outsider focus his observation upon himself. He becomes his own hero, and begins to crowd his other characters into the background. The background takes on a new importance for its influence on his own character. The theme of his novel is the formation of character; its habitual pattern is that of apprenticeship or education; and it falls into that category which has been distinguished, by German criticism at least, as the *Bildungsroman*. The novel of development, when it confines itself to the professional sphere of the novelist, becomes a novel of the artist, a *Künstlerroman*. Goethe's *Wilhelm Meister*, Stendhal's *Vie d'Henri Brulard*, and Butler's *Way of All Flesh* amply suggest the potentialities of the form. /41/

The *Künstlerroman* offered a tentative solution to the dilemma of Joyce's generation, by enabling writers to apply the methods of realism to the subject of art. It enabled Marcel Proust to communicate experience more fully and subtly than had been done before, because it was his own experience that he was communicating, and because he was an artist to his finger-tips. *A la recherche du temps perdu* has been described as a novel that was written to explain why it was written. But, having come to be written, it offers other novelists little stimulus toward self-portraiture. It is singularly fitting that *Ulysses* should have appeared in the year of Proust's death. The perverse logic of André Gide can still present, in his *Journal des faux-monnayeurs,* the diary of a novelist who is writing a novel about a novelist who is keeping a diary about the novel he is writ-

Harry Levin, *James Joyce: A Critical Introduction* (Norfolk: New Directions, 1941), pp. 41-62.

31

ing. Of course, the *Künstlerroman* has no logical limit; but, like the
label on the box of Quaker Oats, it has a vanishing-point. Already
it is beginning to look as old-fashioned as Murger's *Vie de Bohême*.

The *Künstlerroman*, though it reverses the more normal proce-
dure of applying the methods of art to the subject of reality, is the
only conception of the novel that is specialized enough to include
A Portrait of the Artist as a Young Man. In 1913, the year before
Joyce finished his book, D. H. Lawrence had published his own portrait of the artist, *Sons and Lovers.* Both books convey the claustral
sense of a young intelligence swaddled in convention and con-
stricted by poverty, and the intensity of its first responses to esthetic
experience and life at large. The extent to which Lawrence warms
to his theme /42/ is the measure of Joyce's reserve. Characteristically, they may be reacting from the very different institutions behind them—evangelical English protestantism and Irish Catholic
orthodoxy—when Lawrence dwells on the attractions of life, and
Joyce on its repulsions. The respective mothers of the two artists
play a similar role, yet May Dedalus is a wraith beside the full-
bodied realization of Mrs. Morel. The characters in *Sons and Lovers* seem to enjoy an independent existence; in the *Portrait of the
Artist* they figure mainly in the hero's reveries and resentments.
Joyce's treatment of childhood is unrelieved in its sadness: endless
generations of choirs of children sounded, for Stephen Dedalus, the
same note of pain and weariness that Newman had heard in Vergil.
"All seemed weary of life even before entering upon it."

The attitude of the novelist toward his subject is one of the critical questions considered by Joyce's subject. Stephen expounds his
own esthetic theory, which he designates as "applied Aquinas," during a walk in the rain with his irreverent friend, Lynch. *Solvitur
ambulando.* It should be noted that the principal action of the
Portrait of the Artist, whether in conversation or revery, is walking.
The lingering images of *Dubliners* are those of people—often children—in the streets. And it was reserved for Joyce to turn the wanderings of Ulysses into a peripatetic pilgrimage through Dublin.
He was, in that respect, a good Aristotelian. But he added a personal touch to the critical theory of Aristotle and Aquinas, when he
based the distinction between the various literary forms on the relation of the artist to his material. In the lyric, it is immediate; in
the epic, the artist presents his mate- /43/ rial "in mediate relation
to himself and others"; in drama, it is presented in immediate relation to others.

The lyrical form is in fact the simplest verbal vesture of an instant of
emotion, a rhythmical cry such as ages ago cheered on the man who pulled

at the oar or dragged stones up a slope. He who utters it is more conscious of the instant of emotion than of himself as feeling emotion. The simplest epical form is seen emerging out of lyrical literature when the artist prolongs and broods upon himself as the centre of an epical event and this form progresses till the centre of emotional gravity is equidistant from the artist himself and from others. The narrative is no longer purely personal. The personality of the artist passes into the narration itself, flowing round and round the persons and the action like a vital sea. This progress you will see easily in that old English ballad *Turpin Hero,* which begins in the first person and ends in the third person. The dramatic form is reached when the vitality which has flowed and eddied round each person fills every person with such vital force that he or she assumes a proper and intangible esthetic life. The personality of the artist, at first a cry or a cadence or a mood and then a fluid and lambent narrative, finally refines itself out of existence, impersonalizes itself, so to speak. The esthetic image in the dramatic form is life purified in and reprojected from the human imagination. The mystery of esthetic like that of material creation is accomplished. The artist, like the God of the creation, remains within or behind or beyond or above his handiwork, invisible, refined out of existence, indifferent, paring his fingernails.

This progress you will see easily in the succession of Joyce's works. The cry becomes a cadence in *Chamber Music;* the mood becomes a *nuance* in *Dubliners.* If *Exiles* is unsuccessful, it is because the epiphany is not manifest to others; the artist has failed to objectify the relations of his characters with each other or with the /44/ audience. The narrative of the *Portrait of the Artist* has scarcely emerged from the lyrical stage. Whereas *Dubliners* began in the first person and ended in the third, the *Portrait of the Artist* takes us back from an impersonal opening to the notes of the author at the end. The personality of the artist, prolonging and brooding upon itself, has not yet passed into the narration. The shift from the personal to the epic will come with *Ulysses,* and the center of emotional gravity will be equidistant from the artist himself and from others. And with *Finnegans Wake,* the artist will have retired within or behind, above or beyond his handiwork, refined out of existence.

Except for the thin incognito of its characters, the *Portrait of the Artist* is based on a literal transcript of the first twenty years of Joyce's life. If anything, it is more candid than other autobiographies. It is distinguished from them by its emphasis on the emotional and intellectual adventures of its protagonist. If we can trust the dates at the end of the book, Joyce started to write in Dublin during 1904, and continued to rewrite until 1914 in Trieste. There is reason to believe that he had accumulated almost a thousand pages—

and brought Stephen to the point of departure for Paris—when the
idea of *Ulysses* struck him, and he decided to reserve those further
adventures for the sequel. His provisional title, *Stephen Hero,* with
its echo of the ballad of Dick Turpin, marks the book as an early
point in his stages of artistic impersonality. As the hero of a pedagogical novel, Stephen is significantly baptized. Saint Stephen Proto-
martyr was patron of the green on which University College was lo-
cated, and therefore of the magazine with /45/ which Joyce had
had his earliest literary misadventures.

Stephen is ever susceptible to the magic of names—particularly
of his own last name. Names and words, copybook phrases and
schoolboy slang, echoes and jingles, speeches and sermons float
through his mind and enrich the restricted realism of the context.
His own name is the wedge by which symbolism enters the book.
One day he penetrates its secret. Brooding on the prefect of studies,
who made him repeat the unfamiliar syllables of "Dedalus," he tells
himself that it is a better name than Dolan. He hears it shouted
across the surf by some friends in swimming, and the strangeness
of the sound is for him a prophecy: "Now, at the name of the fabulous artificer, he seemed to hear the noise of dim waves and to see
a winged form flying above the waves and slowly climbing the air.
What did it mean? Was it a quaint device opening a page of some
medieval book of prophecies and symbols, a hawklike man flying
sunward above the sea, a prophecy of the end he had been born to
serve and had been following through the mists of childhood and
boyhood, a symbol of the artist forging anew in his workshop out
of the sluggish matter of the earth a new soaring impalpable imperishable being?"

The *Portrait of the Artist,* as we have it, is the result of an extended process of revision and refinement. The original version—if
an *Ur-Portrait* can be remotely discerned—must have been securely
founded upon the bedrock of naturalistic narrative. It must have
been a human document, virtually a diary, to which Joyce con-
fided his notions and reactions not very long after they occurred. In
turning from a reproductive to a selective method, he /46/ has fore-
shortened his work. A fragmentary manuscript, now in the Harvard
College Library, touches only the period covered by the last chapter of the printed book, and yet it is nearly as long as the book itself.
What is obliquely implied in the final version is explicitly stated
in this early draft. The economic situation, for example, as the
Dedalus household declines from the genteel to the shabby, is at-
tested by a series of moving vans. In the book there is just one such
episode, when Stephen arrives home to hear from his brothers and

sisters that the family is looking for another house. Even then the news is not put in plain English, but in evasive pig-Latin. And the book leaves us with only the vaguest impression of the brothers and sisters; Stephen himself is not sure how many there are.

With revision, the other characters seem to have retreated into the background. Stephen's mother, because of the tension between her love and his disbelief, should be the most poignant figure in the book, just as her memory is the most unforgettable thing in *Ulysses*. But the actual conflict is not dramatized; it is coldly analyzed by Stephen in the course of one of his interminable walks and talks —this time with the serious-minded Cranly. In the manuscript it gives rise to a powerful scene, on the death of Stephen's sister, when his mother's orthodox piety is humbled before the mysteries of the body. The heroine of the book has been refined out of existence; she survives only in veiled allusions and the initials E——C——. Emma Clery, in the manuscript, is an enthusiastic young lady with whom Stephen attends a Gaelic class. Their prolonged and pallid romance comes to an /47/ unexpected climax when he sees her mackintosh flashing across the green, and abruptly leaves his lesson to confront her with the proposal that they spend the night together and say farewell in the morning. Her reaction explains the interview so cryptically reported in the book, when Stephen turns on the "spiritual-heroic refrigerating apparatus, invented and patented in all countries by Dante Alighieri."

The esthetic theory plays a more active part in the earlier version. Instead of being dogmatically expounded to Lynch, it is sounded in the debating society, where it occasions a bitter argument. As Joyce rewrote his book he seems to have transferred the scene of action from the social to the psychological sphere. As he recollected his "conflicts with orthodoxy" in the comparative tranquility of exile, he came to the conclusion that the actual struggles had taken place within the mind of Stephen. Discussions gave way to meditations, and scenes were replaced by *tableaux*. Evasion and indirection were ingrained in Joyce's narrative technique. The final effect is that which Shakespearean actors achieve by cutting out all the scenes in *Hamlet* where the hero does not appear. The continuity of dynastic feuds and international issues is obscured by the morbid atmosphere of introspection. Drama has retired before soliloquy.

The Stephen we finally meet is more sharply differentiated from his environment than the figure Joyce set out to describe. How can he be a poet—the other boys have asked him—and not wear long hair? The richness of his inner experience is continually played off against the grim reality of his external surroundings. He is trying "to /48/ build a breakwater of order and elegance against the sordid tide of life without him." He is marked by the aureole of the romantic hero, like Thomas Mann's outsiders, pressing their noses against the window panes of a bourgeois society from which they feel excluded. "To merge his life in the common tide of other lives was harder for him than any fasting or prayer, and it was his constant failure to do this to his own satisfaction which caused in his soul at last a sensation of spiritual dryness together with a growth of doubts and scruples." At school he takes an equivocal position, "a free boy, a leader afraid of his own authority, proud and sensitive and suspicious, battling against the squalor of his life and against the riot of his mind." At home he feels "his own futile isolation." He feels that he is scarcely of the same blood as his mother and brother and sister, but stands to them "rather in the mystical kinship of fosterage, foster child and foster brother."

Joyce's prose is the register of this intellectual and emotional cleavage. It preserves the contrast between his rather lush verse and his rather dry criticism, between the pathetic children and the ironic politicians of *Dubliners*. All his sensibility is reserved for himself; his attitude toward others is consistently caustic. The claims to objectivity of a subjective novel, however, must be based on its rendering of intimate experience. If Joyce's treatment of Stephen is true to himself, we have no right to interpose any other criteria. Mr. Eliot has made the plausible suggestion that Joyce's two masters in prose were Newman and Pater. Their alternating influence would account for the oscillations of style in the *Portrait /49/ of the Artist*. The sustaining tone, which it adopts toward the outside world, is that of precise and mordant description. Interpolated, at strategic points in Stephen's development, are a number of purple passages that have faded considerably.

Joyce's own contribution to English prose is to provide a more fluid medium for refracting sensations and impressions through the author's mind—to facilitate the transition from photographic realism to esthetic impressionism. In the introductory pages of the *Portrait of the Artist*, the reader is faced with nothing less than the primary impact of life itself, a presentational continuum of the tastes and smells and sights and sounds of earliest infancy. Emotion is integrated, from first to last, by words. Feelings, as they filter through Stephen's sensory apparatus, become associated with phrases. His conditioned reflexes are literary. In one of the later dialogues of the book, he is comparing his theory to a trimmed lamp. The dean of studies, taking up the metaphor, mentions the lamp of Epictetus, and Stephen's reply is a further allusion to the stoic doctrine that the soul is like a bucketful of water. In his mind this far-fetched chain of literary associations becomes attached to the sense impressions of the moment: "A smell of molten tallow came up from the dean's candle butts and fused itself in Stephen's consciousness with the jingle of the words, bucket and lamp and lamp and bucket."

This is the state of mind that confers upon language a magical potency. It exalts the habit of verbal association into a principle for the arrangement of experience. You gain power over a thing by naming it; you become mas- /50/ ter of a situation by putting it into words. It is psychological need, and not hyperfastidious taste, that goads the writer on to search for the *mot juste*, to loot the thesaurus. Stephen, in the more explicit manuscript, finds a treasurehouse in Skeat's *Etymological Dictionary*. The crucial moment of the book, which leads to the revelation of his name and calling, is a moment he tries to make his own by drawing forth a phrase of his treasure:

—A day of dappled seaborne clouds.—

The phrase and the day and the scene harmonised in a chord. Words. Was it their colours? He allowed them to glow and fade, hue after hue: sunrise gold, the russet and green of apple orchards, azure of waves, the greyfringed fleece of clouds. No, it was not their colours: it was the poise and balance of the period itself. Did he then love the rhythmic rise and fall of words better than their associations of legend and colour? Or was it that, being as weak of sight as he was shy of mind, he drew less pleasure from the reflection of the glowing sensible world through the prism of a language manycoloured and richly storied than from the contemplation of an inner world of individual emotions mirrored perfectly in a lucid supple periodic prose.

The strength and weakness of his style, by Joyce's own diagnosis, are those of his mind and body. A few pages later he offers a cogent illustration, when Stephen dips self-consciously into his word-hoard for suitable epithets to describe a girl who is wading along the beach. We are given a paragraph of word-painting which is not easy to visualize. "Her bosom was as a bird's, soft and slight, slight and soft as the breast of some dark-plumaged dove," it concludes. "But her long fair hair was /51/ girlish: and girlish, and touched with the wonder of mortal beauty, her face." This is incantation, and not description. Joyce is thinking in rhythms rather than metaphors. Specification of the bird appeals to the sense of touch rather than to the sense of sight. What is said about the hair and face is intended to produce an effect without presenting a picture. The most striking effects in Joyce's imagery are those of coldness, whiteness, and dampness, like the bodies of the bathers who shout Stephen's name.

The most vital element in Joyce's writing, in the *Portrait of the Artist* as in *Dubliners,* is his use of conversation. As a reporter of Irish life, for all his reservations, Joyce is a faithful and appreciative listener. It is a tribute to Stephen's ear that, in spite of the antagonism between father and son, Simon Dedalus is such a ripe and congenial character. Like Sean O'Casey's *Paycock,* with all his amiable failings, he is Ireland itself. Though he takes pride in showing Cork to Stephen, and in showing off his son to his own native city, he is really the embodiment of Dublin: "A medical student, an oarsman, a tenor, an amateur actor, a shouting politician, a small landlord, a small investor, a drinker, a good fellow, a storyteller, somebody's secretary, something in a distillery, a tax-gatherer, a bankrupt and at present a praiser of his own past." The improvident worldliness of John Stanislaus Joyce had made him, in the unforgiving eyes of his son, a foster-parent. So young Charles Dickens, hastening from the blacking-factory to the Marshallsea, came to look upon his father as a horrible example of good-fellowship, a Mr. Micawber. /52/

This disorder, "the misrule and confusion of his father's house," comes to stand in Stephen's mind for the plight of Ireland. Like Synge's *Playboy,* he must go through the motions of parricide to make good his revolt. Religion and politics, to his adult perception, are among the intimations of early childhood: harsh words and bitter arguments that spoil the taste of the Christmas turkey. Again, as in "Ivy Day in the Committee Room," or in Lennox Robinson's *Lost Leader* on the stage, it is the ghost of Parnell that turns conversation into drama. "Dante," the devout Mrs. Riordan, is true to the Catholic Church in denouncing the disgraced nationalist leader. Mr. Casey, the guest of honor, is of the anti-clerical faction. Mr. Dedalus is by no means a neutral, and some of his mellowest profanity is enlisted in the cause of his dead hero. Mrs. Dedalus softly rebukes him:

—Really, Simon, you should not speak that way before Stephen. It's not right.

—O, he'll remember all this when he grows up, said Dante hotly—the language he heard against God and religion and priests in his own home.

—Let him remember too, cried Mr Casey to her from across the table, the language with which the priests and the priests' pawns broke Parnell's heart and hounded him into his grave. Let him remember that too when he grows up.

The *Portrait of the Artist,* as Joyce's remembrance finally shaped it, is a volume of three hundred pages, symmetrically constructed around three undramatic climaxes, intimate crises of Stephen's

youth. The first hundred pages, in two chapters, trace the awakening of reli- /53/ gious doubts and sexual instincts, leading up to
Stephen's carnal sin at the age of sixteen. The central portion, in
two more chapters, continues the cycle of sin and repentance to the
moment of Stephen's private apocalypse. The external setting for
the education of the artist is, in the first chapter, Clongowes Wood
College; in the second, third, and fourth, Belvedere College, Dublin. The fifth and final chapter, which is twice as long as the others,
develops the theories and projects of Stephen's student days in University College, and brings him to the verge of exile. As the book
advances, it becomes less sensitive to outside impressions, and more
intent upon speculations of its own. Friends figure mainly as inter-
locutors to draw Stephen out upon various themes. Each epiphany—awakening of the body, literary vocation, farewell to Ireland—
leaves him lonelier than the last.

A trivial episode at Clongowes Wood seems fraught for Joyce
with a profoundly personal meaning. Young Stephen has been unable to get his lessons, because his glasses were broken on the play-
ing-field. Father Dolan, the prefect of studies, is unwilling to accept
this excuse, and disciplines Stephen with the boys who have shirked
their books. Smarting with pain and a sense of palpable injustice,
Stephen finally carries his case to the rector, who shows a humane
understanding of the situation. Many years later Father Conmee,
the rector, takes a walk through a chapter of *Ulysses;* and Father
Dolan—who was actually a Father Daly—pops up with his "pandybat" in Stephen's nightmare. This schoolboy incident lays down
a pattern for Joyce's later behavior. When he cabled Lloyd George,
who had other things on his /54/ mind during the first World War,
re a pair of trousers and *The Importance of Being Earnest,* he was
behaving like an aggrieved schoolboy unjustly pandied.

The physical handicap, the public humiliation, the brooding sensibility, the sense of grievance, the contempt for convention, the desire for self-justification, and· the appeal to higher authority—these
are all elements of Joyce's attitude toward society and toward himself. He had begun his education by questioning the Jesuit discipline; he would finish by repudiating the Catholic faith. Having re-
sponded to the urgent prompting of his senses, he would be treated
as a sinner; he would refer the ensuing conflict, over the head of religious authority, to the new light of his scientific and naturalistic
studies; he would seek, in the end, to create his own authority by
the light of his senses. In turning away from Ireland toward the
world at large, he would appeal from the parochial Daly to the en-
lightened Conmee. That miserable day at Clongowes Wood, like

that long evening at Combray when M. Swann's visit kept Marcel's mother downstairs, had unforeseen consequences.

Adolescence complicates the second chapter. Stephen is beginning to appreciate beauty, but as something illicit and mysterious, something apart from the common walks of life. Literature has begun to color his experience, and to stimulate his mind and his senses. His untimely enthusiasm for Lord Byron—"a heretic and immoral too"—provokes a beating at the hands of his classmates. Now in jest and again in earnest, he is forced to repeat the *confiteor*. One of his essays had been rewarded with the taunt of heresy from his English master, and he takes /55/ rueful consolation in the self-conscious part of the Byronic hero. He will not agree that Lord Tennyson is a poet, though he gives tacit consent to the assertion that Newman has the best prose style. But it is his other master, Pater, whose influence is felt at the climax of the chapter. Stephen's sexual initiation is presented in empurpled prose, as an esthetic ritual for which his literary heresies have been preparing him. In trying to find a cadence for his cry, he harks back to the lyricism of *Chamber Music* and the anguish of the small boy in *Dubliners:*

> He stretched out his arms in the street to hold fast the frail swooning form that eluded him and incited him: and the cry that he had strangled for so long in his throat issued from his lips. It broke from him like a wail of despair from a hell of sufferers and died in a wail of furious entreaty, a cry for an iniquitous abandonment, a cry which was but the echo of an obscene scrawl which he had read on the oozing wall of a urinal.

The unromantic reader is prone to feel that a scrawl would have been more adequate to the occasion. The incidence of the word "swoon" is a humorless symptom of the Pateresque influence on Joyce's early writing. There is many "A swoon of shame" in *Chamber Music,* and "a slowly swooning soul" in the last paragraph of *Dubliners.* "His soul was swooning" at the end of the fourth chapter of the *Portrait of the Artist,* having been darkened by "the swoon of sin" at the end of the second chapter. Though the scene is clouded with decadent incense, it is clear that Stephen is still a child, and that the woman plays the part of a mother. Joyce's heroes are /56/ sons and lovers at the same time; his heroines are always maternal. It is like him to lavish his romantic sensibility on an encounter with a prostitute and to reserve his acrid satire for the domain of the church. In Stephen's mind a symbolic association between art and sex is established, and that precocious revelation helps him to decide his later conflict between art and religion.

Meanwhile, the third chapter is devoted to his remorse. It embodies at formidable length a sermon on hell, suffered by Stephen and his classmates during a retreat. The eloquent Jesuit preacher takes as his object-lesson the sin of Lucifer, pride of the intellect, his great refusal and his terrible fall. Stephen's repentant imagination is harrowed by the torments of the damned. This powerful discourse provides an ethical core for the book, as Father Mapple's sermon on Jonah does for *Moby-Dick*, or Ivan's legend of the Grand Inquisitor for *The Brothers Karamazov*. Joyce is orthodox enough to go on believing in hell, and—as Professor Curtius recognized— to set up his own *Inferno* in *Ulysses*. Like another tormented apostate, Christopher Marlowe, he lives in a world where there is still suffering, but no longer the prospect of salvation. Like Blake's Milton, he is a true poet, and of the devil's party. Stephen's ultimate text is the defiance of the fallen archangel: *"Non serviam!"*

Temporarily, there is confession and absolution. When Stephen sees the eggs and sausages laid out for the communion breakfast, life seems simple and beautiful after all. For a time his restlessness seems to be tranquilized by church and satisfied by school. Seeking to order his existence, he contemplates the possibilities of the Jesuit /57/ order itself: the Reverend Stephen Dedalus, S. J. After a conference with a member of that order, he is fascinated and terrified by the awful assumption of powers which ordination involves. In the fourth chapter the call comes unexpectedly—the call to another kind of priesthood. Stephen dedicates himself to art, and enters upon his peculiar novitiate. The church would have meant order, but it would also have meant a denial of the life of the senses. A walk along the strand brings him his real vocation—an outburst of profane joy at the bird-like beauty of a girl, a realization of the fabulous artificer whose name he bears, a consciousness of the power of words to confer an order and life of their own. Like the birds that circle between the sea and the sky, his soul soars in "an ecstasy of flight," in a metaphor of sexual fulfilment and artistic creation. "To live, to err, to fall, to triumph, to recreate life out of life!"

The fifth chapter is the discursive chronicle of Stephen's rebellion. He moves among his fellow-students, an aloof and pharasaic figure, unwilling to share their indignation at the first performance of the *Countess Cathleen,* or their confidence in a petition to ensure world peace. His own struggle comes when his mother requests him to make his Easter duty and his diabolic pride of intellect asserts itself. Cranly, with the sharpest instruments of casuistry, tries to probe his stubborn refusal. It is less a question of faith than of observance. Stephen will not, to please his mother, do false homage to the sym-

bols of authority, yet he is not quite unbeliever enough to take part
in a sacrilegious communion. If he cannot accept the eucharist, he
must be anathema; he /58/ respects the forms by refusing to observe them. "I will not serve that in which I no longer believe,
whether it call itself my home, my fatherland or my church: and I
will try to express myself in some mode of life or art as freely as I
can and as wholly as I can, using for my defence the only arms
I allow myself to use, silence, exile and cunning."

With this peremptory gesture, emancipating himself from his
petty-bourgeois family, and from Ireland and Catholicism at the same
time, Stephen stands ready to take his solitary way wherever the creative life engages him. In a previous argument with other friends, he
abandoned the possibility of fighting these issues out at home. "Ireland is the old sow that eats her farrow." Davin, the nationalist, is
willing to admit that Stephen's position is thoroughly Irish, all too
typical of their gifted countrymen. "In your heart you are an Irishman but your pride is too powerful." Stephen is unwilling to compromise: "When the soul of a man is born in this country there are
nets flung at it to hold it back from flight. You talk to me of nationality, language, religion. I shall try to fly by those nets." In exile,
silence, and cunning he trusts to find substitutes for those three
forms of subjection.

On his way to and from Belvedere College, his soul was "dis-
quieted and cast down by the dull phenomenon of Dublin." With
his realization of the end he was soon to serve, a new vista of "the
slowflowing Liffey" became visible "across the timeless air." No-
madic clouds, dappled and seaborne, voyaging westward from Europe, suggested strange tongues and marshalled races. "He heard a
confused music within him as of memories and /59/ names . . ." At
University College, the time-worn texts of Ovid and Horace have
filled him with awe for the past and contempt of the present: ". . . it
wounded him to think that he would never be but a shy guest at
the feast of the world's culture and that the monkish learning, in
terms of which he was striving to forge out an esthetic philosophy,
was held no higher by the age he lived in than the subtle and curious jargons of heraldry and falconry."

English is as strange a tongue as Latin. "His language, so familiar and so foreign, will always be for me an acquired speech," Stephen reflects, while conversing with the dean of studies, an English
convert to Catholicism. "I have not made or accepted its words.
My voice holds them at bay. My soul frets in the shadow of his language." The last pages are fragments from Stephen's notebook, duly

recording his final interviews with teachers and friends, with his family and "her." Spring finds him setting down "vague words for a vague emotion," his farewell to Dublin, and to sounds of the city which will never stop echoing in his ears:

April 10. Faintly, under the heavy night, through the silence of the city which has turned from dreams to dreamless sleep as a weary lover whom no caresses move, the sound of hoofs upon the road.

Toward the end, his purpose stiffens into a flourish of blank verse:

April 26. Mother is putting my new secondhand clothes in order. She prays now, she says, that I may learn in my own life /60/ and away from home and friends what the heart is and what it feels. Amen. So be it. Welcome, O life! I go to encounter for the millionth time the reality of experience and to forge in the smithy of my soul the uncreated conscience of my race.

On the eve of departure he makes his final entry:

April 27. Old father, old artificer, stand me now and ever in good stead.

The mythical and priestly figure of Dædalus is known for more than one work of genius—for a pair of wings, as well as a labyrinth. Stephen invokes his namesake under both aspects, the hawklike man and the fabulous artificer. Sometimes it is the cunning of the craftsman, the smithy of the artist, that is symbolized. At other times, soaring, falling, flying by the nets of Ireland, it is life itself. Yet these images of aspiration can also be associated with Icarus, the son of Dædalus. That ill-fated and rebellious spirit, who borrowed his father's wings and flew too near the sun, is an equally prophetic symbol: in a classical drama, *Icaro,* the young anti-fascist poet, Lauro de Bosis, adumbrated the heroism of his own death. The epigraph of Joyce's book is a quotation from Ovid—or rather a misquotation (the correct reference is to the *Metamorphoses,* VIII, 188). Here we are told that Dædalus abandoned his mind to obscure arts, *"et ignotas animum dimittit in artes."* But Joyce does not tell us Ovid's reason:

> ... *longumque perosus*
> *exsilium, tractusque soli natalis amore* . . . /61/

The artificer was weary of his long exile and lured by the love of his natal soil, the Roman poet and exile goes on to say, and the rest of his myth rehearses the filial tragedy. The father cries out for the son; Joyce's confused recollection, in *Ulysses,* makes the son cry out for the father: *"Pater, ait."* On the brink of expatriation, poised

for his trial flight, Stephen, in the *Portrait of the Artist,* is more
nearly akin to the son. His natural father, Simon Dedalus, is left
standing in the mystical kinship of fosterage. The Jesuit fathers,
who supervised his education, no longer call him son. He has ap-
pealed from Father Dolan to Father Conmee; now he appeals from
the church to another paternity. His wings take him from the fatherland. The labyrinth leads toward a father. /62/

The Portrait in Perspective

HUGH KENNER

LINKING THEMES

In the reconceived *Portrait* Joyce abandoned the original intention of writing the account of his own escape from Dublin. One cannot escape one's Dublin. He recast Stephen Dedalus as a figure who could not even detach himself from Dublin because he had formed himself on a denial of Dublin's values. He is the egocentric rebel become an ultimate. There is no question whatever of his regeneration. "Stephen no longer interests me to the same extent [as Bloom]," said Joyce to Frank Budgen one day. "He has a shape that can't be changed."[1] His shape is that of aesthete. The Stephen of the first chapter of *Ulysses* who "walks wearily", constantly "leans" on everything in sight, invariably sits down before he has gone three paces, speaks "gloomily", "quietly", "with bitterness", and "coldly", and "suffers" his handkerchief to be pulled from his pocket by the exuberant Mulligan, is precisely the priggish, humourless Stephen of the last chapter of the *Portrait* who cannot remember what day of the week it is, P206/201, sentimentalizes like Charles Lamb over the "human pages" of a second-hand Latin book, P209/204, conducts the inhumanly pedantic dialogue with Cranly on mother-love, P281/271, writes Frenchified verses in bed in an erotic swoon, and is epiphanized at full length, like Shem the Penman beneath the bedclothes, F176, shrinking from the "common noises" of daylight:

Shrinking from that life he turned towards the wall, making a cowl [!] of the blanket and staring at the great overblown scarlet /112/ flowers of the tattered wall-paper. He tried to warm his perishing joy in their scarlet glow, imaging a roseway from where he lay upwards to heaven all strewn

Hugh Kenner, *Dublin's Joyce* (Bloomington, Ind.: University of Indiana Press, 1956), pp. 112-33.
[1] Budgen, 107.

45

with scarlet flowers. Weary! Weary! He too was weary of ardent ways.
P260/252.

This new primrose path is a private Jacob's ladder let down to his
bed now that he is too weary to do anything but go to heaven.

To make epic and drama emerge naturally from the intrinsic
stresses and distortions of the lyric material meant completely new
lyric techniques for a constation exact beyond irony. The *Portrait*
concentrates on stating themes, arranging apparently transparent
words into configurations of the utmost symbolic density. Here is
the director proposing that Stephen enter the priesthood:

> The director stood in the embrasure of the window, his back to the
> light, leaning an elbow on the brown crossblind, and, as he spoke and
> smiled, slowly dangling and looping the cord of the other blind, Stephen
> stood before him, following for a moment with his eyes the waning of
> the long summer daylight above the roofs or the slow deft movements of
> the priestly fingers. The priest's face was in total shadow, but the waning
> daylight from behind him touched the deeply grooved temples and the
> curves of the skull. P178/175.

The looped cord, the shadow, the skull, none of these is accidental.
The "waning daylight," twice emphasized, conveys that denial of
nature which the priest's office represented for Stephen; "his back
to the light" co-operates toward a similar effect. So "crossblind":
"blind to the cross";[1] "blinded by the cross". "The curves of the
skull" introduces another death-image; the "deathbone" from Lévy-
Bruhl's Australia, pointed by Shaun in *Finnegans Wake*, F193, is
the dramatic version of an identical symbol. But the central image,
the epiphany of the interview, is contained in the movement of the
priest's fingers: "slowly dangling and looping the cord of the other
blind." That is to say, coolly proffering a noose. This is the lyric
mode of *Ulysses'* epical hangman, "The lord of things as they are
whom the most Roman of Catholics call *dio boia*, hangman god",
U210/201. /113/

THE CONTRAPUNTAL OPENING

According to the practice inaugurated by Joyce when he rewrote
"The Sisters" in 1906, the *Portrait,* like the two books to follow,
opens amid elaborate counterpoint. The first two pages, terminating

---

[1] —You want me, said Stephen, to toe the line with those hypocrites and syco-
phants in the college. I will never do so.
   —No. I mentioned Jesus.
   —Don't mention him. I have made it a common noun. They don't believe in
him; they don't observe his precepts. . . ." S141/124.

in a row of asterisks, enact the entire action in microcosm. An Aristotelian catalogue of senses, faculties, and mental activities is played against the unfolding of the infant conscience.

Once upon a time and a very good time it was there was a moocow coming down along the road and this moocow that was down along the road met a nicens little boy named baby tuckoo. . . .
His father told him that story: his father looked at him through a glass: he had a hairy face.
He was baby tuckoo. The moocow came down along the road where Betty Byrne lived: she sold lemon platt.
> O, the wild rose blossoms
> On the little green place.
He sang that song. That was his song.
> O, the green wothe botheth.
When you wet the bed, first it is warm then it gets cold. His mother put on the oilsheet. That had the queer smell.

This evocation of holes in oblivion is conducted in the mode of each of the five senses in turn; hearing (the story of the moocow), sight (his father's face), taste (lemon platt), touch (warm and cold), smell (the oil-sheet). The audible soothes: the visible disturbs. Throughout Joyce's work, the senses are symbolically disposed. Smell is the means of discriminating empirical realities ("His mother had a nicer smell than his father," is the next sentence), sight corresponds to the phantasms of oppression, hearing to the imaginative life. Touch and taste together are the modes of sex. Hearing, here, comes first, via a piece of imaginative literature. But as we can see from the vantage-point of *Finnegans Wake,* the whole book is about the encounter of baby tuckoo with the moocow: the Gripes with the mookse.[1] The father with the hairy face is the first Mookse-avatar, the Freudian infantile analogue of God the Father. /114/
    In the *Wake*

Derzherr, live wire, fired Benjermine Funkling outa th'Empyre, sin right hand son. F289.

Der Erzherr (arch-lord), here a Teutonic Junker, is the God who visited his wrath on Lucifer; the hairy attribute comes through via the music-hall refrain, "There's hair, like wire, coming out of the Empire."

---

[1] Compare the opening sentence: "Eins within a space, and a wearywide space it wast, ere wohned a Mookse", F152. Mookse is moocow plus fox plus mock turtle. The German "Eins" evokes Einstein, who presides over the interchanging of space and time; space is the Mookse's "spatiality".

Dawning consciousness of his own identity ("He was baby tuckoo") leads to artistic performance ("He sang that song. That was his song.") This is hugely expanded in chapter IV:

Now, as never before, his strange name seemed to him a prophecy . . . of the end he had been born to serve and had been following through the mists of childhood and boyhood, a symbol of the artist forging anew in his workshop out of the sluggish matter of the earth a new soaring impalable imperishable being.   P196/192.

By changing the red rose to a green and dislocating the spelling, he makes the song his own ("But you could not have a green rose. But perhaps somewhere in the world you could." P8/13)

His mother had a nicer smell than his father. She played on the piano the sailor's hornpipe for him to dance.   He danced:

> Tralala lala,
> Tralala tralaladdy,
> Tralala lala,
> Tralala lala.

Between this innocence and its Rimbaudian recapture through the purgation of the *Wake* there is to intervene the hallucination in Circe's sty:

THE MOTHER

(With the subtle smile of death's madness.) I was once the beautiful May Goulding. I am dead. . . .

STEPHEN

(Eagerly.) Tell me the word, mother, if you know it now. The word known to all men. . . .

THE MOTHER

(With smouldering eyes.) Repent! O, the fire of hell! U565/547/115/

This is foreshadowed as the overture to the *Portrait* closes:

> He hid under the table. His mother said:
> —O, Stephen will apologise.
> Dante said:
> —O, if not, the eagles will come and pull out his eyes.—
>
> > Pull out his eyes,
> > Apologise,
> > Apologise,
> > Pull out his eyes.
> >
> > Apologise,
> > Pull out his eyes,
> > Pull out his eyes,
> > Apologise.

The eagles, eagles of Rome, are emissaries of the God with the hairy face: the punisher. They evoke Prometheus and gnawing guilt: again-bite. So the overture ends with Stephen hiding under the table awaiting the eagles. He is hiding under something most of the time: bedclothes, "the enigma of a manner", an indurated rhetoric, or some other carapace of his private world.

THEME WORDS

It is through their names that things have power over Stephen.

—The language in which we are speaking is his before it is mine. How different are the words *home*, *Christ*, *ale*, *master*, on his lips and on mine! I cannot speak or write these words without unrest of spirit. His language, so familiar and so foreign, will always be for me an acquired speech. I have not made or accepted its words. My voice holds them at bay. My soul frets in the shadow of his language. P221/215.

Not only is the Dean's English a conqueror's tongue; since the loss of Adam's words which perfectly mirrored things, all language has conquered the mind and imposed its own order, askew from the order of creation. Words, like the physical world, are imposed on Stephen from without, and it is in their canted mirrors that he glimpses a physical and moral world already dyed the colour of his own mind since absorbed, with language, into his personality. /116/

Words which he did not understand he said over and over to himself till he had learnt them by heart; and through them he had glimpses of the real world about him. P68/70.

Language is a Trojan horse by which the universe gets into the mind. The first sentence in the book isn't something Stephen sees but a story he is told, and the overture climaxes in an insistent brainless rhyme, its jingle corrosively fascinating to the will. It has power to terrify a child who knows nothing of eagles, or of Prometheus, or of how his own grownup failure to apologise will blend with gathering blindness.

It typifies the peculiar achievement of the *Portrait* that Joyce can cause patterns of words to make up the very moral texture of Stephen's mind:

Suck was a queer word. The fellow called Simon Moonan that name because Simon Moonan used to tie the prefect's false sleeves behind his back and the prefect used to let on to be angry. But the sound was ugly. Once has had washed his hands in the lavatory of the Wicklow hotel and his father pulled the stopper up by the chain after and the dirty water

went down through the hole in the basin. And when it had all gone down
slowly the hole in the basin had made a sound like that: suck. Only
louder.

To remember that and the white look of the lavatory made him feel
cold and then hot. There were two cocks that you turned and the water
came out: cold and hot. He felt cold and then a little hot: and he could
see the names printed on the cocks. That was a very queer thing. P6/12.

"Suck" joins two contexts in Stephen's mind: a playful sinner toy-
ing with his indulgent superior, and the disappearance of dirty water. The force of the conjunction is felt only after Stephen has lost
his sense of the reality of the forgiveness of sins in the confessional.
The habitually orthodox penitent tangles with a God who pretends
to be angry; after a reconciliation the process is repeated. And the
mark of that kind of play is disgraceful servility. Each time the sin
disappears, the sinner is mocked by an impersonal voice out of nature: "Suck!"

This attitude to unreal good and evil furnishes a context for the
next conjunction: whiteness and coldness. Stephen finds himself,
like Simon Moonan,[1] engaged in the rhythm of /117/ obedience to
irrational authority, bending his mind to a meaningless act, the
arithmetic contest. He is being obediently "good". And the appropriate colour is adduced: "He thought his face must be white because it felt so cool."

The pallor of lunar obedient goodness is next associated with
damp repulsiveness: the limpness of a wet blanket and of a servant's
apron:

He sat looking at the two prints of butter on his plate but could not
eat the damp bread. The table-cloth was damp and limp. But he drank
off the hot weak tea which the clumsy scullion, girt with a white apron,
poured into his cup. He wondered whether the scullion's apron was damp
too or whether all white things were cold and damp. P8/13.

Throughout the first chapter an intrinsic linkage, white-cold-
damp-obedient, insinuates itself repeatedly. Stephen after saying his
prayers, "his shoulders shaking", "so that he might not go to hell
when he died", "curled himself together under the cold white
sheets, shaking and trembling. But he would not go to hell when he
died, and the shaking would stop." P16/20. The sea, mysterious as
the terrible power of God, "was cold day and night, but it was
cold at night", P14/19; we are reminded of Anna Livia's gesture

[1] Joyce's names should always be scrutinized. Simon Moonan: moon: the heat-
less (white) satellite reflecting virtue borrowed from Simon Peter. Simony, too,
is an activity naturally derived from this casually businesslike attitude to priestly
authority.

of submission: "my cold father, my cold mad father, my cold mad feary father", F628. "There was a cold night smell in the chapel. But it was a holy smell", P14/19. Stephen is puzzled by the phrase in the Litany of the Blessed Virgin: Tower of Ivory. "How could a woman be a tower of ivory or a house of gold?" He ponders until the revelation comes:

> Eileen had long white hands. One evening when playing tig she had put her hands over his eyes: long and white and thin and cold and soft. That was ivory: a cold white thing. That was the meaning of *Tower of Ivory*. P36/40.

This instant of insight depends on a sudden reshuffling of associations, a sudden conviction that the Mother of God, and the symbols appropriate to her, belong with the cold, the white, and the unpleasant in a blindfold morality of obedience. Contemplation focussed on language is repaid:

> *Tower of Ivory. House of Gold.* By thinking of things you could understand them. P45/48.

The white-damp-obedient association reappears when /118/ Stephen is about to make his confession after the celebrated retreat; its patterns provide the language in which he thinks. Sin has been associated with fire, while the prayers of the penitents are epiphanized as "soft whispering cloudlets, soft whispering vapour, whispering and vanishing." P164/163. And having been absolved:

> White pudding and eggs and sausages and cups of tea. How simple and beautiful was life after all! And life lay all before him. . . .
> The boys were all there, kneeling in their places. He knelt among them, happy and shy. The altar was heaped with fragrant masses of white flowers: and in the morning light the pale flames of the candles among the white flowers were clear and silent as his own soul. P168/166.

We cannot read *Finnegans Wake* until we have realized the significance of the way the mind of Stephen Dedalus is bound in by language. He is not only an artist: he is a Dubliner.

THE PORTRAIT AS LYRIC

The "instant of emotion", P251/244, of which this 300-page lyric is the "simplest verbal vesture" is the exalted instant, emerging at the end of the book, of freedom, of vocation, of Stephen's destiny, winging his way above the waters at the side of the hawklike man: the instant of promise on which the crushing ironies of *Ulysses* are to fall. The epic of the sea of matter is preceded by the lyric image of a growing dream: a dream that like Richard Rowan's in *Exiles* dis-

regards the fall of man; a dream nourished by a sensitive youth of
flying above the sea into an uncreated heaven:

The spell of arms and voices: the white arms of roads, their promise of
close embraces and the black arms of tall ships that stand against the
moon, their tale of distant nations. They are held out to say: We are
alone—come. And the voices say with them: We are your kinsmen. And
the air is thick with their company as they call to me, their kinsman,
making ready to go, shaking the wings of their exultant and terrible youth.
P298/288.

The emotional quality of this is continuous with that of the *Count
of Monte Cristo,* that fantasy of the exile returned for vengeance
(the plot of the *Odyssey*) which kindled so many of Stephen's boyhood dreams:

The figure of that dark avenger stood forth in his mind for whatever he
had heard or divined in childhood of the strange and terrible. At night
he built up on the parlour table an image of the wonderful /119/ island
cave out of transfers and paper flowers and strips of the silver and golden
paper in which chocolate is wrapped. When he had broken up this
scenery, weary of its tinsel, there would come to his mind the bright picture of Marseilles, of sunny trellises and of Mercedes. P68/70.

The prose surrounding Stephen's flight is empurpled with transfers
and paper flowers too. It is not immature prose, as we might suppose by comparison with *Ulysses.* The prose of "The Dead" is mature prose, and "The Dead" was written in 1908. Rather, it is a
meticulous pastiche of immaturity. Joyce has his eye constantly on
the epic sequel.

He wanted to meet in the real world the unsubstantial image which his
soul so constantly beheld. He did not know where to seek it or how, but
a premonition which led him on told him that this image would, without
any overt act of his, encounter him. They would meet quietly as if they
had known each other and had made their tryst, perhaps at one of the
gates or in some more secret place. They would be alone, surrounded by
darkness and silence: and in that moment of supreme tenderness he would
be transfigured. P71/73.

As the vaginal imagery of gates, secret places, and darkness implies,
this is the dream that reaches temporary fulfilment in the plunge
into profane love, P113/14. But the ultimate "secret place" is to
be Mabbot Street, outside Bella Cohen's brothel; the unsubstantial
image of his quest, that of Leopold Bloom, advertisement canvasser
—Monte Cristo, returned avenger, Ulysses; and the transfiguration,
into the phantasmal dead son of a sentimental Jew:

Against the dark wall a figure appears slowly, a fairy boy of eleven, a

*changeling, kidnapped, dressed in an Eton suit with glass shoes and a
little bronze helmet, holding a book in his hand. He reads from right to
left inaudibly, smiling, kissing the page.* U593/574.

That Dedalus the artificer did violence to nature is the point of
the epigraph from Ovid, *Et ignotas animum dimittit in artes;*
the Icarian fall is inevitable.

> In tedious exile now too long detain'd
> Dedalus languish'd for his native land.
> The sea foreclos'd his flight; yet thus he said,
> Though earth and water in subjection laid,
> O cruel Minos, thy dominion be,
> We'll go through air; for sure the air is free.
> *Then to new arts his cunning thought applies,*
> *And to improve the work of nature tries.* /120/

Stephen does not, as the careless reader may suppose, become an
artist by rejecting church and country. Stephen does not become an
artist at all. Country, church, and mission are an inextricable unity,
and in rejecting the two that seem to hamper him, he rejects also
the one on which he has set his heart. Improving the work of nature is his obvious ambition ("But you could not have a green rose.
But perhaps somewhere in the world you could"), and it logically
follows from the aesthetic he expounds to Lynch. It is a neo-pla-
tonic aesthetic; the crucial principle of epiphanization has been
withdrawn. He imagines that "the loveliness that has not yet come
into the world", P297/286, is to be found in his own soul. The
earth is gross, and what it brings forth is cowdung; sound and shape
and colour are "the prison gates of our soul"; and beauty is something mysteriously gestated within. The genuine artist reads signatures, the fake artist forges them, a process adumbrated in the obsession of Shem the Penman (from *Jim the Penman,* a forgotten
drama about a forger) with "Macfearsome's Ossean", the most famous of literary forgeries, studying "how cutely to copy all their
various styles of signature so as one day to utter an epical forged
cheque on the public for his own private profit." F181.

One can sense all this in the first four chapters of the *Portrait,*
and *Ulysses* is unequivocal:

Fabulous artificer, the hawklike man. You flew. Whereto? Newhaven-
Dieppe, steerage passenger. Paris and back. U208/199.

The Stephen of the end of the fourth chapter, however, is still unstable; he had to be brought into a final balance, and shown at
some length as a being whose development was virtually ended.

Unfortunately, the last chapter makes the book a peculiarly difficult one for the reader to focus, because Joyce had to close it on a suspended chord. As a lyric, it is finished in its own terms; but the themes of the last forty pages, though they give the illusion of focussing, don't really focus until we have read well into *Ulysses*. The final chapter, which in respect to the juggernaut of *Ulysses* must be a vulnerable flank, in respect to what has gone before must be a conclusion. This problem Joyce didn't wholly solve; there remains a moral ambiguity (how seriously are we to take Stephen?) which makes the last forty pages painful reading.

Not that Stephen would stand indefinitely if *Ulysses* didn't /121/ topple him over; his equilibrium in Chapter V, though good enough to give him a sense of unusual integrity in University College, is precarious unless he can manage, in the manner of so many permanent undergraduates, to prolong the college context for the rest of his life. Each of the preceding chapters, in fact, works toward an equilibrium which is dashed when in the next chapter Stephen's world becomes larger and the frame of reference more complex. The terms of equilibrium are always stated with disquieting accuracy; at the end of Chapter I we find:

> He was alone. He was happy and free: but he would not be anyway proud with Father Dolan. He would be very quiet and obedient: and he wished that he could do something kind for him to show him that he was not proud. P64/66.

And at the end of Chapter III:

> He sat by the fire in the kitchen, not daring to speak for happiness. Till that moment he had not known how beautiful and peaceful life could be. The green square of paper pinned round the lamp cast down a tender shade. On the dresser was a plate of sausages and white pudding and on the shelf there were eggs. They would be for the breakfast in the morning after the communion in the college chapel. White pudding and eggs and sausages and cups of tea. How simple and beautiful was life after all! And life lay all before him. P168/166.

Not "irony" but simply the truth: the good life conceived in terms of white pudding and sausages is unstable enough to need no underlining.

The even-numbered chapters make a sequence of a different sort. The ending of IV, Stephen's panting submission to an artistic vocation:

> Evening had fallen when he woke and the sand and arid grasses of his bed glowed no longer. He rose slowly and, recalling the rapture of his sleep, sighed at its joy. . . . P201/197,

—hasn't quite the finality often read into it when the explicit parallel with the ending of II is perceived:

. . . He closed his eyes, surrendering himself to her, body and mind, conscious of nothing in the world but the dark pressure of her softly parting lips. They pressed upon his brain as upon his lips as though they were the vehicle of a vague speech; and between them he felt an unknown and timid pressure, darker than the swoon of sin, softer than sound or odour. P114/115. /122/

When we link these passages with the fact that the one piece of literary composition Stephen actually achieves in the book comes out of a wet dream ("Towards dawn he awoke. O what sweet music! His soul was all dewy wet", P254) we are in a position to see that the concluding "Welcome, O life!" has an air of finality and balance only because the diary-form of the last seven pages disarms us with an illusion of auctorial impartiality.

CONTROLLING IMAGES: CLONGOWES AND BELVEDERE

Ego *vs.* authority is the theme of the three odd-numbered chapters, Dublin *vs.* the dream that of the two even-numbered ones. The generic Joyce plot, the encounter with the alter ago, is consummated when Stephen at the end of the book identifies himself with the sanctified Stephen who was stoned by the Jews after reporting a vision (Acts VII, 56) and claims sonship with the classical Daedalus who evaded the ruler of land and sea by turning his soul to obscure arts. The episodes are built about adumbrations of this encounter: with Father Conmee, with Monte Cristo, with the whores, with the broad-shouldered moustached student who cut the word "Foetus" in a desk, with the weary mild confessor, with the birdgirl. Through this repeated plot intertwine controlling emotions and controlling images that mount in complexity as the book proceeds.

In chapter I the controlling emotion is fear, and the dominant image Father Dolan and his pandybat; this, associated with the hangman-god and the priestly denial of the senses, was to become one of Joyce's standard images for Irish clericalism—hence the jack-in-the-box appearance of Father Dolan in Circe's nightmare imbroglio, his pandybat cracking twice like thunder, U547/531. Stephen's comment, in the mode of lake's repudiation of the God who slaughtered Jesus, emphasizes the inclusiveness of the image: "I never could read His handwriting except His criminal thumbprint on the haddock."

Chapter II opens with a triple image of Dublin's prepossessions: music, sport, religion. The first is exhibited via Uncle Charles singing sentimental ballads in the outhouse; the second via Stephen's ritual run around the park under the eye of a superannuated trainer, which his uncle enjoins on him as /123/ the whole duty of a Dubliner; the third via the clumsy piety of Uncle Charles, kneeling on a red handkerchief and reading above his breath "from a thumb-blackened prayerbook wherein catchwords were printed at the foot of every page." P67/69. This trinity of themes is unwound and entwined throughout the chapter, like a net woven round Stephen; it underlies the central incident, the Whitsuntide play in the Belvedere chapel (religion), which opens with a display by the dumb-bell team (sport) preluded by sentimental waltzes from the soldier's band (music).

While he is waiting to play his part, Stephen is taunted by fellow-students, who rally him on a fancied love-affair and smiting his calf with a cane bid him recite the *Confiteor*. His mind goes back to an analogous incident, when a similar punishment had been visited on his refusal to "admit that Byron was no good". The further analogy with Father Dolan is obvious; love, art, and personal independence are thus united in an ideogram of the prepossessions Stephen is determined to cultivate in the teeth of persecution.

The dream-world Stephen nourishes within himself is played against manifestations of music, sport, and religion throughout the chapter. The constant ironic clash of Dublin *vs.* the Dream animates chapter II, as the clash of the ego *vs.* authority did chapter I. All these themes come to focus during Stephen's visit with his father to Cork. The dream of rebellion he has silently cultivated is externalized by the discovery of the word *Foetus* carved in a desk by a forgotten medical student:

> It shocked him to find in the outer world a trace of what he had deemed till then a brutish and individual malady of his own mind. His monstrous reveries came thronging into his memory. They too had sprung up before him, suddenly and furiously, out of mere words. . . . P101/102.

The possibility of shame gaining the upper hand is dashed, however, by the sudden banal intrusion of his father's conversation ("When you kick out for yourself, Stephen, as I daresay you will one of these days, remember, whatever you do, to mix with gentlemen . . ."). Against the standards of Dublin his monstrous reveries acquire a Satanic glamour, and the trauma is slowly diverted into a resolution to rebel. After his father has expressed a resolve to "leave him to his Maker" (religion), and offered to "sing a tenor song

against him" (music) or /124/ "vault a fivebarred gate against
him" (sport), Stephen muses, watching his father and two cronies
drinking to the memory of their past:

> An abyss of fortune or of temperament sundered him from them. His
> mind seemed older than theirs: it shone coldly on their strifes and hap-
> piness and regrets like a moon upon a younger earth. No life or youth
> stirred in him as it had stirred in them. He had known neither the
> pleasure of companionship with others nor the vigour of rude male health
> nor filial piety. Nothing stirred within his soul but a cold and cruel and
> loveless lust. P107/108.

After one final effort to compromise with Dublin on Dublin's
terms has collapsed into futility ("The pot of pink enamel paint
gave out and the wainscot of his bedroom remained with its un-
finished and illplastered coat", P110/111), he fiercely cultivates his
rebellious thoughts and moving by day and night "among distorted
images of the outer world", P111/112, plunges at last into the
arms of whores. "The holy encounter he had then imagined at
which weakness and timidity and inexperience were to fall from
him", P112/113, finally arrives in inversion of Father Dolan's and
Uncle Charles' religion: his descent into night-town is accompanied
by lurid evocations of a Black Mass (Cf. *Ulysses*, 583/565):

> The yellow gasflames arose before his troubled vision against the vapoury
> sky, burning as if before an altar. Before the doors and in the lighted
> halls groups were gathered arrayed as for some rite. He was in another
> world: he had awakened from a slumber of centuries. P113/114.

CONTROLLING IMAGES: SIN AND REPENTANCE

Each chapter in the *Portrait* gathers up the thematic material of the
preceding ones and entwines them with a dominant theme of its
own. In chapter III the fear-pandybat motif is present in Father
Arnall's crudely materialistic hell, of which even the thickness of
the walls is specified; and the Dublin-*vs.*-dream motif has ironic in-
flections in Stephen's terror-stricken broodings, when the dream has
been twisted into a dream of holiness, and even Dublin appears
transfigured:

> How beautiful must be a soul in the state of grace when God looked
> upon it with love!
> Frowsy girls sat along the curbstones before their baskets. Their /125/
> dank hair trailed over their brows. They were not beautiful to see as
> they crouched in the mire. But their souls were seen by God; and if their
> souls were in a state of grace they were radiant to see; and God loved
> them, seeing them. P162/160.

A *rapprochement* in these terms between the outer world and

Stephen's desires is too inadequate to need commentary; and it
makes vivid as nothing else could the hopeless inversion of his attempted self-sufficiency. It underlines, in yet another way, his per-
sistent sin: and the dominant theme of chapter III is Sin. A fugue-
like opening plays upon the Seven Deadly Sins in turn; gluttony is
in the first paragraph ("Stuff it into you, his belly counselled him"),
followed by lust, then sloth ("A cold lucid indifference reigned in
his soul"), pride ("His pride in his own sin, his loveless awe of
God, told him that his offence was too grievous to be atoned for"),
anger ("The blundering answer stirred the embers of his contempt
for his fellows"); finally, a recapitulation fixes each term of the
mortal catalogue in a phrase, enumerating how "from the evil seed
of lust all the other deadly sins had sprung forth", P120/120.

Priest and punisher inhabit Stephen himself as well as Dublin:
when he is deepest in sin he is most thoroughly a theologian. A
paragraph of gloomy introspection is juxtaposed with a list of theological questions that puzzle Stephen's mind as he awaits the
preacher:

... Is baptism with mineral water valid? How comes it that while the first
beatitude promises the kingdom of heaven to the poor of heart, the second
beatitude promises also to the meek that they shall possess the land? . . .
If the wine change into vinegar and the host crumble into corruption
after they have been consecrated, is Jesus Christ still present under their
species as God and as man?
—Here he is! Here he is!
A boy from his post at the window had seen the rector come from the
house. All the catechisms were opened and all heads bent upon them
silently. P120/120.

Wine changed into vinegar and the host crumbled into corruption
fits exactly the Irish clergy of "a church which was the scullery-maid
of Christendom". The excited "Here he is! Here he is!" following
hard on the mention of Jesus Christ and signalling nothing more
portentous than the rector makes the point as dramatically as anything in the book, and the /126/ clinching sentence, with the students suddenly bending over their catechisms, places the rector as
the vehicle of pandybat morality.

The last of the theological questions is the telling question. Stephen never expresses doubt of the existence of God nor of the essential validity of the priestly office—his *Non serviam* is not a *non
credo,* and he talks of a "malevolent reality" behind these appearances P287/277—but the wine and bread that were offered for his
veneration were changed into vinegar and crumbled into corruption. And it was the knowledge of that underlying validity clashing

with his refusal to do homage to vinegar and rot that evoked his ambivalent poise of egocentric despair. The hell of Father Arnall's sermon, so emotionally overwhelming, so picayune beside the horrors that Stephen's imagination can generate, had no more ontological content for Stephen than had "an eternity of bliss in the company of the dean of studies", P282/273.

The conflict of this central chapter is again between the phantasmal and the real. What is real—psychologically real, because realized—is Stephen's anguish and remorse, and its context in the life of the flesh. What is phantasmal is the "heaven" of the Church and the "good life" of the priest. It is only fear that makes him clutch after the latter at all; his reaching out after orthodox salvation is, as we have come to expect, presented in terms that judge it:

The wind blew over him and passed on to the myriads and myriads of other souls, on whom God's favour shone now more and now less, stars now brighter and now dimmer, sustained and failing. And the glimmering souls passed away, sustained and failing, merged in a moving breath. One soul was lost; a tiny soul; his. It flickered once and went out, forgotten, lost. The end: black cold void waste.

Consciousness of place came ebbing back to him slowly over a vast tract of time unlit, unfelt, unlived. The squalid scene composed itself around him; the common accents, the burning gasjets in the shops, odours of fish and spirits and wet sawdust, moving men and women. An old woman was about to cross the street, an oilcan in her hand. He bent down and asked her was there a chapel near. P162/160.

That wan waste world of flickering stars is the best Stephen has been able to do towards an imaginative grasp of the communion of Saints sustained by God; "unlit, unfelt, unlived" explains succinctly why it had so little hold on him, once fear had /127/ relaxed. Equally pertinent is the vision of human temporal occupations the sermon evokes:

What did it profit a man to gain the whole world if he lost his soul? At last he had understood: and human life lay around him, a plain of peace whereon antlike men laboured in brotherhood, their dead sleeping under quiet mounds. P144/143.

To maintain the life of grace in the midst of nature, sustained by so cramped a vision of the life of nature, would mean maintaining an intolerable tension. Stephen's unrelenting philosophic bias, his determination to understand what he is about, precludes his adopting the double standard of the Dubliners; to live both the life of nature and the life of grace he must enjoy an imaginative grasp of their relationship which stunts neither. "No one doth well against his will," writes Saint Augustine, "even though what he doth, be well;" and Stephen's will is firmly harnessed to his understanding. And there is no one in Dublin to help him achieve understanding. Father Arnall's sermon precludes rather than secures a desirable outcome, for it follows the modes of pandybat morality and Dublin materiality. Its only possible effect on Stephen is to lash his dormant conscience into a frenzy. The description of Hell as "a strait and dark and foul smelling prison, an abode of demons and lost souls, filled with fire and smoke", with walls four thousand miles thick, its damned packed in so tightly that "they are not even able to remove from the eye the worm that gnaws it", is childishly grotesque beneath its sweeping eloquence; and the hair-splitting catalogues of pains—pain of loss, pain of conscience (divided into three heads), pain of extension, pain of intensity, pain of eternity—is cast in a brainlessly analytic mode that effectively prevents any corresponding Heaven from possessing any reality at all.

Stephen's unstable pact with the Church, and its dissolution, follows the pattern of composition and dissipation established by his other dreams: the dream for example of the tryst with "Mercedes", which found ironic reality among harlots. It parallels exactly his earlier attempt to "build a breakwater of order and elegance against the sordid tide of life without him", P110/111, whose failure, with the exhaustion of his money, was epiphanized in the running-dry of a pot of pink enamel paint. His regimen at that time:

He bought presents for everyone, overhauled his rooms, wrote out /128/ resolutions, marshalled his books up and down their shelves, pored over all kinds of price lists . . .

is mirrored by his searching after spiritual improvement:

His daily life was laid out in devotional areas. By means of ejaculations and prayers he stored up ungrudgingly for the souls in purgatory centuries of days and quarantines and years. . . . He offered up each of his three daily chaplets that his soul might grow strong in each of the three theological virtues. . . . On each of the seven days of the week he further prayed that one of the seven gifts of the Holy Ghost might descend upon his soul. P170/167.

The "loan bank" he had opened for the family, out of which he had pressed loans on willing borrowers "that he might have the pleasure of making out receipts and reckoning the interests on sums lent" finds its counterpart in the benefits he stored up for souls in purgatory that he might enjoy the spiritual triumph of "achieving with ease so many fabulous ages of canonical penances". Both projects are parodies on the doctrine of economy of grace;

both are attempts, corrupted by motivating self-interest, to make peace with Dublin on Dublin's own terms; and both are short-lived.

As this precise analogical structure suggests, the action of each of the five chapters is really the same action. Each chapter closes with a synthesis of triumph which the next destroys. The triumph of the appeal to Father Conmee from lower authority, of the appeal to the harlots from Dublin, of the appeal to the Church from sin, of the appeal to art from the priesthood (the bird-girl instead of the Virgin) is always the same triumph raised to a more comprehensive level. It is an attempt to find new parents; new fathers in the odd chapters, new objects of love in the even. The last version of Father Conmee is the "priest of the eternal imagination"; the last version of Mercedes is the "lure of the fallen seraphim". But the last version of the mother who said, "O, Stephen will apologise" is the mother who prays on the last page "that I may learn in my own life and away from home and friends what the heart is and what it feels". The mother remains.

THE DOUBLE FEMALE

As in *Dubliners* and *Exiles,* the female role in the *Portrait* is less to arouse than to elucidate masculine desires. Hence the complex function in the book of physical love: the physical /129/ is the analogue of the spiritual, as St. Augustine insisted in his *Confessions* (which, with Ibsen's *Brand,* is the chief archetype of Joyce's book). The poles between which this affection moves are those of St. Augustine and St. John: the Whore of Babylon and the Bride of Christ. The relation between the two is far from simple, and Stephen moves in a constant tension between them.

His desire, figured in the visions of Monte Cristo's Mercedes, "to meet in the real world the unsubstantial image which his soul so constantly beheld" draws him toward the prostitute ("In her arms he felt that he had suddenly become strong and fearless and sure of himself", P114/114) and simultaneously toward the vaguely spiritual satisfaction represented with equal vagueness by the wraith-like E—— C——, to whom he twice writes verses. The Emma Clery of *Stephen Hero,* with her loud forced manners and her body compact of pleasure, S66/56, was refined into a wraith with a pair of initials to parallel an intangible Church. She is continually assimilated to the image of the Blessed Virgin and of the heavenly Bride. The torture she costs him is the torture his apostasy costs him. His flirtation with her is his flirtation with Christ. His profane villanelle draws its imagery from religion—the incense, the eucharistic hymn, the chalice—and her heart, following Dante's image, is a rose, and in her praise "the earth was like a swinging swaying censer, a ball of incense", P256/248.

The woman is the Church. His vision of greeting Mercedes with "a sadly proud gesture of refusal":

–Madam, I never eat muscatel grapes. P68/71.

is fulfilled when he refuses his Easter communion. Emma's eyes, in their one explicit encounter, speak to him from beneath a cowl, P76/78. "The glories of Mary held his soul captive", P118/118, and a temporary reconciliation of his lust and his spiritual thirst is achieved as he reads the Lesson out of the Song of Solomon. In the midst of his repentance she functions as imagined mediator: "The image of Emma appeared before him," and, repenting, "he imagined that he stood near Emma in a wide land, and, humbly and in tears, bent and kissed the elbow of her sleeve", P132/131. Like Dante's Beatrice, she manifests in his earthly experience the Church Triumphant of his spiritual dream. And when he rejects her because she seems to be flirting with Father Moran, his anger is couched in /130/ the anti-clerical terms of his apostasy: "He had done well to leave her to flirt with her priest, to toy with a church which was the scullery-maid of Christendom", P258/250.

That Kathleen ni Houlihan can flirt with priests is the unforgivable sin underlying Stephen's rejection of Ireland. But he makes a clear distinction between the stupid clericalism which makes intellectual and communal life impossible, and his long-nourished vision of an artist's Church Triumphant upon earth. He rejects the actual for daring to fall short of his vision.

THE FINAL BALANCE

The climax of the book is of course Stephen's ecstatic discovery of his vocation at the end of chapter IV. The prose rises in nervous excitement to beat again and again the tambours of a fin-de-siècle ecstasy:

His heart trembled; his breath came faster and a wild spirit passed over his limbs as though he were soaring sunward. His heart trembled in an ecstasy of fear and his soul was in flight. His soul was soaring in an air beyond the world and the body he knew was purified in a breath and delivered of incertitude and made radiant and commingled with the element of the spirit. An ecstasy of flight made radiant his eyes and wild his breath and tremulous and wild and radiant his windswept limbs.

– One! Two! . . . Look out!—
—O, Cripes, I'm drownded!—P196/192.

The interjecting voices of course are those of bathers, but their ironic appropriateness to Stephen's Icarian "soaring sunward" is not meant to escape us: divers have their own "ecstasy of flight", and Icarus was "drownded". The imagery of Stephen's ecstasy is fetched from many sources; we recognize Shelley's skylark, Icarus, the glorified body of the Resurrection (cf. "His soul had arisen from the grave of boyhood, spurning her graveclothes", P197/193) and a tremulousness from which it is difficult to dissociate adolescent sexual dreams (which the Freudians tell us are frequently dreams of flying). The entire eight-page passage is cunningly organized with great variety of rhetoric and incident; but we cannot help noticing the limits set on vocabulary and figures of thought. The empurpled triteness of such a cadence as "radiant his eyes and /131/ wild his breath and tremulous and wild and radiant his wind-swept face" is enforced by recurrence: "But her long fair hair was girlish: and girlish, and touched with the wonder of mortal beauty, her face", P199/195. "Ecstasy" is the keyword, indeed. This riot of feelings corresponds to no vocation definable in mature terms; the paragraphs come to rest on images of irresponsible motion:

He turned away from her suddenly and set off across the strand. His cheeks were aflame; his body was aglow; his limbs were trembling. On and on and on and on he strode, far out over the sands, singing wildly to the sea, crying to greet the advent of the life that had cried to him. P200/196.

What "life" connotes it skills not to ask; the word recurs and recurs. So does the motion onward and onward and onward:

A wild angel had appeared to him, the angel of mortal youth and beauty, an envoy from the fair courts of life, to throw open before him in an instant of ecstasy the gates of all the ways of error and glory. On and on and on and on! P200/196.

It may be well to recall Joyce's account of the romantic temper:

. . . an insecure, unsatisfied, impatient temper which sees no fit abode here for its ideals and chooses therefore to behold them under insensible figures. As a result of this choice it comes to disrgeard certain limitations. Its figures are blown to wild adventures, lacking the gravity of solid bodies. . . . S78/66.

Joyce also called *Prometheus Unbound* "the Schwärmerei of a young jew".

And it is quite plain from the final chapter of the *Portrait* that we are not to accept the mode of Stephen's "freedom" as the "message" of the book. The "priest of the eternal imagination" turns out

to be indigestibly Byronic. Nothing is more obvious than his total
lack of humour. The dark intensity of the first four chapters is moving enough, but our impulse on being confronted with the final edition of Stephen Dedalus is to laugh; and laugh at this moment we
dare not; he is after all a victim being prepared for a sacrifice. His
shape, as Joyce said, can no longer change. The art he has elected
is not "the slow elaborative patience of the art of satisfaction". "On
and on and on and on" will be its inescapable mode. He does not *see*
the girl who symbolizes the full revelation; "she /132/ seemed like
one whom magic had changed into the likeness of a strange and beautiful seabird", P199/195, and he confusedly apprehends a sequence
of downy and feathery incantations. What, in the last chapter, he
does see he sees only to reject, in favour of an incantatory "loveliness
which has not yet come into the world", P197/286.

The only creative attitude to language exemplified in the book
is that of Stephen's father:

—Is it Christy? he said. There's more cunning in one of those warts on
his bald head than in a pack of jack foxes.

His vitality is established before the book is thirty pages under way.
Stephen, however, isn't enchanted at any time by the proximity of
such talk. He isn't, as a matter of fact, even interested in it. Without a backward glance, he exchanges this father for a myth. /133/

On *A Portrait of the Artist as a Young Man*

DOROTHY VAN GHENT

One of the oldest themes in the novel is that language is a creator of reality. There is this theme in *Don Quixote*. . . . Quixote is supremely a man animated by "the word"; and as the words he has read in books send him into action—creating reality for him by determining what he sees and what he feels and what he does—so Quixote in turn has a similar effect upon other people, subtly changing their outlook, creating in them new forms of thought and activity. *Don Quixote* may be looked on as an extensive investigation of the creative effects of language upon life. Joyce's *Portrait* is also an investigation of this /264/ kind; appropriately so, for the "artist" whose youthful portrait the book is, is at the end to find his vocation in language; and the shape of reality that gradually defines itself for Stephen is a shape determined primarily by the associations of words. We follow in the circumstances of the boy's life the stages of breakdown and increasing confusion in his external environment, as his home goes to pieces, and the correlative stages of breakdown in his inherited values, as his church and his nation lose their authority over his emotions. Very early the child's mind begins to respond to that confusion by seeking in itself, in its own mental images, some unifying form or forms that will signify what the world *really* is, that will show him the *real* logic of things—a logic hopelessly obscure in external relations. His mental images are largely associations suggested by the words he hears, and in intense loneliness he struggles to make the associations fit into a coherent pattern.

Dorothy Van Ghent, *The English Novel: Form and Function* (New York: Rinehart and Company, Inc., 1953), pp. 264-76.

65

To the very young child, adults seem to possess the secret of the whole, seem to know what everything means and how one thing is related to another. Apparently in command of that secret, they toss words together into esoteric compounds, some words whose referents the child knows and many whose referents are mysterious; and the context of the familiar words guides him in his speculation about the unfamiliar ones, the unfamiliar ones thus taking on their meaning for him in a wondrously accidental and chaotic fashion. These accidents of context, however bizarre, build up his notion of reality and determine his later responses and the bias of his soul. There is the story that Stephen's father tells him about a cow coming down along a road. There is the song about the wild rose blossoming on the green place. He, Stephen, is evidently the "nicens little boy" toward whom the cow designs its path, and he, Stephen, can make the wild rose into a green one by a transposition of adjectives. The world's form, then, is apparently shaped toward him and out from him as its center. But how to put the story and the song intelligibly together, in a superior meaningful pattern of reality, with his father's hairy face looking at him through a glass? or with the queer smell of the oil sheet? or with Dante's two brushes? or with Eileen, the neighbor girl, who has a different father and mother? or with some shadowily guilty thing he has done for which he must "apologize," else eagles will pull out his eyes? In this extremely short sequence at the beginning of the book, the child's sense of insecurity, in a world whose form he cannot grasp, is established—and with insecurity, guilt (he must apologize) and fear (the horrible eagles). With these unpromising emo- /265/ tional elements established in him, the maturing child will try again and again to grasp his world imaginatively as a shape within which he has a part that is essential to its completeness and harmoniousness and meaningfulness.

Immediately there is a transition to the children's playground at Clongowes Wood, the child's earliest experience of a community other than that of the home. Again the auditory impression is predominant—sounds heard, words spoken—and the life-directed attempt of the young mind is to understand their meaning in relation to each other and in relation to a governing design. There are the "strong cries" of the boys and the "thud" of their feet and bodies; then comes a quick succession of references to special oddnesses in the names of things. To the child's laboring apprehension, which assumes all names to have intimate and honest connections with reality, the name "dog-in-the-blanket" for the Friday pudding must represent something about the pudding which is real and which

other people know but which is obscured from him; it may have
more than one meaning, like the word "belt," which means a strap
on a jacket and also "to give a fellow a belt"; or it may have complex, mysterious, and terribly serious associations with destiny, understood by others but dark and anxious to himself, like his own
name, Stephen Dedalus, which Nasty Roche says is "queer" with a
queerness that puts the social status of Stephen's father in doubt.
Through words the world comes to Stephen; through the words he
hears he gropes his way into other people's images of reality. Doubts
and anxieties arise because the words and phrases are disassociated, their context frequently arbitrary, like that of the sentences in
the spelling book:

> Wolsey died in Leicester Abbey
> Where the abbots buried him.
> Canker is a disease of plants,
> Cancer one of animals.

The sentences in the spelling book at least make a rhythm, and a
rhythm is a kind of pattern, a "whole" of sorts; they are therefore
"nice sentences" to think about. But the threatening, overwhelming
problem is the integration of all the vast heap of disassociated impressions that the child's mind is subjected to and out of which his
hopeful urgency toward intelligibility forces him, entirely lonely
and without help, to try to make superior rhythms and superior
unities. /266/

The technique of the "stream of consciousness," or "interior
monologue," as Joyce uses it, is a formal aspect of the book which
sensitively reflects the boy's extreme spiritual isolation. There is a
logical suitability in the fact that this type of technique should arise
at a time of cultural debacle, when society has failed to give objective validation to inherited structures of belief, and when therefore
all meanings, values, and sanctions have to be built up from scratch
in the loneliness of the individual mind. When an author assumes
the right to enter his novel in his own voice and comment on his
characters—as Fielding does or George Eliot does—we are able to
infer a cultural situation in which there are objective points of
reference for the making of a judgment; the author and reader enter into overt agreement, as it were, in criticizing and judging the
character's actions; and where there is this assumption of agreement, we are in a relatively secure social world. The "gregarious
point of view" used by the older novelists reflects a world, comparatively speaking, of shared standards. As the technical point of view
adopted by the novelist more and more tends to exclude the novel-

ist's own expression of opinion from his book, the world which he represents tends more and more to be one whose values are in question; and we have, for instance, in the later work of Henry James, a work such as *The Ambassadors,* where the subjective point of view of the main character is dominant, a concentration on a process of mind in which values are reshifted and rejudged from top to bottom, all in the loneliness of an individual's personal experience. The technique of the "interior monologue" is a modification of the subjective point of view. It is not a departure from traditional convention, for even Fielding used this point of view when he wanted to show "from the inside" how a character's mind worked; but it is an employment of the subjective point of view throughout the entire novel—instead of sporadically, as in the older English novel— and it follows more devious and various paths of consciousness than traditional novelists were concerned with. Joyce's concern, in the *Portrait,* is with the associative patterns arising in Stephen's mind from infancy into adolescence. What we need to emphasize, however, is that he is concerned with these only as they show the dialectical process by which a world-shape evolves in the mind. The process is conducted in the absolute solitude of the inside of the skull, for Stephen has no trustworthy help from the objective environment. The technique of the "interior monologue" is the sensitive formal representation of that mental solitude. /267/

"By thinking of things you could understand them," Stephen says to himself when he arrives at the conclusion that the epithet "Tower of Ivory," in the litany of the Blessed Virgin, means what Eileen's hand felt like in his pocket—like ivory, only soft—and that "House of Gold" means what her hair had looked like, streaming out behind her like gold in the sun. Shortly before, he has been puzzling over the fact that Dante does not wish him to play with Eileen because Eileen is a Protestant, and the Protestants "make fun of the litany of the Blessed Virgin," saying, "How could a woman be a tower of ivory or a house of gold?" Who was right then, the Protestants or the Catholics? Stephen's analytical quandary is resolved by the perception of the identity between the feel of Eileen's prying hand and the meaning of "Tower of Ivory." In the same way, by the same dialectical process, his flooding impressions reach a stage of cohesion from moment to moment, a temporary synthesis in which he suddenly sees what they "mean." As Stephen matures, there is mounted on the early association between the Virgin and Eileen an identification between his dream-Mercedes (ideal girl in a rose-cottage) and a whore. By extension, this association holds in it much of Stephen's struggle between other-worldliness and this-worldliness, for it has identified in his imagination flesh and spirit, while his intellect, developing under education, rebels against the identification.[1] Thus "the word"—Tower of Ivory, House of Gold—creates by accident and at random the reality of suffering and act.

Those moments in the dialectical process when a synthesis is achieved, when certain phrases or sensations or complex experiences suddenly cohere in a larger whole and a meaning shines forth from the whole, Joyce—who introduced the word into literary currency—called "epiphanies." They are "showings-forth" of the nature of reality as the boy is prepared to grasp it. Minor epiphanies mark all the stages of Stephen's understanding, as when the feel of Eileen's hand shows him what Tower of Ivory means, or as when the word "Foetus," carved on a school desk, suddenly focuses for him in brute clarity his "monstrous way of life." Major epiphanies, occurring at the end of each chapter, mark the chief revelations of the nature of his environment and of his destiny in it. The epiphany is an image, sensuously apprehended and emotionally vibrant, which communicates instantaneously the meaning of experience. It may contain a revelation of a per- /268/ son's character, brief and fleeting, occurring by virtue of some physical trait in the person, as the way big Corrigan looked in the bath:

He had skin the same colour as the turf-coloured bogwater in the shallow end of the bath and when he walked along the side his feet slapped loudly on the wet tiles and at every step his thighs shook a little because he was fat.

In this kind of use, as revelation through one or two physical traits of the whole mass-formation of a personality, the epiphany is almost precisely duplicable in Dickens, as in the spectacle of Miss Havisham leaning on her crutch beside the rotten bridecake, or of Jaggers flourishing his white handkerchief and biting his great forefinger. The minor personalities in the *Portrait* are reduced to something very like a Dickensian "signature"—as Heron with his bird-beaked face and bird-name, Davin with his peasant turns of speech, Lynch whose "long slender flattened skull beneath the long pointed cap brought before Stephen's mind the image of a hooded reptile." Or the epiphany may be a kind of "still life" with which are associated deep and complex layers of experience and emotion. In the following passage, for instance, the sordor of Stephen's home,

[1] Irene Hendry points this out in her admirable essay "Joyce's Epiphanies," in *James Joyce: Two Decades of Criticism*, edited by Seon Givens (New York: Vanguard Press, Inc., 1948).

the apprehensive and guilty image of the bath at Clongowes, and the bestiality he associates with the bogholes of Ireland, are illuminated simultaneously by a jar of drippings on the table.

He drained his third cup of watery tea to the dregs and set to chewing the crusts of fried bread that were scattered near him, staring into the dark pool of the jar. The yellow dripping had been scooped out like a boghole, and the pool under it brought back to his memory the dark turf-coloured water of the bath at Clongowes.

Here the whole complex of home, school, and nation is epitomized in one object and shot through with the emotion of rejection. The epiphany is usually the result of a gradual development of the emotional content of associations, as they accrete with others. Among Stephen's childish impressions is that of "a woman standing at the halfdoor of a cottage with a child in her arms," and

it would be lovely to sleep for one night in that cottage before the fire /269/ of smoking turf, in the dark lit by the fire, in the warm dark, breathing the smell of the peasants, air and rain and turf and corduroy . . .

The early impression enters into emotional context, later, with the story Davin tells him about stopping at night at the cottage of a peasant woman, and Stephen's image of the woman is for him an epiphany of the soul of Ireland: "a batlike soul waking to the consciousness of itself in darkness and secrecy and loneliness." The epiphany is dynamic, activated by the form-seeking urgency in experience, and itself feeding later revelations. At the point of exile, Stephen feels, "under the deepened dusk,"

the thoughts and desires of the race to which he belonged flitting like bats, across the dark country lanes, under trees by the edges of streams and near the pool mottled bogs.

The major epiphanies in the book occur as the symbolic climaxes of the larger dialectical movements constituting each of the five chapters. As Hugh Kenner has pointed out, in his essay *"The Portrait* in Perspective,"[2] each of the chapters begins with a multitude of warring impressions, and each develops toward an emotionally apprehended unity; each succeeding chapter liquidates the previous synthesis and subjects its elements to more adult scrutiny in a constantly enlarging field of perception, and develops toward its own synthesis and affirmation. In each chapter, out of the multitude of elements with which it opens, some one chief conflict slowly shapes itself. In the first, among all the bewildering impressions

[2] In *James Joyce: Two Decades of Criticism,* cited above.

that the child's mind entertains, the deeper conflict is that between his implicit trust in the authority of his elders—his Jesuit teachers, the older boys in the school, his father and Mr. Casey and Dante—and his actual sense of insecurity. His elders, since they apparently know the meaning of things, must therefore incarnate perfect justice and moral and intellectual consistency. But the child's real experience is of mad quarrels at home over Parnell and the priests, and at school the frivolous cruelty of the boys, the moral chaos suggested by the smugging in the square and the talk about stealing the altar wine, and the sadism of Father Dolan with his pandybat. With Stephen's visit to the rector at the end of the chapter, the conflict is resolved. Justice is triumphant—even a small boy with weak eyes can find it; he is greeted like a hero on his emergence from the rector's office; his consolidation with his human environment is gloriously affirmed.

The second chapter moves straight from that achievement of emo- /270/ tional unity into other baffling complexities, coincident with the family's removal to Dublin. The home life is increasingly squalid, the boy more lonely and restless. In Simon Dedalus' account of his conversation with the rector of Clongowes about the incident of the pandying, what had seemed, earlier, to be a triumph of justice and an affirmation of intelligent moral authority by Stephen's elders is revealed as cruel, stupid indifference. In the episode in which Stephen is beaten for "heresy," the immediate community of his schoolfellows shows itself as false, shot through with stupidity and sadism. More importantly, the image of the father is corroded. On the visit to Cork, Simon appears to the boy's despairing judgment as besotted, self-deluded, irresponsible—and with the corruption of the father-image his whole picture of society suffers the same ugly damage. On the same visit, Stephen's early dim apprehension of sin and guilt is raised into horrible prominence by the word "Foetus" which he sees inscribed on the desk at Queen's College and which symbolizes for him all his adolescent monstrosity (the more monstrous in that Simon looks with obscene sentimentality on the desk carvings, thus condemning the whole world for Stephen in his own sickened sense of guilt). Meanwhile, his idealistic longings for beauty and purity and gentleness and certitude have concentrated in a vaguely erotic fantasy of the dream-girl Mercedes in her rose-cottage. Again, at the end of the chapter, Stephen's inner conflict is resolved in an emotional unity, a new vision of the relationships between the elements of experience. The synthesis is constituted here by a triumphant integration of the dream of Mercedes with the encounter with the whore. It is "sin" that triumphs, but sublimated as an ideal unity, pure and gentle and beautiful and emotionally securing.

As Hugh Kenner has observed, in the essay cited above, the predominant physical activity in *The Portrait* that accompanies Stephen's mental dialectics, as he moves through analysis to new provisional syntheses, is the activity of walking; his ambulatory movements take him into new localities, among new impressions, as his mind moves correspondingly into new spiritual localities that subsume the older ones and readjust them as parts of a larger whole. Living in Dublin, his walks take him toward the river and the sea —toward the fluid thing that, like the "stream" of his thoughts, seems by its searching mobility to imply a more engrossing reality. At first, in Dublin, the boy

contented himself with circling timidly round the neighbouring square or, at most, going half way down one of the side streets; but /271/ when he had made a skeleton map of the city in his mind he followed boldly one of its central lines until he reached the Custom House . . . The vastness and strangeness of the life suggested to him by the bales of merchandise stocked along the walls or swung aloft out of the holds of streamers wakened again in him the unrest which had sent him wandering in the evening from garden to garden in search of Mercedes . . . A vague dissatisfaction grew up within him as he looked on the quays and on the river and on the lowering skies and yet he continued to wander up and down day after day as if he really sought someone that eluded him.

On his visit to Cork with his father, in his wanderings in the brothel section of Dublin, on his seaward walk at the end of the fourth chapter when his chief revelation of personal destiny comes to him, on his later walks between home and the university, on his walk with Lynch during which he recapitulates his aesthetics, and with Cranly when he formulates his decision not "to serve"—on each of these peripatetic excursions, his mind moves toward more valid organizations of experience, as his feet carry him among other voices and images and into more complex fields of perception.

In the third chapter of the book, the hortations to which he is exposed during the retreat pull him down from his exaltation in sin and analyze his spiritual state into a multitude of subjective horrors that threaten to engulf him entirely and jeopardize his immortal soul. The conflict is resolved during a long walk which he takes blindly and alone, and that carries him to a strange place where he feels able to make his confession. A new synthesis is achieved through his participation in the Mass. Chapter 4 shows him absorbed in a dream of a saintly career, but his previous emotional affirmation has been frittered and wasted away in the performance of pedantically formal acts of piety, and he is afflicted with doubts, insecurities, rebellions. Release from conflict comes with a clear refusal of a vocation in the church, objectified by his decision to enter the university. And again it is on a walk that he realizes the measure of the new reality and the new destiny.

He has abandoned his father to a public house and has set off toward the river and the sea.

The university! So he had passed beyond the challenge of the sentries who had stood as guardians of his boyhood and had sought to keep him among them that he might be subject to them and serve /272/ their ends. Pride after satisfaction uplifted him like long slow waves. The end he had been born to serve yet did not see had led him to escape by an unseen path: and now it beckoned to him once more and a new adventure was about to be opened to him. It seemed to him that he heard notes of fitful music leaping upwards a tone and downwards a diminishing fourth, upwards a tone and downwards a major third, like triple-branching flames leaping fitfully, flame after flame, out of a midnight wood. It was an elfin prelude, endless and formless; and, as it grew wilder and faster, the flames leaping out of time, he seemed to hear from under the boughs and grasses wild creatures racing, their feet pattering like rain upon the leaves. Their feet passed in pattering tumult over his mind, the feet of hares and rabbits, the feet of harts and hinds and antelopes, until he heard them no more and remembered only a proud cadence from Newman:—
—Whose feet are as the feet of harts and underneath the everlasting arms.

The imagery is that of mobile, going things, increasingly passionate and swift—first slow waves, then fitful music leaping, then flames, then racing creatures. A phrase of his own making comes to his lips: "A day of dappled seaborne clouds." The dappled color and the sea movement of the clouds are of the same emotional birth as the images of music and flames. All are of variety and mobility of perception, as against stasis and restriction. Physically Stephen is escaping from his father—and the public house where he has left Simon is the sordid core of that Dublin environment whose false claims on his allegiance he is trying to shake off; at the same time he is realizing a "first noiseless sundering" with his mother, a break that is related to his decision against accepting a vocation in the church. Dublin, the tangible and vocal essence of his nationality, and the Roman church, the mold of his adolescent intellect, have failed to provide him with a vision of reality corresponding with his experience, and he thinks in terms of a movement beyond these—toward another and mysterious possible synthesis. "And underneath the everlasting arms": the phrase from Newman implies an ultimate unity wherein all the real is held in wholeness. Toward this problem-

atic divine embrace Stephen moves, but it is only problematic and
he can approach it only by his own movement. The epiphany which
confronts him in this moment on the beach is a manifestation of his
destiny in terms of a winged movement. He hears his name, Dedalus, called out, and the name seems to be prophetic. /273/

... at the name of the fabulous artificer, he seemed to hear the noise of
dim waves and to see a winged form flying above the waves and slowly
climbing the air ... a hawklike man flying sunward above the sea, a
prophecy of the end he had been born to serve and had been following
through the mists of childhood and boyhood, a symbol of the artist forging anew in his workshop out of the sluggish matter of the earth a new
soaring impalpable imperishable being ...

The ending of Chapter 4 presents this new consciousness in terms
of an ecstatic state of sensibility. It is marked by the radiant image
of the girl standing in a rivulet of tide, seeming "like one whom
magic had changed into the likeness of a strange and beautiful sea-
bird ... touched with the wonder of mortal beauty," while his own
life cries wildly to him, "To live, to err, to fall, to triumph, to recreate
life out of life!" The girl is a "wild angel" that has appeared to him,
to "throw open before him in an instant of ecstasy the ways of error
and glory." The batlike woman-soul of his race, flitting in darkness
and secrecy and loneliness, has given place to this angelic emissary
from "the fair courts of life," of strange seabird beauty, inviting
him to exile across waters and into other languages, as the sun-as-
sailing and perhaps doomed Icarus. And it is in the flights of birds
that Stephen, standing on the steps of the university library, in the
last chapter, reads like an ancient haruspex the sanction of his exile.

With Chapter 5, Stephen's new consciousness of destiny is subjected to intellectual analysis. Here, during his long walks with
Lynch and Cranly, all the major elements that have exerted emotional claims upon him—his family, church, nation, language—are
scrutinized dryly, their claims torn down and scattered in the youth-
fully pedantic and cruel light of the adolescent's proud commitment
to art. Here also he formulates his aesthetics, the synthesis which he
has contrived out of a few scraps of medieval learning. In his aesthetic formulation, the names he borrows from Aquinas for "the
three things needed for beauty"—*integritas, consonantia, claritas*—
are names for those aspects of reality—wholeness, harmoniousness,
significant character—that he has been seeking all his life, from earliest childhood. His aesthetic formulation is thus a synthesis of the
motivations of his psychological life from the beginning; and the
vocation of artist which he has chosen is the vocation of one who
consciously sets himself the task of apprehending and then repre-

senting in his art whatever wholeness, harmony, and meaning the world has./274/

In an earlier version of *The Portrait,* called *Stephen Hero,* it is said that the task of the artist is to

disentangle the subtle soul of the image from its mesh of defining circumstances most exactly and "re embody" it in artistic circumstances chosen as the most exact for it in its new office . . .

The "new office" of the image is to communicate to others the significant character of a complete and harmonious body of experience. The artist is a midwife of epiphanies. Joyce's doctrine of the epiphany assumes that reality does have wholeness and harmony—even as Stephen as a child premises these, and with the same trustfulness—and that it will radiantly show forth its character and its meaning to the prepared consciousness, for it is only in the body of reality that meaning can occur and only there that the artist can find it. This is essentially a religious interpretation of the nature of reality and of the artist's function. It insists on the objectivity of the wholeness, harmony, and meaning, and on the objectivity of the revelation—the divine showing-forth.

At Clongowes Wood, there had been a picture of the earth on the first page of Stephen's geography, "a big ball in the middle of clouds," and on the flyleaf of the book Stephen had written his name and "where he was."

Stephen Dedalus
Class of Elements
Clongowes Wood College
Sallins
County Kildare
Ireland
Europe
The World
The Universe

His ambulatory, dialectical journey is a quest to find the defining unity, the composing harmony, and the significant character of each of these broadening localities containing Stephen Dedalus, and the intelligible relationships making each functional in the next. It is an attempt, by progressive stages, at last to bring the term "Stephen Dedalus" into relationship with the term "The Universe." Through the book he moves from one geographical and spiritual orbit to another, "walking" in lengthening /275/ radius until he is ready to take up flight. As a child at Clongowes it had pained him that he did not know what came after the universe.

What was after the universe? Nothing. But was there anything round the
universe to show where it stopped before the nothing place began? It
could not be a wall but there could be a thin thin line there all round
everything. It was very big to think about everything and everywhere. Only
God could do that. He tried to think what a big thought that must be but
he could think only of God. God was God's name just as his name was
Stephen. *Dieu* was the French for God and that was God's name too; and
when anyone prayed to God and said Dieu then God knew at once that
was a French person that was praying. But though there were different
names for God in all the different languages in the world and God understood what all the people who prayed said in their different languages
still God remained always the same God and God's real name was God.

At the end of the book Stephen is prepared at least to set forth on
the "dappled, seaborne clouds" that float beyond Ireland and over
Europe. His search is still to find out "what came after the universe." The ultimate epiphany is withheld, the epiphany of "everything and everywhere" as one and harmonious and meaningful.
But it is prophesied in "God's real name," as Stephen's personal
destiny is prophesied in his own name "Dedalus." It is to be found
in the labyrinth of language that contains all human revelation
vouchsafed by divine economy, and to be found by the artist in
naming the names. /276/

The Calling of Stephen Dedalus

Stephen Dedalus as he appears in *A Portrait of the Artist as a Young Man* is far from being a godlike hero. Groping painfully toward some understanding of himself and his place in the world, he is sometimes laughable, sometimes pathetic, and nearly always what we should call "difficult." Yet despite his all too human failings he has the almost superhuman courage to face the world alone, and a profound conviction that the artist is quasi-divine. This conviction is brought out in one of the most closely written passages in the novel, the description of Stephen after the composition of his villanelle, standing on the steps of the library, ashplant in hand, watching the flight of some birds which he takes to be swallows. After observing the birds minutely, he begins (characteristically) to observe himself observing the birds and to think of himself as an augur in an ancient temple. As overtones of the supernatural increase in intensity, he thinks of his mythical patron, Daedalus, and then, for several moments, of a god who is closely analogous to Stephen.

A sense of fear of the unknown moved in the heart of his weariness, a fear of symbols and portents, of the hawklike man whose name he bore soaring out of his captivity on osier woven wings, of Thoth, the god of writers, writing with a reed upon a tablet and bearing on his narrow ibis head the cusped moon.

He smiled as he thought of the god's image, for it made him think of a bottle-nosed judge in a wig, putting commas into a document which he held at arm's length. . . .[1]

Eugene M. Waith, "The Calling of Stephen Dedalus," *College English*, XVIII (February, 1957), 256-61.

[1] *A Portrait of the Artist as a Young Man* (Modern Library, 1928), pp. 264-265. All page references are to this edition. See W. Y. Tindall's comment on this passage in his "James Joyce and the Hermetic Tradition," *JHI*, XV (1954), 23-39; see also his *The Literary Symbol* (1955), pp. 57-58, 79-84.

77

Stephen's mental image of Thoth with a headdress suggesting a
judge's wig, the long beak of an ibis, and writing on a tablet held
at arm's length closely resembles depictions of the god in the Book
of the Dead at the ceremony of the weighing of the heart. There
the deceased is assayed while Thoth, an observer slightly removed,
stands ready to add this last judgment to his record of good and evil.
Thoth was the scribe of the gods, but he was also much more: he
was the god of wisdom, the inventor of speech and letters and, somewhat like the divine *logos*, the one at whose word everything was
created. Stephen's "god of writers" is a potent symbol, emblematic
in a number of ways of Stephen himself, the artist as a young man,
observing, recording, creating.

The suggestion of artistic and divine creativity in this allusion is
particularly important as a counterbalance to the suggestion of a
satanic fall made most overtly in Stephen's "I will not serve." Two
stimulating essays on the *Portrait* have emphasized recently the
theme of the fall while neglecting the theme of creativity;[2] the result is a distortion, as it seems to me, of the meaning of the novel.
For example, Caroline Gordon believes that one reason for the superiority of this novel to certain others which have a comparable
theme "is that Joyce is convinced that his hero is damned" (p. 393).
Hugh Kenner, in the course of an excellent demonstration of the
structural complexity of the *Portrait*, says, "Ultimately, as the insistent climax of the overture shows, its [the *Portrait's*] central theme
is Sin: the development of Stephen Dedalus from a /256/ bundle
of sensations to a matured, self-conscious, dedicated, fallen being"
(p. 142). Though the theme of the fall is undoubtedly significant,
it does not occur in isolation, but related and subordinated to what
the title of the novel leads us to expect as its main theme, Stephen's
development as an artist. The fall is assimilated into the preparations for flight—flight from Ireland and flight on the osier wings
of Daedalus, the old artificer to whom Stephen prays in the last words
of the novel.

If the central theme is sin, then these final preparations for
flight are supremely ironic, and in this way they have been interpreted. After commenting on the "instant of promise" at the end,
Kenner goes on to say that in *Ulysses* we see clearly that Stephen's
dream of flight is a delusion. He concludes that we should see Stephen, even at the end of *A Portrait*, as an esthete but no artist—a
would-be flyer whose fall from grace will soon be followed by an-

[2] Caroline Gordon, "Some Readings and Misreadings," *SR*, LXI (1953), 388-
393; Hugh Kenner, "The Portrait in Perspective," *James Joyce, Two Decades
of Criticism*, ed. Seon Givens (1948), pp. 132-174.

other fall like that of Icarus. But there is no indication in *A Portrait* that this kind of irony exists. Ironic detachment there certainly is: no one who has studied the differences between *Stephen Hero* and the final version of the story can doubt that Joyce manipulated the materials of his own life very freely and with great artistic objectivity. He never fails, in painting his final portrait, to indicate what is unlikable, weak, or foolish in his adolescent protagonist. Yet to grant all this is not to say that he brands Stephen as already a failure—still less that he shows the failure to be the consequence of rejecting the church. The entire fabric of the novel seems to proclaim its concern with potentialities, with vocation, with the moments leading to the choice of a career. The depiction of this process is brilliantly successful in making the final choice seem the inevitable outgrowth of character. The time has not come for a final judgment and the book makes none, though every stroke of the depiction is informed by a keen moral awareness.

A Portrait of the Artist as a Young Man defines with elaborate care the conditions of creativity for a particular writer, Stephen Dedalus. Though the action of the novel makes these conditions reasonably clear, the subtlety of the definition lies in a delicate and complex pattern of images reflecting the hero's growing convictions. I propose to examine one part of this pattern—a number of passages related by their imagery and all bearing on the crucial question of the place of Stephen's religious experiences in his artistic development.

Two sets of images appear together in the long description of the bird-watching, part of which I have already quoted: images of flight and images of flow. Their association provides a clue which can profitably be pursued through the novel. After the circling swallows have made Stephen think of the bird-man, Daedalus, and the bird-god, Thoth, they bring to his mind some verses from Yeats's *Countess Cathleen*:

> *Bend down your faces, Oona and Aleel,*
> *I gaze upon them as the swallow gazes*
> *Upon the nest under the eave before*
> *He wander the loud waters.*

A soft liquid joy like the noise of many waters flowed over his memory and he felt in his heart the soft peace of silent spaces of fading tenuous sky above the waters, of oceanic silence, of swallows flying through the seadusk over the flowing waters.

A soft liquid joy flowed through the words where the soft long vowels hurtled noiselessly and fell away, lapping and flowing back and ever shaking the white bells of their waves in mute chime and mute peal and soft low swooning cry.... (p. 265)

As creative power is suggested by the flight of the swallows through Stephen's association with Daedalus and Thoth, so his delight and satisfaction with words—especially the sound of words—are conveyed in the image of the flowing water over which the swallow flies in Yeats's lyric (Stephen's identification of himself with the swallow is suggested by his changing the pronoun in the fourth line /257/ from Yeats's "she" to "he"). When we look at some of the other appearances in the novel of the images of flight and flow we find that they play a major part in the definition of the proper conditions for creativity.

After Stephen's first successful self-assertion, his protest against the injustice of Father Dolan, he is described "alone," "happy and free," and as he listens to the sound of the cricket bats they sound "like drops of water in a fountain falling softly in the brimming bowl" (p. 64). In the second chapter flowing water is associated with both the disorderly life of his father's house and the riotous imagings of his aroused sexual desire. With a little prize money he tries to make a new life, charitable and orderly, but the money is soon gone and the scheme collapses. The end is thus described:

> How foolish his aim had been! He had tried to build a breakwater of order and elegance against the sordid tide of life without him and to dam up, by rules of conduct and active interests and new filial relations, the powerful recurrence of the tide within him. Useless. From without as from within the water had flowed over his barriers: their tides began once more to jostle fiercely above the crumbled mole. (pp. 110-111)

These "sordid tides" seem very different from the dripping water of the fountain, yet in both cases the images of overflowing are related to a rebellion against order, that of a classroom tyrant or of Stephen in his mood of self-reform. The pressure of "a presence subtle and murmurous as a flood" leads finally to the embrace of the streetwalker described at the close of the second chapter. His experience is at least a sort of communication, "a vague speech," and as such is briefly satisfying to the isolated adolescent.

Soon, however, sensual indulgence is presented in images which reflect a great change in attitude: "His soul was fattening and congealing into a gross grease . . ." (p. 127). Once more Stephen's lust is related to the life of his father's house, for he is revolted there by the thick gravies and the grease: in both his inner and his outer life there is viscosity instead of the flowing tide. Throughout the third chapter, from which these quotations are taken, Stephen conceives of his sin as revolting bestiality. In his nightmare after the famous sermons of the retreat these feelings reach a peak of horror

expressed in images of excrement, which follow logically in this
viscous series.

The flow of this rebellion of the senses has coarsened and thick-
ened to the point where it has stopped itself. What was at first a release has become a horrible restraint. Yet before the process is complete there is a hint that the excursion into sensuality is not entirely
worthless. As Stephen sits thinking about his sin and working at a
mathematical problem, an equation in his scribbler begins to look
like the unfolding tail of a peacock, and Stephen sees it as his own
soul, "going forth to experience, unfolding itself sin by sin" (p. 116),
and then folding back and fading. The meaning of the passage
seems to be double: the failure of Stephen's present way of life is
foreshadowed, while at the same time sin is presented as an unfolding, a development. A water image suggests what value the experience may have:

At his first violent sin he had felt a wave of vitality pass out of him, and
had feared to find his body or his soul maimed by the excess. Instead the
vital wave had carried him on its bosom out of himself and back again
when it receded: and no part of body or soul had been maimed, but a
dark peace had been established between them. The chaos in which his
ardour extinguished itself was a cold indifferent knowledge of himself.
(pp. 116-117)

The "chaos" of Stephen's self-knowledge here anticipates his later
break with "the order of life out of which he had come" (p. 265).

The fourth chapter opens with the superbly comic description of
the religious regime Stephen imposes upon himself /258/ after he has
made his confession. It is like the "new life" he began with his
prize money, but far more elaborately contrived. Once more the
temptations of the flesh return to threaten the newly established order and once more they are portrayed in terms of the flood (pp. 176-
177). Stephen now associates the "sluggish turf-coloured water" of
the Clongowes bath with the "grave and ordered and passionless
life" of the priests at the college (pp. 186-187). The standing water
and the "moist unsustaining air" above it symbolize an ordered life,
and they repel Stephen almost as much as the images of grease and
excrement which symbolize complete submission to the flesh. Somewhat later in the book (p. 202), the grease in the kitchen at home
reminds him of the "turfcoloured bogwater," just as the life of the
priests reminds him of it here. This series of associations shows that
the religious life is ultimately as hostile to Stephen's needs as is the
life of worldly self-indulgence exemplified by his brief career in
the brothels and also by the very different but equally self-indulgent

career of his father, Simon Dedalus. The kinds of life associated with images of viscosity and stagnation have one characteristic in common: they seem to Stephen to threaten his freedom of spirit.

The passage in which Stephen makes his choice of an artist's life combines images of flight with those of flowing water. The voices of his friends calling his strange name seem charged with symbolic appeal: he seems "to hear the noise of dim waves and to see a winged form flying above the waves . . . (p. 196). He walks barefoot in the sea-water, "dark with endless drift," and sees the wading girl, who seems "like one whom magic had changed into the likeness of a strange and beautiful sea-bird." Profoundly moved, but not sexually aroused, he looks at her for a few moments, then turns away and strides off across the sand, "singing wildly to the sea" (pp. 199-200). Stephen has "fallen" in that he has taken a beautiful body as an object of contemplation instead of the religious mysteries with which he occupied his mind after his confession and communion, yet his excitement is what he is later to describe as "the esthetic emotion," which is static: "The mind is arrested and raised above desire and loathing" (p. 240). Instead of plunging Stephen again in the mire of sensuality, this "fall" advances him toward the artistic goal he envisages:

Her image had passed into his soul for ever and no word had broken the holy silence of his ecstasy. Her eyes had called him and his soul had leaped at the call. To live, to err, to fall, to triumph, to recreate life out of life! (p. 200)

Not only the arrangement of this series but the association of the girl with a bird and with flowing water shows that the experience, though far removed from the "grave and ordered and passionless life" of the clergy, is equally removed from the life of the senses as it is usually conceived. That the experience and the prose describing it are intensely romantic reveals to the reader that Joyce is contriving with careful particularity the career of a certain artist at a certain time.

Stephen's ecstatic contemplation of the girl on the shore is emblematic of the life which he feels himself destined to lead—in the world but not of it. Twice in Chapter Four, once plainly and once more symbolically, this destiny is described. The first passage comes shortly after his association of the priests' life with the sluggish water of the Clongowes bath:

His destiny was to be elusive of social or religious orders. The wisdom of the priest's appeal did not touch him to the quick. He was destined to learn his own wisdom apart from others or to learn the wisdom of others himself wandering among the snares of the world. (p. 188)

"Elusive" of orders yet "wandering among the snares of the world," uncaught, moving freely. A similar distinction is /259/ made at the moment when Stephen sees his true vocation:

> His throat ached with a desire to cry aloud, the cry of a hawk or eagle on high, to cry piercingly of his deliverance to the winds. This was the call of life to his soul not the dull gross voice of the world of duties and despair, not the inhuman voice that had called him to the pale service of the altar. An instant of wild flight had delivered him. . . . (p. 197)

Stephen's artistic destiny is not to belong exclusively to either the world of the flesh or the world of the spirit. The images of flight, like those of flowing water, suggest the freedom he must have, but their emphasis is not entirely upon escape. The flight of Daedalus is not only an escape but a widening of consciousness, an investigation of the unknown, as Joyce reminds us by quoting on his first page Ovid's line, *"Et ignotas animum dimittit in artes"* (*Met.*, VIII, 18). The images of flight relate freedom, increasing perception, and creativity. In this way part of the novel's statement is made: Stephen seeks freedom from the world and from the church as a condition necessary for new perception and for artistic creation. He sees sin as a stage in the development. The image of the unfolding peacock's tail is related to his thought of his soul, "unfolding itself sin by sin" (p. 116). Another bird image, that of a bat flying in darkness, also presents his association of sin and understanding. It comes to him in connection with the story his friend Davin tells of a country wife who asked him in for the night. For Stephen she is the type of her race and his, "a batlike soul waking to the consciousness of itself in darkness and secrecy and loneliness" (p. 213). Stephen's choice of a vocation may thus be seen as a choice of flux rather than any already created order, of flight into the forbidden and the unknown in order to understand and ultimately to recreate.

The fifth chapter, by far the longest in the novel, elaborates upon the significance of the choice while presenting scenes from Stephen's university life. In the section dealing with Davin, the Irish nationalist, we see Stephen's rejection of the social and political order of his country. In the conversation with Lynch we get the description of the static nature of esthetic experience as Stephen understands it—the artist's dependence upon the stimuli of the senses and the detachment he must yet have from sensual indulgence. As a further example of these complex relationships we have the transmutation of Stephen's jealousy and his longing for "E. C." into his villanelle, "Are you not weary of ardent ways." The composition of the poem begins amid imaginary sensations of music and cool waters and after a significant parody of Scripture, "In the virgin womb of the imagination the word was made flesh." He thinks of "E. C.," like Davin's temptress, as "a batlike soul waking to the consciousness of itself" (p. 259) and surmises that her soul had "begun to live as his soul had when he had first sinned" (p. 261). The composition of the final stanza is described as an imaginary act of sexual intercourse, in which "E. C." is metamorphosed into the words of the poem while both are symbolized by flowing water. No passage in the book links temptation more unequivocally with artistic creativity, and none makes more clear that the emphasis is not finally upon sin.

Immediately following is the scene on the library steps with which I began. With its descriptions of birds and water and music, its allusions to gods and augurs, to the "liquid joy" of words, to the play by Yeats which Dublin noisily rejected, to Daedalus and to Thoth, this passage restates the theme of Stephen's choice of a profession, reminding the reader, more by symbol than by statement, of the meaning and consequences of the choice. Daedalus, always present in the hero's name, referred to in the epigraph and in the last words, belongs to the pattern of imagery we have been tracing, and serves as a con- /260/ stant reminder of the courage and force of artistic endeavor. The artist may be doomed to bitter disappointment as Dedalus was, but even this is not Joyce's subject in *A Portrait of the Artist as a Young Man*. He presents the potential artist, the young man not fallen but girding himself for flight—called but not yet chosen. We are not obliged to take Stephen's exaltation at face value nor, on the other hand, to see in it the corrupt will of a "fallen being." It is part of Stephen's "whatness," portrayed with neither approval nor disapproval by an "indifferent" artist, who has "refined himself out of existence." /261/

The Perceptions of James Joyce

JOHN V. KELLEHER

If the day should come that I walk into the classroom, unfurl my opening lecture on Joyce, and find at the end of the hour that I had as well been talking about Alfred Lord Tennyson, I shall not be unduly surprised. No writer's original fame lasts forever with the young. Joyce has already had an unusually long run with them; and though their interest shows no present signs of weakening, when it does fail it will likely fail suddenly. Everything in literature has its term, and, if worthy, its renewal. That the rediscovery of Joyce will occur, with full fanfare, within a generation after his rejection, may be taken as certain. However, that will be no affair of mine.

Meanwhile, I predict with confidence that when the rest of Joyce's books pass into temporary disfavor *A Portrait of the Artist As a Young Man* will go on being read, possibly as much as ever, by youths from eighteen to twenty-two. They will read it and recommend it to one another just as lads their age do now, and for the same reasons. That is, they will read it primarily as useful and reassuring revelation—not as literature, for they will be blind to its irony and its wonderful engineering, the qualities Joyce most labored to give it. They will use it as a magic mirror: as boys of thirteen use *Huckleberry Finn* and as sixteen-going-on-seventeen looks into the *Rubáiyát of Omar Khayyám* for graceful corroboration of its own grim apprehension of The Meaning of Life. I should think it doubtful that Joyce had these readers in mind when he wrote the book, any more than FitzGerald foresaw for his nearly original poem its permanent audience of callow fatalists; but, like it or not, this is part of his achievement.

Joyce did complain that readers tended to forget the last four words of the title. He could have remarked, too, that the book was

John V. Kelleher, "The Perceptions of James Joyce," *Atlantic Monthly*, CCI (Mar., 1958), 82 ff.

not the *Self-Portrait of the Artist As a Young Man.* All too often it
is read as if it were so named. Then the author himself is belabored
for the sins and the more than occasional priggishness of his hero,
or, conversely, is credited with having possessed in youth the same
astonishing clarity of purpose and action.

Either assumption is unjust to Joyce. True, Stephen Dedalus is
endowed with a personal history quite similar to his creator's; his
experiences are modeled on those Joyce himself suffered or enjoyed
at that age; and as Joyce, writing the book, is the mature artist, so
Stephen is a repre- /82/ sentation of the artist-by-nature as he discovers his vocation, defines his creed, and sets forth to practice it.
There, I think, close resemblance ends. Joyce's life happened to him
as everyone's life happens—at all hours and seasons, any old way,
with chronic inconvenience. Stephen's existence, though presented
in rich detail, is at once the product and the illustration of deliberate
composition in terms of a consciously created aesthetic.

I remember that when I first encountered Stephen Dedalus I was
twenty and I wondered how Joyce could have known so much
about me. That is what I mean by the sort of reading the book will
continue to get, whatever literary fashion may decree. Perhaps
about the third reading it dawned on me that Stephen was, after
all, a bit of a prig; and to that extent I no longer identified myself
with him. (How could I? Quite a while later I perceived that
Joyce knew that Stephen was a prig; that, indeed, he looked on Stephen with quite an ironic eye. So then I understood. At least I did
until I had to observe that the author's glance was not one of un-
mixed irony. There was compassion in it too, as well as a sort of
tender, humorous pride. By this time I was lecturing on Joyce, and
I was having a terrible time with the book. I could not coordinate
what I had to say about it; and the students, as their papers showed,
were mostly wondering how Joyce could have known so much about
them—which was fortunate, for the lectures made very little sense,
and it was well that the victims had their own discoveries to distract
them.

The trouble was, I was trying to examine separate parts of the
book separately. There aren't any separate parts. One might as well
attempt to study a man's gestures by pulling off his arm and dissecting it. The book is all of a piece, one organic whole. It is, as it were,
written backwards and forwards and sideways and in depth, all at
once. A score of premises is laid down in the first twenty-odd pages.
From these, with deliberate and unobtrusive engineering, everything else is developed in the most natural-looking way possible.
The same words or the same basic images in which the premise was

expressed are used over and over again, development usually being measured by the variations of context in which they occur or by new combinations of these identifying words and images.

Described that way, the technique sounds dry as dust. Just some more damned symbolism. Unfortunately I can only suggest the vitality of Joyce's method by illustrating it, and in so short a compass as this essay I can get an illustration only by dissecting it from its text. A curiously uncooperative man he always was.

One early premise is the conjunction of red and green. Stephen, as a baby, has a song:

> O, the wild rose blossoms
> On the little green place.

He sang that song. That was his song.

> O, the green wothe botheth.

The song is an old sentimental favorite, *Lily Dale*. The second line ought to be "On the little green grave," but this is a song taught to a very small child and so for *grave* is substituted the neutral *place*. What counts, however, is that as he sings it he confuses red and green into one image, the green rose.

On the next page the colors are still in proximity but are now separate.

Dante [his grandaunt] had two brushes in her press. The brush with the maroon velvet back was for Michael Davitt and the brush with the green velvet back was for Parnell.

A little later in the chapter the child, now at boarding school, is coming down with a fever and finds it hard to study. He looks at his geography where there is a picture of the earth amid clouds, which another boy, not he, had colored with crayons.

He . . . looked wearily at the green round earth in the middle of the maroon clouds. He wondered which was right, to be for the green or for the maroon, because Dante had ripped the green velvet back off the brush that was for Parnell one day with her scissors and had told him that Parnell was a bad man. He wondered if they were arguing at home about that. That was called politics. There were two sides in it: Dante was on one side and his father and Mr. Casey were on the other side but his mother and Uncle Charles were on no side.

He remembers the song, too. "But you could not have a green rose. But perhaps someplace in the world you could."

At night, sick and very lonely, he dreams of going home for

Christmas; and home is all in terms of a conjunction of green and red.

There were lanterns in the hall of his father's house and ropes of green branches. There were holly and ivy round the pierglass and holly and ivy, green and red, twined round the chandeliers. There were red holly and green ivy round the old portraits on the walls. Holly and ivy for him and for Christmas.

This simple union of red and green—say, of emotion and vitality, though that hardly expresses /84/ the whole meaning—is realized once more, for the last time, at the beginning of the famous Christmas dinner episode.

A great fire, banked high and red, flamed in the grate and under the ivy twined branches of the chandelier the Christmas table was spread.

But from there out, only the red of passion and the black of grief. The argument over Parnell and the bishops cannot be avoided or hushed. Dante, aflame with outraged pietism and heartburn, and the dark-faced Mr. Casey have it out uncontrollably. When Dante stamps from the room shouting, "Devil out of hell! We won! We crushed him to death! Fiend!", the household, like Ireland itself, is split asunder, the soldierly Casey is weeping for his "dead king," all color is crushed out of the scene—and, though the reader, caught up by the wild emotionality, is not likely to remember, confidence in custom has been broken too. Before the argument, Stephen had been thinking how

when dinner was ended the big plum pudding would be carried in, studded with peeled almonds and sprigs of holly, with bluish fire running around it and a little green flag flying from the top.

The pudding is never brought in. Stephen will never see Ireland happily on top of its own world.

Till the book reaches its climax, red and green remain apart. The dominant combination is red, black, and white: a false one for Stephen whether betokened by a red-faced priest with his white collar and black garb or by the dark hair and rosy complexion and white dress of E.C., the wrong girl for him. Meanwhile, half a dozen other themes are being developed through color, the most important being the white, gold, blue, and ivory of the Blessed Virgin to whom Stephen offers a dry and profitless devotion. The same four colors, though never all at once, indicate the image of beauty he must find among mortal women.

The book has five chapters. The first four chronicle Stephen's search for his true identity. As the very first sentence informs us, he is not truly of the family into which he was born—there he is "baby tuckoo," the cuckoo's fledgling in the cowbird's nest. He tries to find himself through obedience, through disobedience, through the family, through dream, through precocious sexuality, and finally and most earnestly through rigorous piety. Each attempt fails. He only learns in recurrent weariness and despair that he is not this, not that. Then suddenly, a little after he has refused to be trapped by vanity into falsely admitting a vocation for the priesthood, freedom possesses him. Freedom and expectation. He wanders out onto the strand at the north side of the river mouth where presentiment had long since warned him he would meet his love. Bond after bond falls away from him. Weariness is banished. Joyfully he feels his final separation from all that does not truly and wholly pertain to himself. He knows with absolute certainty that he is approaching his destiny in the "wild heart of life." Suddenly, too, color—all significant color—is around him, every hue transformed, red to russet and green to emerald. Almost on that instant he meets his Muse.

A girl stood before him in midstream: alone and still, gazing out to sea. She seemed like one whom magic had changed into the likeness of a strange and beautiful seabird. Her long slender bare legs were delicate as a crane's and pure save where an emerald trial of seaweed had fashioned itself as a sign upon the flesh. Her thighs, fuller and softhued as ivory, were bared almost to the hips where the white fringes of her drawers were like feathering of soft white down. Her slate-blue skirts were kilted boldly about her waist and dovetailed behind her. Her bosom was as a bird's, soft and slight, slight and soft as the breast of some dark-plumaged dove. But her long fair hair was girlish: and girlish, and touched with the wonder of mortal beauty, her face.

They look at each other without speaking. Then the girl withdraws her glance and begins to stir the water with her foot

hither and thither, hither and thither: and a faint flame trembled on her cheek.

Heavenly God! cried Stephen's soul, in an outburst of profane joy.

Here, then, the Virgin's colors and green and red, the strand of seaweed and the flame upon the cheek, are fused with the bird imagery that continues throughout the book from "baby tuckoo" on the first page to Dedalus, the winged artificer, who is evoked in the final sentence. The whole thus created is greater than the sum of its parts and has a new and greater meaning. Stephen's joy when he recognizes that meaning must be profane. The identity, the vocation, and the destiny here revealed to him are those of the artist. They demand a dedication as absolute as that of the priest—directed, however, not to the sacred and infinite, but to that sensual reality which is the artist's sole material. Now all that remains for Stephen to do is to free himself in actuality, work out the theology of his devotion, and after that, well, everything—with no flinching or excuses. It will be lucky for him that he has had at least this one moment of undiminished exultation.

I chose color for my illustration because, though it is much more elaborate than I have managed /86/ to indicate, it is the simplest continuing imagery in the book and because it is resolved. Other images convey more and are harder to follow, especially those based on abstract concepts like sphericity, extension, or systole and diastole (whether as the ebb and flow of tides, or the lengthening and shortening of lines in the solution of an algebraic problem, or a reaching out to infinity and a swift instinctive recurrence to self). Nearly as difficult are pair-words like "difference" and "indifference," or the notion of the "bounding line," or what seems mere natural description like the falling of rain or light, or the smell of turf smoke, or mist and vapors rising, or, in every instance, the moon. The very aesthetic that Stephen outlines to his sounding board, Lynch of the withered soul, employs a vocabulary already saturated with meaning from repeated use. When he says

The artist, like the God of the creation, remains within or behind or beyond or above his handiwork, invisible, refined out of existence, indifferent, paring his fingernails,

we may note that fingernails have been pared before—and will be again, as in *Ulysses* where Bloom looks out of the funeral coach, sees his wife's seducer, and looks at his own nails to see if they are pared, which they are.

This way of writing—I suppose we shall have to call it symbolism, though the word has been beaten shapeless—is, I believe, Joyce's natural and most central method. It antedates the *Portrait*. There are hints of it in the first story in *Dubliners;* and in the last, "The Dead," where the ubiquitous Mr. Brown is Death himself, it has already become systematic. At the same time, symbolism is never Joyce's sole method; it is always employed in conjunction with means which, though they receive reinforcement from it, are themselves self-sustaining.

Thus the *Portrait* functions well enough simply as a naturalistic novel. It was meant to. The book has several levels, each with a workable meaning of its own; and yet, since the containing form is the same for all levels, each meaning necessarily relates to the one overall statement. The irony that we remarked before depends on this. In the final chapter we have Stephen theorizing a little too positively about what he has not yet actually tried. This is his prig-gishness which, if honesty is to be complete, is inescapably part of the statement too. Proudly Stephen declares what qualities—forti-tude, discipline, detachment—characterize the true, and the very rare, artist. The novel, telling his story so intricately and simply, is the proof of those qualities. And the proof itself is a measure of how far Stephen has yet to travel, through how much discouragement and pain, before he can practice what he so confidently preaches: Again let us remember that this is not Stephen's self-portrait. When the book is written Stephen no longer exists.

Still, does even this achievement justify so much complexity? Or as the question is more usually put, has Joyce the right to demand so much of the reader? The answer, I think, is that he demands no more than the serious artist normally expects is due his work. All that he wrote can be validly appreciated as what it outwardly ap-pears to be, because it is what it outwardly appears, as well as much else. His short stories, his play, his novels are all true specimens. As a matter of fact, he was aggrieved that readers, probing worriedly for deeper significances, should so consistently miss what lay on the surface. He pointed out in exasperation that *Ulysses* was, after all, a funny book. It is indeed. And if the reader gets the symbolic mean-ings but misses the fun, he has missed a good third of what the au-thor was at pains to provide. Again, if the reader exploits the sym-bolism only for its meaning and fails to grasp its structural function, he has missed the deepest pleasure of all, the apprehension of pure form purely realized.

Not that such form is always achieved. The *Portrait* is Joyce's one perfected work, evenly sustained and controlled from end to end by a talent in calm dominion over its theme, its instruments, and itself. The books that followed were quite different. Joyce saw no point in doing the same job twice. In *Ulysses* he attempted much more, succeeded with more, and I feel, produced a book spotted with failure. *Finnegans Wake,* in which he tried to encompass nearly all that he considered humanly applicable reality, succeeded almost beyond imagination and failed frequently and flatly. In neither case is the success contradicted by the failure which it out-weighs quantitatively and morally—not to mention that the success could not be, and was not, predictable, being wholly novel.

The quantity and novelty of Joyce's achievement are obvious. Its moral quality is not so readily agreed on. Critics in a surprising variety have spoken as if the indifference Joyce enjoins upon the artist continues, with him, into a callous indifferentism toward all moral value. Some of his warmest admirers have sadly admitted his gamin irresponsibility and have sought cause or extenuation for it in the unideal circumstances of his life. A more frequent charge is "emptiness of content."

If an artist is to be judged by the positiveness of his advice on politics, quotidian morality, education, or what have you, Joyce does not rank very high. There is, however, the possibility that his /88/ silence on these matters may have been due to modesty. As an artist he was anything but modest—he simply regarded himself as the best of the age—but I see little in his work to indicate that he felt that the gift of expression carried with it the duty to express quotable judgments on what he knew no more about than the next man. And there are times, as when I read Yeats on government or Shaw on child-rearing, when I think Joyce's reticence is rather commendable.

Often, though, it is a painful reticence. He was past master of the confessorial technique that confesses nothing because it blabs too much. He could rarely permit himself to write simply from the heart, though when he did—as in the ending of *Finnegans Wake* or in the poem, "Ecce Puer," on his father's death and his grandson's birth—a most poignant power was released. Such passages give the lie to his usual affectation of wearing his heart up his sleeve. Why, then, the affectation? Partly, perhaps, because his artistic discipline was primarily late nineteenth century, art for art's sake, absolute subordination of subject to form, and because his subject was usually his own, often bitterly unhappy experience. What impelled him, I think, to choose and continue such a discipline was not just his artistic proclivities or the fact that he grew up in a cultural province where that view of art and the artist was still high fashion, but rather that he had a very Irish nature (counter to another Irish nature) that instinctively chose mockery if the alternative was tears. It is useless to observe that tears might often have been better for his health or that there are many places in his work where open emotion could have been admitted without loss of integrity. He was what he was. He hated what he called the "whine" in Irish poetry. When he noticed the impulsive tear and smile mingled in Ireland's eye his instinct was to give it a rough wipe. He did his best to keep his own eye dry in public. If he sometimes succeeded all too well, that was only what he intended.

We must be careful not to confuse that innate stoicism with despair. He is not a comforting writer. He seems to have viewed life as a sort of epic drama composed of details almost indifferently tragic and farcical and acted by involuntary comedians, of whom he was himself one. If so, he could stand it and, when opportunity offered, enjoy it. There is one condition that holds true in art as in politics: you can't ask favors from a man who wants none for himself.

When Yeats declared in the Irish Senate that Joyce had "an heroic mind," he made an understanding estimate. Joyce's heroism was partly this toughness and partly that his mind drove continually beyond itself in an ever-widening effort to define, through appropriate means, its own perceptions. The nature of those perceptions can be seen clearly in the *Portrait:* secret relationships, impalpable yet vitally communicative, sensed as existing between man and man, age and age, world and man, and, of course, between word and word. Most of them could be expressed only indirectly through symbol, for they are very curious relationships. Few are obvious. A lot of them would never occur to the reader independently; and after Joyce has pointed them out they still don't occur. Some, like the endless punning upon mere sound in *Finnegans Wake,* can only be judged trivial and compulsive. Yet, time and again, just as the mind is about to turn away from some dull obscurity, one discovers that the artist has turned the trick, the commonest clay of experience made magically luminous with fresh meaning and oldest sympathy. And suddenly all the individual strands of technique and attitude subsumed in Joyce's approach to his subject are seen moving together like muscles working under the skin, and the impact is multiple and one. We perceive what the adjective "organic" is supposed to indicate in a work of art.

His failure is heroic too, a tremendous try that doesn't come off. There is no mistaking it when it happens. Often enough when his skill fails, his taste fails with it, as in those godawful gooey embarrassing soliloquies of the girl Isobel in *Finnegans Wake* or, again in the *Wake,* in long, long passages where ingenuity, mistaking itself for humor, produces the most intricate tedium achieved by non-Marxist man. But, turn the page, and you are back in the midst of magic and delight. Many a grave writer who never loses control cannot promise you that. To reveal the wonders of the great deep involves the risk of going overboard.

Stop in them where one will, subtract from them what one will, by any measure Joyce's works are those of a very big writer. Even the most narcissistic youth looking into the *Portrait* as his own must realize at last that the mirror owes something to its maker. Yet I discover that it can be long before one realizes whence Joyce's bigness derives. The source is indicated in his recently published letters. For the most part these annotate what his formal writings have amply documented: his courage, independence, humor, honor, and his curiousness, for he was a very curious man. They also demonstrate, for the first time fully, how deeply seated was his possession of his virtues. The proof is in the letters he wrote to his only daughter when she was sinking into insanity, letters so compounded of easy fun and mortal agony and iron control that only the fun shows. Let any of us try that on for size. He was, it seems, a big man too. /90/

PART IV

ART AND AUTOBIOGRAPHY /
AUTOBIOGRAPHY AND ART

[Ten Passages from the Life of the Artist]

RICHARD ELLMANN

[1. SIMON DEDALUS]

This reckless, talented man, convinced that he was the victim of circumstances, never at a loss for a retort, fearfully sentimental and acid by turns, drinking, spending, talking, singing, became identified in his son James's mind with something like the life-force itself. His expressions, 'With the help of God and a few policemen,' 'Like a shot off a shovel,' ''Twixt you and me, Caddereesh,' and the like, echo in James's books. He appeared in them more centrally, in fact, than anyone except their author. In the early stories in *Dubliners*, 'The Sisters' and 'Araby,' he is considerately disguised as an uncle; in the later stories, besides contributing to Farrington, he is also in Henchy, Hynes, Kernan, and Gabriel Conroy. In *A Portrait of the Artist* he is Simon Dedalus, described by his son Stephen as having been 'A medical student, an oarsman, a tenor, an amateur actor, a shouting politician, a small landlord, a small investor, a drinker, a good fellow, a storyteller, somebody's secretary, something in a distillery, a tax- /20/ gatherer, a bankrupt and at present a praiser of his own past.' In *Ulysses* he is Simon again and also enters into Bloom and the narrator of the *Cyclops* episode; in *Finnegans Wake*, John Joyce is the chief model for Earwicker. Most of his children grew to dislike him intensely, but his eldest son, of whom he was most fond, reciprocated his affection and remembered his jokes. When John Joyce died in 1931, James told Louis Gillet, 'He never

Richard Ellmann, *James Joyce* (New York: Oxford University Press, 1959), pp. 20-21, 24-25, 37, 39-40, 48-50, 62-66, 120-21, 149-54, 306-09.

said anything about my books, but he couldn't deny me. The humor of *Ulysses* is his; its people are his friends. The book is his spittin' image.' In *A Portrait* Stephen denies that Simon is in any real sense his father, but James himself had no doubt that he was in every way his father's son. /21/

[2. DANTE]

Soon after the Joyces moved to Bray they were joined by Mrs. 'Dante' Hearn Conway from Cork, who was to act as governess to the children. A fat, clever woman, she was too embittered by a disastrous marriage to fit easily into the tolerant, gay household. She had been on the verge of becoming a nun in America when her brother, who had made a fortune out of trading with African natives, died and left her 30,000 pounds. She came back to Ireland to settle her inheritance, and instead of returning to the United States, gave up the convent and settled in Dublin to find a husband. She allowed herself to be won by an overdressed employee of the pillared Bank of Ireland. Soon after their marriage, to culminate a fine show of considerateness and good manners, Conway ran off to South America with her money tucked away in his pockets, and quickly ceased to write her promises to return. For the rest of her life Dante Conway remained the abandoned bride, and her burning memories of being deserted joined remorse at having left the convent to make her overzealous, in both religion and nationalism. She had, as James Joyce wrote, two brushes, one backed in maroon for Davitt and his Land League, the other in green for Parnell. Her loyalties clashed bitterly when Parnell was found to have been an adulterer, but it is not hard to see why she should have at once abandoned this betrayer of marriage ties and torn off the green backing from her second brush.

Mrs. Conway was fairly well educated and evidently a competent teacher. Sitting on a throne-like arrangement of chair and cushions to soothe her chronically ailing back, wearing a black lace cap, heavy velvet skirts, and jeweled slippers, she would ring a little bell. James would then come and sit at her feet for a lesson in reading, writing, geography, or arithmetic; or he would listen to her recite poetry. Her /24/ piety affected him less than her superstition; she talked a good deal about the end of the world, as if she expected it any moment, and when there was a flash of lightning she taught James to cross himself and say, 'Jesus of Nazareth, King of the Jews, from a sudden and unprovided for death deliver us, O Lord.' The thunderstorm as a vehicle of divine power and wrath moved Joyce's imagination so profoundly that to the end of his life he trembled at the sound. When a friend asked him why he was so affected, he replied, 'You were not brought up in Catholic Island.'* /25/

[3. EILEEN]

Across the street, at 4 Martello Terrace (not 7, as *A Portrait of the Artist* says), lived a chemist named James Vance with his family, and although the Vances were Protestant, the families were quickly drawn together. Vance's bass voice boomed against John Joyce's light tenor in 'Come-all-ye's.' The Vances' eldest child, four months younger than James, was a pretty girl named Eileen, and the two fathers often spoke half-seriously of uniting their first-born. Dante Conway warned James that if he played with Eileen he would certainly go to hell, and he duly informed Eileen of his destination but did not cease to merit it. /25/

[4. CORK]

While James was bolstering his position at Belvedere, his father's was deteriorating at home. Their house for over a year remained 14 Fitzgibbon Street, for John Joyce gave this address in February 1894, when he disposed of his remaining Cork properties. He took James down to Cork with him, and in *A Portrait of the Artist* Stephen is represented as increasingly alienated from his father, his father's friends, and his father's youth. There were probably many such moments of melancholy, but not undiluted. Stanislaus Joyce remembers that his brother's letters home indicated also that he followed his father about with considerable amusement. In later life he always showed a fellow feeling for Cork men, and would ask them about the Imperial Hotel, where he stayed, about the Mardyke, a fine promenade, and about the special Cork dish, drisheens. Beyond these, he made Stephen remember the word FOETUS inscribed on one of the desks at Queen's College, Cork,

---

* In *A Portrait of the Artist*, (514 [359]), Stephen Dedalus says that he fears 'dogs, horses, firearms, the sea, thunderstorms, machinery, the country roads at night'; his fears of dogs and thunderstorms is illustrated in *Ulysses*, his fear of thunderstorms gives (with the assistance of Vico) a prominent theme to *Finnegans Wake*.

The fear of dogs originated in childhood too, but without Dante's aid. James and Stanislaus were playing one day on the strand, throwing stones in the water, when a dog bit James, as he said later, on his chin. Stanislaus thought it was on the back of his brother's leg. From then on Joyce took precautions against dogs that would seem more absurd if he had not been bitten again, in 1927, at Scheveningen. /25/

the scene of John Joyce's unsuccessful effort to become a doctor. *A Portrait* makes the word concentrate Stephen's sense of puberty, in which sex was reproachful, irresistible. Self-consciously prudish about girls himself, Stephen mulled over his father's reputation as a great flirt, which Cork friends still jollied him about. (Eleven years later James Joyce was still to boast to an Italian friend that his father was a *conquistatore di dame.*) It was now, too, that John took his son to Crosshaven to the Presentation Convent to try, unsuccessfully, to get two of his daughters accepted as free boarders. Unperturbed, they listened to an O'Connell cousin there sing 'The Fisherman's Goodnight,' and both expertly criticized the song as unsuitably low in range for her voice. /37/

[5. BYRON HERESY]

The immediate change that the lack of funds brought about was another move, this time to Millbourne Lane in Drumcondra. Stanislaus Joyce describes this house as 'a small semi-detached villa . . . at the foot of a low hill' not far from woods and the river Tolka. Their neighbors, farmhands and navvies, resented the arrival of this family that had known better days. Stanislaus had a fight with one of the local boys, 'Pisser' Duffy, and was amused when his unforgetting brother gave the name of Duffy to the hero of 'A Painful Case,' who in most respects was modeled on Stanislaus. James too had a fight, but not with the local boys. It began at school, according to *A Portrait,* when 'Mr Tate' read out a sentence from 'Stephen's' weekly theme: 'Here. It's about the Creator and the soul. Rrm . . . rrm . . . Ah! *without a possibility of ever approaching nearer.* That's heresy.' Joyce, in using the incident in his book, says Stephen murmured (so that the value of the Church as /39/ intercessor might be preserved), 'I meant *without a possibility of ever reaching.*' In real life, Dempsey was appeased in some such manner, but his fellow-students, who had envied Joyce his success at themes, were not. Several of them took the same route home as he did, and that afternoon, as Stanislaus Joyce helps to establish, they were quick to seize the advantage offered them by Dempsey. They turned the subject to literature, and argued whether Marryat was the greatest writer or not. Then Joyce was asked his opinion. The greatest prose writer, he said, was Newman, a choice that sounded goody-goody but was really stylistic. 'And who is the best poet?' Albrecht Connolly, an excellent student, named Tennyson as he ought, but Joyce named Byron.* 'Byron was a bad man,' said one, and

---

* Joyce held to these opinions of Newman and Byron in later life.

Connolly called out, 'Here, catch hold of this heretic.' They seized him and demanded he admit that Byron was no good, hitting him meanwhile with a stick and bearing him back against a barbed wire fence that tore his clothes. Joyce would no more have judged Byron by his love affairs than he would have Parnell. He did not submit, but, as Stanislaus remembered, went home crying to his mother, who comforted him and mended his clothes. So his sufferings for his art began.† /40/

[6. THE SODALITY OF THE BLESSED VIRGIN MARY]

Joyce was moving closer to that moment which could, as he later held, be pinpointed in a man's psychic as well as physical development, when boyhood changes to adolescence. For some months yet he was still a boy, though with a secret unwillingness to remain so. His conduct was irreproachable enough to earn him admission on December 7, 1895, to the Sodality of the Blessed Virgin Mary, and on September 25, 1896, he was chosen prefect or head. During his fourteenth year (as he told Stanislaus later), and very possibly between these two events, he precociously began his sexual life. *A Portrait* has to represent this 'fall' with dramatic suddenness, but it came about in actuality with at least one incident to herald it. This was a flirtation with a young maid servant. Stanislaus Joyce describes a scene between the two as 'a kind of catch-as-catch-can cum-spanking match,' and prefers, since it came to the notice and disapproval of the Jesuits, to find in it more innocence than perhaps it had. At any rate, it was followed by a more serious episode. On his way home from the theater, where he had seen a performance of *Sweet Briar*, Joyce walked along the canal bank and met a prostitute. Reckless, curious, and valuing any expression of his own temperament, he experimented, and the experiment helped to fix his image of the sexual act as shameful, an image suppressed but never quite abandoned later. Returing to his house, Joyce found Bergan and his father talking gaily about the play, which they also had attended, and kept his feelings to himself.

† Another indignity of this spring is perhaps described much as it happened in a story of *Dubliners*. The bazaar *Araby* came to Dublin on May 14-19, 1894. The boy fixed his mind with accustomed intensity upon the bazaar, and won his uncle's (his father's?) consent to go. But his uncle did not return with money until it was too late, and then said, 'The people are in bed and after their first sleep now.' The boy went anyway, and by the time he arrived, the bazaar was virtually over; the lights were going out, the merriment had ceased. There is perhaps then a particular irony when in *A Portrait* a schoolmate accuses Stephen of not being the sort to go to bazaars. Joyce, like Stephen, seems in some moods to have encouraged other people to regard him as a very virtuous boy. /40/

Yet his demeanor was not so impeccable as he probably wished. Father Henry, the rector of Belvedere, prided himself on his ability to judge character, and Joyce aroused his suspicions. Henry had a convert's harshness, and his students were often perplexed to see him suddenly stop in the middle of a class to pray down some suspect thought. James's manner was too impenetrable for the rector to hope to get anything out of the boy himself, but he cannily called Stanislaus into his office and questioned him first about himself and then, more deviously, about his brother. Stanislaus, intimidated by the rector's reminders of the dangers of telling a lie to the Holy Ghost, mentioned the one thing he knew of—the incident between his brother and the maid. Father Henry pounced on this corroboration of his suspicion, and the next day sent for Mrs. Joyce. Without offering any particulars, and thus alarming her further, he warned her, 'Your son is inclined to /48/ evil ways.' She returned home very disturbed, and Stanislaus, who by this time bemoaned his own candor, confessed to both his mother and brother what he had told the rector. James merely laughed and called him a fathead, while Mrs. Joyce blamed the servant and discharged her. To Brendan Gallaher's mother she said that some woman had tried to seduce her son.

She must have shown enough signs of dismay to arouse the suspicions of John Joyce, who asked his son what the trouble was. 'I am under a cloud at school,' he replied, as Stanislaus remembered. 'What about?' asked his father. 'I don't know. You had better ask the rector.' John Joyce did so, but Father Henry remained vague and monitory. 'That boy will give you trouble,' he warned him, but John Joyce replied with aplomb, 'No, he won't, because I won't let him.'

Joyce did not heed the rector's warnings, and he was not removed from his position as prefect of the sodality. The position suited him very well; he had an adolescent thrill in adoring the Virgin Mary while his lips still savored 'of a lewd kiss.' His mind longed to adore and to desecrate. Yet virginity still engrossed him, and he was readier than he knew for the retreat which began on November 30, 1896. In charge of the retreat was Father James A. Cullen,* and his ser-

---

* In identifying Father Cullen as the preacher of the sermons in the retreat, Thomas Bodkin says: 'Father Cullen's phrasing was characteristic. Where most preachers would begin their sermons on such occasions by saying "Dear boys," he had a habit of addressing his congregation as "My dear little brothers in Jesus Christ," which always struck me as a repellent mode of address. Moreover, he used to wear as few Jesuits do on such occasions, the heavy cloak over his

mons, delivered, as was customary, according to the prescription of St. Ignatius Loyola's *Spiritual Exercises,* elicited a more than customary number of twinges from hell-fire. All Joyce's mounting scruples against his own conduct found a fierce justification. He saw himself as a beast, eating like a beast, lusting like a beast, dying like a beast, and dreamed of pure love for a virgin heart. /49/

He did not confess in the college chapel; to abase himself before Father Henry was still too much to bear. He went instead, according to a sister, to the Church Street chapel. A Capuchin there listened to the tale from a boy of a man's sins with sympathy rather than indignation. It was Joyce's first confession since Easter, and it brought about an eager spirituality in his conduct which heightened his reputation, secured until then by hypocrisy, for piety. He prayed interminably, mortified himself and labored to achieve a virtue as extreme as his sinfulness seemed to him before to have been. In *A Portrait of the Artist* Joyce later mocked his own religious revival a little by a commercial metaphor dressed out in purple rhythm: 'His life seemed to have drawn near to eternity; every thought, word and deed, every instance of consciousness could be made to revibrate radiantly in heaven: and at times his sense of such immediate repercussion was so lively that he seemed to feel his soul in devotion pressing like fingers the keyboard of a great cash register and to see the amount of his purchase start forth immediately in heaven, not as a number but as a frail column of incense or as a slender flower.' He was a miser of grace.

The reformation lasted some months, probably well into 1897; his sister Eileen saw him saying his rosary piously on the way to school, and Stanislaus, who was losing his faith with less compunction, watched his brother in perplexity. Then James began to bethink himself once again. It seemed to him now that the sermons during the retreat had played on the weakest part of his nature, and that the confession wrung from him by such methods could

---

gown of which Joyce speaks. Like a good many of the community of Belvedere at that time he had a distinct trace of sadism in his character, e.g., he found it humorous to offer to shake hands with young boys and then squeeze their hands until they yelled with pain. Belvedere, during the period when Joyce and I were there as pupils, was not a happy school. In that it was quite unlike Clongowes which we both also attended. Father Henry was the rector of Belvedere then, a harsh insensitive man. This, I think, was ultimately recognised generally by all who had dealings with him and I for one, who owe a great deal to the Jesuits and regard the order with affection and esteem, never met among them anyone else of the type.' /49/

only be insincere. What had seemed piety now seemed only the last spasm of religious terror. This point of view, which he gives Stephen in *A Portrait,* was growing in his own mind, as later letters and re- marks confirm. It was also true, as he declared flatly some time aft- erwards to a friend, that sexual continence was impossible for him. He felt he must choose between continual guilt and some heretical exoneration of the senses. By conviction Joyce could not abase him- self before Catholic doctrine; by temperament he could not abase himself before other men. /50/

[7. UNIVERSITY COLLEGE]

Joyce and another student, George Clancy, liked to rouse Cadic to flights of miscomprehension. In a favorite little drama, Joyce would snicker offensively at Clancy's efforts to translate a passage into Eng- lish. Clancy pretended to be furious and demanded an apology, which Joyce refused. Then Clancy would challenge Joyce to a duel in the Phoenix Park. The horrified Cadic would rush in to concili- ate the fiery Celts, and after much byplay would persuade them to shake hands.

The students at University College were more unusual than their professors. Three of Joyce's close friends, Clancy, Francis Skeffing- ton, and Thomas Kettle, indicated the extent of the earnestness of their youth by losing their lives in battle, each for a different cause. Clancy was to end as a victim of the Black and Tans, murdered while he was mayor of Limerick. His unfortunate death was ap- propriate in that, even as a young man, Clancy subscribed ardently to every aspect of the national movement. He helped form a branch of the Gaelic League at University College, and persuaded his friends, including even Joyce for a time, to take lessons in Irish. Joyce gave them up because Patrick Pearse, the instructor, found it necessary to exalt Irish by denigrating English, and in particular denounced the word 'Thunder'—a favorite of Joyce's—as an exam- ple of verbal inadequacy. Clancy was an enthusiast also for Gaelic sports like hurling, and therefore a great friend of Michael Cusack, the founder of the Gaelic Athletic Association. He brought Joyce to meet Cusack a few times, and Joyce liked /62/ him little enough to make him model the narrow-minded and rhetorical Cyclops in *Ulysses*. Clancy appears in Joyce's early work as Madden; he is the only friend who calls Stephen by his first name, and Joyce later confirmed that Clancy alone among his classmates did so. Madden (called Davin in *A Portrait*) labors with rustic sincerity to make

Stephen more Irish, and Stephen's relations with him are simpler
and more relaxed than with his other friends. There is no indication, however, that Joyce ever called Clancy 'George.'

After himself, James Joyce told Stanislaus, the cleverest man at
University College was Francis Skeffington. Skeffington, like Clancy,
died at the hands of the British, but a few years sooner, during the
Easter Rebellion of 1916, when he quixotically tried to dissuade the
soldiers from looting. As a young man Skeffington, four years Joyce's
senior, was the college iconoclast. To protest against uniformity in
dress he wore plus fours and was known as 'Knickerbockers.' To
protest against shaving he grew a beard, then went on to denounce
smoking, drinking, and vivisecting. Joyce called him 'Hairy Jaysus.'
Skeffington demanded equal rights for women, and supported paci-
fism and vegetarianism with equal fervor. A great framer and signer
of petitions, he sought to persuade Joyce to sign a petition to encourage the Czar in his pursuit of universal peace, but Joyce re-
torted, according to *A Portrait*, 'If you must have a Jesus, let it be a
legitimate Jesus.'

Joyce took pleasure in so puncturing Skeffington's armor, in ask-
ing Socratic questions of Socrates. If Skeffington was so rational, how
had he managed to preserve his belief in Catholicism? To this Skeffington would reply earnestly, but with some discomfort, that he intended before long to take a year off to study the religious question.
He did in fact give up the Church later. If Skeffington believed in
feminism, did he think the police force should be composed of
women? In *A Portrait* Skeffington appears as McCann, anxious to
dispute, very serious, and, with a chocolate bar always in one pocket,
a little /63/ absurd, a less agile debater in fiction than he was in
fact. He in turn was always trying to draw Joyce out with some direct question. Once he asked him, according to Stanislaus, 'Have
you ever been in love?' Joyce replied with an evasive shift of tense,
'How would I write the most perfect love songs of our time if I
were in love? A poet must always write about a past or a future emotion, never about a present one. If it is a regular, right-down, hon-
est-to-God, "till-death-us-two-part" affair, it will get out of hand and
spoil his verse. Poetry must have a safety valve properly adjusted.
A poet's job is to write tragedies, not to be an actor in one.' This
kind of answer, which turned the argument to abstraction, played
neatly on Skeffington's own tendency.

In spite of intellectual differences Joyce and Skeffington got on
well enough. Joyce devised an amusing test of Skeffington's dogged
insistence upon all kinds of rights; he offered to give him a half

crown if Skeffington would buy a halfpenny worth of gooseberries at the most expensive fruit shop in Sackville Street and offer a sovereign in payment. Skeffington agreed, and from the doorway Joyce watched the irritated salesgirl and the unintimidated libertarian, and whooped with glee. He met Skeffington chiefly at the Sheehys' house; eventually Skeffington was to marry Hannah Sheehy and, refusing to allow marriage even nominally to compromise the equality of the sexes, he changed his name to Sheehy-Skeffington.

Another gifted friend, whom Joyce alone seems to have rated below Skeffington, was Thomas Kettle, killed while fighting in the British army in 1916. Kettle followed Skeffington in marrying into the Sheehy family, his wife being Mary, the girl whom Joyce during his university days had not forgotten. Kettle was an intellectual Catholic and nationalist; soon after his graduation he became a Member of Parliament and the spokesman for the younger intellectuals. In the university he was already saying, 'If Ireland is to become a new Ireland she must first become European,' an idea that was Joyce's too, but Kettle's passionate and courageous (or, as Joyce put it, 'too demonstrative') concern with the national question prevented his assuming Joyce's cosmopolitanism. He later disapproved of the unpatriotic candor of *Dubliners.* Kettle does not appear in *A Portrait,* but some of his attitudes, such as the necessity of making Ireland European, are used in *Exiles.* He was the only other student with whom Joyce discussed Thomas Aquinas, and he pleased Joyce with the remark that 'The difficulty about Aquinas is that what he says is so like what the man in the street says.' In Paris later someone was to object to Joyce, who was discussing Aquinas, 'That has nothing to do with us,' and /64/ Joyce replied, perhaps recalling Kettle, 'It has everything to do with us.'

There were three other young men whom Joyce knew well at University College: Curran, Cosgrave, and Byrne. The first two were almost opposites: Constantine P. Curran was goodhearted and controlled; Joyce granted his cleverness as well. *A Portrait* represents him as interested in food (he was inclined to be fat); he was also well-versed in literature and architecture. Afterwards he became Registrar of the Supreme Court. He shared Joyce's taste for trips to the continent, but he was pious, and more pious than continental, as he demonstrated by sympathizing with the mob who jerred in outrage at the first production of Synge's *The Playboy of the Western World.* Joyce respected his critical judgment, however, and in the course of his lifetime was to owe Curran a great many kindnesses.

Vincent Cosgrave had a ruddy Neronic face and careless habits. He had a good mind but did not train it; he appraised Joyce shrewdly and early, and said to Byrne, 'Joyce is the most remarkable man any of us have met.' He was committed to idleness and rancorous unsuccess. As he grew older his character was to deteriorate further, and his death in the Thames, presumably from suicide, was a blunt admission of futility. Cosgrave gratified Joyce by always being ready to walk with him, talk with him, or (if they had money) to accompany him to a Tyrone Street brothel. His talk, whether of religion or women, was coarse and witty; Joyce, who had not yet begun to drink, affected along with abstemiousness a disdain for low talk and public misbehavior that gave him the appearance almost of virtue. He liked the appearance, and enjoyed taking sometimes the anomalous role of chiding schoolmaster with Cosgrave.

But Joyce's closest friendship at the College was with John Francis Byrne, the 'Cranly' of his novels. Though he had known Byrne casually at Belvedere, he did not see much of him until later. 'It was in favor of this young man,' says Joyce in *Stephen Hero,* with deference for his own youthful pomposity, 'that Stephen decided to break his commandment of reticence.' Byrne was handsome, athletic, and clever; he excelled at chess and handball, and disregarded his studies even more cavalierly than Joyce. He had been brought up by two older sisters after the early death of his parents, and during the summer disappeared into Wicklow, where his activities were so unaffectedly rural as to puzzle his city friend. Byrne's distinction was not in his speech; his ideas, said Stanislaus Joyce to his brother, were commonplace, and the best defense James could think of was that they were 'daringly commonplace'; in a world of foppishness, Byrne had the /65/ courage to be plain. But it was his manner that attracted: he moved about with the air of a man who knows all the secrets but disinclines to exercise the power he thereby possesses. Standing among other young men on the steps of the National Library or of University College, he listened to their small fallacies and did not deign to correct them. His power over Joyce came from his habit of refraining from comment: Joyce's admissions about his feelings towards family, friends, and church, about his overweening ambitions, struck like waves against Byrne's cryptic taciturnity. Byrne listened to Joyce's confidences without offering any of his own, and, as Joyce noted, without conferring absolution.

Joyce needed no other friend as he did Byrne. He would wait for an hour for Byrne to win a chess game, as he usually did, so that afterwards he might capture that receptive but neutral ear for new disclosures. For his part, Byrne was as fascinated by Joyce's unabashed speech as Joyce was by Byrne's intimidating silences. The friendship was of such importance to Joyce that when it dwindled, as it did later, he felt less at home in Ireland. /66/

[8. CRANLY]

In Dublin he discovered he had lost a friend. The photo-postcard which he had sent to Byrne, with the poem written in the space for a message, had pleased Byrne very much. He showed it to Cosgrave and said proudly that no man in Dublin knew more about Joyce than he did. Cosgrave, making the retort irresistible, slyly took a similar photograph from his pocket and showed it to Byrne saying, 'Perhaps that's something you didn't know.' Byrne read Joyce's description in dog-Latin of Paris whoredom with consternation; he had explicitly warned Joyce not to confide in Cosgrave, and the details were evidently shocking to him. He handed both post cards to Cosgrave saying, 'You can have this one, too.'

Cosgrave told Stanislaus Joyce in great amusement what had happened, and gave him Byrne's card, saying he didn't need two. Joyce heard the story on his return, and experienced some snub from Byrne, for he said rather pompously to Stanislaus, 'I think I have been mistaken in Byrne.' Stanislaus, who had been jealous of Byrne's pre-eminence in his brother's intimacy, took off his hat and solemnly began to intone the *Te Deum*. James began to refer to Byrne as 'His Intensity' and 'the Sea-Green Incorruptible.'

What made the collapse of his principal friendship more serious was that Joyce had no relationships with women that were not coarse or distant. In his writing more is at stake in the friendship of Stephen and Cranly (Byrne) than in the relationship of Stephen and Emma Clery. Friendship becomes, in fact, a focal point, for if friendship exists, it impugns the quality of exile and of lonely heroism. If the world is not altogether hostile, we may forgive it for having mistreated us, and so be forced into the false position of warriors without adversaries. Joyce allows his hero to savor friendship before discovering its flaws, and then with the theme of broken friendship represents Stephen's broken ties with Ireland and the world.*

In actual life Joyce searched in vain for any foundation for his feeling that Byrne's change in attitude toward him was a betrayal,

* 'Away then; it is time to go. . . . His friendship was coming to an end. Yes; he would go. He could not strive against another. He knew his part.' *A Portrait of the Artist* (516 [360-61]). /120/

but /120/ in his books he propounded various theories to explain it. The first, suggested by Stephen's brother Maurice, is that 'Cranly wants to become more and more necessary to you until he can have you in his power.' Stephen repudiates this analysis, which he contends is based upon a 'novel' conception of friendship. The second reason appears on the surface to be an esthetic disagreement, Cranly's cool reception of Stephen's paper on 'Drama and Life.' Stephen now detects 'in Cranly's attitude toward him a certain hostility, arising out of a thwarted desire to imitate.' The third is Cranly's growing interest in Emma Clery.* These three reasons, the desire to domi-nate, to emulate, and to steal away his friend's girl, have in com-mon the fact that it is Cranly who takes the first steps towards en-mity, and that all explanations of his behavior are essentially proof of his dependence upon Stephen. In *A Portrait* Joyce goes further to evolve the total fiction that Cranly's motivation is homosexual.† To Stanislaus, James Joyce owned himself baffled by Byrne's be-havior, though he said, too, that Byrne must accept him whole, in the words of *Ulysses:* 'As I am. All or not at all.' The incident of the post card kept the friends at odds, so that they did not meet any more during Joyce's Dublin holiday. /121/

[9. STEPHEN HERO]

At the beginning of 1904 he learned that Eglinton and another writer he knew, Fred Ryan, were preparing to edit a new intellec-

---

* In *Stephen Hero* (215 [220]) Emma Clery walks by the two men, and when they bow to her she disregards Stephen to bow only to Cranly. To Cranly's ques-tion, 'Why did she do that?' Stephen replies with a laugh, 'Perhaps she meant it as an invitation.' What in *Stephen Hero* is only a suspicion becomes in *A Por-trait of the Artist* (501 [350]) a virtual certainty. Stephen asks Cranly to come and talk with him, but Cranly delays. During the delay Emma Clery passes by, and again bows across Stephen in response to Cranly's greeting. Stephen is affronted and pounces upon this deliberate misdirection of her favor. 'Was there not a slight flush on Cranly's cheek?' he asks himself. 'Did that explain his friend's listless silence, his harsh comments, the sudden intrusions of rude speech with which he had shattered so often Stephen's ardent wayward confessions?' In the last pages of the book he writes in his journal of Cranly's growing intimacy with Emma, 'Is he the shining light now? Well, I discovered him. I protest I did. Shining quietly behind a bushel of Wicklow bran.' (522 [365])

† Cranly reminds Stephen that if he leaves his country he will be alone. 'And you know what that word means? Not only to be separated from all others but to have not even one friend . . . And now to have any one person . . . who would be more than a friend, more even than the noblest and truest friend a man ever had.' Stephen looks at him and wonders if he has spoken of himself. 'Of whom are you speaking?' he asks at last, and receives no answer. (519 [362–3])
/121/

tual journal named *Dana* after the Irish earth-goddess. On January 7 he wrote off in one day, and with scarcely any hesitation, an autobiographical story that mixed admiration for himself with irony. At the suggestion of Stanislaus, he called it 'A Portrait of the Artist,' and sent it to the editors. This was the extraordinary beginning of Joyce's mature work. It was to be remolded into *Stephen Hero*, a very long work, and then shortened to a middle length to form *A Portrait of the Artist as a Young Man*. But this process took ten years.

In 'A Portrait of the Artist,' for the first time since writing *A Brilliant Career,* Joyce was willing to attempt an extended work, to give up the purity of lyrics and epiphanies. He was resolved to gather the stages of his spiritual experience together in a connected pattern. It is difficult to say whether what he wrote was essay or story, for it has elements of both, the essay strained by apostrophe and dramatic exhortation, the narrative presented for the most part discursively. At the age of twenty-one Joyce had found he could become an artist by writing about the process of becoming an artist, his life legitimizing his portrait by supplying the sitter, while the portrait vindicated the sitter by its evident admiration for him. That admiration was already a little complicated by the attitude which, in the later book *A Portrait of the Artist as a Young Man,* has led some readers to suppose that Joyce could not bear /149/ his own hero. But in both portraits, as well as in the intermediate *Stephen Hero,* there is no lack of sympathy on the author's part; he recognizes, however, that earlier stages of the hero's life were necessarily callow, and makes the callowness clear in order to establish the progression towards the mature man.

The tone of this first draft is belligerent. Joyce begins by insisting on the psychological theory that 'the features of infancy' belong to a portrait as much as the features of adolescence. The past has no 'iron memorial aspect,' but implies 'a fluid succession of presents.' What we are to look for is not a fixed character but an 'individuating rhythm' not 'an identificative paper but rather the curve of an emotion.' This conception of personality as river rather than statue is premonitory of Joyce's later view of consciousness.

The development of the unnamed hero is already stylized, though the stages are less clearly marked than in the final *Portrait* they became. The hero first enters upon a period of religious zeal: 'He ran through his measure like a spendthrift saint, astonishing many by ejaculatory fervors, offending many by airs of the cloister. One day in a wood near Malahide a labourer had marvelled to see a boy of fifteen praying in an ecstasy of oriental posture.' This zeal steadily diminishes and ends after he enters the university. It is followed by his creation of 'the enigma of a manner' to protect from intrusion 'that ineradicable egoism which he was afterwards to call redeemer.' While the writing exhibits both candor and presumption, presumption has the better of it:

Is the mind of boyhood medieval that it is so divining of intrigue? . . . For this fantastic idealist, eluding the grunting booted apparition with a bound, the mimic hunt was no less ludicrous than unequal in a ground chosen to his disadvantage. But behind the rapidly indurating shield the sensitive answered. Let the pack of enmities come tumbling and sniffing to the highlands after their game. There was his ground and he flung them disdain from flashing antlers.

What is astonishing about this passage, however, is something else: the prose has been infected by the hero's mind. With symbolist reticence hunter and deer are not named, but their attendant metaphors, 'the grunting booted apparition' and 'flashing antlers,' are weighted with the hero's attitude toward them. The resultant bias colors phrases which might otherwise seem derogatory, 'this fantastic idealist' and 'the sensitive.' The prose works through emotional image rather than /150/ through idea, and, without admitting sympathy for the hero, implies it by allowing him, as it were, to describe himself. Though the technique is not impeccable—the facile heroics of 'flashing antlers,' for example—Joyce's discovery of it made possible *A Portrait of the Artist as a Young Man*. In *Ulysses* and *Finnegans Wake* he carried the discovery further; there the language reflects not only the main characters, as when the river is described in words which sound like rivers or when the style tumesces with Gerty MacDowell's sexual excitement, but also the time of day or night, as when, late in the evening at 7 Eccles Street, the English language is as worn-out as the day and can produce only clichés, or when, early in the morning at the end of Earwicker's dream, the style dies away with the night. Joyce even learned to make language reflect aspects of the setting, as when, in a butcher shop, Bloom's mind unconsciously borrows metaphors from meat even when he is thinking of quite other things. This magnetization of style and vocabulary by the context of person, place, and time, has its humble origin in the few pages Joyce wrote for *Dana*.

Joyce's hero chooses his ground 'to his disadvantage' because he wishes to be hunted so as to defy his pursuers; he seeks not loyalty but betrayal. He is sharply differentiated from silly fellow-students and from worldly Jesuit masters; against both groups Joyce poses the artist's holy office, which the young man accepts in two stages. In the first he searches for 'an arduous good,' and his mind, like that of Yeats's alchemical heroes, is 'ever trembling towards its ecstasy.' Over his soul 'the image of beauty had fallen as a mantle,' and he leaves the church through the gates of Assisi to find in art an unworldly bliss.

Searching for sanctions he studies not St. Francis but the heresiarchs Joachim Abbas, Bruno, and Michael Sendwogius. He seeks with their help to 'reunite the children of the spirit, jealous and long-divided, to reunite them against fraud and principality. A thousand eternities were to be reaffirmed, divine knowledge was to be reestablished.' The plan has Yeats, the Theosophists, and Blake behind it, but Joyce plunges away: 'Alas for fatuity! as easily might he have summoned a regiment of the winds.' The treasons of the heretics were too 'venial.' The disconsolate young man meditates on the strand like Stephen Dedalus after him, and gradually loses interest in 'an absolute satisfaction' to become instead 'conscious of the beauty of mortal conditions.'

This is the second stage, and in it he develops a great interest in sexual freedom and a concomitant spiritual freedom. There follows a lyrical apostrophe of an unidentified female figure, his secular correlative of the Virgin Mary. It is she, presumably the girl that Joyce had seen at the sea's edge in 1898, who has led his soul to exfoliation. Like /151/ Sudermann's Magda, she has taught him that he must sin if he wishes to grow, and enabled him through sin to discover his self. 'Thou wert sacramental,' he tells her, 'imprinting thine indelible work of very visible grace. A litany must honour thee. Lady of Apple Trees, Kind Wisdom, Sweet Flower of Dusk.' In imagined intercourse with her, in actual intercourse with prostitutes, he establishes that he must go forward 'to the measurable world and the broad expanse of activity.' He bursts with new life and endeavor. He will change the world, not by violence, but by subtlety, by 'urbanity.' His audience will not be those already born; they, like Yeats, are too old for him to help; it will be those 'surely engenderable.' In a stirring peroration compounded of Zarathustra, a dash of Marx, and Joyce, he calls to these: 'Man and woman, out of you comes the nation that is to come, the lightening of your masses in travail. The competitive order is employed against itself, the aristocracies are supplanted; and amid the general paralysis of an insane society, the confederate will issues in action.'

The essay narrative was duly submitted to Eglinton and Ryan, and by them duly rejected. Eglinton told Joyce, 'I can't print what I can't understand,' and objected to the hero's sexual exploits, whether with the dream lady of his litany or with the real prostitutes. Joyce took this rejection as a challenge to make the fictional history of his own life the call to arms of a new age. Stanislaus, in his diary for February 2, 1904, shows James's response most intimately:

2nd February: 1904: Tuesday. Jim's birthday. He is twenty-two [to] day. He was up late and did not stir out all day, having a bad cold. He has decided to turn his paper into a novel, and having come to that decision is just as glad, he says, that it was rejected. The paper . . . was rejected by the editors, Fred Ryan and W. Magee ('John Eglinton') because of the sexual experiences narrated in it. Jim thinks that they rejected it because it is all about himself, though they professed great admiration for the style of the paper. They always admire his style. Magee has an antipathy for Jim's character, I think. Magee is a dwarfish, brown-clad fellow, with red-brown eyes like a ferret, who walks with his hands in his jacket pockets and as stiffly as if his knees were roped up with sugauns.* He is sub-librarian in Kildare Street, and I think his mission in Ireland is to prove to his Protestant grandaunts that unbelievers can be very moral and admire the Bible. He is interested in great thoughts and philosophy, whenever he can understand it. Jim is beginning his novel, as he usually begins things, half in anger, to show that in writing about himself he has a subject of more interest than their aimless discussion. I suggested the title of the paper 'A Portrait of the Artist', and this evening, sitting in the kitchen, Jim told me his idea for the novel. It is to be almost autobiographical, and naturally as it comes from Jim, /152/ satirical. He is putting a large number of his acquaintances into it, and those Jesuits whom he has known. I don't think they will like themselves in it. He has not decided on a title, and again I made most of the suggestions. Finally a title of mine was accepted: 'Stephen Hero,' from Jim's own name in the book 'Stephen Dedalus.' The title, like the book, is satirical. Between us we rechristened the characters, calling them by names which seemed to suit their tempers or which suggested the part of the country from which they come. Afterwards I parodied many of the names: Jim, 'Stuck-up Stephen'; Pappie, 'Sighing Simon'; myself, 'Morose Maurice'; the sister, 'Imbecile Isobel'; Aunt Josephine (Aunt Bridget), 'Blundering Bibby'; Uncle Willie, 'Jealous Jim.'

Pappie came in very drunk, and—an unusual thing for him—went straight up to bed. Today we have had a grand dinner and tea. It rained heavily after dark. We spent the evening playing cards—in honour of the occasion—Jim and Charlie smoking. Jim wanted to ask Pappie to come down but it was thought better to let him sleep.

Abruptly within a month, for Joyce always moved very quickly when the matter was crucial, he recognized his theme, the portrait of the renegade Catholic artist as hero. He could draw upon two types of books he had read: the defecter from religion and the in-

* Hay ropes (Irish). /152/

surgent artist. He joined the two together. His own conflict with
the Church, his plunge into callow sexuality, his proud recalci-
trance in the name of individuality and then of art, his admiration for Parnell, for Byron, for Ibsen and Flaubert, his Parisian
exile, all began to merge as parts of this central conception in which
the young man gives up everything for art. But Stephen's esthetic
notions are not renunciant; he becomes an artist because art opens
to him 'the fair courts of life' which priest and king were trying to
keep locked.

Joyce finished the first chapter of his book by February 10, 1904,
and by midsummer he had written already a large volume. The
earliest chapters, now lost, were lyrical, according to C. P. Curran,
the tone becoming more bitter and realistic as Joyce proceeded. But
there was a limitation upon even his candor; as Stanislaus said
shrewdly in his diary, 'Jim is thought to be very frank about himself but his style is such that it might be contended that he confesses
in a foreign language—an easier confession than in the vulgar
tongue.' To suggest the Christian and pagan elements in his mind,
even to the point of absurdity, Joyce called himself Stephen Daedalus (then, to make it a little less improbable, Stephen Dedalus)
after Christianity's first martyr and paganism's greatest inventor.
Stephen would be a saint of literature, /153/ and like Dedalus
would invent wings to soar beyond his compatriots, and a labyrinth,
a mysterious art based on great cunning. The choice of the hero's
name determined the bird imagery of the book, though Joyce did
not fully develop that in the chapters we have of Stephen Hero; it
became more thematic in *A Portrait of the Artist as a Young Man*
where he was willing to parade his symbols with greater audacity.
He had not yet decided that the book would end with his departure
for the continent in 1902, and before long had carried it beyond
that date. But the convergence of its plot upon alienation probably
encouraged him, as he adjusted his life to art's exigencies, to consider leaving Dublin again and for good.

In later life Joyce, in trying to explain to his friend Louis Gillet
the special difficulties of the autobiographical novelist, said, 'When
your work and life make one, when they are interwoven in the same
fabric . . .' and then hesitated as if overcome by the hardship of his
'sedentary trade.' The fact that he was turning his life to fiction at
the same time that he was living it encouraged him to feel a certain
detachment from what happened to him, for he knew he could re-
consider and re-order it for the purposes of his book. At the same
time, since he felt dependent for material upon actual events, he
had an interest in bringing simmering pots to a strong boil, in making the events through which he lived take on as extreme a form

as possible. The sense that they were characters in his drama annoyed some of his friends, especially Gogarty, who did not much care for the role of culprit in a court where Joyce was both judge and prosecuting attorney. Joyce did not keep his book to himself; he showed the manuscript to chosen friends, and, without perhaps saying so directly, threatened some of them with the punishments he would mete out for slights suffered at their hands. They became, as Gogarty said, 'accessories before the fact.' His art became a weapon which had an immediate effect upon his circle of acquaintances, and so altered the life it depicted. At first he allowed Stephen to have one loyal adherent, his brother Maurice, modeled on Stanislaus, but later he virtually obliterated him too, feeling that his hero must be entirely alone. He waited in trepidation for Cosgrave, Gogarty, and others to betray him as he imagined Byrne had done, and so to earn their places in the circles of his hell. He himself was a blend of celebrated victims (Christ and Parnell), light-bringing malefactors (Lucifer and Giordano Bruno), and exiles (Dante and Daedalus), while they were Intensities and Bullockships. /154/

[10. "LIKE THE GOD OF THE CREATION"]

To write *A Portrait of the Artist as a Young Man* Joyce plunged back into his own past, mainly to justify, but also to expose it. The book's pattern, as he explained to Stanislaus, is that we are what we were; our maturity is an extension of our childhood, and the courageous boy is father of the arrogant young man. But in searching for a way to convert the episodic *Stephen Hero* into *A Portrait of the Artist,* Joyce hit upon a principle of structure which reflected his habits of mind as extremely as he could wish. The work of art, like a mother's love, must be achieved over the greatest obstacles, and Joyce, who had been dissatisfied with his earlier work as too easily done, now found the obstacles in the form of a most complicated pattern.

This is hinted at in his image of the creative process. As far back as his paper on Mangan, Joyce said that the poet takes into the vital center of his life 'the life that surrounds it, flinging it abroad again amid planetary music.' He repeated this image in *Stephen Hero,* then in *A Portrait of the Artist* developed it more fully. Stephen refers to the making of literature as 'the phenomenon of artistic conception, artistic gestation and artistic reproduction,' and then describes the progression from lyrical to epical and to dramatic art:

The simplest epical form is seen emerging out of lyrical literature when the artist prolongs and broods upon himself as the centre of an epical event and this form progresses till the centre of emotional gravity is equidistant from the artist himself and from others. The narrative is no longer purely personal. The personality of the artist passes into the narration itself, flowing round and round the persons and the action like a vital sea. . . . The dramatic form is reached when the vitality which has flowed and eddied round each person fills every person with such vital force that he or she assumes a proper and intangible esthetic life. . . . The mystery of esthetic like that of material creation is accomplished.

This creator is not male but female; Joyce goes on to borrow an image of Flaubert by calling him a 'god,'* but he is really a goddess. Within this womb creatures come to life. No male intercession is necessary /306/ even; as Stephen says, 'In the virgin womb of the imagination the word was made flesh.'

Joyce did not take up such metaphors lightly. His brother records that in the first draft of A Portrait, Joyce thought of a man's character as developing 'from an embryo' with constant traits. Joyce acted upon this theory with his characteristic thoroughness, and his subsequent interest in the process of gestation, as conveyed to Stanislaus during Nora's first pregnancy, expressed a concern that was literary as well as anatomical. His decision to rewrite Stephen Hero as A Portrait in five chapters occurred appropriately just after Lucia's birth. For A Portrait of the Artist as a Young Man is in fact the gestation of a soul, and in the metaphor Joyce found his new principle of order. The book begins with Stephen's father and, just before the ending, it depicts the hero's severance from his mother. From the start the soul is surrounded by liquids, urine, slime, seawater, amniotic tides, 'drops of water' (as Joyce says at the end of the first chapter) 'falling softly in the brimming bowl.' The atmosphere of biological struggle is necessarily dark and melancholy until the light of life is glimpsed. In the first chapter the foetal soul is for a few pages only slightly individualized, the organism responds only to the most primitive sensory impressions, then the heart forms and musters its affections, the being struggles toward some unspecified, uncomprehended culmination, it is flooded in ways it cannot understand or control, it gropes wordlessly toward sexual differentiation. In the third chapter shame floods Stephen's whole body as conscience develops; the lower bestial nature is put by. Then at the end of the fourth chapter the soul discovers the goal towards which

---

* Stephen says the artist is 'like the God of the creation,' remaining 'within or behind or beyond or above his handiwork, invisible, refined out of existence, paring his fingernails.' But Lynch sardonically qualifies this statement by saying, 'Trying to refine them [the fingernails] also out of existence.' Stephen makes no reply. A Portrait (481-2 [336-7]). /306/

it has been mysteriously proceeding—the goal of life. It must swim no more but emerge into air, the new metaphor being flight. The final chapter shows the soul, already fully developed, fattening itself for its journey until at last it is ready to leave. In the last few pages of the book, Stephen's diary, the soul is released from its confinement, its individuality is complete, and the style shifts with savage abruptness.

The sense of the soul's development as like that of an embryo not only helped Joyce to the book's imagery, but also encouraged him to work and rework the original elements in the process of gestation. Stephen's growth proceeds in waves, in accretions of flesh, in particularization of needs and desires, around and around but always ultimately forward. The episodic framework of *Stephen Hero* was renounced in favor of a group of scenes radiating backwards and forwards.* In the /307/ new first chapter Joyce had three clusters of sensations: his earliest memories of infancy, his sickness at Clongowes (probably indebted like the ending of 'The Dead' to rheumatic fever in Trieste), and his pandying at Father Daly's hands. Under these he subsumed chains of related moments, with the effect of three fleshings in time rather than of a linear succession of events. The sequence became primarily one of layers rather than of years.

In this process other human beings are not allowed much existence except as influences upon the soul's development or features of it. The same figures appear and reappear, the schoolboy Heron for example, each time in an altered way to suggest growth in the soul's view of them. Eileen Vance, a partner in childhood games, becomes the object of Stephen's adolescent love poems; the master at Clongowes reappears as the preacher of the sermons at Belvedere.† The same words, 'Apologise,' 'admit,' 'maroon,' 'green,' 'cold,'

---

* It is a technique which William Faulkner was to carry even further in the opening section of *The Sound and the Fury,* where the extreme disconnection finds its justification, not, as in Joyce, in the haze of childhood memory, but in the blur of /307/ an idiot's mind. Faulkner, when he wrote his book, had read *Dubliners* and *A Portrait;* he did not read *Ulysses* until a year later, in 1930, but knew about it from excerpts and from the conversation of friends. He has said that he considered himself the heir of Joyce in his methods in *The Sound and the Fury.* /308/

† In both these instances Joyce changed the actual events. His freedom of recomposition is displayed also in the scene in the physics classroom in *A Portrait* (453 [319]), where he telescopes two lectures, one on electricity and one on mechanics, which as Professor Felix Hackett remembers, took place months apart. Moynihan's whispered remark, inspired by the lecturer's discussion of ellipsoidal balls, 'Chase me, ladies, I'm in the cavalry!', was in fact made by a young man named Kinahan on one of these occasions. In the same way, as

'warm,' 'wet,' and the like, keep recurring with new implications. The book moves from rudimentary meanings to more complex ones, as in the conceptions of the call and the fall. Stephen, in the first chapter fascinated by unformed images, is next summoned by the flesh and then by the church, the second chapter ending with a prostitute's lingual kiss, the third with his reception of the Host upon his tongue. The soul that has been enraptured by body in the second chapter and by spirit in the third (both depicted in sensory images) then hears the call of art and life, which encompass both without bowing before either, in the fourth chapter; the process is virtually complete. Similarly the fall into sin, at first a terror, gradually becomes an essential part of the discovery of self and life.

Now Stephen, his character still recomposing the same elements, leaves the Catholic priesthood behind him to become 'a priest of eternal imagination, transmuting the daily bread of experience into the /308/ radiant body of everlasting life.' Having listened to sermons on ugliness in the third chapter, he makes his own sermons on beauty in the last. The Virgin is transformed into the girl wading on the strand, symbolizing a more tangible reality. In the last two chapters, to suit his new structure, Joyce minimizes Stephen's physical life to show the dominance of his mind, which has accepted but subordinated physical things. The soul is ready now, it throws off its sense of imprisonment, its melancholy, its no longer tolerable conditions of lower existence, to be born.

Joyce was obviously well-pleased with the paradox into which his method had put him, that he was, as the artist framing his own development in a constructed matrix, his own mother. The complications of this state are implied in Stephen's thought of himself as not his parents' true son, but a foster-son. In *Ulysses* Joyce was to carry the method much further; he makes that book the epic of the whole human body, the womb being the organ only of the *Oxen of the Sun* episode. In that episode, as Joyce said later, Stephen is again the embryo. But, in a parody of the method of *A Portrait*, Stephen emerges not to life but to Burke's pub. The theme of *Ulysses*, Joyce intimates, is reconciliation with the father. Of course, the father whom Joyce depicts in Bloom is in almost every way the opposite of his own father, and is much closer to himself. Insofar as the movement of the book is to bring Stephen, the young Joyce, into *rapport*

J. F. Byrne points out in *Silent Years*, the long scene with the dean of studies in *A Portrait* (446-51 [313-17]) happened not to Joyce but to him; he told it to Joyce and was later displeased to discover how his innocent description of Father Darlington lighting a fire had been converted into a reflection of Stephen's strained relations with the Church. /308/

with Bloom, the mature Joyce, the author becomes, it may be said, his own father. Stephen is aware enough of the potential ironies of this process to ponder all the paradoxes of the father as his own son in the Trinity, and of Shakespeare as both King Hamlet and Prince Hamlet. Yet the book is not without its strong woman; Bloom is appropriately under the influence of his wife, whom he dissatisfies (to some extent intentionally), and wishes to bring Stephen under her influence too.

In both these books Joyce seems to reconstitute his family relationships, to disengage himself from the contradictions of his view of himself as a child and so to exploit them, to overcome his mother's conventionality and his father's rancor, to mother and father himself, to become, by the superhuman effort of the creative process, no one but James Joyce. /309/

[Clongowes Wood and Belvedere]

KEVIN SULLIVAN

[1. CLONGOWES WOOD]

But in September, 1888, even the boys in the third or lowest line at Clongowes were, most of them, four or five years older /30/ than Joyce. The Jesuits, therefore, prudently arranged that his contact with these older, bigger boys be limited. He did not live among them in the dormitories, but was assigned a room in the infirmary—"quite distinct from the rest of the college buildings"[38]—where a nurse, Nanny Galvin, doubling as a governess, took him in charge. Miss Galvin was not a trained nurse, but she is reported to have been fully experienced in looking after the ordinary ailments and mishaps of boyhood.[39] It was she who, during Joyce's first two years at Clongowes, seems to have acted *in loco parentis*. She did so, however, under the direct supervision of the Jesuit laybrother, John Hanly, S.J., official infirmarian.

Brother Hanly is the first Jesuit whom young Joyce could and presumably did come to know at all intimately. Brother Michael, his counterpart in the *Portrait,* is there described as a tall man—"He had a long back like the back of a tram horse"—with "reddish

Kevin Sullivan, *Joyce among the Jesuits* (New York: Columbia University Press, 1958), pp. 30-41, 48-49, 85-93, 107-10, 119-24.

[38] *Prospectus*, Section 1.

[39] Father P. A. Baggot, S.J., present rector at Clongowes, supplied this information about Nanny Galvin and Joyce's residence in the infirmary in his letter to me on August 19, 1954. Baggott gives as his authority Father George Redington Roche, S.J., "who was a boy at Clongowes from 1883 to 1889 . . . and during his life as a Jesuit spent very many years at the school, being Higher Line prefect, Rector (1927-1933), as well as having a very intimate knowledge of the traditions of the College and of its past pupils."

hair mixed with grey and a queer look." To young Dedalus, down that morning with an attack of the "collywobbles," everything looked queer, even the sunlight. But what was queer about Brother Michael was "that he would always be a brother" and "that you could not call him sir because he was a brother and had a different kind of look." Still he was "very decent," passing along to the boys in the infirmary news out of the paper about sports and politics. And in Stephen's dream it is, significantly, Brother Michael's sorrowing face and his loud voice of mourning that is heard telling the death of Parnell (P 20-21, 25).

Technically, at this point in the novel Stephen's dream pre-/31/ pares the ground for the heart-rending argument over Parnell in the following episode. The implication is that Brother Michael was a Parnellite, one with Mr. Casey and Mr. Dedalus, and opposed to the full-blown clericalism of Dante. During the latter's bitter defense of priestly authority, young Stephen, in so far as he understood at all the issues at stake, could only have associated that authority with the priests and prefects at Clongowes. These gentlemen, politically impossible by tradition, represented the only such authority the boy had yet known. But Brother Michael was not like the priests and the prefects: he was not called "sir," and compassion not authority, sorrow not severity, surround his image in Stephen's troubled dream. He was a representative of that people, a race of servants, for whom Parnell had struggled and whom he might have saved had he not been betrayed by their "betters." This, too, is a reason why Brother Michael had for Stephen "a different kind of look."

His original, Brother John Hanly, was in real life a tall rugged man in his middle fifties who, before becoming a Jesuit, had been a pharmaceutical chemist.[40] At the time that Joyce came under his care he had already served the order as a lay brother for more than thirty years.[41] Like all Jesuit brothers (or temporal coadjutors, as their grade is designated in the order) he had, after entering the novitiate, received no special training. He and his fellows constitute a sort of Jesuit proletariat, and, though there would be small likelihood of any of them desiring it, they are neither encouraged nor afforded much opportunity to cultivate an intellectual life. But though they are servants, they are not menials. Guarded by their peculiar vocations from the temptations of pride, ambition, and sense of power, which are not unknown in higher circles of Jesuitdom, these humble men frequently serve their order more usefully

[40] Letter from Father Baggot, August 19, 1954.
[41] *Catalogus S.J.*, 1888.

than many of the priests and scholastics who pass as their social and
intellectual superiors. /32/

Brother Hanly appears to have been such a man. In addition to
his duties as infirmarian, there were a dozen other chores he might
be expected to perform around Clongowes: those of porter, coach-
man, general handyman, and supervisor of the workmen and labor-
ers employed on the college grounds. But the only other office, besides infirmarian, to which he was assigned in the Jesuit *catalogus*
was that of sacristan. In this capacity, too, in so far as he was responsible for the corps of Clongownian altarboys, he would have
had young Joyce in charge. The boy, during his first years at Clongowes, was probably considered too young to assist the priest at
mass; there is no evidence that he ever did so either then or later
at Belvedere. But it is quite certain that, like Stephen Dedalus, he
often served as boat-bearer at Benediction of the Blessed Sacrament. As the smallest boy in the school he would have been Brother
Hanly's natural choice for this minor honor, for it was an office that
always devolves on tiny fellows, just as that of thurifer goes to the
tall spare boys. The tall boy in this instance was George Redington
Roche, later ordained a Jesuit, and later still appointed rector of
Clongowes, who was in his last year at the college when Joyce was
in his first. Many years later, when Joyce's notoriety had penetrated
even the solemn dullness of Jesuit recreation rooms, Father Roche
might add a fillip to the conversation by recalling that Joyce and
he, the short and the long of it, boat and thurifer, had been altarboys together back in Clongowes Wood.[42]

III

Of the other Jesuits who are mentioned in the *Portrait*, only one,
besides Father Conmee, appears under his own name. This /33/
is Mr. Gleeson—William Gleeson, S.J.—a scholastic who, while a
member of the Jesuit community at Clongowes Wood, was preparing for his matriculation examinations at the Royal University.[43]
The description given of him is curious:

But Mr. Gleeson had round shiny cuffs and clean white wrists and fattish
white hands and the nails of them were long and pointed. Perhaps he
pared them too like Lady Boyle. But they were terribly long and pointed
nails. So long and cruel they were though the white fattish hands were not
cruel but gentle. And though he trembled with cold and fright to think

[42] Father R. P. Roche, S.J., rector of Belvedere College in Dublin, supplied this
information about his namesake and young Joyce in an interview during August,
1954. An obituary and "an appreciation" of Father George Roche appeared in
The Clongownian, 1954, but contained, not unexpectedly, no mention of James
Joyce.
[43] *Catalogus S.J.*, 1888.

of the cruel long nails and of the high whistling sound of the cane and
of the chill you felt at the end of your shirt when you undressed yourself
yet he felt a feeling of queer quiet pleasure inside him to think of the
white fattish hands, clean and strong and gentle. And he thought of what
Cecil Thunder had said; that Mr. Gleeson would not flog Corrigan hard.
And Fleming had said he would not because it was best of his play not to.
But that was not why.   [P 48]

The innocence of this is sinister, and sinister perhaps because
ambiguous. At first reading the suggestion of effeminacy, and of
something worse—a hint of perversion—seems inescapable. But
there is more to it than that. The image of Gleeson's hands pick up
and relate two conflicting impressions already made on Stephen's
slowly emerging consciousness. The cruel pointed nails are the
talons of those eagles, symbols of a Roman authority, whom Dante,
defender of clerical authority, had threatened would come and pull
out his eyes if Stephen did not apologize (P 2).[44] They are the instruments of a justice that is swift, sharp, and implacable. But the
cruelty of the nails is mitigated by the clean strength and gentleness
of the hands. They are soft and white like those of the little girl in
Bray. /34/

Eileen had long white hands. One evening when playing tig she had put
her hands over his eyes: long and white and thin and cold and soft. That
was ivory: a cold white thing. That was the meaning of *Tower of Ivory*.
                                                                             [P 36]

This sudden association of Eileen's white hands with the Mother
of God, who under another title in the same litany is also the
Mother of God, who under another title in the same litany is also the
Mother of Mercy, provides Stephen with an insight into a quite
different aspect of religious authority. Though it is blinding in the
obedience it elicits, it is also merciful and meaningful, an imaginative influence in the hearts of her children.[45] Mr. Gleeson represents
both aspects of authority at once. As justice he is masculine and
fear-inspiring, his nails pointed and cruel; as mercy he is feminine
and gentle, his hands white and soft. He will flog Corrigan, but he
will not flog him hard. Because it was best of his play not to? The
passage ends on a note that sustains the ambiguity: "that was not
why."

[44] These eagles, instruments of the "Allhighest," reappear—as what does not?—
in *Finnegans Wake*, p. 80.

[45] See Joyce's *Epiphanies*, ed. by O. A. Silverman, p. 15. The subject of the
epiphany to which reference is made here is the Blessed Virgin. The full context of the reference is: "She comes from her ancient seat to visit the least of her
children, mother most venerable, as though he had never been alien to her. She
knows the inmost heart; therefore she is gentle, nothing exacting; saying, I am
susceptible of change, an imaginative influence in the hearts of my children."

There was nothing ambiguous about the real-life Mr. Gleeson. He was an athlete who "excelled in all games but especially in cricket."[46] Young Joyce must often have watched him and Jimmy Magee (mentioned in the *Portrait*, p. 9), captain of the team in 1891-92, perform brilliantly at the wicket, on one occasion setting up a score of 212 which remained a record for inmatches. This talent alone was enough to make Gleeson a hero to young Clongownians. They nicknamed him "Ormonde" after the great Jacobite champion of Stuart times, and champion he was. A year or so after Joyce left the college, in June, 1893, "Ormonde," then prefect of the third line, turned in the most /35/ memorable performance of his career. The occasion was an outmatch with British officers from the Curragh, Clongowes' neighbors in Kildare. The impression made upon another young Clongownian at that time reads somewhat differently from that of Stephen Dedalus, shivering pleasurably at the thought of Mr. Gleeson's fattish white hands.

We third Liners knew that Mr. Gleeson was the best cricketer in Ireland! We knew that he was on the "Gentlemen of Ireland," or that if he was not, it was simply due to the fact that he was a Jesuit[47]. . . . The match began with a calamity! In the very first over, our captain was out, l.b.w. for zero! Then, mid the encouraging cheers from the whole House, Mr. Gleeson walked calmly to the wicket. . . . With varied, brilliant strokes, he scattered the field in all directions. The score mounted rapidly. Bowlers were changed, but all in vain. We were victorious. When stumps were drawn at 5:15, the House swept across the pitch, wildly cheering Mr. Gleeson and his fellow-batsman, as they moved to the marquee. We had three or four wickets to fall, and Mr. Gleeson was 120 not out. What a victory! What a hero![48]

One wonders why Joyce chose, and identified by name, William Gleeson, S.J., for the dubious, even if symbolic, role that he briefly plays in the *Portrait*. Gleeson had not been either his master or prefect at Clongowes. His prefect, at least on "walking-out" days, was Mr. Andrew Macardle, S.J., and during Joyce's time at the school the masters of the two lowest grades, rudiments and elements, were respectively Mr. James Jeffcoat, S.J., and Father William Power, S.J.[49]

Jeffcoat, a young scholastic barely turned twenty-two, was at the start of the Michaelmas term in 1888 beginning his first year of

[46] "Analecta Cluenensia," *The Clongownian,* 1953, p. 76.
[47] *Ibid.* At this point the editor, tongue-in-cheek, interpolates the remark that there is no incompatibility between Jesuit and gentleman. The "Gentlemen of Ireland" are the cricketing equivalents of our "All-Americans" in football.
[48] *Ibid.,* pp. 76-77.
[49] *Catalogus S.J.,* 1888.

regency at Clongowes. When he first begins to teach, a Jesuit's patience and idealism are, like those of most new teachers, un- /36/
tried and untireable. This may explain why Jeffcoat's stand-in in
the *Portrait,* Mr. Harford, is described briefly as a master who was
"very decent and never got into a wax" (P 48). Father Power—the
Father Arnall at Clongowes, but probably not the Arnall who later
directs the boys' retreat at Belvedere[50]—after twelve years of teaching small boys at Clongowes Wood, would be quite capable of get-
ting into "dreadful waxes." But that he was also a kindly, understanding man, with a knowledge of a boy's heart and sympathy for
his hurt, is indicated by his assignment as confessor to students. He
is almost certainly the priest to whom young Joyce confessed in
preparation for his First Holy Communion, which he would have
received in the spring of 1889 after having reached the canonical
"age of reason." In this connection it is perhaps significant that
when, in the *Portrait,* Stephen Dedalus for the first time reflects
upon the mystery of sin and the sacrament of penance (P 51), it is
Father Arnall (Power) who occasions his reflections. The McGlade
of the novel, the prefect whom Simon Moonan is accused of sucking
up to and who leads Stephen down to the infirmary when he gets
the "collywobbles" (P 6, 19-20), is Andrew Macardle, S.J. A young
man in his late twenties, seven years a Jesuit, Macardle was possibly Joyce's first Jesuit teacher, in charge of his instruction while
the boy was still living in the infirmary and before he was admitted
on a regular basis to scheduled courses of instruction.[51] Unfortunately there is no record of these earliest studies of Joyce at Clongowes, but considering his age and circumstances at this time it is
not perhaps a very significant gap in knowledge.

These three Jesuits, Jeffcoat, Power, and Macardle, were all more
closely associated with young Joyce than was Mr. Gleeson; yet all
three are disguised in aliases, and Gleeson is made to appear under
his own name. Why? The question might be dismissed as /37/
trivial—none of the four is of major interest or importance in the
novel—were it not for the fact that the trivial was always interesting
and important to Joyce. He had, moreover, an astonishing memory,
nor would any serious critic accuse him of being casual or slipshod
in designing and executing his effects. He had a reason for identifying Gleeson by name, and the reason would seem to be that, like
Conmee who afterwards had a distinguished career as a Jesuit,
Gleeson had also, though in a quite different way, made a name for
himself. His reputation as an athlete, admittedly an odd sort of dis-

---

[50] See below, p. 128.
[51] *Catalogus S.J.,* 1888.

tinction for a Jesuit, was not confined to Clongowes Wood. It would at one time have been known and talked about all over Ireland wherever there was the slightest interest in cricket, and presumably in parts of England as well. The British officers whom he had defeated that memorable day in June, 1893, were, one may be sure, as impressed with Gleeson's performance as were the young Clongownians who idolized him for it. It is possible, then, that Joyce was trading on this reputation when he identified Gleeson by name in the *Portrait*. That it would be some years after his completion of the first draft, and years after final publication of the novel, that Irish readers might have the opportunity to read and recognize Gleeson's name, Joyce could not have forseen.

Joyce had none of the artist-in-the-garret indifference to fame and fortune. Apart from his work, even after that work was widely acclaimed, he took pains to propagandize it further and win a still wider publicity for his current writing.[52] He knew too, /38/ in blunt terms of the market place, the value of jarring his readers into a shock of recognition—or of revulsion—by means of his work. Gleeson's name is only a minor case in point, but it is a significant point. Joyce's effects were calculated, his intentions ulterior, and the results rewarding. The identities of Jeffcoat, Power, and Macardle, unlighted by the dimmest glow of fame, might be decently draped in convenient aliases. It did not matter one way or the other.

Father James Daly, S.J., the Father Dolan of the *Portrait*, was similarly disguised. He had come to Clongowes the year before Joyce entered the college, and he was to remain as prefect of studies for the next thirty years.[53] As a Jesuit he seems to have conformed perfectly to that ideal embodied in the Ignatian formula "totus ad laborem." He devoted himself single-mindedly to the task of so raising the academic standards of the college that it would be known throughout Ireland as something more than the country's most fashionable school. In this he very largely succeeded. Two years after his arrival Clongowes Wood College "went to the top of the

[52] Joyce at one point apparently solicited the aid of so unlikely a person as H. G. Wells. There is a letter from Wells to Joyce (now in the Lockwood Memorial Library of the University of Buffalo), dated November 23, 1928, which begins:

"My dear Joyce: I've been studying you and thinking over you a lot. The outcome is that I don't think I can do anything for the propaganda of your work. I've an enormous respect for your genius etc. . . ." (Published by Stuart Gilbert in *Letters of James Joyce*, pp. 274-75).

See also the use Joyce made of the Transition crowd in Paris as reported and /38/ interpreted by Kenner in *Dublin's Joyce*, pp. 360-61. For other examples of Joyce's earliest efforts to publicize his own work, see Tindall's edition of *Chamber Music*, p. 20 and note.

[53] Corcoran, *Clongowes Record*, p. 149.

list, and during the following score of years and more, if not absolutely first, it was always well within the very best group of Irish schools judged by the public examination records."[54] To his reorganization of the Clongowes curriculum Father Daly brought the experience gained as prefect of studies in two other Jesuit schools, Belvedere College, Dublin, and Crescent College, Limerick.[55] These were day schools, and socially not in the same class as Clongowes. But Father Daly, in his process of revitalizing the academic life of the college, would have taken small note of social distinctions. He was interested in scholarship, and scholarship is what he produced. The sons of /39/ gentlemen were expected to study just as hard and as long as the sons of shopkeepers and artisans. The record indicates that they did.

Though Father Daly's success was real, it was not of a kind to bring him, even had he desired it, any appreciable fame. Fame, anyhow, is not the usual lot of schoolmasters. Their success is often in proportion to their severity, and this generally wins them little more than brief notoriety in an ephemeral community of schoolboys. Father Daly's name might still be forgotten had not Herbert Gorman chosen to identify him—the only Jesuit at Clongowes whom he does identify—as a clerical "martinet" and the persecutor of young James Joyce.[56] There would be little point in objecting to the epithet, which is gratuitous, but a reasonable doubt may be cast on the report of persecution. The account of the unwarranted punishment meted out to Stephen Dedalus (P 51-55) may possibly have some basis in Joyce's own experience at Clongowes. However, it would be a mistake to read this passage in the *Portrait* as a simple transcript of an actual event. There is at present no evidence either to prove or to disprove it. But it is worth pointing out that in the organization of a Jesuit school, the disciplining of students, especially when it is corporal discipline, is specifically excluded from the provinces of the prefect of studies. Usually some person not a master is designated for this unpleasant duty.[57] From the internal evidence of the *Portrait* itself,[58] it would seem that the man so designated during Joyce's time at Clongowes was none other than William Gleeson, S.J. This does not of course exclude the possibility that Father Daly may on occasion have taken matters into his own hands. /40/

[54] *Ibid.*, p. 151.
[55] *Ibid.*, p. 149.
[56] Gorman, *James Joyce*, pp. 29, 33-34.
[57] Fitzpatrick, *St. Ignatius*, pp. 187, 206, 242.
[58] The passage describing Gleeson quoted earlier. At the time, Gleeson was not a master at Clongowes; while assigned to the Jesuit community there he was preparing for his matriculation examinations at the Royal University.

There was, finally, no reason, as there was with Conmee and Gleeson, for Joyce to identify Daly by name. As a small boy, first living in the infirmary, and then a member of the lowest line in the school, his contacts with the prefect of studies must have been few indeed. Even Daly's reorganization of the program of studies, carried out chiefly in the higher lines, would not have affected Joyce in any marked degree. Daly was only another name, remembered perhaps by a few hundred schoolboys, forgotten by hundreds of others; there was no special reason why anyone in Ireland or elsewhere should remember it. But "Dolan: it was like the name of a woman who washed clothes" (P 60). /41/

.   .   .   .

The horizons of boyhood are limited. The boy returning to college in January, 1891, could not have foreseen that before the calendar year was out he would be leaving Clongowes Wood for the last time. He was still a small boy, still shy in company, reserved with his schoolfellows, obedient and dutiful with his masters. A slight curve of scar on his chin, left there by a mongrel dog nearly as big as he when he was only five, was still visible.[70] Years later, when his face would be familiar to the large world beyond Clongowes, that scar would still persist. But by then he would have grown a beard to hide it, a light but adequate beard, like that of a thoughtful but unsorrowing Christ. Now he was just turned nine years of age and, scar or no scar, was quite undistinguishable from the rest of the schoolboys around him.

They were a good set of fellows. Their names are set like unobtrusive stones through the first chapter of the *Portrait,* the real names of real boys—Rody Kickham, Cecil Thunder, Jack Lawton, Jimmy Magee, and the rest. But of the sixteen boys who appear or are mentioned in this chapter, the names of four are pure invention, and these are the only boys who are shown in a really unflattering light: Simon Moonan is a "suck," Athy an obnoxious goldbrick, Tusker Boyle a sissy, and Corrigan the perpetrator of a scandalous and mysterious offense bordering on sacrilege. Two other actual Clongownians, Wells and Nasty Roche, are not portrayed as the most pleasant sort of fellows, but /48/ neither can the identity of either be established with complete certainty. Roche, a trifling snob, can be the name of any of four boys who were in school at the same time as Joyce, three of them having entered in the same year. There

[70] "Portrait of James Joyce," edited by W. R. Rodgers, produced by Maurice Brown, broadcast by the British Broadcasting Commission, Third Program, February 13 and 17, March 22, 1950. Hereafter cited as BBC.

were two boys by the name of Wells, Charles Wells and H. Wells, who, though they also entered Clongowes in 1888, left in 1890, a year before the events narrated in the *Portrait* are supposed to have occurred. Furthermore, the Wells of the novel, something of a bully, has the decency later to apologize to Stephen for elbowing him into the ditch, and though his decency is undoubtedly motivated by fear, it is perhaps enough to redeem him in his author's eyes and in those of the reader. In the light of all this it seems not too much to claim that in writing, or in revising, the first chapter of the *Portrait* Joyce remained loyal to the ties which bound him, if only in memory, to Clongowes Wood.[71]

These were the boys with whom he shared his earliest experiences in and out of the classroom. He was only nine years old, but he had known most of these fellows for almost a third of his life. He was a good student, but this year, despite his natural shyness, he was to share in more of their outside activities. Not sports of course—he was never to be much at that—but extracurricular activities. Third Liners were not eligible for the debating society, or the sodality, or any of the other clubs at Clongowes except dramatics. Dramatics, then, it must be for young Joyce. He played his first and only role on the Clongowes stage during the Easter holidays of 1891. /49/

[2. BELVEDERE]

Joyce mentions none of his Belvedere masters by name in the *Portrait*. George Dempsey, his English teacher, appears briefly as Mr. Tate: he points out a near heresy in one of Dedalus's essays (P 88), chats quietly with Vincent Heron (Albert Connolly) during the famous retreat (P 143), and is not seen or heard of again. Physically, Mr. Dempsey appears to have been an imposing figure. A tall thin man with gray hair and a mustache the color of old hay, he reminded Eugene Sheehy of a retired brigadier and J. F. Byrne of Mr. Justice Holmes.[36] The accounts agree in the impression of dignity conveyed, a dignity that seems not to have been impaired by the slight stoop, becomingly pedagogical, with which he moved among the boys at Belvedere. But he is remembered best for the caustic judgments pronounced on the English themes read in class on Monday afternoons. It is easy now to imagine him standing by one of the great second-floor windows overlooking Great Denmark Street, staring down on the broad tongue of /85/ pavement that George's Street dips into the pool of Dublin, listening with feigned inatten-

[71] The names of the boys mentioned here may be checked on the school lists provided by Corcoran in *Clongowes Record*, pp. 165-297.

[36] Sheehy, *May It Please the Court*, p. 4; Byrne, *Silent Years*, p. 147.

tion to a schoolboy's voice elaborating more or less grammatically
the praises of A Favorite Hero or Heroine.[37] And while the boy read,
Mr. Dempsey's right hand would be working the hay of his mustache, twisting it into a sugan and shaping and reshaping it with
patient care. Almost under the shadow of that mustache, in the first
seat in the first row next to the great window, sat young Joyce, a
small blond boy, delicate but not unmanly, precocious but strangely
simple, listening, too, to the schoolboy voice repeating the theme,
observing the odd behavior of Mr. Dempsey, waiting for the end
and the flick or flash of the master's comment. The boy was a favorite of Dempsey's, for he was personable as well as proficient, and
when his turn came to read the master, more deliberately attentive
now, "would literally wriggle and chuckle with delight."[38] George
Dempsey was indeed Joyce's first critical and appreciative audience,
and he was to remain so long after the boy had gone from Belvedere.
According to Gorman he continued always a strong partisan of
Joyce, forwarding reference books when the latter was in the midst
of work in progress and urging publication of Joyce's verse in the
college magazine.[39]

Dempsey's brother-in-law, P. Bertram Foy, who taught chemis-
try and physics (known in the curriculum of the day as "natural
philosophy") has been singled out by Byrne as the best of the
teachers then at the school.[40] But, Byrne admits, his judgment in
this may well have been guided by his predilection for the subject
matter of Foy's course. Joyce, whose grades in natural phi- /86/
losophy indicate a profound lack of interest in the subject, did not,
one feels sure, think one way or the other about P. Bertram Foy.
Nor could he have worked up any great enthusiasm for the physical
culture program of Sergeant Major Wright. Athletic boys like Byrne
and Sheehy might be expected to enjoy their sessions in the new
gymnasium behind Belvedere House, twirling Indian clubs and
hoisting dumbbells and playing monkey on parallel and horizontal
bars. But poor Joyce was no gymnast. "His legs just wouldn't behave
in the ordinary way, no muscles at the hip you see."[41] It is easy
to believe that, like Dedalus, he got through these sessions by

[37] This title is included in a comic list of essay assignments in *Finnegans Wake*,
p. 306. Gorman says (*James Joyce*, p. 45) that for this assignment Joyce wrote on
Ulysses, and so indeed he may have. But it is unlikely that the boy's choice of
subject was thought "not quite orthodox, at least from the point of view of the
Society of Jesus."

[38] Byrne, *Silent Years*, p. 147.

[39] Gorman, *James Joyce*, p. 42.

[40] Byrne, *Silent Years*, p. 23.

[41] Hutchins, *James Joyce's Dublin*, p. 33. For a different account of Joyce's
athletic abilities, see Stanislaus Joyce, *My Brother's Keeper*, pp. 41-42.

assuming the painless role of "secretary to the gymnasium" (P 81).

With the exception, then, of George Dempsey, Joyce seems to have had little to do with any of the lay instructors at Belvedere. On the evidence of the *Portrait* alone, it would also seem that he had about as little to do with his Jesuit instructors. All the Jesuits in the Belvedere chapters of the novel, with the exception of the retreat master, are cast in minor roles. Only one is introduced by name; all the others, even the rector, remain anonymous. The Jesuit who is named is the object of Heron's contemptuous irreverence— "Will you tell Doyle with my best compliments that I damned his eyes?" (P 92)—an irreverence not shared on the occasion by Stephen Dedalus. This Doyle is described as "a plump freshfaced jesuit" (P 94) in charge of the Whitsuntide play at Belvedere who, in contrast with the cold unconcern of Dedalus, is in "a great bake" about his young actor. His original is Charles Doyle, S.J., a scholastic assigned in 1897 to teach Third of Grammar at Belvedere.[42] He was not, then, one of Joyce's teachers (Joyce having completed this grade of Grammar in 1893), but he /87/ was well enough remembered by Joyce that, twenty-five years later, the artist could write to the Jesuit, long since ordained and assigned again to the same college, enquiring into the past history of Belvedere House. Father Doyle's answer, already quoted, appears to have been prompt and cordial, and one wonders now how well the priest remembered Joyce as a boy or whether he recognized the sketch of himself in the *Portrait,* had he the luck to read it.

The Jesuit whom Joyce probably knew more intimately than any other at Belvedere was the rector, Father William Henry, S.J. He is unnamed in the *Portrait,* where he is introduced only to announce to Dedalus and his school fellows the schedule for the retreat and to deliver a brief devotional exhortation to the boys on St. Francis Xavier. But Father Henry seems to have played a somewhat larger part in Joyce's life at school. He was not only rector of the college, he served also as procurator, prefect of studies, and instructor in Latin in the higher grades.[43] It was his prelection in Horace that prepared Joyce for his translation of *O Fons Bandusiae* into English verse. It was to his office, as prefect of studies, that he summoned Joyce to receive the prizes won in scholastic competition. It was in the same office, but now in his capacity as rector, that Father Henry discussed with Joyce, prefect of the sodality and virtual head of the school, plans for college activities and perhaps, at times, more personal plans for the boy's future. For in addition to their vari-

[42] *Catalogus S.J.,* 1897.
[43] *Ibid.*

ous official connections, a friendly, even familiar relationship seems to have existed between the boy and the priest.

In the *Portrait,* on the night of the Whitsuntide play, Heron suggests that "it would be a ripping good joke" (P 83) if Dedalus took off the rector in the part of the schoolmaster. There is no indication in the novel that Dedalus did so, for Joyce does not /88/ allow this solemn adolescent to step out of character even for a moment. But the mimicry that was foreign to the solemnity of Dedalus was natural and spontaneous in Joyce. On the occasion of one such Belvedere play the boy, cast in the role of a farcical pedagogue, did turn his performance into an impersonation of the reverend rector. The story is that Father Henry, a small, precise, bewhiskered man, master of the cliché and the Delsarte gesture, sat in the front row of the audience that night and, before the assembly of students, parents and friends, laughed as heartily at the joke against himself as any of the boys or parents present.[44] It may be true that, under the circumstances, there was not much else he could do without appearing even more ridiculous than Joyce had made him out. But it is more probable that he honestly enjoyed the jape, for Joyce was not reprimanded then or later for this piece of talented impudence.

If one wonders why he was not reprimanded, the answer must be, first, that Belvedere was an Irish school. It is difficult to imagine Dr. Arnold of Rugby reacting like Father Henry of Belvedere. It is even more difficult to imagine an audience of Victorian parents joining in a laugh had at the headmaster's expense. Indeed, it is quite impossible to imagine a contretemps of this kind even occurring at an English public school, where, however much the boys might bully or jolly or fag one another, the attitude toward masters was one of relentless respect stamped into the students by a code of behavior as stiff and confining as an Eton collar. But Irish schoolboys were not groomed by so fine or stern a code. They were trained to reverence rather than respect, the impulse of belief starting from the heart being held more significant than the gesture of the hand touched to one's cap. Disrespect was not to be condoned, but neither was its appearance /89/ to be mistaken for irreverence. Joyce and Father Henry and the audience present at the Whitsuntide play knew what reverence was, took it indeed for granted, and so did not have to make a great show of respect for themselves or for each other. Joyce's mimicry of the rector, juxtaposing a show of disrespect against this fundamental reverence, struck among them

[44] Sheehy, *May It Please the Court,* p. 8. Stanislaus Joyce (*My Brother's Keeper,* p. 88) identifies the play as Anstey's farce *Vice Versa* and corroborates Sheehy's report of the rector's amusement.

the essential note of laughter—*on se moque de ce qu'on aime.* The same note is sounded throughout Joyce's work where too often the respectable reader, lacking perhaps in reverence, responds to it in shock or in outrage—if indeed he is aware of it at all.

The most immediate significance of this episode is the light it casts on the relationship between Joyce and Father Henry. Even in an Irish school boys are not likely to joke or trifle with an unpopular master, and no master, unless he is sure of his students' devotion, will endanger discipline and decorum by submitting to schoolboy bantering even when it is less pointed and public than that reported of Joyce. Father Henry, then, may be supposed to have known his boy, to have liked him, to have been on easy and cordial terms with him, and even perhaps to have been more than ordinarily interested in his future. On his part, Joyce was certainly fond of Father Henry, and though he had reason to believe that he was the rector's favorite, he also knew that he was not his toady. He could ape his mannerisms because he admired his man. And the characteristic trait of this man, like that of Joyce's former rector, Father Conmee, was fairness, that quality in a master valued above all others by schoolboys.

There is another story told of Father Henry that in class one day, receiving what he thought to be a wrong answer from a pupil, he ordered the boy to write out the correct answer a hundred times. When the boy stubbornly insisted that he was right, the rector doubled the penalty. When the boy still refused to yield, the rector raised it another hundred—agreeing, however /90/ to write out the penalty himself should he be proved wrong and the boy right. So it turned out, and before classes were dismissed that afternoon Father Henry presented the boy with several sheets of paper on which the penalty was inscribed three hundred times in a neat priestly hand.[45]

This was not the act of a "harsh and warped" character, as Father Henry is depicted by Joyce's biographer.[46] It was the act of a man whom boys could recognize, beneath his mask of professional severity, as eminently just and fair, worthy of admiration and even of affection. This estimate of the man would seem closer to Joyce's opinion of Father Henry than Gorman's dismissal of him as "a fanatical Roman Catholic convert who wore whiskers."[47] That the boy who figures in this story was a lad named Lenehan and not

[45] Sheehy, *May It Please the Court*, p. 5.

[46] Gorman, *James Joyce*, p. 41.

[47] *Ibid.;* echoed by Stanislaus Joyce: "a fanatical convert from Protestantism." *My Brother's Keeper*, p. 68.

Joyce himself, as one version has it,[48] does not alter the point of the story.

None of the other teachers at Belvedere appears to have known Joyce quite so well at this time, and their influence on him was probably negligible. Of some all that is now known is their names, and in at least one case even this may be inaccurate. For example, there was a layman called Loup who is said to have first taught Joyce Italian at the age of twelve.[49] Of this Mr. Loup there is now no trace, but it is interesting to note that his name may be anglicized as "error" or "trick" (literally "wolf"), and Joyce, who /91/ was presumably Gorman's authority in this, was not beyond having a bit of fun at the expense of his biographer. But if Mr. Loup did exist, he shared the burden of teaching Italian to not more than three or four out of approximately one hundred and twenty boys[50] with Father Francis Ryan, S.J., who was officially assigned to teach Italian and French at Belvedere from 1894 to 1898.[51] Another Jesuit, Father Richard Campbell[52]—"whom some of the boys called Lantern Jaws and others Foxy Campbell"—is mentioned only in passing in the *Portrait* (p. 187), where Stephen Dedalus remembers him as "eyeless and sourfavoured and devout." But such descriptions, it should be remembered, are Stephen's impressions, invented rather than recollected by Joyce himself. So, in the first chapter of the novel, the author can locate another Jesuit, the scholastic Patrick Barrett, at Clongowes Wood where he is depicted as one of the more ingenuous and formidable of the prefects (P 29, 46). Actually, Barrett was stationed at Belvedere, and though he was not one of Joyce's own masters, he taught his younger brother Stanislaus in the class of Elements in 1893-94.[53]

In the novel the Belvedere Jesuits are dimly, vaguely drawn. They are names without faces, like Charles Doyle, or faces without identity, like Richard Campbell, or personifications of authority without

[48] Hutchins, *James Joyce's Dublin*, p. 48.

[49] Gorman, *James Joyce*, p. 43. The biographer also states that only one other boy, "Albrecht" Connolly, was studying Italian at this time. If this is so, there seems to have been a superfluity of Italian masters at Belvedere—each with one pupil apiece. To add to the confusion, Stanislaus Joyce speaks of "a young Jesuit, MacErlaine, the professor of French . . . whose best pupil my brother was in those years . . ." (*My Brother's Keeper*, p. 89). But, according to the official records, there was no Jesuit of that name at Belvedere during the year in question, 1897-98.

[50] Sheehy, *May It Please the Court*, p. 1.

[51] *Catalogus S.J.*, 1897. This would appear to be the same Ryan who is mentioned in "An Encounter."

[52] *Ibid.*

[53] *Catalogus S.J.*, 1894.

name or definition like William Henry. None of them is a person in his own right—neither a pleasant person, like Father Conmee, nor unpleasant, like Father Dolan. They exist only as modifications of Stephen's consciousness. At Clongowes the child Stephen had sensed the opposition between ego and nonego, between self and the world, and though it had puzzled and /92/ frightened him, he had not had to choose between them or to deny one or the other. His innocence preserved the world within and the world without in delicate balance, and the latter world was peopled by real persons who had names and faces and identities of their own. But at Belvedere, after a futile attempt at religious surrender of self, the frightened adolescent drew more and more into himself: "he drew less pleasure from the reflection of the glowing sensible world . . . than from the contemplation of an inner world of individual emotions" (P 194). The balance tipped inward, the conflict resolved in favor of ego, and the nonego then appears as a *veiled, grey, dim haze* (P 194). In this progressive idealization of experience, the identity of individual Jesuits blurs and becomes lost, for in the world in which Stephen Dedalus now moves the only individual that really exists is Stephen himself, and the only identity that matters is his own. /93/

.   .   .   .

While at Belvedere, the boy's response to the Jesuit prescription was pronounced. Even Dedalus had been infected briefly by the virus of Jesuit idealism and in his quieter moments could reflect dispassionately, even admiringly, on those "intelligent and serious priests and highspirited prefects" who had guarded and guided him thus far through life. James Joyce cannot be thought less sensitive or intelligent or responsive than Stephen Dedalus, and his thought about his Jesuit masters and about himself as a Jesuit must be taken at least as seriously, and perhaps a good deal more seriously, than the somber solipsistic reflections of the Dedalus. In want of any more intimate record, the quality of his response at this time may be deduced from what is known of his experience—apart from his purely scholastic achievements—while at the college. What, to begin with, were his relations with his fellows, his family, and his superiors in the schoolboy world of Belvedere?

Of all the boys who are mentioned in the Belvedere chapters of the *Portrait* only one may be said to figure more than incidentally.[1]

[1] J. F. Byrne entered Belvedere on September 3, 1892, and, according to his own account, left the school in 1895 after he had taken and passed the autumn matriculation examination in the old Royal University. His last two years at the

This is Albert Connolly, who appears under the *nom de guerre* of Vincent Heron. The name is significant because of the impression the boy makes on Stephen Dedalus:

He had often thought it strange that Vincent Heron had a bird's face as well as a bird's name. A shock of pale hair lay on the forehead like /107/ a ruffled crest: the forehead was narrow and bony and a thin hooked nose stood out between the closeset prominent eyes which were light and inexpressive.   [P 84]

This description of Heron relates him to Dante's eagles (P 2) and to Mr. Gleeson (P 48), both taloned symbols of authority. But where Dante symbolized domestic authority (with strong clerical overtones), and Gleeson is an obvious representative of ecclesiastical authority (whose justice is tempered with gentleness), Heron stands for a kind of self-justifying lay or civil authority. Stephen—"this heretic"—is delivered into his power by his two henchmen and fellow inquisitors, and the punishment that Stephen had trembled to consider at the hands of Mr. Gleeson is in fact meted out at Heron's hand (P 91). And during this caning the exchange between Stephen and Heron ("Admit," "No," "Admit," "No. No.") distantly echoes the cruel antiphon of the encounter with Dante: "Apologise, / Pull out his eyes, / Pull out his eye, / Apologise." The episode does point up the cowardice and cruelty of Heron and his two lieutenants, Nash and Boland; and Stephen at the time is reduced to tears by their malice. But, though the details of the incident are painfully clear in Stephen's recollection (it is presented in the *Portrait* as a flashback; P 87-91), "the memory of it called forth no anger in him." This is because Stephen is already beginning to feel the stirrings of a more profound unrest which is eventually to carry him beyond the bounds of all authority.

But this does not mean that Joyce is branding his own companions at Belvedere as fools and cowards. Who Nash and Boland were is not known, nor does it now seem of much importance. But Albert Connolly's relation with Joyce would seem to be much like that between Dedalus and Heron in the *Portrait*:

The rivals were school friends. They sat together in class, knelt together in the chapel, talked together after beads over their lunches. /108/ As the fellows in number one were undistinguished dullards Stephen and Heron had been during the year the virtual heads of the school. It was they who went up to the rector together to ask for a free day or to get a fellow off.   [P 84]

---

college coincided, therefore, with Joyce's first two; but, though the two boys were doubtless acquainted at this time, they did not become close friends until they met again at University College.

Albert Connolly was in fact Joyce's scholastic rival at Belvedere. The two boys appear to have been in the same class until 1896. That year, the year in which Joyce was held back because of his age and did not compete in the Intermediate examinations, Connolly won an exhibition. This he retained the following year when Joyce and he were the only boys from Belvedere so honored. The closeness of their rivalry may be measured by their respective ranks in the order of merit: of the 64 students who won honors in 1897, Joyce was 54th and Albert Connolly 57th. The rivalry was, however, friendly. They did "kneel together in the chapel" where Joyce served as prefect of the Sodality and Connolly was his first assistant prefect:[2] the former led one group of boys in recitation of the Little Office B.V.M., and the latter led another group in antiphonal response. As prefect and assistant prefect respectively, they were indeed "virtual heads of the school."

As the Jesuits in the Belvedere chapters of the *Portrait* are more dimly drawn than the Clongowes Jesuits, so too are the schoolboys in their charge. Only one student, W. G. Fallon, is clearly identified by name (P 189), but the passing mention of him is of no significance to the narrative.[3] Moreover, one must again be constantly on guard against confusing Dedalus's response to the "undistinguished dullards" around him with the attitude of the adolescent James Joyce to his own schoolfellows. /109/ Dedalus at Belvedere goes into a solipsistic spin in which the objective realities of existence recede from the tightening center of his sensibility like a universe of fading stars. When he does not deliberately shun the community of his fellows, he is enduring their company passively and reluctantly. Only once is he drawn back briefly into a sense of oneness with those about him. The occasion is again the Whitsuntide play.

Another nature seemed to have been lent him: the infection of the excitement and youth about him entered into and transformed his moody mistrustfulness. For one rare moment he seemed to be clothed in the real apparel of boyhood: and, as he stood in the wings among the other players, he shared the common mirth amid which the drop scene was hauled upwards by two ablebodied priests with violent jerks and all awry. [P 95]

This "rare moment" in Dedalus's experience would seem to have been the more habitual mood of Joyce himself. The other nature

[2] Annals of the Congregation of the Blessed Virgin Mary, a record of the sodality at Belvedere, now in the Rector's archives at the college.

[3] This William Fallon was frequently one of Joyce's fellow guests at the Sheehy parties on Belvedere Place. During one evening of charades he and Joyce did a burlesque of *Hamlet,* Joyce playing the queen mother to Fallon's Ophelia. See Sheehy, *May It Please the Court,* p. 22.

here lent to him may well be Joyce's own nature, "clothed in the
real apparel of boyhood," and the passage, contrasting the living
boy with the literary portrait, may be read as more authentically
autobiographical than other more dramatic passages in these Belvedere chapters. For if Joyce, like Dedalus, was different from his fellows, it was not that he stood apart from them in mysterious and
surly aloofness, but that he stood superior to most of them in ways
at once understandable, acceptable, and admirable in their eyes and
in the eyes of their Jesuit masters. *At this time* the boy is not to be
thought of as a budding artist whose Dedalean eccentricities were
also at the bud; he was an exceptional schoolboy of proved scholastic superiority, of sound if fragile health, and, to all outward appearances, of substantial moral and religious disposition. As such,
he had all the physical, intellectual, and moral qualities prerequisite
for a vocation to the priesthood. /110/

.   .   .   .

Joyce at Belvedere was certainly not the rebel some have thought
him. For that matter, neither was Stephen Dedalus. The latter, for
example, despite Heron's spirit of quarrelsome comradeship, never
allows himself to be seduced "from his habits of quiet obedience"
(P 93). Obedience, significantly, is that characteristically Jesuit
virtue to which St. Ignatius especially exhorted his companions.
"Above all," he wrote to the scholastics at Coimbra, "I desire that
you be most outstanding in the virtue of obedience. . . . Let other
religious orders surpass us in fasts and vigils and in all things else
that, according to their own rule and discipline, they piously undertake; but in true and perfect obedience, and in the abdication
of your own will and judgment, I especially desire that you who
serve God Our Lord in this Society, be outstanding."[15] Again and
again Ignatius stresses the im- /119/ portance and preeminence of
obedience, and his words are fully familiar to Stephen Dedalus who,
observing the Jesuit dean of studies at the University, can repeat to
himself the original simile of Ignatius from the *Summarium Constitutionum:*[16] "*Similiter atque senis baculus,*" he was, as the founder
would have had him, like a staff in an old man's hand . . ." (P 217).

[15] "Atque ego sane . . . imprimis obedientiae virtute praestantissimos esse
cupio. . . . Ab aliis religiosis ordinibus facilius patiamur superari nos jejuniis,
vigiliis, et cetera victus cultusque asperitate, quam suo quique ritu ac disciplina
sancte suscipiunt: vera quidem ac perfecta obedientia, abdicationeque voluntatis
atque judicii maxime velim, fratres charissimi, esse conspicuos, quicumque in
hac Societate Deo Domino nostro deserviunt." "Epistola S. Ignatii de virtute
obedientiae," in *Thesaurus Spiritualis S.J.*, pp. 428-29.
[16] ". . . vel similiter atque senis baculus, qui ubicumque et quacumque in re
velit eo uti, qui eum manu tenit, ei inservit." *Ibid.*, p. 397.

But if Stephen at the University was already beyond the bounds
of obedience, he was never so at Belvedere, and the Jesuits, sensible
of the boy's merits, might naturally be expected to see in him a
prospective candidate for the order. For here was a young man of
obviously superior intellectual capacity, who enjoyed a reputation
for solid and unassuming virtue, and who, though not robust, was
in unquestionably good health. Unless one believes that every call
to the religious life must, like that of St. Paul, be accompanied by
a bolt of thunder and a flash of lightning, these three qualities—
brains, character, and health—are in the natural order and in an
otherwise uninvolved Catholic all that is necessary for a vocation.
And in the supernatural order they will also be deemed sufficient
when there is evidence of a sincere desire to devote such talents to
the service of God. Joyce clearly had all the necessary qualifications,
and the Jesuits may well have believed that there was sufficient evidence for a vocation in the boy's habitual demeanor. For a firm
habit of obedience—that virtue by which the order was supposed to
be especially distinguished—was indeed especially marked in Joyce,
and seemed to indicate a vocation not merely to the religious life
in general, but quite specifically to the Society of Jesus.

In the *Ratio Studiorum* Jesuit masters are urged to converse frequently with their students about spiritual things, but at the same
time they are admonished not "to entice anyone into our /120/
order."[17] The admonition, however, as any Jesuit alumnus might
testify, is one of those more honored in the breach than in the observance. One of the annotations to *The Spiritual Exercises* also
forbids the director to urge upon his retreatants any special advantages of the religious life over another. But the same annotation
continues: "Outside the Exercises, it is true, we may lawfully and
meritoriously urge all who probably have the required fitness to
choose continence, virginity, and religious life, and every form of
religious perfection."[18] The director is further advised that he should
act "as a balance at equilibrium, without leaning to one side or the
other, and that he should permit the Creator to deal directly with
the creature, and the creature directly with his Creator and Lord."[19]

[17] Fitzpatrick, *St. Ignatius and the Ratio Studiorum,* p. 196.
[18] *Thesaurus Spiritualis S.J.,* p. 23: "Decima quinta, ille, qui tradit exercitia,
non debet ea accipientem movere magis ad paupertatem neque ad promissionem
quam ad opposita, neque ad unum statum vel modum vivendi quam ad alium:
quia licet, extra Exercitia, possimus licite ac meritorie movere omnes, qui proba-
biliter idoneitatem habeant, ad eligendam continentiam, virginitatem, religionem
et omnem modum perfectionis evangelicae. . . ."
[19] *Ibid.,* p. 24: ". . . qui tradit Exercitia, non divertat, nec se inclinet ad unam
neque ad alteram partem: sed consistens in medio, ad instar bilancis, sinat Crea-

In the *Portrait* it is, appropriately, the director who, after the retreat, speaks to Stephen about the possibility of a vocation. He is
acting entirely in the spirit of *The Spiritual Exercises,* and he presents the life of a Jesuit in terms calculated to affect the imagination
and idealism of an adolescent. His simple arguments are weighted
on the side of a vocation, but toward the close of his remarks he
makes a gesture of restoring "a balance of equilibrium": "But you
must be quite sure, Stephen, that you have a vocation because it
would be terrible if you found afterwards that you had none"
(P 185). The balance is more than restored and, with a pious promise and exhortation to pray, the director releases Ste- /121/ phen
in order to "permit the Creator to deal directly with the creature,
and the creature directly with his Creator."

In the *Portrait* the issue is never in doubt. The opening lines of
the episode, descriptive of the director, adumbrate the decision
that is already in the back of Stephen's mind and which later, passing the Jesuit residence in Gardiner Street, he does not so much
will as recognize.

The director stood in the embrasure of the window, his back to the light,
leaning an elbow on the brown crossblind, and, as he spoke and smiled,
slowly dangling and looping the cord of the other blind, Stephen stood
before him, following for a moment with his eyes the waning of the long
summer daylight above the roofs or the slow deft movements of the priestly
fingers. The priest's face was in total shadow, but the waning daylight
from behind him touched the deeply grooved temples and the curves of
the skull.   [P 178]

The embrasure (that is, recess or crypt), the crossblind, the other
blind, the waning daylight, the total shadow, the skull, all of these
evoke a joyless, sepulchral mood in which the person of the priest
suggests to Stephen a figure of death, and his invitation to the priesthood a temptation to deny nature and life. The director's "back to
the light" contributes to the same effect. The repetition of the image
of the waning daylight, of the words "crossblind" and "blind," and
later of the words "gravely" and "grave," deepen the mood with
incantatory echoes as if indeed this were the opening of a chant for
the dead. One wonders whether Joyce, in presenting the Jesuit director here as a symbol of death, had again in mind that passage in
the *Summarium Constitutionum* from which Stephen afterward
quotes. Just preceding the simile of the old man's staff, the *Summarium* presents a far more graphic image of Jesuit obedience.

---

torem cum creatura, et creaturam cum suo Creatore ac Domino immediate
operari."

"Let each one," it reads, "persuade himself that he ought to allow himself to be ruled and governed . . . as if he were a dead body that suffers /122/ itself to be turned this way and that and to be treated in any manner whatsoever."[20] If the *Summarium* did suggest to Joyce his treatment of the director, then the significance of the latter "slowly dangling and looping the cord of the other blind" is abundantly clear and may be rightly identified as the central image, the epiphany of the interview.[21] Stephen is indeed receiving an invitation to death, to hang himself on the crossblind of obedience, and his executioner is that representative of the *"dio boia* hangman god"* (U 210), the Jesuit director.

But Stephen, who even before this interview acknowledged that "to merge his life in the common tide of other lives was harder for him than any fasting or prayer" (P 175), was temperamentally incapable of following this ideal or of accepting this destiny. It was not for him to be "made obedient unto death, even to the death of the cross."[22] After the interview, on his way homeward, he wondered vaguely "at the frail hold which so many years of order and obedience had on him" (P 188) when once his personal freedom was threatened. And at home, in the squalor and disorder of the family kitchen, the weary voices of his brothers and sisters sounded for him a note which, "like the voice of nature herself" (P 190), despite pain and weariness, gave utterance to a kind of hope which was not to be heard in "the voice of the director urging upon him the proud claims of the church and the mystery and power of the priestly office" (P 188). That voice was the voice of death, to be echoed a little later by the mocking voices of his schoolfellows on the beach at Dollymount. But by /123/ then Stephen's "soul had arisen from the grave of boyhood, spurning her graveclothes" (P 197). He heard now only the affirmative cry of his own heart, and listened now only for the wild cry of the voice of Nature herself. This came to him in the image of a girl standing, alone and still, by the sea, in "the likeness of a strange and beautiful sea-bird" (P 199). Always before the image or suggestion of a bird—Dante's eagles, Gleeson's taloned hands, Heron's ruffled crest—had symbolized a cruel and repressive authority. All these are now submerged and transmuted in the dark-

[20] *Ibid.*, p. 397: "Quisque sibi persuadeat, quod qui sub obedientia vivunt, se ferri ac regi a Divina providentia per Superiores suos sinere debent perinde, ac si cadaver essent, quod quoquoversus ferri, et quacumque ratione tractari se sinit. . . ."

[21] Kenner in *Dublin's Joyce*, p. 113, does so identify it, but without calling attention to this relevant passage in the *Summarium Constitutionum*.

[22] A significant text (*Phil.* 2:8) quoted by St. Ignatius in his "Letter on Obedience" with which Joyce was doubtless familiar.

plumaged dove of a girl rising, like love, from the sea. The symbols are transmuted—authority into loveliness, obedience into liberty, repression into joy. Stephen is transfigured. The call, the vocation he had awaited has come to him: "Her eyes called him and his soul had leaped at the call. To live, to err, to fall, to triumph, to recreate life out of life!" (P 200). Out of the death of the priest who might have been is now born the artist who is never entirely to be. /124/

[Limerick for Ezra Pound]

JAMES JOYCE

There once was a lounger named Stephen
Whose youth was most odd and uneven.
He throve on the smell
Of a horrible hell
That a Hottentot wouldn't believe in.

James Joyce, letter to Ezra Pound, 9 April 1917, in Stuart Gilbert (ed.), *Letters of James Joyce* (New York: The Viking Press, 1957), p. 102. /143/

PART V

ON THE ESTHETIC THEORY

The Joycean epiphany in literature may be described as a formulation through metaphor or symbol of some luminous aspect of individual human experience, some highly significant facet of most intimate and personal reality, some particularly radiant point to the meaning of existence.

—William T. Noon, S.J., *Joyce and Aquinas* (New Haven: Yale University Press, 1957), p. 70.

[The "Eagle" Epiphany]

JAMES JOYCE

[Bray: in the parlour of the house in Martello Terrace]

Mr. Vance—(*comes in with a stick*) . . . O, you
know, he'll have to apologise, Mrs. Joyce.
Mrs. Joyce—O yes . . . Do you hear that,
Jim?
Mr. Vance—Or else—if he doesn't—the
eagles'll come and pull out his eyes.
Mrs. Joyce—O, but I'm sure he will apologise.
Joyce—(*under the table, to himself*)

> —Pull out his eyes,
> Apologise,
> Apologise,
> Pull out his eyes.

> Apologise,
> Pull out his eyes,
> Pull out his eyes,
> Apologise.

James Joyce, *Epiphanies*, with Introduction and Notes by O. A. Silverman
(Buffalo, N.Y.: Lockwood Memorial Library, University of Buffalo, 1956), p. 6.

147

[Passing through Eccles' St]

JAMES JOYCE

He was passing through Eccles' St one evening, one misty evening,
with /210/ all these thoughts dancing the dance of unrest in his
brain when a trivial incident set him composing some ardent verses
which he entitled a "Vilanelle of the Temptress." A young lady was
standing on the steps of one of those brown brick houses which seem
the very incarnation of Irish paralysis. A young gentleman was leaning on the rusty railings of the area. Stephen as he passed on his quest
heard the following fragment of colloquy out of which he received
an impression keen enough to afflict his sensitiveness very severely.

The Young Lady—(drawling discreetly) . . . O, yes . . . I was . . .
at the . . . cha . . . pel . . .

The Young Gentleman—(inaudibly) . . . I . . . (again inaudibly)
. . . I . . .

The Young Lady—(softly) . . . O . . . but you're . . . ve . . . ry . . .
wick . . . ed . . .

This triviality made him think of collecting many such moments
together in a book of epiphanies. By an epiphany he meant a sudden spiritual manifestation, whether in the vulgarity of speech or
of gesture or in a memorable phase of the mind itself. He believed
that it was for the man of letters to record these epiphanies with
extreme care, seeing that they themselves are the most delicate and
evanescent of moments. He told Cranly that the clock of the Ballast
Office was capable of an epiphany. Cranly questioned the inscrutable dial of the Ballast Office with his no less inscrutable counte-
nance:

—Yes, said Stephen. I will pass it time after time, allude to it, refer to it, catch a glimpse of it. It is only an item in the catalogue
of Dublin's street furniture. Then all at once I see it and I know
at once what it is: epiphany.

James Joyce, *Stephen Hero*, ed. by John J. Slocum and Herbert Cahoon (New
Edit.; New York: New Directions, 1955), pp. 210-13.

—What?

—Imagine my glimpses at that clock as the gropings of a spiritual eye which seeks to adjust its vision to an exact focus. The moment the focus is reached the object is epiphanised. It is just in this epiphany that I find the third, the supreme quality of beauty.

—Yes? said Cranly absently. /211/

—No esthetic theory, pursued Stephen relentlessly, is of any value which investigates with the aid of the lantern of tradition. What we symbolise in black the Chinaman may symbolise in yellow: each has his own tradition. Greek beauty laughs at Coptic beauty and the American Indian derides them both. It is almost impossible to reconcile all tradition whereas it is by no means impossible to find the justification of every form of beauty which has ever been adored on the earth by an examination into the mechanism of esthetic apprehension whether it be dressed in red, white, yellow or black. We have no reason for thinking that the Chinaman has a different system of digestion from that which we have though our diets are quite dissimilar. The apprehensive faculty must be scrutinised in action.

—Yes . . .

—You know what Aquinas says: The three things requisite for beauty are, integrity, a wholeness, symmetry and radiance. Some day I will expand that sentence into a treatise. Consider the performance of your own mind when confronted with any object, hypothetically beautiful. Your mind to apprehend that object divides the entire universe into two parts, the object, and the void which is not the object. To apprehend it you must lift it away from everything else: and then you perceive that it is one integral thing, that is *a* thing. You recognise its integrity. Isn't that so?

—And then?

—That is the first quality of beauty: it is declared in a simple sudden synthesis of the faculty which apprehends. What then? Analysis then. The mind considers the object in whole and in part, in relation to itself and to other objects, examines the balance of its parts, contemplates the form of the object, traverses every cranny of the structure. So the mind receives the impression of the symmetry of the object. The mind recognises that the object is in the strict sense of the word, a *thing,* a definitely constituted entity. You see?

—Let us turn back, said Cranly.

They had reached the corner of Grafton St and as the foot- /212/ path was overcrowded they turned back northwards. Cranly had an inclination to watch the antics of a drunkard who had been ejected from a bar in Suffolk St but Stephen took his arm summarily and led him away.

—Now for the third quality. For a long time I couldn't make out what Aquinas meant. He uses a figurative word (a very unusual thing for him) but I have solved it. *Claritas* is *quidditas*. After the analysis which discovers the second quality the mind makes the only logically possible synthesis and discovers the third quality. This is the moment which I call epiphany. First we recognise that the object is *one* integral thing, then we recognise that it is an organised composite structure, a *thing* in fact: finally, when the relation of the parts is exquisite, when the parts are adjusted to the special point, we recognise that it is *that* thing which it is. Its soul, its whatness, leaps to us from the vestment of its appearance. The soul of the commonest object, the structure of which is so adjusted, seems to us radiant. The object achieves its epiphany.

Having finished his argument Stephen walked on in silence. He felt Cranly's hostility and he accused himself of having cheapened the eternal images of beauty. For the first time, too, he felt slightly awkward in his friend's company and to restore a mood of flippant familiarity he glanced up at the clock of the Ballast Office and smiled:

—It has not epiphanised yet, he said. /213/

Introduction

THEODORE SPENCER

There is one aspect of Stephen's aesthetic theory which appears in the manuscript alone, and is left out of the *Portrait* entirely. In my opinion the passage describing it is the most interesting and revealing in the entire text. It is the passage on pp. 210 ff. beginning with the words, "He was passing through Eccles Street," which explains Joyce's theory of epiphanies.‡

I ask the reader to turn to this passage, and read it.

This theory seems to me central to an understanding of Joyce as an artist, and we might describe his successive works as illustrations, intensifications and enlargements of it. *Dubliners,* we /16/ may say, is a series of epiphanies describing apparently trivial but actually crucial and revealing moments in the lives of different characters. The *Portrait* may be seen as a kind of epiphany—a showing forth—of Joyce himself as a young man; *Ulysses,* by taking one day in the life of the average man, describes that man, according to Joyce's intention, more fully than any human being had ever been

Theodore Spencer, "Introduction," in *Stephen Hero,* ed. by John J. Slocum and Herbert Cahoon (New Edit.; New York: New Directions, 1955), pp. 16-17.

‡ This theory is mentioned once in *Ulysses.* . . . Stephen is meditating: "Remember your epiphanies on green oval leaves, deeply deep, copies to be sent if you died to all the great libraries of the world, including Alexandria?" Dr. Gogarty also refers to it in his autobiography, *As I was Walking down Sackville Street.* . . . Gogarty is spending the evening with Joyce and others; Joyce says "Excuse me," and leaves the room. "I don't mind being reported," Gogarty writes, "but to be an unwilling contributor to one of his Epiphanies is irritating.

"Probably Fr. Darlington had taught him, as an aside in his Latin class—for Joyce knew no Greek—that 'Epiphany' meant 'a showing forth.' So he recorded under 'Epiphany' any showing forth of the mind by which he considered one gave oneself away.

"Which of us had endowed him with an 'Epiphany' and sent him to the lavatory to take it down?"

described before; it is the epiphany of Leopold Bloom, just as, years earlier, the trivial conversation overheard on a misty evening in Eccles Street (where, incidentally, Mr. Bloom lived) was the epiphany of those two people's lives, shown forth in a moment. And *Finnegans Wake* may be seen as a vast enlargement, of course unconceived by Joyce as a young man, of the same view. Here it is not any one individual that is "epiphanized"; it is all of human history, symbolized in certain types the representatives of which combine with one another as the words describing them combine various meanings, so that H. C. Earwicker and his family, his acquaintances, the city of Dublin where he lives, his morality and religion, become symbols of an epiphanic view of human life as a whole, and the final end of the artist is achieved.

And if we keep this theory in mind, as a further aspect of the static theory of art developed throughout the present text, it helps us to understand what kind of writer Joyce is. A theory like this is not of much use to a dramatist, as Joyce seems to have realized when he first conceived it. It is a theory which implies a lyrical rather than a dramatic view of life. It emphasizes the radiance, the effulgence, of the thing itself revealed in a special moment, an unmoving moment, of time. The moment, as in the macrocosmic lyric of *Finnegans Wake,* may involve all other moments, but it still remains essentially static, and though it may have all time for its subject matter it is essentially timeless. /**17**/

Joyce's Epiphanies

IRENE HENDRY CHAYES

By an epiphany he meant a sudden spiritual manifestation, whether in the vulgarity of speech or of gesture or in a memorable phase of the mind itself. He believed that it was for the man of letters to record these epiphanies with extreme care, seeing that they themselves are the most delicate and evanescent of moments.—Stephen Hero

Stephen Dedalus' esthetic in *A Portrait of the Artist as a Young Man* has the same specious quality as his Hamlet thesis in *Ulysses* and is a product of the same talent for parody; as Stephen's friend Lynch remarks, it has "the true scholastic stink." Both theories are, of course, more than parody: the speculations on Hamlet serve to crystallize Stephen's broodings on his spiritual parentage, and the esthetic is actually Joyce's, which he followed faithfully in his own literary method. Just how closely method and principle were related in Joyce's work is shown by his little-noticed theory of epiphanies, which is mentioned fleetingly in *Ulysses,* but is given explicit statement only in *Stephen Hero,* the fragmentary first draft of the *Portrait* recently published in book form for the first time.[1]

The theory of epiphanies, presented as Stephen's, is /448/ bound up with the three cardinal esthetic principles, or conditions of beauty, that he expounds to Lynch in one of their dialogues in the *Portrait.* (In *Stephen Hero,* the passive listener is Cranly, a character apparently based on Joyce's own college friend Byrne.) These principles have a respectable philosophic origin in the *integritas, consonantia* and *claritas* of Aquinas. *Integritas* Stephen explains in

Irene Hendry, "Joyce's Epiphanies," *Sewanee Review,* LIV (July, 1946), 449-67. Mrs. Chayes' article was published under her maiden name, retained here for bibliographical accuracy.

[1] James Joyce, *Stephen Hero, A Part of the First Draft of A Portrait of the Artist as a Young Man,* edited from the manuscript in the Harvard College Library by Theodore Spencer (New York: New Directions, 1944).

pseudo-scholastic language as "wholeness"—the perception of an esthetic image as *one* thing, "self-bounded and self-contained upon the immeasurable background of space or time /449/ which is not it." *Consonantia,* similarly, is symmetry and rhythm of structure, the esthetic image conceived as "complex, multiple, divisible, separable, made up of its parts and their sum, harmonious"; "the synthesis of immediate perception is followed by the analysis of apprehension." The third principle, *claritas,* is given the approximate meaning of "radiance" and equated with another Thomistic term, *quidditas,* or the "whatness" of a thing. *Quidditas* is the link with the theory of epiphanies; in this case, the definition in *Stephen Hero* is the more revealing:

> *Claritas* is *quidditas.* After the analysis which discovers the second quality the mind makes the only logically possible synthesis and discovers the third quality. This is the moment which I call epiphany. First we recognise that the object is *one* integral thing, then we recognise that it is an organized composite structure, a *thing* in fact: finally, when the relation of the parts is exquisite, when the parts are adjusted to the special point, we recognise that it is *that* thing which it is. Its soul, its whatness, leaps to us from the vestment of its appearance. The soul of the commonest object, the structure of which is so adjusted, seems to us radiant. The object achieves its epiphany.

Joyce's epiphanies are mentioned by Harry Levin, who had access to the manuscript of *Stephen Hero* in preparing his New Directions study, and by Theodore Spencer, who edited and wrote the preface to the published version of the fragment. Both Levin and Spencer, however, emphasize only the obvious aspect of the epiphany: its effect on the observer and his relation to the object "epiphanized." Spencer calls the theory one which "implies a lyrical rather than a dramatic view of life," thinking apparently of Stephen's defintion of the "lyrical" form of art as "the form wherein the artist presents his image in immediate relation to himself." Levin takes the stories in *Dubliners* as pure examples of epiphany and the collection of which Stephen resolves (in *Ulysses*) to leave copies to all the libraries of the world; Joyce's /450/ later works, he says, are "artificial reconstructions of a transcendental view of experience," and his "dizzying shifts" of technique "attempt to create a literary substitute for the revelations of religion."

But these descriptions do justice to neither the concept nor Joyce's use of it. In the first place, of course, the epiphany is not peculiar to Joyce alone. Virtually every writer experiences a sense of revelation when he beholds a fragment of his ordinary world across what Bullough has called "psychic distance"—dissociated from his subjective and practical concerns, fraught with meaning beyond itself, with every detail of its physical appearance relevant. It is a revelation quite as valid as the religious; in fact, from our present secular viewpoint, it perhaps would be more accurate to say that the revelation of the religious mystic is actually an esthetic revelation into which the mystic projects himself—as a participant, not merely as an observer and recorder—and to which he assigns a source, an agent and an end, called God. What Joyce did was give systematic formulation to a common esthetic experience, so common that few others—writers, if not estheticians—have thought it worth considering for its own sake.

Again, many writers use "revelation" as a technical device in achieving their effects; Joyce, however, used it more consciously and with greater variation than anyone with whom he can be compared. More than a "transcendental view of experience" is involved in Joyce's application of his theory of epiphanies, just as there is more than mysticism in religion, particularly the Roman Catholicism that shaped his whole outlook as a young man. The theory furnished Joyce with a technique of characterization which evolved generally in the "lyrical-epical-dramatic" progression that Stephen describes: from the first person to the third, from the personal to the impersonal, from the kinetic to the static. It is a technique in which *integritas* and *consonantia* are always necessary to *claritas,* and *claritas* itself comes more and /451/ more to reside in *quidditas,* the soul, the essential identifying quality of the thing, than in a mystic, emotional exhilaration on the part of someone who looks on. *Claritas* is *quidditas* is the key the theory itself gives us.

In *Dubliners, claritas* is achieved most often, although not always, through an apparently trivial incident, action, or single detail which differs from the others making up the story only in that it illuminates them, integrates them, and gives them meaning. It is like the final piece which is added to the child's pile of lettered blocks and completes the spelling of a word or gives form to the "house" or "tower" he is building. Farrington's treatment of his son attaches to himself the petty tyranny we recognize first in his employer. Little Chandler's brief rebellion against domesticity frightens his child, and his dreams of being a poet are swept away by his remorse. After a drinking bout, Mr. Kernan is persuaded by his friends to take part in a retreat, at which Father Purdon's metaphor of the "spiritual accountant" crystallizes a businessman's religion that is only a reflection of their daily lives. And in *The Dead,* the artistic highpoint of the collection, the conviviality of the banquet, Gabriel Conroy's confident rejection of the dead past,

his scorn for Irish nationalism, and his desire of his wife are ironically drawn together and then dispersed by the story of Michael
Furey.

Joyce used the *Dubliners* "block" technique again, with some
modification, in the Nausicaa episode in *Ulysses,* where, after having sexually aroused Leopold Bloom and indulged in erotic day-
dreams of her own, Gerty MacDowell walks away with a limp. It is
a technique that is obvious to us because it is familiar; although
their origin is probably Katherine Mansfield or Chekhov rather
than Joyce, similar "revelations" of character are vouchsafed regu-
larly by the *New Yorker* and its imitators. Such stories are usually
considered to be "objective" because the author offers no overt interpretation of his material but merely arranges it so that its meaning is "revealed" directly to the reader. /452/ The *Dubliners* stories
seem to conform to Stephen's definition of "dramatic" art as the
form in which the artist "presents his image in immediate relation
to others"; "life purified in and reprojected from the human imagination." Joyce was not satisfied with such an easy attainment of the
esthetic stasis, however, and this may have been because the "block"
technique did not fulfill equally all three of his basic principles of
art. *Claritas* is achieved, but the *quidditas* that constitutes it is di-
lute; *consonantia,* the parts and their sum, is in evidence, but *integritas* is not, at least to the same degree.

II

The example of epiphany which Joyce employs in *Stephen
Hero*—a fragment of conversation between a girl and a young man,
overheard on Mr. Bloom's own Eccles Street—is actually the final
"block" of the *Dubliners* method without the foundation; one may
guess that the foundation in each story was laid down later, in an
effort to insure the impersonality of the epiphany Joyce originally
experienced in a very personal fashion. It may be, too, that the collection of epiphanies Stephen wishes to leave to posterity is not
Dubliners at all but a collection of just such fragments as the one
he acknowledges.

A number of these "most delicate and evanescent of moments"
occur throughout both *Stephen Hero* and the *Portrait,* taking up
residence in Stephen's consciousness with neither elucidation nor
relation to anything beyond themselves: factory girls and boys coming out to lunch; the witless laughter of an old woman; the screech-
ing of a mad nun; a servant singing; the salutation of a flower girl.
In *Ulysses,* too, the peregrinations of Bloom and Stephen about
Dublin are rich in epiphanies of this sort; the shout Stephen hears

in the street and calls a "manifestation of God" is only the most obvious.

Occasionally we are given a suggestion of what is "revealed" in Joyce's epiphanies. The black straw hat and the greeting of /453/ the prostitute in *Stephen Hero* have an inordinate fascination for Dedalus; "mustn't the devil be annoyed to hear her described as an evil creature?" he asks. In order to fill in the background of an epiphany, he sometimes makes a reconstruction of an event in the past: a forgotten medical student cutting the word *Foetus* in the wooden surface of his desk, or an imagined incestuous meeting in the rain, suggested by the dwarfish reader in the library and the rumors about his birth. And in at least three instances an epiphany helps Stephen to decide on the future course of his life: the snatch of song from the street, contrasting suddenly with the unsmiling face of the Jesuit who has been urging him to enter a novitiate; the vision of the girl wading at the shore; and the flight of birds about the college library, symbolizing the "fabulous artificer" after whom he is named.

The moment of revelation without its narrative base is the most conventional of Joyce's epiphanies; we find it elsewhere even in fiction which does not make use of revelation as a specific technique in the *Dubliners*-Chekhov-Mansfield-*New Yorker* manner. This is particularly true among writers who, like Virginia Woolf and John Dos Passos, have modified Joyce's stream-of-consciousness method. And in poetry the isolated moment of revelation dates at least from Wordsworth's experiences in the presence of mountains, leech-gatherers, and the lights about Westminister Bridge. The epiphanies in Joyce's own poetry, in such pieces as "The twilight turns from amethyst," "My love is in a light attire," "A Flower Given to My Daughter," "On the Beach at Fontana," fit so well into the familiar lyric pattern that the poetry is usually dismissed as something outside the main stream of his work.

Joyce's second epiphany technique does quite clearly conform to Stephen's definition of lyrical art. Although *claritas* is ultimately generated by *quidditas*, we are first aware of an effect on the beholder—Stephen, or ourselves through Stephen—not of an objectively apprehensible quality in the thing revealed; if we /454/ are to penetrate through to the *quidditas*, we must try to identify ourselves with Stephen or wrest a meaning of our own from the revelation. From the standpoint of eliminating the artist's personality from his work, this particular technique was a retrogression from the method of *Dubliners*, but it did have the advantage—in Joyce's esthetic theory, an extremely important one—of realizing the three principles, *integritas, consonantia,* and *claritas,* in a single image. The next step toward impersonal creation was to modify the image so that its *quidditas* would be unmistakable, with its radiance attached to itself rather than to a perceiving consciousness: Joyce's third epiphany technique, which explains the differences between *Stephen Hero* and *A Portrait of the Artist.*

In the *Portrait,* which covers in 93 pages events that require 234 pages in the *Hero* fragment, the original elements of Joyce's first novel, particularly the characters, are subjected to a process of compression and distillation that rejects all irrelevancies, all particularities and ambiguities, and leaves only their pure essence. In *Stephen Hero,* the common people at the Good Friday service are diverse in their submissive ignorance and their unquestioning respect for the clergy; the old women scrape their hands over the dry bottom of the holy-water font and speak in broad, realistic dialect. But in the *Portrait* the simple faithful are represented by pious sighs and a peasant smell "of air and rain and turf and corduroy," or by kneeling forms and whispering voices in the confessional box—"soft whispering cloudlets, soft whispering vapour, whispering and vanishing." In the first draft of the novel, Maurice and Isabel Dedalus appear specifically as characters; in the *Portrait,* Stephen's brothers and sisters are merely voices at the tea-table, replying to his questions in pig-latin or singing with an "overtone of weariness behind their frail fresh innocent voices." "He heard the choir of voices in the kitchen echoed and multiplied through an endless reverberation of the choirs of endless generations of children: /455/ and heard in all the echoes an echo also of the recurring note of weariness and pain. All seemed weary of life even before entering upon it."

The character of Stephen itself undergoes a transformation. The *Hero* draft is often marred by adolescent particularities: Stephen baiting his cruder classmates, sneering at his mother's pious superstitions, or trying to convert his parents to Ibsen. In the *Portrait,* however, the Ibsen episode is omitted entirely, the intellectual distance between Stephen and his contemporaries is given less emphasis, and the quarrel with his mother over his failure to do his Easter duty is mentioned only indirectly. The details of Stephen's debauches similarly remain obscure; what we are shown, in the boy's dreams of temptation, the sermons he listens to during the retreat, and his hallucinations of damnation and punishment, is actually an apotheosis—or epiphany—of sin and repentance, far removed from the adventures of the Eugene Gants who for a generation have been storming the brothels of the world in imitation of Stephen.

But the most striking attenuation occurs in the character of
Emma Clery. In the *Hero* fragment, she is a healthy, middle-class
girl who studies Gaelic with enthusiasm, flirts with priests, and is
only confused and offended by Stephen's unconventional offer of
himself. In the *Portrait*, however, we are told nothing of her appearance and are never allowed a clear conception of her as an individual. The Gaelic lessons shrink to an Irish phrasebook, the
flirtation becomes a bitter recollection in Stephen's mind, associated with the scorn he feels for the Church, and there is only the
barest hint of the circumstances of the rejection. The girl herself
is never more than a shadowy presence—a provocative glance or
speech, a shawled head, "fresh warm breath," laughter and tapping
footsteps, a sash or a nodding hair ornament. Her etherialization
extends even to her name, which in the *Portrait* becomes "E— C—."

In Stephen's discussion of *quidditas,* the necessary condition to
/456/ radiance is a perfection of formal organization, or *consonantia* itself; "when the relation of the parts is exquisite, when the parts
are adjusted to the special point, we recognize that it is *that* thing
which it is." The formal adjustment in the examples of *quidditas* I
have been citing is simpler and more tangible than the metaphors
"distillation," "essence" and "etherealization" might suggest; it consists in nothing more mysterious than the division of a whole character into its separate parts, analogous to the "analysis of apprehension" Stephen matches up with *consonantia*. Although she
represents an almost opposite conception of woman, Emma is an
essence by virtue of the same process of formal disintegration as
Molly Bloom, whom we know through most of *Ulysses* as drowsy
breathing, untidily scattered garments, the rattling of the brass
quoits on her bed, an odor, or a chance remark, when we know her
directly, and as a collection of separate physical charms when we
know her through Bloom. Stephen, only somewhat less than Bloom
in his celebrated stream of consciousness, is the sum of fleeting
memories, sense impressions, shifting thoughts, and associations,
each "a memorable phase of the mind itself." The *integritas* of the
character is sacrificed to the *integritas* of the esthetic image, and we
are presented with generalities resynthesized from individuals: not
the pious poor, but Faith; not Stephen's brothers and sisters, but
Childhood; not Emma Clery, but Virginity. In *A Portrait of the
Artist,* Stephen Dedalus and Emma already foreshadow the great
male and female abstractions of Joyce's later work, which express
on successively higher levels of sublimation the *quidditas* of each
sex.

Emma's etherealization is, incidentally, suggested in other figures of women in Joyce's early work: Gretta Conroy in *The Dead*; the "memories of the girls and women in the plays of Gerhart Hauptmann" and "their pale sorrows," which the wet branches of trees call forth in Stephen's mind; the boyish figure of the Virgin in the liturgy, which Stephen visualizes as he listens to a servant singing *Rosie O'Grady*. Joyce's feminine characters /457/ in general tend to become essences before his men. In fact, he conceived of only three types of woman, the Virgin, the Temptress, and the Mother—all curiously Catholic, all complementing the naïve misogyny of *Stephen Hero,* where Stephen sneers at the notion of "votes for the bitches" and refers to women inaccurately but with effective insult as "marsupials." Anna Livia Plurabelle ranges through all three essences; Molly Bloom combines the qualities of temptress and mother; and Emma is transformed into a temptress in Stephen's dreams, so that the boy's abortive passion becomes a conflict between carnal and spiritual love, centered in one object. This is the conflict that is made part of a "problem" formula in Joyce's play *Exiles,* with Bertha Rowan set off against the consumptive music teacher, who is significantly named Beatrice. (In at least one scene of the *Portrait,* incidentally, there is also a suggestion of *La Vita Nuova,* with ironic overtones: Emma standing silently in the school porch surrounded by her girl companions, while Stephen regards her from a distance, remembering her flirtatiousness in the presence of Father Moran.)

And when a character is broken down into its parts and resynthesized, what is the new integrating agent which assists the "synthesis of immediate perception" and serves both *consonantia* and *claritas?* Appropriately enough in Joyce's case, it is language itself. We are most familiar with the plays on etymology and multiple accretions of meaning in his later work, but at first he achieved his effects through all the poet's or orator's traditional devices of cadence and balanced period, metaphor and apostrophe, verbal connotation and subtle variation of sound. This is apparent in the examples of *quidditas* that have been cited ("soft whispering cloudlets," "frail fresh innocent voices"), where we are given auditory impressions rather than adequate visual description. Epiphany is, in fact, one purpose of Joyce's amazing virtuosity of language, which grows as much between *Stephen Hero* and the *Portrait* as between the *Portrait* and *Ulysses* or /458/ *Ulysses* and *Finnegans Wake*. It is not an attempt to "create a literary substitute for the revelations of religion"; it is the vehicle of the radiant esthetic experience itself, and at the same time it is intimately related to the plan of Joyce's work as a whole.

It has not been sufficiently emphasized, I think, that the three major books, as well as the play and the poetry, together repeat on the scale of the author's entire career the childhood-adolescence-maturity pattern of the *Dubliners* stories. Youth—hope and rebellion; maturity—disillusion and repentance; middle age—conformity and loneliness; age—resignation and death; in spite of palimpsests of Vico and Homer, psychoanalysis and Irish history, there is a clear and continuous line of development in Joyce's literal subject matter from his first writings to his last. His theme is, quite simply, the life of man, and his own life was devoted to writing piece by piece a vast Human Tragedy, an epiphany of all mankind, in which a profound anthropological sense of the mystery and power of death takes the place of the Christian's traditional faith in union with God and the life everlasting. It was mainly in the service of his theme, I believe, that Joyce incorporated smaller "growth" patterns (often regarded as mere pedantic conceits) in his separate works: the passage of the day from morning to night, a river flowing to the sea, a child growing to manhood. One of the most prominent of these is the Oxen of the Sun episode in *Ulysses,* where the successive stages of the child's development in the womb are paralleled by successive stages of the development of the English language; but there are other examples of the adaptation of linguistic techniques to his theme as well as to the epiphany principle. Even in the early works there is a lyrical or rhetorical passage wherever there is a climactic epiphany of particular emotional significance, or where a generalized rather than an individual *quidditas* is revealed. In *Dubliners* we find the disillusion of *Araby* and the elegiac closing pages of *The Dead.* Ste- /459/ *phen Hero* has Stephen's rhetorical outbursts against the Church and the "nocturne" scene just preceding Isabel's death, which in mood and setting is very like Joyce's lyric "The twilight turns from amethyst," while passage after passage in *A Portrait of the Artist,* some frankly dyed with purple, make Joyce's first novel as much a vocal book as *Ulysses* or *Finnegans Wake.*

The final epiphany in the *Portrait* is Stephen's famous journal entry marking the point at which the young man becomes an artist: "Welcome, O life! I go to encounter for the millionth time the reality of experience and to forge in the smithy of my soul the uncreated conscience of my race." Although we are supposed to think of it as written, this is pure oratory (Joyce refused to set off the written word from the spoken and exploited the possibilities of both to the utmost) and an exact formal counterpart of both Molly Bloom's remembered affirmation as she sinks into sleep and Anna Livia

Plurabelle's valediction at dawn. Moreover, it is balanced by the fragmentary, unpersonalized impressions of the infant Stephen at the beginning of the book precisely as the soliloquies of Molly and Anna Livia are balanced by the impersonal narrative beginnings of *Ulysses* and *Finnegans Wake*. In a reversal of the progression in Stephen's theory (which actually describes the relation of the artist to his work rather than artistic form), Joyce moves from the third person to the first, and achieves in each case a simultaneous progression on another level. In the *Portrait,* the biological development from child to man becomes also a psychological and moral development, from passive receptivity to the self-conscious will. In *Ulysses* with the progress of the day we are taken from the matter-of-fact blasphemies of Buck Mulligan to the nostalgia of middle age, a development away from the delusive optimism of the will. (For the eagerness of youth which Molly Bloom celebrates belongs as much to the past as the dead son Bloom himself has been seeking during the day, and Molly's memories—Anna Livia has them also—serve to bring into focus, or "reveal," what /460/ has gone before in much the same way as Gretta Conroy's story in *The Dead*.) And in *Finnegans Wake* the concluding first-person passage is the final epiphany of the generalized human *quidditas,* the thinking and feeling soul (Joyce shows sensibility surviving will), before it enters a new cycle of existence and is dissolved in the inorganic beginnings we encountered on the first page of the book: "riverrun, past Eve and Adam's, from swerve of shore to bend of bay," the river flowing through the city. Here at last is a perfect unity of technique, theme and esthetic principle, and a distillation of essence so complete that Being becomes quite literally the Word.

III

Joyce's work is a tissue of epiphanies, great and small, from fleeting images to whole books, from the briefest revelation in his lyrics to the epiphany that occupies one gigantic, enduring "moment" in *Finnegans Wake,* running through 628 pages of text and then returning upon itself. His major technique and the best illustration of his theory is the one just discussed, revelation through distillation of the pure, generalized *quidditas* from an impure whole, by which *consonantia* (here analysis of the whole into its parts) and *integritas* (resynthesis of the parts into a larger whole through the agency of language itself) interact to produce *claritas* directly. It is also his best-known technique (anyone who has grown up since the publication of *Ulysses* knows in advance, for instance, that Molly Bloom is female essence—Magna Mater and all that!) and in its high points it is his most spectacularly successful. It has, however, the defects of virtuosity. Usually the scale is too large to comprehend with ease, and the means to unity and diffusion, even in the intricate Joycean patterns of language, tend to become too mechanically ingenious, like Tchelitchew's devices for hiding children's figures among the images of trees. In spite of the author's intention, his method often separates from his meaning and actually becomes /461/ an obstacle to it, turning a serious work of art (which one cannot doubt *Finnegans Wake* is) into a parlor game.

Although it is less conspicuous and plays a fixed and minor role in the larger scheme of his work, Joyce makes use of one more epiphany technique which is worth considering because it is his closest approach to that austere impersonality of creation Stephen describes to Lynch: when "the artist, like the God of the creation, remains within or behind or above his handiwork, invisible, refined out of existence, indifferent, paring his fingernails." Under this, the intervention of a consciousness, even indirectly through the medium of language, is ruled out. A character is broken down into its separate parts, as it is under the "distillation" technique, but only one or two of the detached "parts"—"the vulgarity of speech or of gesture," a detail of figure or expression, an item of clothing—are recombined. Although it is free of irrelevancies, the *quidditas* represented by the recombination is not the *quidditas* of a generality but an individual; its function is to identify rather than to abstract.

In *Stephen Hero* to some degree, and especially in *A Portrait of the Artist*, we can watch this technique take form. A priest is invariably marked by the fluttering of his soutane. Father Dolan steadies Stephen's hand before administering the pandying, and the cruelty of his gesture extends to his "firm soft fingers," "his greywhite face and the no-coloured eyes behind the steel-rimmed glasses"; when the priest reappears in *Ulysses*, he is signified only by the pandybat. In the same way, Mr. Casey's three cramped fingers symbolize his activities as an Irish patriot and hence his loyalty to Parnell, which for the boy Stephen is the peculiar essence of his father's friend. Again, the humility and joylessness of the church office are represented in the movements of the Jesuit dean of studies as he lights the fire, in his old, lean body—literally *similiter atque senis baculus*—and his face, compared by Stephen to "an unlit lamp or a reflection hung in a false focus." /462/

Gesture and clothing, in particular, are as important in creating an individual *quidditas* as voice and breathing in creating a generalized *quidditas*. "There should be an art of gesture," Stephen tells Cranly in *Stephen Hero*. In the *Portrait*, he finds his "image of the

soul in prayer" in "the raised and parted hands, the parted lips and
eyes of one about to swoon" of religious art, and during his period
of repentance visualizes himself "accomplishing the vague acts of
the priesthood which pleased him by reason of their semblance of
reality and of their distance from it." Clothes, in their turn, are
true repositories of the soul, as they are for Lévy-Bruhl's primitives.
When he comes upon his schoolmates, swimming, Stephen thinks
pityingly of their nakedness: "How characterless they looked! Shuley
without his deep unbuttoned collar, Ennis without his scarlet belt
with the snaky clasp, and Connolly without his Norfolk coat with
the flapless sidepockets!" In *Stephen Hero,* he is first impressed by
the prostitute's black straw hat, the outward and visible sign of her
essence, and the clothes of the characters in Joyce's play *Exiles* are
so important that they are not only described in the stage directions
but are mentioned by the characters themselves, with a green velvet
jacket playing a significant part in the action. Finally, in the night-
town episode of *Ulysses,* changes of costume are as frequent as in the
charades in which Stephen takes part at Mr. Daniel's house (*Stephen Hero*), and the hallucinatory images of Bloom at successive
stages of his past are all carefully dressed for their rôles.

Gesture and clothing, details of physical appearance, peculiari-
ties of speech, and intimate material appurtenances all serve to
identify Stephen's friends in the *Portrait,* in dialogue passages which
might be scenes from a play. Amid the profane, witty, or banal conversations of the students, the author intervenes only as a sort of
property man, to mark each one with his objectified *quidditas,*
which adheres to him from scene to scene virtually without change
and in some instances even carries over into /463/ *Ulysses:* Cranly's "iron crown" of hair and priestly pallor, his profanity and Latin
affectation of speech; Lynch's whinnying laugh, his habit of swear-
ing "in yellow," and his gesture of putting out his chest; the shoot-
ing-suit and fair goatee of McCann, the reformer; Davin's brogue
and Dixon's signet ring; Heron's cane and smile; the pedant Glynn's
umbrella. In these scenes Stephen himself, the individual Stephen,
is often a participant; he has his ashplant, his "familiar," which he
carries also in *Ulysses,* and his soul moves rapidly and elusively
through a series of metamorphoses which never quite leave the
realm of the literal: the lamp mentioned in his conversation with
the dean of studies; Epictetus' bucketful of water; Cranly's handball; the louse he picks from his neck; the fig Cranly tosses into the
gutter.

This technique represents the ultimate in "objective" characterization, "revealing" an individual essence by means of a detail or an

object to which it has only a fortuitous relation; the pandybat expresses Father Dolan's soul not because it resembles him in any way but because it is associated with him in an act that marks him forever in Stephen's eyes. Through Joyce's fourth epiphany technique (in which *claritas* is a tiny, perfunctory flash, all but absorbed by *quidditas*) we can trace out a virtual iconography of the characters, like the systematic recurrence of emblems and attitudes among the figures in sacred art. This was probably intentional on the part of Joyce, who was curiously "influenced" by medieval concepts and methods, probably more so than any other writer of our time, and whose preoccupation with symmetry and correspondence and the-microcosm-within-the-macrocosm would have been worthy of Dante. (There are indications in the *Portrait* of his attraction to religious iconography, which itself had a literary origin in the Middle Ages. During his period of sin, the adolescent Stephen still delights in the traditional symbols of Mary, and saints and their emblems—St. Ignatius Loyola with his book, St. Francis Xavier indicating his chest, Lorenzo Ricci and his berretta—are noted with particular /464/ interest by Stephen the boy in the paintings at Clongowes.) In *Ulysses,* where the individual Mr. Bloom is signified variously by his hat, his newspaper and cigar, the lemon soap, the yellow flower, and the pork kidney, much of the medieval flavor of the Witches' Sabbath passages is due to the highly formalized iconography of the apparitions: King Edward with his bucket ("for identification bucket in my hand," the king explains himself), the dead Rudy with his Eton suit and his lambkin (a genuine epiphany to Bloom as he appears over the prostrate body of Stephen), Gerty MacDowell with her bloody clout, Lord Tennyson and his Union Jack blazer, the corpse of Stephen's mother with her faded orange blossoms and torn bridal veil, her breath of "wetted ashes" and *Liliata rutilantium.*

The emblematic *quidditas* is used with greatest virtuosity in *Ulysses,* but it is a technique of characterization that runs through all of Joyce's work. There are remnants of it in *Finnegans Wake,* in the signatures (tree and stone, river and hill, H.C.E. and A.L.P.) of Anna Livia and Earwicker, and it appears even in *Dubliners.* Father Flynn's chalice and old Maria's saucer of clay are clear examples; in *Two Gallants,* the coin takes part in the conventional narrative "revelation" and at the same time serves as the *quidditas* of the gallants; in *The Dead,* the absent Michael Furey is represented obliquely and ironically by the snow, *The Lass of Aughrim,* the overshoes, and the sore throat of Bartell D'Arcy, the vain concert tenor. In Joyce's poems we have the flower in "A Flower Given to My Daughter" and the snood "that is the sign of maidenhood" in "Bid adieu, adieu, adieu." *Exiles* has already been mentioned: its detailed descriptions of the dress and attitudes of the characters are not so much evidence of meticulous naturalistic accuracy as an effort to transmit to the actors the special objectified *quidditas* of each character as the author conceived it; the play is a failure largely because the stage directions cannot take the place of Joyce's own handling of the scenes. And finally, I think the same iconographic technique was ultimately /465/ responsible for the Joycean compound epithet that has now seeped down into Mr. Luce's editorial offices. In "shameclosing eyes," "dewsilky cattle," "saltwhite corpse," "snotgreen sea," modeled on the "winedark sea" and "rosy-fingered dawn" that have been deified by scholars, a unique quality is wedded to its counterpart to produce a compact representation of *quidditas* in its smallest unit.

And so the individual *quidditas* is concentrated in a physical image, often, though not always, visual, as the generalized *quidditas* is diffused in a stream of sound. The soul of the thing, its whatness, truly "leaps to us from the vestment of its appearance." Basically, perhaps, there is no difference between Joyce's final epiphany technique and the symbolism of other writers—such as the *leitmotiv* of Thomas Mann—but in its development and its use there are very real differences. Following Freud, we have come to think of a symbol chiefly in terms of its representational qualities (Pribislav Hippe's pencil in *The Magic Mountain*); through a combination of experimental science and philosophical idealism, we tend also to find a value of their own in "things," which we conceive more or less as absolutes. Joyce's conception of the symbol is much closer to the conception of the medieval Church: a symbol has a specific function to perform in a given situation, and, when that function has been performed, nothing prevents the use of the symbol again in a totally different context. This flexibility results eventually in the intimate interpenetration of the parts and the whole that is one of the chief manifestations of Joyce's principle of *consonantia,* reaching a high degree of complexity in his later work. In *Finnegans Wake,* where, as the writers of exegeses remind us, every part presupposes every other part and their sum as well, it is difficult to separate out the individual threads of the pattern. But we can see its outlines already in the "Christmas" symbolism of the *Portrait,* where the significance of the velvet-backed brushes (maroon for the *quidditas* of Michael Davitt, green for the *quidditas* of Par- /466/ nell) is expanded in Stephen's "red and green" impressions as he anticipates the school holiday, and the Irish church and Irish politics are ironically united at the dinner party on Christmas day in the violent quarrel between Aunt Dante and Mr. Casey; we see it also in the "bowl" symbolism in the early pages of *Ulysses*, where the bowl of shaving-lather, introduced as the *quidditas* of Buck Mulligan, becomes successively the bay, the bowl of incense Stephen carried at Clongowes, and the bowl of green bile at his mother's deathbed. Although these are only minor examples of Joyce's method, few could illustrate it more effectively. /467/

Quidditas in the Tragi-Comedy of Joyce

RUDD FLEMING

In *A Portrait of the Artist as a Young Man* Stephen Dædalus improves as follows upon Aristotle's definition of the tragic emotions:

> Aristotle has not defined pity and terror. I have. I say . . . Pity is the feeling which arrests the mind in the presence of whatsoever is grave and constant in human sufferings and units it with the human sufferer. Terror is the feeling which arrests the mind in the presence of whatsoever is grave and constant in human sufferings and unites it with the secret cause.

Stephen's concern is to point to some unchanging essence in human sufferings and to show how the active and passive aspects of this essence (respectively "secret cause" and "human sufferer") unite in the mind to produce an arrested state which Stephen, after Luigi Galvani, calls "the enchantment of the heart." This is Stephen's equivalent for the catharsis of Aristotle. The enchantment or catharsis is conceived as a balanced state between equal tensions. Stephen says: "The tragic emotion, in fact, is a face looking two ways, towards terror and towards pity."

Particularly interesting in Stephen's definitions is his statement that terror unites the mind with the secret cause of whatsoever is grave and constant in human sufferings. It is easy to see how the mind may unite itself with the human sufferer, but it is strange, perhaps, to think of the mind as uniting itself with the secret cause of the suffering. Aristotle says that terror is what we feel when we see persons like ourselves suffering misfortune, and this is only to say that we fear lest misfortunes like those arousing our sympathy overtake us in our own persons and circumstances; but Joyce must

Rudd Fleming, "*Quidditas* in the Tragi-Comedy of Joyce," *University of Kansas City Review*, XV (Summer, 1949), 288-96.

have felt that Aristotle was stepping out of bounds at this point and bringing in a non-tragic sort of terror, kinetic rather than static— which, instead of arresting the mind of the spectator, might be expected simply to make him more careful in the management of his affairs. This, according to Stephen, would be an effect of improper art. The terror in Stephen's definition is not terror lest we come to suffer this or that misfortune; it is terror felt in the face of what is constant and unchanging in our sufferings. The cause of this suffering is "secret" and yet we may unite ourselves with it; this is to say that, in some manner, we ourselves are this secret cause; for whatsoever is grave and constant in human sufferings remains always available to our minds and so is always "essentially" present in us, "proceeding" from us, to use a scholastic term, in self-generating constancy.

Stephen's definitions of tragic terror and pity show the two emotions in the relationship to each other of introversion and extraversion. The terror of tragedy is the terror of being obliged to approach oneself as the "secret cause" of one's own sufferings—an act of the mind /288/ magnificently symbolized by the self-discovery of Oedipus; but this tragic introversion is opposed, or balanced, by an extraversion through pity, away from oneself toward the "human sufferer." Thus the tragic emotion, which, Stephen says, is a face looking two ways, arises between "human sufferers" and is, therefore, not unlike the emotion of love when love is not "kinetic" as Lynch would have it but "static," an "enchantment of the heart."

II

Stephen's exposition of his aesthetic begins thus abruptly with an effort to prove that the "tragic emotion," while it contains an inner characteristic dynamics, arrives nevertheless at stasis. He then goes on to show that all aesthetic apprehension is a stasis, taking here as his point of departure Aquinas' abbreviated statement: *ad pulchritudinem tria requiruntur integritas, consonantia, claritas;* and translating it: three things are needed for beauty, wholeness, harmony and radiance. These terms correspond to "stages" or "phases" in the process of aesthetic apprehension, and Stephen's special interest is the final term *claritas:*

> It baffled me for a long time . . . I thought he might mean that *claritas* was the artistic discovery and representation of the divine purpose in anything or a force of generalization which would make the esthetic image a universal one, make it outshine its proper conditions. But that is literary talk. I understand it so. When you have apprehended that basket as one thing and have then analyzed it according to its form and apprehended it

as a thing, you make the only synthesis which is logically and esthetically permissible. You see that it is that thing which it is and no other. The radiance of which he speaks is the scholastic *quidditas* or *whatness* of a thing.

In *Stephen Hero* appears an earlier version of this analysis:

Now for the third quality. For a long time I couldn't make out what Aquinas meant. He uses a figurative word (a very unusual thing for him) but I have solved it. *Claritas* is *quidditas*. After the analysis which discovers the second quality the mind makes the only logical synthesis and discovers the third quality. This is the moment which I call epiphany. First we recognize that the object is *one* integral thing, then we recognize that it is an organized composite structure, a *thing* in fact: finally, when the relation of the parts is exquisite, when the parts are adjusted to a special point, we recognize that it is *that* thing which it is. Its soul, its whatness, leaps to us from the vestment of its appearance. The soul of the commonest object, the structure of which is so adjusted, seems to us radiant. The object achieves its epiphany.

The important word seems to be "epiphany" and Theodore Spencer, in editing the manuscript of *Stephen Hero,* takes his word to be explanatory of Joyce's purpose in *Finnegans Wake:*

Here is not any one individual that is "epiphanized"; it is all the human history, symbolized in certain types, the representatives of which combine with one another as the words describing them combine various meanings, so that H. C. Earwicker and his family, his acquaintances, the city of Dublin where he lives, his morality and religion, become symbols of an epiphanic view of human life as a whole, and the final end of the artist is achieved.

But there is still a puzzle in this word "epiphany" and certainly "epiphanized" is not the same as "symbolized," as Spencer recognizes in the phrase, "symbols of an epiphanic view." Joyce himself omits the word "epiphany," as well as the distinction between "soul" /289/ and "vestment of appearance," from his later discussion of Aquinas' definition of beauty; I think his reason may have been that the word "epiphany" suggests a dynamic movement of vision through, or beyond, the thing itself. At any rate Stephen does insist on plain *quidditas*[1] or *whatness;* although, as he himself says, he was not always of one mind in this matter:

It baffled me for a long time . . . I thought he might mean that *claritas* was the artistic discovery and representation of the divine purpose in anything or a force of generalization which would make the esthetic image a universal one, make it outshine its proper conditions.

[1] Like Aristotle's *catharsis* this term of Joyce's cannot be quite fixed from any one point of approach. Irene Hendry, in the essay *Joyce's Epiphanies,* suc-

But Stephen emphatically repudiates any movement toward universality and finds the "only logical synthesis" to conclude in a static apprehension of the thing itself.

In actual experience, however, we and all we see are continually undergoing metamorphosis, and since this is so, the "object" or "thing" which Stephen abstracts from the metamorphosis of experience can be maintained only by ceaseless struggle. Stephen says:

Your mind to apprehend that object divides the entire universe into two parts, the object, and the void which is not the object.

It appears, then, that in order to create in this manner the "whatness" of a thing, one must undertake at the same time an enormous act of obliteration. But this act is only the first stage in the process of aesthetic apprehension; for if the "thing" is to remain intact, held back from metamorphosis, it must be immediately subjected to analysis. This analysis will be rhythmical: for rhythm, according to Stephen, "is the first formal esthetic relation of part to part in any esthetic whole or of an esthetic whole to its part or parts or of any part to the esthetic whole of which it is a part."

But when "the parts are adjusted to a certain point" the *claritas* of the experience is finally apprehended and the aesthetic stasis achieved. This process of adjustment is itself, of course, not static but kinetic; although in a work of art the process is, as it were, pre-arranged for the spectator by the artist, who uses various conventions, systems and techniques to guide and regulate this process of the "adjustment" of parts. But in nature any object may by a subjective act be brought into this kind of "epiphanic" focus; as Stephen suggests when glancing up at the clock of the Ballast Office, he remarks that the face of the clock "has not yet epiphanized."

Subjectively, then, this adjusting of the parts "to a certain point" may be understood as a rhythmic balancing of opposing attitudes engendered by contemplation of the object, held in constant isolation from the rest of the "universe," so /290/ that all possible move-

---

cessfully analyzes Joyce's technic by taking *quidditas* to mean not only "moment of revelation" but more basically the symbolic *leitmotiv* presentation of a whole by some one of its vividly perceived parts: "Basically, perhaps, there is no difference between Joyce's final epiphany technique and the symbolism of other writers—such as the *leitmotiv* of Thomas Mann—but in its development and its use there are very real differences. Following Freud, we have come to think of symbol chiefly in terms of its representational qualities (Pribislav Hippe's pencil in *The Magic Mountain*); through a combination of experimental science and philosophical idealism, we tend also to find a value of their own in "things," which we conceive more or less as absolutes." [*The Sewanee Review*, Summer, 1946.]

ments of the mind are obliged to focus on this particular object and be, in that process, cancelled out, or brought into a moment of equipoise; at which moment the tension which we have been maintaining between the object and the void we have created around it also vanishes—the puzzling relationship of part to whole no longer troubles the mind—and the moment of aesthetic stasis, the moment of apprehended *quidditas,* is achieved.

In order to bring this general aesthetic concept back to Stephen's theory of tragedy, we may appeal to Stephen's own exploratory question: Is a chair finely made tragic or comic? This question acquires its significance when we consider that although a chair is neither tragic nor comic, we can hardly bring ourselves to any full awareness of a chair which is totally without dramatic setting; the *whatness* of a chair must be approached *through* some measure or implication of tragedy or comedy.

From this point of view both tragedy and comedy appear as means of working toward the effect of epiphany. In works which are predominantly tragic or comic this effect is achieved through an elaborate rhetoric involving laughter and tears. The unhappy reversal of tragedy acts as a rhetorical device to persuade us, so to speak, that in the midst of life there is death, that even in those moments when we are most alive, death is "essentially" present. In this way we are led to discover the tragic "terror" in ourselves and are prepared for the compensating extraversion of "pity." In accordance with this rhetoric, the tragic chorus begins by advising simple prudence and concludes by telling us to count no man happy until he is dead; this, we are told, is to see life steadily and see it whole, and we are deeply moved by this rhetoric; but if it is successful, that is, if it ends in catharsis or, as Stephen would have it, aesthetic stasis at the moment of balanced tension between the terror and the pity, we are released from the rhetorical movements and brought into the epiphanic light where there is no longer tension between part and whole; where, therefore, we no longer *need* to see life steadily and see it whole. But as this moment of tragic epiphany fades, another and quite different rhetoric may be imagined to begin—we do not live life all at once, why then should we see it all at once? The tragic rhetoric is pious; the rhetoric of comedy is impious. And from the comic point of view, to count no man happy until he is dead is a very trim reckoning. We know well enough (like Falstaff) that we owe God a death, but may we not be loathe to pay him before his day, even "essentially"?

In some such mood as this, perhaps, the rhetoric of comedy begins its search for an "essential life" to counterpoise the "essential death" of tragedy. The basic comic rhetoric is very similar to the tragic rhetoric; for comedy also uses reversal, but this time it is a happy reversal, aiming to show us that although the characters of the story underwent all sorts of hardships, they were "essentially" well-off the whole time.

If we return then to Stephen's question: is a chair finely made tragic or comic, we should say again /291/ that the chair is neither tragic nor comic, but that freedom from tragic and comic tensions necessary to an epiphanic view of the chair requires a full play of both the tragic and the comic rhetorics and is, perhaps, best achieved at a "moment of metamorphosis" between them.

III

The general development of Joyce's style, from the motionless, strict "objectivity" of some of the *Dubliners* stories and of *Exiles* to the elaborately intellectual and emotional, tragi-comic, lyric-dramatic style of *Finnegans Wake,* suggests that Joyce, while always seeking "epiphany" or *quidditas,* came to think that it could be best achieved by allowing full rhythmic play to all conceivable oppositions, intellectual or emotional, which might be brought to bear upon the object and which, if unresolved, must cloud the "epiphanic" vision.

In addition to the question: is a chair finely made tragic or comic, Stephen asks the parallel question: Is the bust of Sir Phillip Crampton lyrical, epical or dramatic? And in response to this question Stephen develops a theory of relationship between lyric, epic and dramatic literary forms which reflects the same basic search for *quidditas* and the same concept of a dynamic relationship and possible poise between introversion and extraversion which underlie his theory of tragedy:

Lessing—said Stephen—should not have taken a group of statues to write of. The art, being inferior, does not present the forms I spoke of distinguished clearly one from another. Even in literature, the highest and most spiritual art, the forms are often confused. The lyrical form is in fact the simplest verbal vesture of an instant of emotion, a rhythmical cry such as ages ago cheered on the man who pulled at the oar or dragged stones up a slope. He who utters it is more conscious of the instant of emotion than of himself as feeling emotion. The simplest epical form is seen emerging out of lyrical literature when the artist prolongs and broods upon himself as the center of an epical event and this form progresses till the centre of emotional gravity is equidistant from the artist himself and from others. The narrative is no longer purely personal. The personality of the artist passes into the narration itself, flowing round and round the persons and the action like a vital sea. . . . The dramatic form is reached when the vitality which has flowed and eddied round each person fills every person with such vital force that he or she assumes a proper and intangible esthetic life. The personality of the artist, at first a cry or a cadence or a mood and then a fluid and lambent narrative, finally refines itself out of existence, impersonalizes itself, so to speak. The esthetic image in dramatic form is life purified in and reprojected from the human imagination. The mystery of esthetic like that of material creation is accomplished. The artist, like the God of creation, remains within or behind or beyond or above his handiwork, invisible, refined out of existence, indifferent, paring his fingernails.

This concept of fluid relationship between the lyric introversion and the dramatic extraversion is evident throughout Joyce's writing. In *A Portrait of the Artist as a Young Man* there is a continual weaving back and forth between "lyric" and "dramatic" through "epic"; that is to say, "lyric" introspective passages open out through narrative into dramatic scenes and back again into the "lyric" originating subjectivity; and the book ends with a device which combines the dramatic and lyric forms—in the perfectly objective presentation of lyric entries from Stephen's dairy. In *Ulysses* the dynamic relation between lyric and /292/ dramatic, between inner and outer, subject and object, personal and impersonal, is symbolized in many ways, but chiefly by the "atonement" of Stephen and Bloom; and *Ulysses* also ends with a device combining the dramatic and the lyric—in Molly Bloom's lyric soliloquy. In *Finnegans Wake* the dynamic relationship of lyric and dramatic is given a much freer play; and it becomes apparent in this work that if, in following the movement from personal to impersonal, the poet does, so to speak, "refine himself out of existence," the traditional dramatic form, which requires fixed perspective, also vanishes; for there is now no distance between the poet and his creatures, who are now themselves all poets or lyric voices seeking, as it were, their own dramatic objectivity through each other, all appearing at once to be both speaking and listening, until finally it is as if the language itself were developing the memories of its infinite past occasions. Jolas says of Joyce that he seemed "constantly *à l'affût*, always to be listening rather than talking." And he quotes Joyce as having said: "Really, it is not I who am writing this crazy book . . . It is you, and you, and you, and that man over there, and that girl at the next table."[2]

If the tragic emotion is "a face looking two ways, towards terror and towards pity, both of which are phases of it," the emotion engendered by the mature style of Joyce is a face looking at once in-

[2] Eugene Jolas, "My Friend James Joyce," *The Partisan Reader* (1946), p. 464.

ward and outward; inward toward the "secret cause" of human sufferings, the tragic source of the lyric cry, to the discovery of "self"; and then outward through pity to the discovery of "others" and the identification of oneself with others—an identification which has its comic aspect in a phase of irresponsible "detachment" from oneself as the source of tragic terror—but which, in the passing of this moment of irresponsible self-detachment, returns again to the lyric and the tragic; the "emotion" itself being static, neither tragic nor comic, lyric nor dramatic.

But in addition to the two exploratory questions already examined, Stephen asks two others: Is the portrait of Mona Lisa good if I desire to see it? If a man hacking in fury at a block of wood make there an image of a cow, is that image a work of art?

These, as well as the other two questions, are aimed at the discovery of that static quality of *whatness* or *quidditas,* which is for Joyce the center of truth, beauty, and goodness. A chair finely made is neither tragic nor comic; the portrait of Mona Lisa is neither good nor bad because Stephen does or does not desire to see it; the bust of Sir Philip Crampton is neither lyrical, epical, nor dramatic; and the image of the cow is neither a work of art nor a simple product of nature. But in order to "epiphanize" the chair, the portrait, the bust, the wooden cow (all of which are at once "things" and in some manner works of art), the mind must not only know the correct answer to these questions but must work out their implied dynamics in actual poetic experience.

As for the portrait of Mona Lisa, Stephen says: "The feelings excited /293/ by improper art are kinetic, desire or loathing. Desire urges us to possess, to go to something; loathing urges us to abandon, to go from something."

If, then, Joyce's style in *Finnegans Wake* is a kind of dynamics of disillusionment, making possible the stasis of aesthetic apprehension, we should expect the "improper" movements of desire and loathing, as well as the movements of tragedy and comedy, lyric and dramatic, to be allowed their full rhetorical play, and it seems to me that this is so; indeed, for some readers Joyce's style is chiefly characterized by his continual practice of mingling the most highly desirable with the most immediately disgusting; as, for example, in the line: "Lord help you, Maria, full of grease, the load is with me!"

The oddest of the four questions asked by Stephen is the last: If a man hacking in fury at a block of wood make there an image of a cow, is that image a work of art? This question arouses the admiration of Lynch: "That's a lovely one—said Lynch, laughing again. That has the true scholastic stink." But the serious bearing of this question on the development of Joyce's style may, perhaps, be suggested by his remark to Jolas: "Really, it is not I who am writing this crazy book . . ." And certainly the reader of *Finnegans Wake* will find no easy resting place in any expressed intention of the author. The peculiar absence of "intentionality" in *Finnegans Wake,* with its effect of throwing the reader inward upon himself, is evident if we contrast Joyce's tone of strangely harmonious coincidence with the clear, single-minded, powerfully "intentional" tone of Yeats:

> I have prepared my peace
> With learned Italian things
> And the proud stones of Greece

Jolas says of Joyce's method of working:

He never changed a single word. There was always a certain inevitability, an almost volcanic affirmativeness about his primal choice of words. To me, his deformations seemed to grow more daring. He added, ceaselessly, like a worker in mosaic, enriching his original pattern with ever new inventions. [P. 463]

But this "volcanic affirmativeness" is not personal affirmation; indeed, it more nearly resembles, as Jolas seems to be suggesting by the word "volcanic,"—"a man hacking in fury at a block of wood." Nevertheless, the author is always intimately, if obscurely, present, and sometimes he speaks out plainly in his own person as author to discuss with the reader this very complexity of style and its probable effect on him: "You is feeling like you was lost in the bush, boy? You says: It is a puling sample jungle of words. You most shouts out." [*Finnegans Wake* (New York, 1939), p. 112.]

But this also is part of the play between personal and impersonal, lyric and dramatic, tragic and comic; and if Joyce can prevent it, we shall not by looking into *Finnegans Wake* find any underlying purpose which may supplant the balanced *whatness* of the whole. Joyce himself, according to Jolas, seems to have felt in *Finnegans Wake* the presence of a kind of "prophetic" and essentially unintended type of /294/ significance; at least it is clear that he regarded the book not only as a "work of art" but as an "event." Jolas quotes from a letter of Joyce:

It is strange, however, that after publication of my book, Finland came into the foreground suddenly. First by the awarding of a Nobel Prize to a Finnish writer, and then by the political door. The most curious comment I have received on the book is a symbolical one from Helsinki . . . [P. 467]

Nor in *Finnegans Wake* may we find rest from the movement of this cathartic rhetoric in any statement of philosophical truth, but only in the poise of aesthetic *claritas*. Stephen says:

Truth is beheld by the intellect which is appeased by the most satisfying relations of the intelligible: beauty is beheld by the imagination which is appeased by the most satisfying relations of the sensible. The first step in the direction of truth is to understand the frame and scope of the intellect itself, to comprehend the act itself of intellection.

Stephen here discovers a kind of intellectual stasis comparable to the aesthetic stasis, an "enchantment of the mind" to match the "enchantment of the heart," and if, accordingly, we model an analy sis of this intellectual stasis on Stephen's analysis of the tragic stasis, we might say that truth, or satisfaction of the "intellectual appe- tite," is achieved when the mind is arrested in the presence of some grave and constant intellectual tension, some unavoidable self-gen- erated conflict, essential in the mind and driving it alternately back into itself as ultimate, incomprehensible point of view and forth again into union with external objects—in an opposition (or sub- stantial union) of the intellectual introversion and extraversion, of *noesis* and *noema,* comparable to the opposition (or substantial union) of terror and pity, desire and loathing, active and passive, lyric and dramatic, tragic and comic.

IV

At any rate, although we may regard Joyce as a philosophical poet (he himself in his early essay on Mangan assumes the union of poetry and philosophy), we may expect that in his work philo- sophical statements, as of the doctrine of reincarnation or of Vico's theory of history, will subsist only in relation to an intellectual dy- namics and will be inextricably woven into the comic-tragic di- lectic, usually in the form of comic parody of their underlying tragic seriousness, as:

Phall if you but will, rise you must.

The intellect as well as the emotions must be engaged, but the end of this dialectic is not exposition of any kind, either philosophical or psychological, but only the achievement of "epiphany."

The lyric cry in its first purity is impersonal and, as it were, the beginning or source of extraverted vision: "He who utters it is more conscious of the instant of emotion than of himself as feeling the emotion." It is through brooding introversion that the artist dis- covers himself as the residence of this impersonal emotion, and then, working through himself outward, discovers the objective resi- dence of the lyric emotion, the final artistic shape of which is drama. The lyric emotion has not necessarily undergone any /295/ change in itself, but only, so to speak, in its artistic residence—a modifica- tion of residence which was, in fact, already implicit within it. The crucial moment in this action is the return *outward* from the tragic introversion. In pure contemplation, which is to say contemplation free from the tragic-comic dialectic, there is no introversion but only an enlarging of contemplative scope to include not only the realms of natural objectivity but also the "subjective," that is, the as yet unperceived "envelope" surrounding the "object" or "thing"; this enlargement of scope does not transcend or pass beyond the "thing" but merely shows the full "content" or *quidditas* of the original "point of origin"; tragic inwardness, however, fixes this "subjectivity" into the shape of "self" and it becomes necessary to clear up the resulting "ontological confusion" and return the "self" to its pure condition as "point of view"; which is to say (in a language less awkward than this derivation from the method of discourse of Edmund Husserl): "A condition of complete simplicity (costing not less than everything)." /296/

James Joyce: Esthetic Freedom and Dramatic Art

JAMES R. BAKER

In reviewing the mass of critical literature which has appeared on James Joyce in the last few years it is surprising to find that no one has as yet thoroughly investigated the theories that underlie his productions. There are three main sources available for such an investigation—the esthetic theory which appears in the fragmentary *Stephen Hero* manuscript, the esthetic which appears in *A Portrait of the Artist as a Young Man,* and the excerpts from the young Joyce's esthetic notebooks which Herbert Gorman chose to include in his biography. The present essay makes no attempt to examine the deficiencies of the esthetic but will be concerned with unifying, in a short space, the major theoretic ideas found in these three books.

I

In *A Portrait of the Artist as a Young Man* Stephen Dedalus' esthetic theory emerges in the course of a long conversation with his friend, Lynch. His explanations are frequently interrupted by Lynch's satirical and comical remarks. This device was no doubt intended to relieve the reader from constant concentration on Stephen's abstractions. And since all of Lynch's objections are adeptly overcome, the device also serves to demonstrate Stephen's confidence and rather arrogant certainty in regard to his artistic creed.

In *Stephen Hero,* however, the young theorist is far from dogmatic. He is seen preparing with great care for the presentation of his esthetic to the "University College Literary and Historical So-

James R. Baker, "James Joyce: Esthetic Freedom and Dramatic Art," *Western Humanities Review,* V (Winter 1950-51), 29-40.

ciety." With the aid of his brother, Maurice, he finally produces a manifesto which he considers satisfactory for the critical ears of the "Society." The chief ideas contained in this paper, in which Stephen ". . . intended to define his own position for himself," are conveniently summarized for us by the author. Within the space of four pages, and two additional pages which appear near the end of the manuscript, are set down the fundamental principles which were later modified and made the theoretical basis of Joyce's works. No reader who wishes to gain a comprehensive understanding of Joyce's esthetic development can afford to neglect these pages. It is true that some of the terminology employed is vague and quite immature. But the *Stephen Hero* thesis /29/ does contain certain remarks on the relationship of the artist to the general public, and on the all-important idea of "epiphany," which are omitted in the dialogue version of the novel.

Stephen begins his essays by defining art as ". . . the human disposition of intelligible or sensible matter for an esthetic end. . . ."[1] Thus he makes it clear at the outset that art is concerned with both idea and sensation. The definition does not say that art cannot be absorbed with one matter to the exclusion, or rather near exclusion, of the other. But, as will be seen later, Joyce regarded the ideational and sensory elements of art as inseparable. The disposition or arrangement of these matters is undertaken for an "esthetic end." Esthetic pertains to the beautiful. It is distinguished from the moral and, especially, the useful. The sole purpose of the artist, therefore, is to create beautiful things.

It seems at first that the possibilities for the "disposition of intelligible or sensible matter for an esthetic end" are infinite. But according to Stephen there are only three:

. . . all such human dispositions must fall into the division of three distinct natural kinds, lyrical, epical and dramatic. Lyrical art . . . is the art whereby the artist sets forth his image in immediate relation to himself; epical art is the art whereby the artists sets forth his image in mediate relation to himself and to others; and dramatic art is the art whereby the artist sets forth his image in immediate relations to others.[2]

These forms, proceeding from the lyric to the epic to the dramatic, are representative of degrees of detachment. Stephen's definitions do not deny that the three modes of artistic disposition are often merged or used in conjunction with one another. They merely state that there is an intimate relationship existing between the degree of

[1] James Joyce, *Stephen Hero* (New York: New Directions, 1944), p. 77.
[2] *Ibid.*

development of the writer's esthetic consciousness and the form of his artistic productions.

It was Stephen's belief that the literary arts reveal these three natural types of human expression with the greatest degree of clarity. And because these distinctions are more easily seen in literature than in music, painting, sculpture, etc., he thought literature to be the most "excellent" of the arts. Excellence, in this case, is evidently determined by the manifest distinctness of the particular form employed. The quality of a literary lyric, by this standard, would apparently be judged, at least in part, by the accuracy with which it reflects the personal reaction of the artist. The quality of an epic would depend on the /30/ artist's ability to relate his reaction to the reactions of others. And the quality of dramatic art would be dependent upon the ability of the artist to present the reactions of others without explicitly relating them to himself. It is readily apparent that dramatic art requires the greatest degree of detachment on the part of the artist. The dramatic artist is capable of employing the lyrical or epical forms wherever they may be appropriate to his material. And for this reason, although it is not specifically stated in the *Stephen Hero* version of the esthetic, Joyce regarded dramatic art as the highest form of achievement.

In the process of creation—be the result lyric, epic, or dramatic— the artist attempts to cast in the proper form that which has been selected from the "world of experience" and the "world of dreams." Perhaps the vagueness of the terms "experience" and "dream" will be clarified by the following interpretation. In the finished writing the realistic detail will have been drawn from "experience." Those vital symbols which interpret the significance of the realistic detail will have been drawn from the "world of dreams." It will be seen later that the "world of dreams" refers to those universal and constant motifs which underlie all human activities and which are manifested in the "world of experience." The function of the artist is to correlate in the appropriate manner realistic detail with symbol, or as Stephen says, to re-embody in one image experience and dream.

Since the artist acts as mediator between the world of experience and the world of dreams, and since his task is to re-embody in one image elements from these two worlds, he has both a selective and reproductive task to perform.

. . . to equate these faculties [selective and reproductive] was the secret of artistic success: the artist who could disentangle the subtle soul of the image from its mesh of defining circumstances most exactly and "re-embody" it in artistic circumstances chosen as the most exact for it in its new office, he was as the supreme artist. This perfect coincidence of the two artistic faculties Stephen called poetry and he imagined the domain of art to be cone-shaped. . . .[3]

Poetry, at the apex of the cone, links that which it has selected from the world of experience with the "unalterable laws" or universal and constant motifs which compose the world of dreams. "Literature," the term which designates the large middle region of the art cone, portrays only "externals"—the manners and customs of societies. The base of the cone represents the "chaos of unremembered writing." This last category of writing fails to survive because it neither deals with the "unalterable laws" nor accurately describes the manners and /31/ customs of the society in which it is produced. "Literature" survives because it faithfully records the manners and customs of the particular age which happen to be its subject. It is inferior to "poetry," however, because it derives its symbolism from the changing manners and customs of its time rather than by reference to the "unalterable laws" of the world of dreams.

The attempt of the poet to distinguish or separate the unalterable laws from the complex of experience in which they are obscured might well result in the creation of vague and confused images. Insistence on a classical style provides the only means of avoiding disorder in practice. By classical, Stephen did not mean the manner of a particular age in a particular country. The classical style he defined as the ". . . syllogism of art, the only legitimate process from one world to another. . . . It is a temper of security and satisfaction and patience." Unlike romanticism, "the classical temper . . . ever mindful of limitations, chooses rather to bend upon these present things and so to work upon them and fashion them that the quick intelligence may go beyond them to their meaning which is still unuttered."[4] The meaning of the classicist or poet, it follows, must be implicit in his style—"experience" and "dream" must be unified in one image.

The romantic temper, on the other hand, ". . . is an insecure, unsatisfied, impatient temper which seeks no fit abode here for its ideals and chooses therefore to behold them under insensible figures."[5] In its desire to speak of unearthly matters romanticism disregards the limitations of its images. Romantic figures are, therefore, ". . . blown to wild adventures, lacking the gravity of solid bodies. . . ."[6]

[3] Ibid., p. 78.
[4] Ibid.
[5] Ibid.
[6] Ibid.

These two tempers are, of course, in conflict. Classicism insists that the artist control his images. Romanticism demands freedom from all restriction. The disagreements of the two tempers are often criticized unjustly. Many critics have treated the reserve and materialism of the classicist and the chaos and imagistic excesses of the romanticist too harshly. The two tempers are frequently charged with deviation from what is all too commonly assumed to be the limits of sane artistic endeavor. Stephen defined the just critic as ". . . he who is able, by means of the signs which the artist affords, to approach the temper which has made the work and to see what is well done therein and what it signifies."[7] The critic fails to be fair unless he can maintain the tolerance and objectivity demanded by this definition. To approach a work of art with a preconceived idea of what is permissible and valuable is to "profane" art. Chief among the false principles which /32/ profane art, and prompt unjust criticism, is the ancient maxim that the end of art is to instruct, to elevate, or to amuse. To justify this assertion Stephen refers to his master, Saint Thomas Aquinas.

". . . I am unable to find even a trace of this Puritanic conception of the esthetic purpose in the definition which Aquinas has given of beauty . . . or in anything which he has written concerning the beautiful. The qualifications he expects for beauty are in fact of so abstract and common a charter that it is quite impossible for even the most violent partizan to use the Aquinatian theory with the object of attacking any work of art that we possess from the hand of any artist whatsoever." This recognition of the beautiful in virtue of the most abstract relations afforded by an object to which the term could be applied so far from giving any support to a commandment of *Noli Tangere* was itself no more than a just sequence from the taking-off of all interdictions from the artist. . . .[8]

The artist who operates within the poetic apex of the art cone, is, of course, free from all "profanities." As a result, much of what he writes does not meet with the favor of the public or of those critics who defend public taste. Their unwillingness to accept his efforts, however, has little to do with their worth. The value of art cannot be measured in terms of conventions. The artist seeks to faithfully reproduce what he selects from the world of experience and the world of dreams. He should not be required to select and reflect only those elements which meet with public or critical pleasure. The public, and the critics who ally themselves with public standards, must realize that the tradition of art is in the hands of the art-

[7] *Ibid.*, p. 79.
[8] *Ibid.*, p. 79-80.

ists. It is absurd for a criticism founded on homilies to prohibit the chosen course of the artist, even though he outrages what the critic or the public considers the "limits of decency."

Stephen believed that only the artist is capable of absorbing the life around him and of finding the truths (the unalterable laws) that lie buried within it. "The poet is the intense centre of the life of his age to which he stands in a relation than which none can be more vital."[9] This is true, not because the artist is a naturally superior being, but because he has successfuly emancipated himself from the confines of conventional thought. And even though the public may criticize or condemn the artist, his views are ultimately indispensable.

> . . . The age, though it bury itself fathoms deep in formulas and machinery, has need of these realities which alone given and sustain life and it must await from those chosen centres of vivification the force to life, the security for life which can come to it only from them. Thus the spirit of man makes a continual affirmation.[10] /33/

One of the most important features of the esthetic is not discussed in connection with the essay which Stephen read before the "University College Literary and Historical Society." The concept of epiphany, which contributes more to an understanding of Joyce's works than any single principle in the above material, appears near the end of the *Stephen Hero* manuscript. "By an epiphany he meant a sudden spiritual manifestation, whether in the vulgarity of speech or of gesture or in a memorable phase of the mind itself."[11]

Saint Thomas Aquinas, who is the source for this important idea, lists in his *Summa Theologica* three requisites for beauty: integrity or wholeness, symmetry, and radiance. The meaning of these terms can best be understood by examining the processes of the mind "when confronted with any object, hypothetically beautiful." The first function the mind performs is to separate this object from the remainder of the universe. By this means it recognizes the object as an integral thing. Its "wholeness" becomes apparent. The mind next examines the parts of which the object is constructed in their relations to each other and to the whole, thereby perceiving its "symmetry" or rhythm of structure. After recognizing the object as "one integral thing," then as a composite structure, the mind makes the only logically possible step—which is a resynthesis—and discovers the third quality of the object, its "radiance." This is the moment

[9] *Ibid.*, p. 80.
[10] *Ibid.*, p. 80.
[11] *Ibid.*, p. 211.

of epiphany, the supreme instant in which the essential spirit or "soul" of the thing is revealed.[12]

It is the duty of the artist, Stephen concludes, to become a collector of epiphanies, a watcher for those "sudden spiritual manifestations" which reveal the true nature and meaning of all phenomena that he observes.

II

Many of the esthetic principles that appear in *A Portrait of the Artist as a Young Man* are identical with those set forth in *Stephen Hero*. The different order of their appearance, however, coupled with the omission of some of the earlier concepts and the inclusion of certain new ones, is of value in determining the more mature Joyce's esthetic position.

In rewriting and condensing *Stephen Hero* Joyce gave the esthetic a new significance. As Theodore Spencer has pointed out in his illuminating introduction to the manuscript, the presentation of the theory in that book is given no more importance than the many incidents depicting Stephen's clashes with his family, his friends, the Catholic /34/ Church, and the conventions of Dublin life. But in *A Portrait of the Artist as a Young Man* the emergence of Stephen's theory represents the climax of the young artist's intellectual struggles. The esthetic itself, as it is given in the novel, not only implies the necessity of rejecting the uncongenial creative atmosphere of Dublin but provides the logical basis for doing so.

Stephen begins the exposition of his theory this time with definitions of pity and terror, dramatic emotions which he says Aristotle neglected to define.

—Pity is the feeling which arrests the mind in the presence of whatsoever is grave and constant in human sufferings and unites it with the human sufferer. Terror is the feeling which arrests the mind in the presence of whatsoever is grave and constant in human sufferings and unites it with the secret cause.—[13]

The use of the word "arrests" in defining these dramatic emotions is of peculiar significance. Joyce believed that true art creates an esthetic stasis.

. . . Beauty expressed by the artist cannot awaken in us an emotion which is kinetic or a sensation which is purely physical. It awakens, or ought to awaken, or induces, or ought to induce, an esthetic stasis, an

[12] *Ibid.*, pp. 212-213.
[13] James Joyce, *A Portrait of the Artist as a Young Man* (New York: The Modern Library, 1928), p. 239.

ideal pity or an ideal terror, a stasis called forth, prolonged and at last dissolved by . . . the rhythm of beauty.[14]

The improper arts—pornographic and didactic—are kinetic, they urge us to either possess or abandon. The response to them is little more than physical. And because they urge us to act, to alter in some way the circumstances they describe, they therefore excite desire or loathing, and cannot result in the stasis which is characteristic of a genuine esthetic experience. Desire and loathing, unlike pity and terror, are thus not esthetic emotions at all.

The production of a stasis, as has been said, is dependent on the "rhythm of beauty." This rhythm, or harmony of construction, arises out of the relations of the whole to the parts, the parts to the parts, and the parts to the whole of the total art work. In order to understand the function of this essential rhythm it will be necessary to trace from the beginning the stages of artistic apprehension.

It will be remembered that Stephen defines art as ". . . the human disposition of sensible and intelligible matter for an esthetic end."[15] The mind, then, comprehends an art work through both intellectual and sensory channels. /35/

> . . . Truth is beheld by the intellect which is appeased by the most satisfying relations of the intelligible; beauty is beheld by the imagination which is appeased by the most satisfying relations of the sensible.[16]

These statements are not intended to dichotomize truth and beauty. The intellect is appeased by finding certain ideas or classes of ideas logically juxtaposed in an organic whole. The imagination is appeased if it finds the relations of the concomitant sensible paraphernalia rhythmical or harmonious. Both the intellect and the imagination are participants in the apprehension of an art object.

In its progress toward artistic apprehension, or appeasement, the mind ("intellect" and "imagination" as a cooperative unity) performs the three distinct functions—synthesis, analysis and resynthesis —described in *Stephen Hero*. Now if the mind detects a flaw in the relations of the sensible or intelligible matters or in their relations to each other while engaged in the process of analysis it will not experience an esthetic stasis. Unless it perceives a *rhythm of beauty*, an order everywhere consistent in the context of the work, the mind will be excited to desire or loathing, which, of course, negates the possibility of stasis.

These three phases of artistic apprehension—synthesis, analysis

---

[14] *Ibid.*, p. 241.
[15] *Ibid.*, p. 242.
[16] *Ibid.*, p. 243.

and resynthesis—can be equated with Saint Thomas' three requisites for beauty—wholeness, harmony and radiance. And even though what is called beautiful varies, in its particulars, from age to age and from culture to culture, the three basic constituents of beauty, and the three processes by which it is recognized, remain constant and universal.

In order to make his images accessible to others the artist must set them between his own mind or senses and the mind or senses of others. This necessity involves the choice of an arrangement or form. Again, there are but three possibilities. If the artist remains the "centre of emotional gravity" his images will be set forth in immediate relation to himself, and his work will be called lyric. If the artist pauses in meditation, and thus perceives his reaction as it relates to others, he will produce epical art. If he makes others the center of emotional gravity without *explicitly* relating them to himself he will produce a dramatic work.

These three forms or modes of arrangement are practically indistinguishable in all of the arts except literature. But though the literary arts manifest these divisions most clearly, they are often found to merge and combine in a confusing and somewhat uncontrolled fashion within the framework of a single unit of writing. The artist should strive, /36/ however, to achieve an objective state in which he becomes capable of setting forth his images in immediate relations to others and thus of utilizing the other modes at will. The lyric and epic points of view should be regarded as phases of an esthetic evolution that has as its goal dramatic detachment.

. . . The personality of the artist, at first a cry or a cadence or a mood and then a fluid and lambent narrative, finally refines itself out of existence, impersonalizes itself. . . . The esthetic image in the dramatic form is life purified in and reprojected from the human imagination. The mystery of esthetic like that of the material creation is accomplished. The artist, like the God of the creation, remains within or behind or beyond or above his handiwork, invisible, refined out of existence, indifferent, paring his fingernails.[17]

III

The essential spirit of Joyce's esthetic philosophy has never been more accurately summarized than in the lines which conclude the presentation of the *Portrait* theory. The artist who successfully disentangles himself from the restrictive web of conventional thought and rises to this position of godlike objectivity gains the insights necessary for the creation of dramatic art. Joyce, throughout his literary career, never ceased to struggle for this goal. His successive

[17] *Ibid.*, p. 252.

works are representative of his progress toward detachment. This lifelong struggle for objectivity is central to an understanding of Joyce the artist and Joyce the man.

Through a study of his life it becomes apparent that the basic attitudes implied in the esthetic had evolved in his thinking by the time he was twenty years old. The theory, as it appears in *Stephen Hero* and *A Portrait of the Artist as a Young Man,* is largely a product of Joyce's early years in Dublin. It is true that his many years of residence in various European cities had a profound effect on his artistic tenets. This fact, however, does not place the esthetic of the manuscript and of the novel in an entirely juvenile light. None of the devices adopted by the older Joyce is basically inconsistent with these theories. The major premises which they have in common were never discarded. There is no evidence that he came to consider Stephen's ideas on art wholly childish and impracticable.

Preceding his success in the art world were years of painful search for confidence and certainty. The esthetic is one of the products of this search. If we view the theory in terms of the behavior it would require of its follower, Joyce's progressive rejection of the ideals of his church, /37/ his country, and his people is not without a logical basis. His rebellion, seen in this light, was not due to conceit or neurotic inability but to what he considered esthetic necessity.

The young Joyce quite naturally looked elsewhere for the intellectual companionship and accordance which he failed to receive from his schoolmates and other Dubliners. His emerging esthetic, criticized by teachers and fellow students, was encouraged and reenforced by certain of the writings of Aristotle and Saint Thomas Aquinas. From their works he derived justifications for setting up art values divorced from the conventional standards of his society, from the nationalism of his country, and from the puritanical codes of the church. Joyce's study of these two writers was not confined to his college career but accompanied his progress toward maturity. Constant reading and rereading of Aristotle provoked meditation on the various forms of the literary arts and on the subject matters and methods of treating those matters in comedy and tragedy. Joyce's concern with the lyric, epic, and dramatic forms was probably inspired by Aristotle. His use of these terms in *Stephen Hero* and the *Portrait* to denote points of view or states of the creative mind, however, should be credited with some originality. The demand that art result in an esthetic stasis sounds somewhat like a restatement of Aristotle's insistence on the purgation of pity and fear, but in reality Joyce's idea of stasis was deduced from Aquinas, not Aristotle.

Saint Thomas Aquinas was the chief source for Joyce's ideas on the nature of Beauty. In both *Stephen Hero* and the *Portrait* Joyce says that Stephen's esthetic is largely "applied Aquinas." This remark is not an exaggeration if we consider the concepts of stasis and epiphany, and the steps which lead to them, as the philosophical core of the theory. It will be remembered that Stephen equated Aquinas' three requisites for beauty—wholeness, symmetry, and radiance—with the three phases of artistic apprehension—synthesis, analysis, and resynthesis. The production of a stasis depends on what the mind discovers in the process of analysis. If the construction is perfectly harmonious, if it lends a "rhythm of beauty," the mind will not be urged to desire and loathing but will willingly resynthesize and thus experience an emotional stasis. It is perhaps by this means (at least this is a possible interpretation) that Aristotle's catharsis of pity and fear is accomplished.

The counsel of Aristotle and Aquinas was also of great personal worth to Joyce. They not only aided him in the formulation of an esthetic, but, as has been said, helped him understand the relations of the artist to the culture in which he exists. /38/

The most explosive of Joyce's remarks on this problem are found in a youthful essay on the new Irish Literary Theatre. This organization, which had come into being in 1898, was the predecessor of the famous National Theatre. The following is from Joyce's article called "The Day of the Rabblement."

No man . . . can be a lover of the true or the good unless he abhors the multiude; and the artist, though he may employ the crowd, is very careful to isolate himself. This radical principle of artistic economy applies specially to a time of crisis, and today when the highest form of art has just been preserved by desperate sacrifices, it is strange to see the artist making terms with the rabblement. The Irish Literary Theatre is the latest movement of protest against the sterility and falsehood of the modern stage. . . . The Irish Literary Theatre gave out that it was the champion of progress, and proclaimed war against commercialism and vulgarity. It had partly made good its word . . . when after the first encounter it surrendered to the popular will . . . the Irish Literary Theatre must now be considered the property of the most belated race in Europe. . . .

In such circumstances it has become imperative to define a position. If an artist courts the favor of the multitude he cannot escape the contagion of its fetichism and deliberate self-deception, and if he joins in a popular movement he does so at his own risk. Therefore, the Irish Literary Theatre, by its surrender to the trolls, has cut itself adrift from the line of advancement. Until he has freed himself from the mean influences about him—sodden enthusiasm and clever insinuation and every flattering influence of vanity and low ambition—no man is an artist at all. . . .[18]

[18] Herbert Gorman, *James Joyce* (New York: Rinehart & Company, 1948), pp. 68-73.

At this point in his career Joyce was strong enough to alienate himself from popular enthusiasms; but the religious and social obligations insisted on by his family and friends continued to anger and inhibit him. It was rapidly becoming apparent that his ability to tolerate the requirements not only of his family, but of the general milieu in which he moved, would soon expire. His faith in Catholicism had waned almost to the point of extinction. He despised the spiritual restrictions of his home and his school and the many nationalisms of his country, both political and literary. His emerging esthetic was definitely non-Irish. It had little in common with the romantic nationalism of the Irish Literary Renaissance. The more he pondered the literature of his own country, the more sure he became that only in Europe would he find the freedom of thought requisite for the superior quality of artistic activity he had set for his goal. According to his theories the artist should work only for an esthetic end. His sole purpose is to create beautiful things— not to confirm religious teachings, support national movements nor amuse the public. "Until /39/ he has freed himself from the mean influences about him . . . no man is an artist at all." The quality and extensiveness of synthesis and analysis is dependent on the degree of objectivity to which the artist has attained. Since true objectivity, and the experience of significant epiphany, can be obtained only through freedom from conventions, Joyce is very insistent on the necessity for spiritual exile. His departure from Dublin was not only a revolt against the notorious restrictions imposed upon the artist there, but, in a broader sense, was symbolic of a desire to escape the strictures of the common sensibility wherever it existed.

By the fall of 1902 (Joyce was twenty at the time) the intensity of his disgust with the Dublin scene had reached a peak. To remain in the city would mean creative paralysis. Flight was inevitable.

. . . I will not serve that in which I no longer believe whether it call itself my home, my fatherland or my church: and I will try to express myself in some mode of life or art as freely as I can and as wholly as I can, using for my defense the only arms I allow myself to use, silence, exile and cunning.[19]

It is with this declaration that we may mark the end of Joyce's struggle to justify his rebellion and the debut of Joyce the dramatic artist. /40/

[19] Joyce, *Portrait of the Artist*, p. 291.

Joyce's Categories

ELLSWORTH MASON

Critics who write more than hit-and-run articles on Joyce, and some critics who write much less, get around sooner or later to classifying his own works in terms of his lyric-epic-dramatic categories of art. The temptation to slice up his career into a neat progression from one category to another has proved too strong for a generation of critics overmuch concerned with pattern. He has, after all, written lyric poems, a novel which has been hailed as the modern epic, and a drama—that is to say, lyric, epic, and drama in the ordinary meaning of these terms. Or, since Joyce's definition of the categories is stated in terms of the artist's relation to his material, he has written a novel which is completely personal, one which is partly personal, and one which is impersonal—that is to say, the *Portrait* is completely about Stephen, *i.e.* Joyce, *Ulysses* is partly about Stephen-Joyce, and in *Finnegans Wake* Stoyce is nowhere to be found (although, to be sure, there is that annoying fellow, Shem). So the arguments of the commentators go. Such misconceptions, based on a confusion of Joyce's esthetic terms with their ordinary meanings or a confusion of the character Stephen with the writer Joyce (a booby trap which has led one commentator to the astounding conclusion that Stephen goes off at the end of *Ulysses* to write *Ulysses*) have produced neat critical patterns at the expense of a sensible understanding of Joyce. But an examination of his works in the light of his definition of the categories shows that Joyce has refused to oblige these critics.

The difficult passage in the *Portrait* in which Stephen discusses the categories is actually Joyce's third attempt over a period of about ten years to define the lyric, epic, and dramatic. Taken /427/ together, these attempts to establish artistic categories throw

Ellsworth Mason, "Joyce's Categories," *Sewanee Review*, LXI (Summer, 1953), 427-32.

considerable light on each other and on Joyce's mind as it moved step by step toward a greater esthetic clarity. During his preface to exile in the spring of 1903, Joyce wrote in his Paris notebooks:

> That art is lyrical whereby the artist sets forth the image in immediate relation to himself; that art is epical whereby the artist sets forth the image in mediate relation to himself and to others; that art is dramatic whereby the artist sets forth the image in immediate relation to others.

Joyce savored the true scholastic stink, and his Jesuitic mentality was apparently satisfied with this definition, as far as it went, for he later repeated it twice with only insignificant modifications in wording. But despite its longwindedness, the definition was too laconic to make much sense to a reader (and it is a mistake to believe that Joyce wrote his works without regard for the reader), and despite its appeal to the philosophical side of Joyce, such an abstract definition was too far removed from the working level to satisfy his practical side. It obviously needed elaboration and extension. It needed to be put to work in terms of literature.

In *Stephen Hero* Joyce repeated the definition almost verbatim from the notebooks and then proceeded to explore the function of the artist in the artistic process. This exploration focused on the artist's relation to his subject matter. The artist, according to Joyce's theory, has to work with his experience of life around him; however, his proper realm is not this experience itself but its essence, its soul, which he extracts and reprojects by his gifts of selectivity and reproductivity. This theory began to relate the artist to both his raw material and his finished product, but it was not yet sufficiently developed to be of much practical use, and it was not yet tied in with the definition /428/ of the categories. It supplied no basis for categorizing an art work as lyric, epic, or dramatic.

The classic definition of the categories in the *Portrait* is a much more mature consideration and extension of that first set forth in the notebooks. To be sure, the definition is shaped artistically to emphasize the dual role of the artist as young man, but it springs so directly from Joyce's earlier gropings toward an esthetic theory and it is reflected so consistently in his work as a whole that it can safely be taken as a theory to which Joyce held with varying degrees of intensity throughout his life. In the *Portrait* Joyce's earliest definition is again supplemented by a consideration of the artist's function in the artistic process, but now these two factors are fused into a full-fledged genetic theory of art which defines the terms in which an art work is to be categorized.

The passage in *Stephen Hero* helps to clarify this part of the *Portrait*. Here again the artist's emotions grow out of his experience with life, but quite properly these emotions should not be embodied in the art work. Rather, an essential vitality should be extracted from them to be incorporated in the work of art. The artist, as Joyce conceives of him, seems to be garbed in Wordsworth's coat with two pairs of pants and a heavily classical vest. He is two people in one—an unconscious receptor, who reacts emotionally to the world around him, and a conscious converter, who depersonalizes these emotions into an independent artistic vitality and projects them in different art forms. The lyric form of art is little more than the raw personal emotion of the artist garbed in a filmy vesture of rhythm, a mood or a cry caught in a cadence. There is very little conscious control exercised in its creation. There is very little depersonalization of the artist's emotion. Consequently, the lyric form of art contains less independent vitality than the other forms. The creation of the epic form of art involves a considerable amount /429/ of conscious control and depersonalization of the artist's emotion. The increased independent vitality which results takes the shape of the epical narration. The dramatic form of art is the result of complete conscious control in the creative process and complete depersonalization of the artist's emotion. Its independent vitality, which is greater than that of the other art forms, takes the shape of living characters. The dramatic form, in Joyce's estimation, is the highest form of art.

Although this discussion in the *Portrait* emphasizes the importance of conscious control in the process of creation, its primary emphasis lies elsewhere. If we turn the definitions around, we can see more clearly what Joyce is setting up as criteria for categorizing art. Characters are a sign of dramatic art, narration is a sign of epic art, and the artist's emotion hanging out in plain sight, too direct to take the form of narration or character, is a sign of lyric art. Or, to make the criteria a little easier to handle, a work of art which is primarily concerned with character is dramatic, one which is primarily concerned with plot is epic, and one which is primarily concerned with the artist's personal emotions is lyric.

Now, in the light of these terms, it is quite clear that Joyce conceived of himself as a dramatic writer. His fifty poems are lyric moods and cadences, and perhaps in "Ecce Puer" a cry. But in *Dubliners, Stephen Hero,* the *Portrait, Exiles, Ulysses,* and *Finnegans Wake* Joyce is working with the dramatic form. None of these works is concerned with Joyce's personal emotions or with plot; all are concerned with presenting character. The degree of success achieved varies among these works, and they can be graded according to their artistic excellence; but they all belong to the category of dramatic art, according to Joyce's definition.

For instance, a comparison of *Stephen Hero* with the *Portrait* shows that the earlier work suffers from immaturity and infla- /430/ tion. It presents its material in cruder form with much less economy and selectivity. Moreover, Joyce is less objective in his treatment of Stephen in the early work, and the early character is a less vital figure than the Stephen of the *Portrait*. *Stephen Hero* is obviously inferior to the *Portrait* as a dramatic work of art, but this fact does not relegate it to another esthetic category. It, as well as the *Portrait*, is centrally concerned with creating a character. It is not concerned with the ends of lyric or epic art and it does not take the form of a lyric emotion or an epic narration. In Joyce's meaning of the term, it is a dramatic work of art.

These categories of art which Joyce defined for himself at an early age thus can be described as a result of the attempt of a very cocky young man to establish the extreme limits of his ambition. Since he wanted to write nothing but the best, he first had to decide in his own mind which art form was the best. But no sluggard he—even when he had defined and evaluated the lyric, epic, and dramatic art forms, the job was not finished. The categories had yet to be categorized. Dramatic art, with which he was principally concerned, could be divided quite naturally into the broad categories of comedy and tragedy, and, although not so naturally, so could lyric and epic art. In the Paris notebooks Joyce went on to define and evaluate these broad categories, with a nod in the direction of Aristotle and a curious twist of his own. Tragedy, he said, aims to arouse pity and terror, whereas comedy aims to arouse the feeling of joy; but since the act of apprehending a tragedy also arouses in us a kind of joy, tragedy is the imperfect manner and comedy is the perfect manner in art.

Joyce used the imperfect manner in two of his works, *Dubliners* and *Exiles;* but the comic manner which makes its early appearance in the poems, in *Stephen Hero*, and in the *Portrait* achieves its great flowering in *Ulysses* and *Finnegans Wake*. The /431/ richness, variety, and central importance of comedy in these two mature works is a subject yet to be explored. Leopold Bloom gradually becomes an object of deep human compassion, despite his absurdities and obscenities, because he is seen continually in a comic light. And Finnegan's whirligig of time is kept from ever becoming a harsh fatalism or a meaningless void by a comic spirit which, holding nothing sacred, yet enjoys everything. A great deal of misunderstanding of Joyce's works, especially of the *Portrait* and *Ulysses,* which are particularly abused, could be averted by a realization of two facts. Joyce is a dramatic writer who always stands aloof from his characters, and he is primarily a comic writer with one of the greatest gifts for comedy in English literature. Joyce is not Stephen. *Ulysses* is not a tragedy.

Dramatic, lyric, epic, comedy, tragedy—these terms were, for Joyce, portals of discovery through which he glimpsed reality, and in arriving at an understanding of what they had to mean to him, he supplied for his later career a footing whose importance cannot be overestimated. The Paris notebooks record the fruition of his attempt to work out an esthetic creed to replace the Credo which he had abandoned. By 1903, a year before he first turned his hand to writing short-stories or novels, Joyce had formulated his esthetic values into a rounded theory. On this bedrock of faith was founded the enormous self-confidence and sense of direction that carried Joyce through the overwhelming difficulties which beset him during most of his life. His definitions of the categories set up five requirements for the perfect work of art. It should be a comedy; it should be concerned with character, rather than narrative; it should work with material drawn from the artist's experience with life around him; it should contain the author's emotions depersonalized; it should be written with conscious artistry. Time brought later accretions in Joyce's esthetic conceptions, especially in the realm of technique, but the road from the categories to *Ulysses* and *Finnegans Wake* is a straight line. /432/

Bergson and Stephen Dedalus' Aesthetic Theory

SHIV K. KUMAR

Although the aesthetic theory of Stephen Dedalus is "in the main applied Aquinas"[1] with a few tags of "Aristotle's poetics and psychology,"[2] it is possible to interpret it in terms of Bergsonism.

In the course of a scholarly exposition to Lynch of his conception of beauty, Stephen cites *integritas, consonantia,* and *claritas* as its three main attributes, corresponding to the three necessary phases of artistic apprehension. *Integritas* implies that each aesthetic image is apprehended as "self-bounded and self-contained upon the immeasurable background of space or time which is not it."[3] Then we pass on to the next phase of artistic apprehension, *consonantia,* which signifies a rhythmic relationship between the various parts constituting the image. In brief, an integral perception is succeeded by "the analysis of apprehension." *Claritas,* the third attribute of beauty, Stephen admits, is at best a rather vague and inexact term, but he proceeds to interpret it as "the scholastic *quidditas . . .* the clear radiance of the esthetic image . . . apprehended luminously by the mind which has been arrested by its wholeness and fascinated by its harmony . . ."[4] This supreme aspect of beauty resembles, in certain respects, Bergson's *l'intuition philosophique* which enables a person to enter into the heart of an aesthetic image and apprehend it, in a single effort, as a rhythmic synthesis of its organically related components.

Shiv K. Kumar, "Bergson and Stephen Dedalus' Aesthetic Theory," *Journal of Aesthetics and Art Criticism,* XVI (Sept., 1957), 124-27.

[1] James Joyce, *Stephen Hero,* ed. Theodore Spencer (London, 1950), p. 64. (First published July 1944.)

[2] *A Portrait of the Artist,* etc., p. 200.

[3] *Ibid.,* p. 241.

[4] *A Portrait of the Artist,* etc., p. 242.

Let us now examine the first two essentials of beauty: *integritas* and *consonantia* in terms of Bergson's aesthetic. In one of his most illuminating essays entitled "Intellectual Effort," Bergson, like Stephen Dedalus, describes the different phases of artistic awareness.[5] According to him, every artist first conceives his subject as a whole scheme or apprehends his aesthetic image, to borrow Stephen's terminology, as *integritas* and then proceeds to realize it analytically as comprising parts in a harmonious relationship. The entire progression in the process of literary composition is thus from "scheme to image."[6]

"It must necessarily be assumed, then," observes Bergson, "that the whole is presented as a scheme, and that invention consists precisely in converting the scheme into image," in realizing the rhythmic relationship between parts con- /124/ stituting the whole.[7] He then proceeds to illustrate his aesthetic theory: "The author writing a novel, the dramatist creating his characters and situations, the musician composing a symphony,[8] the poet composing an epic, all have in mind first of all, something simple and abstract, something, so to say incorporeal. For the musician and poet it is a new impression, which they must unfold in sounds or in imagery. For the novelist and the dramatist it is a theme to be developed into events, a feeling, individual or social, to be materialised in living personages. They start work with a scheme of the *whole,* and the end is obtained when they reach a distinct image of the elements."[9]

The "end" signifies here nothing else than an apprehension of the aesthetic image as "the result of its parts and their sum, harmonious. That is *consonantia.*"[10]

Consonantia, Stephen further amplifies, is the passing from one element to another, till all is held together in a balance and one feels "the rhythm of its structure." It is the same rhythmic essence underlying every work of art, hidden behind its various parts to which Bergson refers in his essay "The Life and Work of Ravais-

[5] It may here be interesting to compare these three "phases of artistic apprehension" with Spinoza's three levels of knowledge. *Imaginatio, Ratio,* and *Scientia Intuitiva, Claritas, l'intuition philosophique,* and *Scientia Intuitiva* appear to belong to the same category. "Intellectual Effort" was first published as an article in the *Revue Philosophique,* Paris, January 1902, later included in *Mind-Energy.*

[6] Bergson's 'scheme' and 'image' seem to be synonymous respectively with Stephen's 'wholeness' and 'parts.'

[7] Bergson, *Mind-Energy,* trans. Wildon Carr (London, 1920), p. 173.

[8] *Cf.* William James' description of Mozart's method of composition, *The Principles of Psychology,* Vol. 1 (London, 1890), p. 255.

[9] *Mind-Energy,* pp. 173-174. (Italics mine.)

[10] *A Portrait of the Artist,* etc., p. 242.

son": "True art aims at portraying the individuality of the model
and to that end it will seek behind the lines one sees the movement
the eye does not see, behind the movement itself something even
more secret, the original intention, the fundamental aspiration of
the person: a simple thought equivalent to all the indefinite richness of form and colour."[11] The "simple thought" behind the multi-
plicity of lines and curves represents the "scheme" or integral apprehension of the aesthetic image. When the beholder of a beautiful
object realizes this basic impulse, his response may be likened to
"that cardiac condition which," cites Stephen, "the Italian physi-
ologist Luigi Galvani . . . called the enchantment of the heart."[12]
This attribute of beauty, says Stephen, is *claritas*. It may be seen
that *claritas* bears a certain resemblance to Bergson's *l'intuition
philosophique,* with the only difference that whereas the former is
the culmination of the two preceding phases—*integritas* and *consonantia*—the latter signifies an immediate identification with the
image to realize it in its entirety.

This resemblance between Stephen's aesthetic and Bergson's assumes still more significant proportions when the former elaborates
his theory of art as progressing through three distinct forms: the
lyrical, the epical, and the dramatic.[13]

These forms of art, as we shall now try to indicate, can be interpreted in terms of progressive awareness of aesthetic experience
from its being a loose assemblage of discrete emotions to its realization as a process of fluid continuity. /125/

The lyrical form, it may be seen, represents, according to Stephen
Dedalus, the most elementary phase of literary creation, being in
fact "the simplest verbal vesture of *an instant of emotion,* a rhythmical cry such as ages ago cheered on the man who pulled at the
oar or dragged stones up a slope. He who utters it is more conscious
of the instant of emotion than of himself as feeling emotion."[14] In
other words, every lyrical outburst of feeling remains a discrete and
independent entity not completely related to the person who experiences it. This, according to Bergson, would be symbolical of a
mechanistic conception of experience constituting instants of emotion as spatial elements not lending themselves to a process of creative interpenetration of the "instant of emotion" and the artist

---

[11] Bergson, *The Creative Mind,* trans. M. L. Andison (N.Y., 1946), p. 273.

[12] *A Portrait of the Artist,* etc., pp. 242-243.

[13] It may be here noted that Stephen's conception of art as *progressing* through
three different forms is described only in the *Portrait;* in *Stephen Hero,* these
forms are presented only as "three distinct natural kinds," p. 64.

[14] *A Portrait of the Artist,* etc., p. 244. (Italics mine.)

"himself as feeling emotion." This marks the first stage in the development of artistic modes of expression, and the epical form emerges from it "when the artist prolongs and broods upon himself as the centre of an epical event." The unrelated instant of emotion has now lengthened itself into "an epical event," and the artist by virtue of prolonged brooding upon himself, is able to let his personality flow into his work, giving to the experience therein represented a dynamic aspect. To quote Stephen Dedalus again, "the personality of the artist passes into the action like a vital sea."[15]

The dramatic form, Stephen further adds, "is reached when the vitality which has flowed and eddied round each person fills every person with such *vital force* that he or she assumes a proper and intangible esthetic life. The personality of the artist, at first a cry or a cadence or a mood and then a fluid and lambent narrative, finally refines itself out of existence, impersonalises itself, so to speak. The esthetic image in the dramatic form is life purified in and reprojected from the human imagination."[16] This is how, he concludes, "the mystery of esthetic, like that of material creation," is consummated.

This seems to be an interesting counterpart to Bergson's theory of creative evolution in which the dramatic form signifies the culmination of the *élan vital* ("vital force") injecting itself into matter and transforming it into living organism. The dramatic form implies, however paradoxical it may seem, the immanence of the creative spirit in every character or situation. The artist, through a stupendous intuitive effort, succeeds so completely in identifying himself with his character and scene that he remains, like God Almighty, "within or behind or beyond or above his handiwork, invisible, refined out of existence . . ."[17] This attitude of the dramatic artist is often misunderstood to signify conventional objectivity, whereas it implies, in fact, the culmination of the literary process when the artist, after having injected something of his *élan vital* into each of his characters, finally emerges as a cosmic spirit, "indifferent, paring his fingernails."

Joyce's own development as a novelist may be explained in terms of these progressive forms of literary composition. *Stephen Hero* and *A Portrait of the Artist as a Young Man* represent the earliest phase of literary development, both novels being, in a sense, a series of discrete instants of emotion or rhythmical /126/ cries, not cohering into any ostensible pattern of dynamic continuity. The main

[15] *A Portrait of the Artist,* etc., p. 244.
[16] *A Portrait of the Artist,* etc., p. 244. (Italics mine.)
[17] *Ibid.,* p. 245.

episode in the *Portrait,* when Stephen in the course of his rambles on the beach suddenly realizes his aesthetic ideal of using words in their multiple meanings and associations, centers round an intense lyrical cry of spiritual anguish. "His throat ached with a desire to cry aloud, the cry of a hawk or eagle on high, to cry piercingly of his deliverance to the winds . . . An instant of wild flight had delivered him and the cry of triumph which his lips withheld cleft his brain.—Stephaneforos!"[18]

As he breaks away in freedom from "the pale service of the altar," he feels "his throat throbbing with song . . . a lust of wandering in his feet," and a few paces further, his eyes fall on a girl whose "bosom was as a bird's, soft and slight, slight and soft as the breast of some darkplumaged dove . . . Heavenly God! cried Stephen's soul, in an outburst of profane joy."[19]

These moments of lyrical intensity, like discrete drops of water, seem to become larger and heavier and then fall down without flowing into a continuous stream.

Ulysses emerges from the *Portrait* as Joyce "prolongs and broods upon himself as the centre of an epical event."[20] The narrative ceases to be a mere pseudo-biography, with the center of interest shifting from Stephen Dedalus to Leopold Bloom. But Joyce's vicarious experience appears to flow round each of his characters and episodes like "a vital sea." *Ulysses,* unlike the *Portrait,* is not a series of lyrical outbursts, but progresses organically with an epical design imposed upon its continuous flow. Leopold Bloom's commonplace experiences of a single day have the same epical significance as the adventures of Ulysses, his Greek prototype. *Ulysses,* in a sense, is a vast epic of the Common Man of today.

But Stephen Dedalus in *Ulysses* still strongly suggests the personal point of view of his creator, and therefore, it is only in *Finnegans Wake* that Joyce completely refines himself "out of existence" and achieves an impersonal presentation of experience. In this sense, *Finnegans Wake* is a "dramatic" work, because the writer's personality does not intrude into the narrative which flows on, as it were, by itself. Characters and situations, mythical or symbolical, culled from the summation of human experience, blend ceaselessly into each other in a process of "constant fluxion." /127/

[18] *A Portrait of the Artist,* etc., p. 193.
[19] *A Portrait of the Artist,* etc., p. 195.
[20] *Ibid.,* p. 244.

A Pennyworth of Thomism

WILLIAM T. NOON, S.J.

Stephen confuses, it would seem, the Scholastic analysis of the act of apprehension with this act itself. Adequately to analyze the simplest act of apprehension requires many concepts in any epistemology, but the ordering of the concepts of analysis is not a substitute for the act which is under analysis. The concept of beauty is far from simple. As Aquinas conceives it, it is truly complex, with an onto-logical-psychological polarity which defies simple definition. The best one can do is to describe it, /45/ and the description must necessarily be complicated. But neither the complexity of this concept nor the complications which arise in a description of its genesis warrant one on Thomist grounds to speak as though it were generated in three stages by the mind. The integrity, consonance (or harmony), and clarity of which Aquinas speaks are all three known simultaneously by the viewer or reader or listener in one *intuitive* act.[4]

As has already been noted, Stephen seems to be thinking of the phantasm of the Scholastics when he describes integritas as the first phase of apprehension, which draws a bounding line, as he says, about the object to be apprehended. "An esthetic image is presented to us either in space or in time."[5] The phantasm, or imaginative

William T. Noon, S. J., *Joyce and Aquinas* (New Haven: Yale University Press, 1957), pp. 45-56.

[4] "Intuitive" is here used in a general sense, and not in the special sense that one can have knowledge without *any* intellectual abstraction. The latter is much disputed by Scholastics when they concern themselves with the "natural" powers of the intellect. All I mean to imply is "that there is no need for *effort* at abstraction, no *labor*, no *discursus* of reasoning." *Cf.* John L. Callahan, O.P., "The Esthetic Doctrine of the *Summa*." Supplement to the *Summa Theologiae* of St. Thomas Aquinas, *3* (New York, Benziger, 1948), 3342, col. 1. Cf. also *S.T.*, I, p. 58, a. 3, and 1ᵐ: "Si autem uno inspecto, simul aliud inspiciatur, sicut in speculo inspicitur simul imago rei et res, non est propter hoc cognitio discursiva."

[5] Pp. 248-9.

representation, of Scholastic psychology has, it is true, an ontological priority in the genesis of the act of knowledge. Stephen interprets this ontological priority as though it were a question of temporal sequence. But ontological and temporal priority are not the same thing: one must have light before the act of vision can take place, but the light does not come first and then the act of vision. Granted that there is light, one sees both the light and the object which the light illuminates not in stages but simultaneously. In some respects the aspect of light does not fit the case of the phantasm. Stephen goes on to say: "The esthetic image is first luminously apprehended as selfbounded and selfcontained." But the phantasm, or image of Thomist psychology is not pure luminosity. It is inchoative cognition or symbolization, and like all imaginative symbolization, though it presents the concrete and the particular for the intellect to scrutinize,[6] it does so tentatively and obscurely. The truth of reality is germinally present, but a simultaneous, not subsequent, immanent operation of the intellect is necessary for this truth to be conceived in the mind.

Even the concept, the *verbum mentis,* though it perfects the image which the imagination has elaborated, makes no commitment or enunciation about the abstract nature of this mental image, or about the nature of the reality which the mind grasps (that is, "apprehends," or knows) through the instrumentality of the image. The Thomist concept is not a /46/ mirror of reality, as though one knew the object by knowing its representation in the mind. In Scholastic terminology, the concept is not a *medium quod of cognitionis* but a *medium quo* or *in quo:*[7] that is, the mind knows not concepts but things.[8] Explicitly to affirm the conformity or nonconformity of

---

[6] Cf. Frederick D. Wilhelmsen, "The Aesthetic Act and the Act of Being," *Modern Schoolman,* 29 (May 1952), 277-91, esp. 282-3. Cf. too *De Ver.,* q. 2, a, 6, ad 3[m]: "Homo cognoscit singularia per imaginationem et sensum; et ideo potest applicare universalem cognitionem quae in intellectu, ad particulare: non enim, proprie loquendo, sensus aut intellectus cognoscunt, sed homo per utrumque."

[7] Scholastics are not in agreement as to whether the concept is a *medium quo* or *medium in quo.* All agree that it is not a *medium quod*—that is, that one does not "know" the concept but the thing. Whether one knows the thing without any knowledge of the concept, as one might look at an object through a perfectly transparent glass without adverting to the medium, or whether one knows the object with some advertence to the presence of the medium is the point in dispute. A medium quod here might roughly be likened to a mirror.

[8] Cf. Albert J. Steiss, "Outline of a Philosophy of Art," *Thomist,* 2 (Jan. 1940), 21: "The concept is not to be thought of as an object of knowledge; an image, as it were, which the mind sets up in lieu of the external object; or as a mirror in which the mind sees the object indirectly. The mind does not know the concept: the action of conceiving *is* knowledge. The concept, or expressed species, is the Form of the object existing by an act of the knower (i.e., intentionally) whereas outside the knower it exists by its own act (i.e., substantially)."

the concept with reality, and a fortiori to predicate such abstract qualities as *wholeness* or *oneness* of an apprehended object, the mind needs two concepts and an act of the judgment, an act which Stephen never explicitly mentions and which he seems to confound now with the phantasm, now with the concept. Furthermore, to affirm the identity of a being with itself "as selfbounded and selfcontained," distinct from all "which is not it,"[9] is to predicate of it, in Thomist terms, not integritas but *unitas,* a transcendental property of every being, so far as a being is conceived of as *aliquid,* that is, a being distinct and apart.[1]

Integritas has for Aquinas a perfectly definite and different meaning which Stephen appears not to have noticed in his breezy citation of the Thomist text. "Nam ad pulchritudinem tria requiruntur: Primo quidem integritas sive perfectio." To one familiar with the language of Aquinas, it is clear that by integritas (sive perfectio) he has in mind the completeness or perfection which a being possesses when it is all that it ought to be. Aristotle had much the same thing in mind when, for example, he "required" that the drama have a beginning, a middle, and an end: Did it grow out of something, did it grow toward something, did it finally reach the term of its growth? Was it an organism (in the analogous sense proper to literature)? Was it, as we might say, a mature work of art? In one of his earliest book reviews, Joyce defines "the first quality of beauty" as "the quality of being separate and whole"[2] which comes closer to Aquinas' integritas than Stephen with his talk of the "synthesis" and "analysis" of "immediate apprehension." /47/

Stephen's description of consonantia (or debita proportio) as "rhythm of . . . structure"[3] is Thomistically accurate, though here again Stephen speaks for himself and not for Aquinas when he calls it a "stage" or "phase" of apprehension rather than an existential quality inherent in the object apprehended. Also one is surprised to hear Stephen say: "Having first felt that it is *one* thing you feel now that it is a *thing.*"[4] Inasmuch as Stephen himself describes consonantia as that by which the object is apprehended as "harmonious," "made up of its parts, the result of its parts and their sum," it would seem more consistent to apply his distinction in reverse. Then we should say that integritas is that in virtue of which one comes to

[9] P. 249.

[1] Cf. Emmanuel Chapman, "The Perennial Theme of Beauty and Art," *Essays in Thomism,* ed. Robert E. Brennan, O.P. (New York, Sheed and Ward, 1942), p. 340.

[2] "An Irish Poet," *Dublin Daily Express,* Dec. 11, 1902. A review of *Poems and Ballads of William Rooney.*

[3] P. 249.

[4] Ibid.

know the object as one *thing* (aliquid), and consonantia is that which enables one to see the object's *oneness,* since consonantia (or proportio) is the principle of order, *quaelibet habitudo unius ad alterum.*[5] Aquinas at any rate states the matter in exactly the reverse order, and does so in the paragraph which immediately precedes the enumeration of the three qualities, which Stephen quotes: the object, as he says, must be first conceived of as a *thing (ens quoddam)* before one can think of it as *one,* "a thing" (*in quantum est una*).[6]

Stephen's account of consonantia presents this quality as a rather static, completed or pre-established harmony in constructed things, whereas the account of Aquinas pays more attention to it as a dynamic principle of order operative throughout all reality.[7] In his commentary on the *Sentences,* Aquinas applies consonantia to the immanent procession of the Son from the Father within the unity of the Divine Trinity, as well as to the immanent, dynamic presence of God in all creatures, and to the union of all creatures among themselves, which has the Divine Trinity as its ideal analogate.[8] The consonantia of a poem, a verbal act, would seem to postulate some such principle of fluid order, or dynamic structure, more "energetic" than the static structure of the basket which Stephen uses for an example. An account of consonantia which fails to take into consideration the asymmetrical function of dissonance or discontinuity in the rhythm of the whole would not be a very valuable tool for literary criticism or interpretation; it would ignore the existence of the real toads in so much of the world's imaginary garden of poetry.[9] Such a tool would be particularly inept for a critical understanding of Joyce's own significant contributions to modern literature. /48/

When Lynch interrupts Stephen after the latter's account of consonantia, he remarks, "Tell me now what is claritas and you win the cigar."[1] Lynch's wager is a better calculated risk than he himself might have realized. Aquinas' theory of claritas or *resplendentia* is the most crucial and subtle element in Stephen's "Aquinatian" theory of art. With the usual reminder that Aquinas presents this third quality of the beautiful as an existential property in the object rather than as a "stage" or "phase" of the mind's own act of know-

---

[5] *S.T.,* I, q. 12, a. 1, ad 4[m].

[6] "Nam primo consideratur res ipsa absolute in quantum est ens quoddam. Secunda autem consideratio rei est in quantum est una." *S.T.,* I, q. 39, a. 8 (corp.).

[7] Cf. De Bruyne, *Études d'esthétique médiévale, 3,* 303.

[8] *I Sent.,* dist. 31, q. 2, a. 1, conclus. of solutio.

[9] Cf. Marianne Moore, "Poetry," *Collected Poems of Marianne Moore* (New York, Macmillan, 1953), p. 41.

[1] P. 249.

ing, most Thomists would probably agree that in the main Stephen gives at this point the most satisfactory interpretation of Aquinas' thought.

Stephen prefaces his own interpretation of claritas by setting aside another possible interpretation which, as he admits, "baffled me for a long time. It would lead you to believe that he [Aquinas] had in mind symbolism . . . a light from some other world." Inasmuch as Aquinas holds that "every form through which anything has existence is some kind of participation in the divine clarity,"[2] it follows that Aquinas' understanding of claritas is more compatible with a "sacramentally" symbolic view of poetry than Stephen suspects. Dante, whose Thomism is admitted by most of his commentators, certainly seems to understand the radiance of created beauty in some such anagogical sense.[3]

The identity which Stephen establishes between claritas and the Scholastic *quidditas,* the "whatness" of a thing, is also questionable if Stephen claims Aquinas as his authority. Unlike the Suarezian Scholastics (and Joyce's Jesuit professors in Dublin at the turn of the century would presumably have been followers of Suarez), Thomists in general insist on the "real" (or actual), as opposed to the "rational" (or notional), distinction between the essence (or the quiddity, whatness) of a thing and its existence. Stephen certainly places his emphasis on the quiddity or essence as actuated, as "existential," as a structurally intelligible whole belonging to that order where "existence is prime among perfections."[4] Even if one allows that as a good Suarezian Thomist Stephen did not need to concern himself about the nice refinement of a "real distinction" between essence and existence, it is still difficult to see on what /49/ Scholastic grounds, Thomist or otherwise, he means "claritas is quidditas." Aquinas, to be sure, considers quidditas in the existential order when he talks about existent things, but even in this existential order the existent quidditas is conceived of as the nature

---

[2] *In Div. Nom.,* c. 4, lect. 5.

[3] Cf. Karl Vossler, *Mediaeval Culture. An Introduction to Dante and His Times,* tr. William Cranston Lawton (New York, Harcourt, Brace, 1929), *1,* 107, 127-8.

Curtius asserts (*European Literature,* p. 595): "The Thomism of Dante is an exploded myth." I must leave it up to the Dante specialists to decide whether Vossler or Curtius is more nearly correct. The famous letter of Dante to Can Grande would incline one to suspect that Dante, like Joyce, was accommodating his Thomism to his poetics rather than "exploding" it.

[4] "Prima quidem [perfectio est] secundum quod in suo esse constituitur." *S.T.,* I, q. 6, a. 3.

"Unde patet quod hoc quod dico esse est actualitas omnium actuum, et propter hoc est perfectio omnium perfectionum." *De Pot.,* q. 7, a. 2, ad 9^{m}.

of a thing, or the principle of operation which the thing possesses in virtue of its "substantial" form. The *forma substantialis* is not a principle of individuation; it is sometimes called the "specific form," or *forma specifica,* but the specification is to species, or class. Though Stephen alleges that he is following Aquinas, he clearly has more than that in mind: "You see that it is that thing which it is and no other."[5]

So far as Stephen is talking about poetry, and his citation of Shelley at this point suggests that he is, he must intend to include in his notion of quiddity some "accidental" or secondary form over and above the "specific form," some intrinsic modification imposed from within. Though Stephen cites Shelley's comparison in *A Defence of Poetry* between the creative mind and "a fading coal,"[6] he is throughout his exposition of the Scholastic quidditas much more of a realist than Shelley ever was. The symbolism which Stephen advocates is tied down to the objects of this world, like the butcher boy's basket, much more than Shelley's symbolism could be: a knowledge (root, blossom, fruit, and seed, as Shelley says) "from those eternal regions where the owl-winged faculty of calculation dare not ever soar."[7] Shelley's "transcendental" symbolism would seem, from Stephen's calculated analysis of quidditas, to be a kind of symbolism which Joyce did not particularly like. It was too much "out in the yonder," too much inclined to evaporate the things of this world, to be quite congenial to Joyce. Besides, when Joyce speaks of poetry he appears to be thinking of a knowledge which does not come from the "yonder" but is constructed through a careful molding by words. This interest in a claritas of the here and now shows how close is Joyce's own affinity with Aquinas even when he portrays Stephen as a kind of nineteenth-century idealistic symbolist eager to cite Shelley in support of his Scholastic views.

The claritas which a poem possesses is a most individual and

---

[5] P. 250: "The radiance of which he [Aquinas] speaks is the scholastic *quidditas,* the *whatness* of a thing." Cf. *Stephen Hero,* p. 213: "*Claritas* is *quidditas.*"

[6] This image of the mind in creation being like "a fading coal" is a favorite one with Joyce. He uses it in his college essay in *St. Stephen's* (May 1902), p. 8, applying it to James Mangan; in the *Portrait* (p. 250) he uses it to illustrate claritas; in *Ulysses* (p. 192) he incorporates it into his theory of *Hamlet.* In all three cases the mind is "the fading coal," but in the Mangan essay the mind is considered as creative under the breath of the imagination; in the *Portrait* the mind is considered as apprehending beauty, not creating it; and in *Ulysses* the mind is identified with the creative imagination such wise that its light, though fadng, not only illuminates what we see and what we are but is prophetic and reflective of what we are ourselves fated to become.

[7] "A Defence of Poetry"; see John Shawcross, ed., *Shelley's Literary and Philosophical Criticism* (London, Henry Frowde, 1909), pp. 152, 153.

concrete /50/ concentration of meaning brought to some particular point of intellectual focus. In this sense the poem's quidditas might be likened to a prism which gathers in light from various sources—metaphors, images, antitheses, rhythm, syntax, and so forth—but which is cut in such wise by the poet's craft that all the light is brought to a point of radiant intuition, the claritas, for the mind to see. It is this concrete, individual quidditas of an existent thing which has always defied precise philosophical analysis, be the thing a poem or a basket or anything else.

What Stephen seems to mean by claritas may have been expressed better by the *haecceitas* of Duns Scotus than by the quidditas of Aquinas. Étienne Gilson, an authority on both Aquinas and Scotus, has described the haecceitas of Scotus as "l'extrême point d'actualité qui détermine chaque être réel à la singularité"[8] and he goes on to say. "Même si nous connaissions le singulier, nous pourrions le voir, mais non le définir."[9] Or in the words of Heidegger, "Das Individuelle ist ein unzurückführbar Letzes."[1]

Stephen's final summary of claritas as an "enchantment of the heart," though it is easily explicable in an "Aquinatian" context, has also even greater affinities with Scotus' principles. It is interesting to speculate whether the poet Gerard Hopkins, who died while a professor at University College, may have left behind him a little of his love for the *Doctor Subtilis,* strong enough to keep alive a modest tradition of Scotist poetics in Joyce's student days. Be that as it may, the affective, aesthetic affinities of Joyce's Stephen are better described as Scotist than as "Aquinatian." The actual composition or interpretation of poetry, with which Stephen is not much concerned, would seem to be largely the same whether one's bias in poetics was Scotist or Aquinan.

Aquinas would have said that quidditas is a condition for claritas, rather than claritas itself, but in either case the claritas is to be explained as a radiance of the form, and Stephen is correct in describing it as a synthesis of integritas and consonantia.[2] It is the form of an object, according to the Scholastic account of cognition, which the intellect assimilates when it knows the object. The assimilation to be sure is an intentional and not physical appropriation of the object and owes as much to the intrinsic finality of the knowing mind as to the principle of intelligibility, the form, which is in the

[8] Étienne Gilson, "Jean Duns Scotus," *Études de philosophie médiévale,* No. 42 (Paris, Librairie Philosophique J. Vrin, 1952), p. 464, n. 2.
[9] Ibid., 466.
[1] Quoted, ibid.
[2] P. 250.

object known. Ultimately any theory of knowledge must admit that it is up against one of the irreducibles of human experience. The Scholastic account, like others, makes the effort to describe upon reflection what must take place, or at least what must /51/ be accounted for, without claiming to explain it. Some union between object and mind is to be described: the Scholastics begin by looking for a principle of intelligibility in the object, and this they discover in the form, the intrinsic principle of organization, which determines that the object exists in this way and not in another. Between the form of an object and the clarity there is, therefore, a most intimate connection: the claritas is nothing else but the *irradiatio formae:* "For every essence either is a simple form or has its completion through the form. The form, however, is a certain radiance flowing from the first clarity. Clarity, moreover, is one of the aspects of the beautiful."[3] So Aquinas expresses himself in his *Commentary on the Divine Names.* The Dedalan exposition of claritas would have gained in precision had it taken up Aquinas' notion of claritas as the irradiatio formae. Forma and quidditas are not convertible notions as Aquinas uses them. He conceives of the quidditas or essence of an angel as being the same as its form, but in the case of all other creatures the essence is regarded as compounded of matter as well as of form, and it is obvious that a poem or any other work of art cannot be judged as though it were pure form.

Inasmuch as a poem is not something which is found in nature as is, for example, a tree, there is no particular advantage in talking about its forma substantialis. The form a poem has is a "secondary" form. Its intelligibility is man-made, contrived; there is no reason why a poem as a human utterance may not have, may not be, an aggregate of forms. It must have unity, and here precisely the work of the poet (and his reader) with language begins: to discover some principle of organization, some pattern according to which the insights and suggestions associated with individual words and collocations of words may be utilized so as to offer a new verbal dramatization of experience. It is in this way, is it not, that the claritas of a poem, its "radiance of form," manifests itself to the mind?

When Stephen speaks about the claritas of a being as the only logically and aesthetically permissible synthesis of integritas and consonantia, he would seem to be echoing the Scholastic theory of the form, though he does not mention it. So far as the existential form of a being successfully manifests itself to the mind, the full per-

[3] "Omnis enim essentia vel est forma simplex, vel habet complementum per formam. Forma autem est quaedam irradiatio proveniens ex prima claritate. Claritas autem est de ratione pulchritudinis." *In Div. Nom.,* c. 4, lect. 6.

fection (integritas) of the being is revealed, and the principle of
order (consonantia) in the midst of multiple, even discordant or
asymmetrical, elements is discovered. To talk about the "substantial
form" of a poem manifesting itself to the mind would not, however,
take one very far; at most the disclosure would reveal that one was
reading a poem, and even this disclosure would be assuming that
the reader knew the "specific essence" of poetry /52/ as distinct
from all that is not poetry. Theories of la poésie pure are not easy to
defend, and one may presume that Joyce would have been least of
all likely to wish to defend them. For Stephen the case is not so
clear; his romantic version of the neo-Thomist aesthetic, couched as
it is in literary language and not, as he tells us, in the language of
the market place,[4] sounds at times like a plea for the refined essence
of poetry, pure and distilled.

On the analogy of the irradiatio formae of Scholastic psychology,
it would be legitimate and perhaps helpful for the literary critic or
aesthetician to speak of the work of the poet as a preparation
through the "formal" organization of his language for the moment
of illumination, or clarity. In this sense, the meaning or the idea of
a poem is comparable to Aquinas' (and Aristotle's) material cause,
and the poem's style is comparable to their formal cause. W. Y. Tindall has noted that the aesthetic theory of the Portrait is a definition of significant form.[5] A theory of literature in the light of the
Thomist texts de pulchro seems to move toward some such solution
of the question of content and style. If our analysis of the form be
correct, then it would seem as if one should conceive of the words
or the language as the formal, determing principle of embodiment,
and that the meaning or the poetic truth should be regarded as
"the potential" waiting to be actuated by the form. It is, of course,
possible to view this application of matter and form to literature,
as the Chicago critics have done, in just the opposite light.[6] It goes
without saying that any application of the hylomorphic theory at
this point must necessarily be analogous, but the analogy may be in-
structive so long as one remembers that in the Thomist cosmology
the matter and the form are never conceived of as independent
causes but always as "co-causes," con-causae, which interpenetrate
at every point.

Stephen sums up this account of claritas ("the only synthesis

[4] P. 250.

[5] W. Y. Tindall, James Joyce, His Way of Interpreting the Modern World
(New York, Scribner's, 1950), p. 119.

[6] Cf. W. K. Wimsatt, Jr., "The Chicago Critics," Comparative Literature, 5
(Winter 1953), 50-74.

which is logically and esthetically permissible") by remarking: "The instant wherein that supreme quality of beauty, the clear radiance of the esthetic image, is apprehended luminously by the mind which has been arrested by its wholeness and fascinated by its harmony is the luminous silent stasis of esthetic pleasure . . . the enchantment of the heart."[7] In spite of the stress which the intellectualist Aquinas places on the cognitive aspect in his analysis of beauty, he sees no difficulty in accounting for the overflow of the mind's joy into the emotions, so that they too are *actively* engaged, even though silently, as long as the harmonious vision of the mind endures. In response to a difficulty proposed against /53/ the argument of the *de Veritate,* Aquinas speaks, for example, much as Stephen does when he describes the intellectual meditation on the meaning of the beautiful as an "enchantment of the heart." Man is an *unum per se,* as the Scholastics say, and it is a common experience of men whose attention is absorbed by the forms of art to experience this "intransitive attention" and affective enchantment which Stephen's phrase expresses so well. In the words of Aquinas: "Insofar as one desires the good, he desires at the same time beauty and peace: . . . for it is with one and the same longing that one wishes for goodness, for beauty, and for peace."[8] The *Summa Theologiae* makes the same correlation between knowledge and joy: "It appertains to the nature of beauty that in the sight of it—or in the knowing of it—yearning should come to rest."[9] This aspect of joy in knowledge, contemplative joy, had a special relevance for Joyce's early theory of poetry, as his youthful essay on the Irish poet James Clarence Mangan shows: "Beauty, the splendour of truth, is a gracious presence when the imagination contemplates intensely the truth of its own being or of the visible world, and the spirit which proceeds out of truth and beauty is the holy spirit of joy."[1] From what Stephen has said, it is clear that his aesthetic emotion of joy is different, or at least distinct, from the emotions represented in the poem, which may be quite sorrowful (as they often are in Mangan's verse). The

---

[7] P. 250.

[8] "Ex hoc enim ipso quod aliquid appetit bonum, appetit simul pulchrum et pacem: . . . Unde et codem appetitu appetitur bonum, pulchrum, et pax. *De Ver.,* q. 22, a. 1, ad 12^m.

[9] "Ad rationem pulchri pertinet quod in ejus aspectu seu cognitione quietetur appetitus." *S.T.,* I-II, q. 27, a. 1, ad 3^m.
Cf. Maritain, *Creative Intuition in Art and Poetry,* p. 58: ". . . in the last analysis, in art as in contemplation, intellectuality at its peak goes beyond concepts and discursive reason, and is achieved through a congeniality or connaturality with the object, which love alone can bring about."

[1] "James Clarence Mangan," *St. Stephen's,* p. 15.

joy of listening to *Dark Rosaleen* comes not from sharing the joy of the speaker, who "night and noon" is in "pain and woe," nor from sharing the joy of Rosaleen herself, who sighs and weeps without hope. The listener (or reader) overhears and rejoices not at the speaker's or Rosaleen's sorrows but at Mangan's perfect expression of their sorrows through the "truth and beauty" of his vision elaborated in *words*. It is there that the "gracious presence" of the aesthetic emotion of joy in the poem resides.

All that Stephen has said in the *Portrait* on the nature of beauty and the nature of art leads in the end to his division of art into three forms: "Art necessarily divides itself into three forms progressing from one to the next. These forms are: the lyrical form, the form wherein the artist presents his image in immediate relation to himself; the epical form, the form wherein he presents his image in mediate relation to himself and to others; the dramatic form, the form wherein he presents his image in /54/ immediate relation to others."[2] From the corresponding account in *Stephen Hero*[3] it comes out that Stephen is thinking of literature and that he considers the other forms of art which do not "offer this division with the same clearness" as on this account less excellent. Having taken the position that the reality of art is apprehended in a moment of detached and silent stasis, he does not surprise us in describing as profanities "the antique principle that the end of art is to instruct, to elevate, and to amuse." As any student or alumnus of a Jesuit college ought to know, the aims of rhetoric and of poetic do not coincide.[4] Having based his aesthetic of poetry on a theory of contemplative joy, a *revelatio,* as he says, analogous to the Thomist *contemplatio pulchri,* Stephen feels justified on Aquinas' authority in dismissing the aims of rhetoric as Puritanic, as absurd, as a criticism established not on poetry but on homilies.[5]

The "impersonal" theory of poetry which emerges from Stephen's threefold division is a logical development from the premises of aesthetic distance and detachment which Stephen imagined that Aquinas had established. Aquinas has so little to say about poetry

[2] Pp. 250-1.

[3] *Stephen Hero*, p. 77.

[4] The last two years of the Jesuit course of study in "colleges" organized on the European plan are devoted respectively to "poetry" and "rhetoric." (Jesuit houses of study in America also have "a poetry year," and "a rhetoric year," and the students are referred to as "poets" and "rhetoricians" respectively.) Cf. *Portrait*, p. 13: "He felt small and weak. When would he be like the fellows in Poetry and Rhetoric?"

[5] *Stephen Hero*, pp. 79-80.

that it is difficult at this point to decide how he might have felt about the Flaubertian principle back of Stephen's three-form theory, the artist's progressively refining himself out of existence in his work.

Though Stephen's particular division of literature into lyric, epic, and dramatic is as old as Plato's and Aristotle's "manners of imitation," he describes these three forms in such a way as to suggest that he is strongly influenced here by Hegelian theories of art's progressively transcending itself through the symbolic, classical, and romantic forms.[6] There seems to be some echo too of Schelling's concept of art in the sphere of ideality as progressing through the stages of lyric finiteness and particularity, to epic infiniteness and generality, and finally to dramatic union, where the particular is lost in the general and the real is totally taken up into the ideal.[7] It would seem to be only in virtue of Stephen's Scholastic training in rhetoric and poetic (a sturdy ballast) that he is saved at this /55/ point in his discussion from being carried off into the idealistic empyrean of German romantic aestheticism.

It would not be too much to say that the problem of rhetoric versus poetic is the underlying aesthetic problem which the young man of the *Portrait* sets himself to solve. In Stephen's terms, rhetoric aims at forming the man of action through a kinesis of the will in the presence of good and evil; poetic aims at leading a man to contemplation, to a stasis of the mind before the *visum placens*.[8] The moral claims of theology are viewed by the youthful Stephen as compatible with the aims of rhetoric but not with those of poetic. After listening to the retreat-master's rhetorical peroration calling to repentance—the conclusion of the lurid sermon on hell—Stephen returns to his room despondent. His heaviness of heart is not caused by an onrush of penitential sorrow but rather by his disappointment when he fails to feel any penitential emotion at all: "Could it be that he, Stephen Dedalus, had done those things?"[9] He is torn between two impulses: the explicit, rhetorical demands of the sermon ("to meet

---

[6] Cf. Bosanquet, *The Introduction to Hegel's Philosophy of Fine Art*, pp. 145-57.

[7] Cf. Katherine E. Gilbert and Helmut Kuhn, *A History of Aesthetics* (New York, Macmillan, 1939), p. 433. Also see Joyce's early review, "George Meredith," in *Dublin Daily Express*, Dec. 11, 1902, in which he remarks that Meredith "is plainly lacking in that fluid quality, the *lyrical* impulse," and goes on to say that "Meredith's novels . . . have no value as *epical* art, and Mr. Meredith has not the instinct of the *epical* artist." (A review of Walter Jerrold's *George Meredith: An Essay toward Appreciation*. Italics mine.)

[8] P. 243.

[9] Pp. 157-8.

his sins face to face, to recall their times and manners and circumstances, to weep over them") and his implicit, poetic refusal to assume kinship with so "leprous" a company ("He could not weep, he could not summon them to his memory"). The conflict is resolved not on the level of rhetoric, a conversion of the will into action, but on the level of poetic: "He saw." He begins to consider the subject aesthetically and it comes into focus. This is the key to his understanding it—to understanding, so he imagines, his life: "He wept for the innocence he had lost."[1]

Seen in this light, the "conversion" of the *Portrait* needs to be qualified. It is not theological in the strict sense of the word: a turning to God; much more, it is a turning to art, a commitment to the life beautiful, to the life of the artist, seen perhaps for a time in theological perspectives but accepted here and now because it is a solution congenial to art: "It would be beautiful to die if God so willed. It was beautiful to live in grace."[2] This is not to impugn Stephen's sincerity or to deny that God might have used Stephen's passion for the beauty of art as an occasion for grace. When the practical demands of living this life beautiful grow too exigent for the artist to heed, Stephen turns from the vision of his retreat to the vision of "mortal youth and beauty," and in an instant of ecstasy is prepared to follow this "envoy from the fair courts of life" into "all the ways of error and glory."[3] The break with theology and with rhetoric is complete, but the solution of the *Portrait* is not final.
/56/

[1] P. 160.
[2] P. 168.
[3] P. 200.

PART VI

SEVEN FURTHER CONSIDERATIONS

The Role of Structure in Joyce's "Portrait"

GRANT H. REDFORD

A close look at *The Portrait of the Artist as a Young Man* by James Joyce reveals a relationship between artistic proposition and structure which has either been overlooked or too-little emphasized. Yet unless the book is seen as both definition and demonstration, its subject matter cannot be properly evaluated. It will be seen merely as a thinly-veiled autobiographical record of an arrogant, somewhat ridiculous, even "insufferable" (says Hugh Kenner) young man with artistic pretensions who is not understood by his family nor appreciated by his society, and who turns his back on "all that" and decides to remake the world nearer to his heart's desire. This partial and inexact view supported by considerable comment over the years does disservice to the book. The present paper proposes to show how the book's themes—Search and Rebellion—are made meaningful through structure, and how the structure is the embodiment of an artistic proposition proclaimed by the central character himself as being basic to a work of art.

As a useful step toward this purpose, a word of reminder needs to be said about Joyce's method of work. Frank Budgen visited him while he was writing *Ulysses* and was told that though he had been working hard all day he had written only two sentences. "I have the words already," he told Budgen. "What I am seeking is the perfect order of the words in the sentence. There is an order in every way

Grant H. Redford, "The Role of Structure in Joyce's 'Portrait,'" *Modern Fiction Studies*, IV (Spring, 1958), 21-30.

appropriate." This search for the perfect order is revealed throughout Joyce's work, both indirectly and directly: In *Stephen Hero*,
Stephen "sought in his verses to fix the most elusive of his moods
and he put his lines together not word by word but letter by letter"
(69). In *The Portrait*, he is trying to write a poem about a girl and
a party; an earlier effort to write a poem about Parnell had foun-
dered: "Now it seemed as if he would fail again, but by dint of brooding on the incident, he thought himself into confidence. During this
process all those elements which he deemed common and insignificant fell out of the scene" (77-8). This process is dramatically demonstrated in the transformation of a manuscript, *Stephen Hero*,
estimated by Joyce to be 150,000 words covering twenty-five chapters— /21/ about half the projected work—into five chapters total-
ling less than 90,000 words, *The Portrait*.

A characteristic of this process is a more precise use and inter-
weaving, as in music, of symbol and motif; e.g., the family name,
Dedalus, is retained, but made the defining symbol of *The Portrait*—
note the scene, pages 196-7; the motif of the bat-like soul of Ireland
and thus of Stephen waking to consciousness is used at least seven
times at important junctures (e.g., pp. 213, 226, 237, 238, 259, 280,
299). Everything is made to serve the "perfect order" of Joyce's vision.

The vision, the proposition which underlies the book, is stated
by Stephen near the end of the book as the climax of his Search:
"Truth is beheld by the intellect which is appeased by the most
satisfying relations of the intelligible: beauty is beheld by the imagination which is appeased by the most satisfying relations of the
sensible" (243). Such a work, he concludes, will have "wholeness,
harmony and radiance." How then does the book conform to this
requirement of having the most satisfying relation of the intelligible
and the sensible, of attempting to be both true and beautiful?

The first two pages introduce the major subject-matter motifs:
family, friends, country, church (embodied in the aunt), and Stephen's special responsiveness to music and language. Each of the
book's five chapters presents an aspect of these materials in relation
to Stephen's growth, i.e. in relation to his rebellion from them—
family, church, etc.—and in relation to his search for something
more satisfying to the artist's necessity. The length, treatment and
special emphasis given each of the chapters is a key to how Joyce
wanted the reader to regard the material and to view the total work.

Considerably more than half of Chapter I is devoted to religion
and politics as factors destructive of family harmony, personal dignity and justice. Sixteen pages in full scene, a method employed no-

where else in the book, reveal the harrowing experience of the bitterly ironic family Christmas dinner. Four pages concentrate the injustice of a whipping administered by a priest, Father Dolan. Stephen's attempt to obtain justice from the Rector turns out, he discovers later, to be an ironic gesture, for it merely causes laughter among the authorities. Expanded through the remaining chapters, these elements constitute part of that against which Stephen eventually rebels.

The Search is also embodied in this first chapter but indirectly as an expression of the child's, then young boy's, growing awareness of the "outside world"—a term used often and with special significance throughout the book. These beginnings of the Search are revealed through Stephen's unusual sensitivity to language. /22/ Dorothy Van Ghent goes so far as to say that *The Portrait* is an investigation of the creative effects of language upon life: "and the shape of reality that gradually defines itself for Stephen is a shape determined primarily by the association of words." In addition to the verse "apologize" and its implications on page 2, examples of his preoccupation with language are found on pages 5, 11, 13, 22, 25, 45, 49 and others, all in Chapter I. But most directly related to the Search are pages 11-12. They present Stephen not only concerned with language but seeking to *place* himself. He writes his name and then his address progressively until he asserts himself in the universe. This is Joyce announcing in full scale the Search theme.

Chapter II extends his experience with the "outer world" and his recognition and reaction to the continuing disintegration of his family's financial and social condition. Ten pages of the fifty are devoted to a reiteration of the "apologize" theme; here it involves his judgments and the writing and speaking of them. In class his instructor, Mr. Tate, forces submission from him regarding the phrasing of a relationship between the Creator and the soul. Mr. Tate says that the phrase "without a possibility of ever approaching nearer" was heresy. Stephen murmurs: "I meant without a possibility of ever reaching. . . . Mr. Tate, appeased, folds up the essay and passes it across to him, saying,—O . . . Ah! *ever reaching*. That's another story." But boys from the class use the incident as an excuse to attempt to force an admission from him that Byron was no good. They pinioned his arms and whacked him with a cabbage stump. But at last "after a fury of plunges he wrenched himself free" (91).

His second attempt to wrench himself free—this time from the grip of the squalid family circumstances—was not successful. He had won an exhibition and essay prize of thirty and three pounds and with it had embarked on a "swift season of merrymaking" of loaning money, buying presents, groceries and delicacies, buying pink paint for his room, etc.

How foolish his aim had been! He had tried to build a breakwater of order and elegance against the sordid tide of life without him and to dam up, by rules of conduct and active interests and new filial relations, the powerful recurrence of the tide within him. Useless. From without as from within the water had flowed over his barriers. . . .

By day and by night he moved among distorted images of the outer world. (110-11)

In this chapter he writes the poem about the girl and the party and defines his method of composition: by dint of brooding on the incident, etc. In addition to this significant act we find him testing and responding to words and conducting his search: /23/

Words which he did not understand he said over and over to himself till he had learnt them by heart: and through them he had glimpses of the real world about him. The hour when he too would take part in the life of that world seemed drawing near and in secret he began to make ready for the great part which he felt awaited him the nature of which he only dimly apprehended. (68)

He sat listening the the words and following the ways of adventure that lay open in the coals, arches and vaults and winding galleries and jagged caverns. (74)

Here, indirectly through the architecture of the fire's action, Joyce introduces the major motif of the Search theme, Dedalus, the Artificer, with whom Stephen aligns himself more and more throughout the work and dramatically at the climax and the book's end.

As did the first and as do all the others, this chapter ends with a seeming of order and satisfaction: his nocturnal wanderings, which are a manifestation of his seeking of solace from inner and outer turmoil, land him in the arms of a prostitute who is kind and gentle with him. "In her arms he felt that he had suddenly become strong and fearless and sure of himself" (114).

Chapter III presents a concentration of his emotional involvement with sin on the one side and the Church on the other. Over one sixth of the book is devoted directly to this conflict. It is an intense and harrowing experience for Stephen to find himself involved in more, and more nerve-wracking, excursions into the sins of the flesh while at the same time he is confronted with the celebration of a Retreat in honor of the school's patron saint, Xavier, wherein Stephen is subjected to a most devastating view of hell, the horror into which he, Stephen, is to be cast as the reward of his multiple sins. The length and intensity of this section is proportional to its effect on Stephen. Joyce is careful to show that others took it more casually (143). However, in spite of the terror of the experience, as the artist-becoming, he does not judge. This is made clear in an earlier sequence where he is angry for being young and being a victim of a world of squalor and insincerity. "Yet his anger lent nothing to the vision. He chronicled with patience what he saw, detaching himself from it and testing its mortifying flavour in secret" (73). Later he states directly that detachment, impersonalization of the artist, is a necessity for art (252).

Simply as a human being, however, the terrified young man of sixteen seeks solace in confession in an out-of-the-way, unpretentious chapel. Here, though edged with irony, Joyce presents a quiet, gentle sequence to contrast with the cacophony and stridency of the Retreat. Stephen returns to his school a lifted soul and partakes of the sacrament. The chapter ends on a note of peace, Stephen apparently safe in the arms of the Church. /24/

But as neither the arms of a prostitute nor the bosom of the Church gave him the satisfaction that his heart desired—"the loveliness which has not yet come into the world"—the next chapter, IV, a short one of thirty pages, reveals him still searching. One of the most enticing of all the nets held out to him is offered in this chapter. The director of the school calls Stephen in and asks him if he has ever had a desire to join the order. "To receive that call, Stephen . . . is the greatest honour that the Almighty God can bestow upon a man. No king or emperor . . . no angel or archangel . . . no saint, not even the Blessed Virgin herself has the power of a priest of God . . ." (183).

Pondering this possibility and after an encounter with his mother, which ends with him "aware dimly and without regret of a first noiseless sundering of their lives," (191), he wanders by himself to a headland overlooking the sea. "Disheartened, he raised his eyes toward the slow-drifting clouds, dappled and seaborne. They were voyaging across the deserts of the sky, a host of nomads on the march, voyaging high over Ireland, westward bound." He hears "confused music within him" that recedes, recedes. He hears the call with his whole being, paying little heed that the call also sounds from bantering school acquaintances on the beach, shouting, "Hello, Stephanos! Here comes The Dedalus!" Caught and held in the mystic moment of an overpowering vision, he sees himself the artificer winging to whatever artistic forgings his soul could achieve: "This was the call of life to his soul not the dull gross voice of the world of duties and despair, not the inhuman voice that had called him to the pale service of the altar . . ." (197).

He lies down in a hidden sandy nook "that the peace and silence of the evening might still the riot of his blood. . . . He felt above him the vast indifferent dome and the calm processes of the heavenly bodies: and the earth beneath him, the earth that had borne him, had taken him to her breast" (200). This embrace of earth is within three paragraphs of the end of the chapter. It makes a dramatic contrast with the earlier embraces of prostitute and church, which ended chapters two and three. Chapter IV ends, significantly enough, with Stephen awakening from the breast of earth. "He rose slowly and, recalling the rapture of his sleep, sighed at his joy." But this is no seeming. This is the awakening to true joy, the product of his Search and Rebellion.

Though this awakening is the climax of the book, and four of the book's five chapters have been used in arriving at this point, the Search, in a real sense, has just begun. Now he has simply discovered "the end he had been borne to serve." How to serve that end, /25/ the responsibilities and limitations of his calling are yet to be discovered.

It is something that he should know what he will *not* serve; but from here on it is absolutely necessary that he know what he *will* serve and that he discover how to serve; he must perform an extended and laborious apprenticeship before he achieves the certitude of understanding and skill which Stephen says is the gift of the artist to his generation: "He was persuaded that no one served the generation into which he had been born so well as he who offered it, whether in his art or in his life, the gift of certitude" (*Stephen Hero,* 76).

In view of this necessity, it can be understood why the last chapter covers a third of the book; why its length, subject matter, and emphasis are necessary to the completion of its structure and the achieving of the wholeness, harmony, and radiance requisite to a work of beauty. Hugh Kenner finds this last third unsatisfactory: "The insufferable Stephen of the final chapter is explicable on the assumption that Joyce is preparing his bridge into *Ulysses;* but the moral difficulty of accepting the *Portrait* as satisfactorily finished off in its own right imposes an intolerable strain on the reader." As I've explained, however, the length and emphasis of this portion of the book are necessary to complete the satisfying relations of the intelligible and of the sensible. They are necessary to the completion of Stephen's proposition and Joyce's artistic problem when he assigned himself the task of transforming *Stephen Hero* into *A Portrait of the Artist as a Young Man.* Stephen, having had the vision of himself as the Artificer, the winged man climbing the air of certitude and the wide glimmering vistas of art, must make sure of his wings before flight. So it is that Joyce presents him during this last third of the book completing the severing of ties and analyzing, defining, testing the artistic and intellectual equipment which is to bear him up in his flight.

But it is not easy. The fine confidence that was born with the vision and Rebellion is often assailed. Early in this last chapter, after drinking watery tea and chewing on crusts of fried bread preparatory to his going to morning classes at the university, he leaves by the back lane and hears a mad nun crying, "Jesus! O Jesus!" beyond the wall.

. . . stumbling through the mouldering offal, his heart [was] bitten by an ache of loathing and bitterness. His father's whistle, his mother's mutterings, the screech of an unseen maniac were to him now so many voices offending and threatening to humble the pride of his youth. (204)

Later, standing on the steps of the library and seeing birds in flight, he was moved to doubt. /26/

A sense of fear of the unknown moved in the heart of his weariness, a fear of symbols and portents, of the hawklike man whose name he bore soaring out of his captivity on osier woven wings. . . .
. . . was it for this folly that he was about to leave forever the house of prayer and prudence into which he had come? (264)

There are also other periods of frustration and self-doubt. But from them all he emerges stronger, surer. Buoyed up by the necessity of his developing wings, he continues to serve his apprenticeship, to forge out his own concepts.

Touched by the spirit of Ibsen "like a keen wind" or the "silver-veined prose of Newman" or a song by Ben Jonson, he wanders the dark streets of Dublin "among heaps of dead language."

His own consciousness of language was ebbing from his brain and trickling into the very words themselves which set to band and disband themselves in wayward rhythms:

> *The ivy whines upon the wall,*
> *And whines and twines upon the wall,*
> *The yellow ivy upon the wall*
> *Ivy, ivy up the wall.*

Did any one over hear such drivel? Lord, Almighty!
Who ever heard of ivy whining on a wall? Yellow ivy: that was all right. Yellow ivory also. And what about ivory ivy?
The word now shone in his brain, clearer and brighter than any ivory sawn from the mottled tusks of elephants. (208)

(Here, Joyce picks up an image made use of early in the book, on page 45. Thinking of Eileen's hands, "They were like ivory; only soft. That was the meaning of *Tower of Ivory* but protestants could not understand it and made fun of it.")

In this quotation—the one just quoted from page 208—is revealed the change taking place in Stephen's relationship to language. When, in the forepart of the book, he travels the countryside with his uncle he listens to the talk. "Words which he did not understand he said over and over to himself till he had learnt them by heart: and through them he had glimpses of the real world about him" (68). He still responds to language; its phrases and rhythms have been the core around which much of his knowledge of places and events has accreted. But now, as he says, language is beginning to form shapes of idea and sound in his mind. He is beginning to cross over from the passive recipient to the active maker, the artificer.

It is easy to understand, therefore, why this section presents Stephen in the act of composing a poem. Nearly ten pages are devoted to this emotion-charged event (254-63). The poem, in keeping with the rigorous self-discipline of the artist-becoming, is one of the more demanding of verse forms, the villanelle. And as would be expected, it makes use of a motif introduced earlier in the /27/ book, an echo of Stephen's reading of Shelley, lines about the moon "pale for weariness? Of climbing heaven and . . . Wandering companionless" (108). When first used, these lines were more or less passively repeated by Stephen as an embodiment of his mood, but now the motif is used aggressively; now is the act of making:

Towards dawn he awoke. O what sweet music! His soul was all dewy wet. Over his limbs in sleep pale cool waves of light had passed. He lay still, as if his soul lay amid cool waters, conscious of faint sweet music. His mind was waking slowly to a tremulous morning knowledge, a morning inspiration. A spirit filled him, pure as the purest water, sweet as dew, moving as music. . . . [As has been noted, music accompanies almost every major event of vision or "awakening" in the book.]

O! In the virgin womb of the imagination the word was made flesh. Gabriel the seraph had come to the virgin's chamber. An afterglow deepened within his spirit, whence the white flame had passed, deepening to a rose and ardent light. . . .

> Are you not weary of ardent ways,
> Lure of the fallen seraphim?
> Tell no more of enchanted days.

The verses passed from his mind to his lips and, murmuring them over, he felt the rhythmic movement of a villanelle pass through them. The roselike glow sent forth its rays of rhyme; ways, days, blaze, praise, raise. . . . (255)

Fearing to lose all, he raised himself suddenly on his elbow to look for paper and pencil. . . . His fingers found a pencil and then a cigarette packet. He lay back and . . . began to write out the stanzes . . . in small neat letters on the rough cardboard surface.

Having written them out he lay back on the lumpy pillow, murmuring them again. (256-7)

The completed poem is full of literary echoes and self-consciousness, but it achieves an objectification of the artist at his work serving his apprenticeship; it reveals discipline, knowledge of his craft, imagination and passion.

Further, it is dramatized by Joyce into a significant, semi-climactic segment of the book's structure. It follows immediately Stephen's enunciation to his friend Lynch of the principles and definitions of his esthetic philosophy. He defines pity and terror, the rhythm of beauty; he answers the question "What is art? What is the beauty it expresses?" by saying, "Art is the human disposition of sensible or intelligible matter for an esthetic end." He then defines truth and beauty and states that the form of the art is of major significance.

"The image, it is clear, must be set between the mind or senses of the artist himself and the mind or senses of others. If you bear this in memory you will see that art necessarily divides itself into three forms progressing from one to the next. These forms are: the lyrical form, the form wherein the artist presents his image in immediate relation to himself; the epical form, the form wherein he presents his image in mediate relation to himself and to others; /28/ the dramatic form, the form wherein he presents his image in immediate relation to others. . . . Even in literature, the highest and most spiritual art, the forms are often confused. The lyrical form is in fact the simplest verbal vesture of an instant of emotions, a rhythmical cry. He who utters it is more conscious of the instant of emotion than of himself as feeling emotion." (250-51)

The "instant of emotion, the rhythmical cry"—his poem—follows two and a half pages later. Here in embryo—the statement by Stephen of artistic principles followed by his objectifying them in his poem—is what characterizes the book. Joyce seems to have proceeded from definition—Stephen's—to demonstration—his own.

Before this "rhythmical cry" Stephen had made his choice between the Church and Art, but he had not overtly, publicly done so. To have declined the invitation to join the order did not mean that he was breaking with the Church. It is significant that he does not do so until he has evolved his own statement of esthetic truths. Once he has defined what the artist can and must do, once he has demonstrated to himself that his principles have validity in action—the composition of the lyric, among other things—he is ready for the more vital severing, the cutting off of himself from the Church and his family and his friend Cranly, the "unfrocked priest" who hears confesssions but cannot absolve.

These three "severings" occur in the same scene near the end of the book: Stephen is talking to his friend Cranly, after conversations with others on all subjects relevant to the situation, on Universal Peace, nationalism, and a national language—with cold violence he had told his friend Davin that "Ireland is the old sow that eats her farrow" (238)—on art, truth and beauty, and personal love of women. The scene continues at some length and Stephen is forced to state precisely what his relationship to the church and his family is, whether he loves his mother, etc. This results in Stephen's saying rather sharply,

"I will not serve that in which I no longer believe, whether it call itself my home, my fatherland or my church: and I will try to express myself in some mode of life or art as freely as I can and as wholly as I can. . . . I do not fear to be alone or to be spurned for another or to leave whatever I have to leave. And I am not afraid to make a mistake, even a great mistake, a lifelong mistake and perhaps as long as eternity too." (291-2)

Following this scene, the book consists of six and a half pages of diary entries. These are in the main impersonal, thus conforming to Stephen's observation: "The personality of the artist, at first a cry or a cadence or a mood and then a fluid and lambent narrative, finally refines itself out of existence, impersonalizes itself, so to speak" (252). These diary entries also conform to his conclusion that art progresses from the personal to the impersonal, from first to third /29/ person. The book is indeed a definition by example or a philosophy of art that its central figure espouses.

The entries cover two months and a week. The night after his talk with Cranly, Stephen writes in his diary: "Free. Soul free and fancy free. Let the dead bury the dead. Ay. And let the dead marry the dead."

April 6, he writes: ". . . I desire to press in my arms the loveliness which has not yet come into the world."

Ten days later he writes: "Away! Away!"

The spells of arms and voices: the white arms of roads, their promise of close embraces and the black arms of tall ships that stand against the moon, their tale of distant nations. They are held out to say: We are alone—come. And the voices say with them: We are your kinsmen. And the air is thick with their company as they call to me, their kinsman, making ready to go, shaking the wings of their exultant and terrible youth. (298)

Ten days later, April 26: "Mother is putting my new secondhand clothes in order. She prays now, she says, that I may learn in my own life and away from home and friends what the heart is and what it feels. Amen. So be it" (298). This has the bravado and terrible confidence of youth which knows all the answers. In Stephen's case, he has made an attempt at all the answers relevant to himself, the artist soul awakening to a consciousness of itself, so there is nothing left but to depart and to test in the crucible of himself the values and vision which experience and exceptionally alert and sensitive capabilities have made available to him. For him there is nothing else to say but what he says next:

"Welcome, O life! I go to encounter for the millionth time the reality of experience and to forage in the smithy of my soul the uncreated conscience of my race. *April 27*. Old father, old artificer, stand me now and ever in good stead.'" (299)

His Rebellion may be done, but his Search for and the achievement of form sufficient to forge the uncreated conscience of his race is just begun. The book has become the objectification of an artistic proposition and a method announced by the central character. The book has achieved its form, the most satisfying relations of the intelligible and the sensible, its wholeness, harmony, and radiance. /**30**/

[Stream of Consciousness in the "Portrait"]

MELVIN FRIEDMAN

This loosely autobiographical novel continues the poetic tendency of *The Dead*. It is a kind of lyrical biography, with the structure determined as much by the caprices of the developing sensibility of the artist as by the growth of Stephen Dedalus from infancy to young manhood. There is little in Joyce's previous work to prepare one for the surprising first paragraph, which is not bracketed by quota- /214/ tion marks although it is excerpted from a story being read to the infant, Stephen: ["] Once upon a time and a very good time it was there was a moocow coming down along the road and this moocow that was down along the road met a nicens little boy named baby tuckoo. ["][9] One is aware immediately of Joyce's method. His intention is to quote from the mind of an infant. The style of the remainder of the first chapter parallels Stephen's development from infancy to boyhood. The chapter reads like an extended interior monologue, through the indirect presentation of the third person. One can determine Stephen's age, at a given moment, by the construction of the sentences and by the maturity of the language. Just after his arrival at Clongowes Wood School, there is this passage of reflections of a boy about six or seven:

It would be nice to lie on the hearthrug before the fire, leaning his head upon his hands, and think on those sentences. He shivered as if he had

Melvin Friedman, *Stream of Consciousness: A Study in Literary Method* (New Haven: Yale University Press, 1956), pp. 214-219.
[9] Joyce, *A Portrait of the Artist as a Young Man,* p. 245.

cold slimy water next his skin. That was mean of Wells to shoulder him into the square ditch because he would not swop his little snuffbox for Wells's seasoned hacking chestnut, the conqueror of forty. How cold and slimy the water had been! A fellow had once seen a big rat jump into the scum. Mother was sitting at the fire with Dante waiting for Brigid to bring in the tea. She had her feet on the fender and her jewelly slippers were so hot and they had such a lovely warm smell! Dante knew a lot of things. She had taught him where the Mozambique Channel was and what was the longest river in America and what was the name of the highest mountain in the moon. Father Arnall knew more than Dante because he was a priest but both his father and Uncle Charles said that Dante was a clever woman and a wellread woman. And when Dante made that noise after dinner and then put up her hand to her mouth: that was heartburn.[10]

Until the sentence beginning "Mother was sitting," the thoughts are entirely concerned with a present happening: Stephen's unfortunate encounter with the school bully. Then there is a sudden /215/ change in setting to a moment in the past, occasioned by the child's irresistible impulse to warm himself. This is prepared for by the opening sentence, which expresses the wish realized imaginatively four sentences further on. (Joyce has not yet eliminated the stage directions; one can still follow a clear development in the mind of the monologueur.) The thought of Mother and Dante sitting together extends the digression to Dante's expert tutelage. The comparison between Father Arnall (an instructor at Clongowe's Wood) and Aunt Dante is not quite enough to refocus Stephen's mind on the present situation; in fact, it occasions a further aside about a peculiar characteristic of Dante. The wish fulfillment (to use a favorite expression of Freud) is sufficient in this instance to distract the reverie from the unpleasant encounter. By a series of associations in his mind, Stephen is able to tip the balance in favor of a cherished memory.

The child's sureness with his medium is really the subject of this first chapter. Whenever the young Stephen feels the urge, he can conveniently transplant himself to some moment in the past. Often reality and imagination become hopelessly confused. The thought of returning home for the holidays is sufficient to produce the event in Stephen's reverie: one is convinced that he is at home, until the monologue is suddenly interrupted:

All the people. Welcome home, Stephen! Noises of welcome. His mother kissed him. Was that right? His father was a marshal now: higher than a magistrate. Welcome home, Stephen!

[10] *Ibid.,* p. 249.

Noises . . .
There was a noise of curtain rings running back along the rods, of
water being splashed in the basins. There was a noise of rising and
dressing and washing in the dormitory: a noise of clapping of hands as
the prefect went up and down telling the fellows to look sharp [p. 261].

The transition from the scene created by Stephen's imagination to
the scene of objective detail is cleverly managed by the insertion of
the word "noises" which is part of each tableau. The first chapter is
thus precariously balanced between the conflicting tendencies of
Stephen's mind, now oriented toward the vagaries of the imagina-
/216/ tion, now brought back forcibly to the details of the waking
world. This is the first genuine use Joyce makes of his combined
gifts as poet and novelist. In the first chapter especially he succeeds
in reducing the novel of analysis to an enumeration of the movements of the sensibility.

The opening section of *A Portrait of the Artist as a Young Man*
is written in something very close to the later stream of consciousness method. Indeed there is a resemblance in technique between
these pages and the Nausicaa episodes of *Ulysses*. Both use the device
of indirect interior monologue. Although the writing is entirely in
the third person, there is a genuine attempt, in each instance, to reproduce the mentality of the character. The first chapter of *A Portrait of the Artist* presents Stephen Dedalus as the environment im-
pinges directly on his consciousness; the mind of the infant and
young boy is opened on a strange, very new experience, which his
consciousness does not yet subject to questioning, selection, or judgment.

The following chapters desert this region and rely almost entirely on objective detail. The style changes from the chastened impressionism of the opening pages to a fuller and more rhythmical
prose, which seems much closer to indirect narrative than to stream
of consciousness. In the second chapter Stephen has a fairly lengthy
first-person monologue, which is diligently prefixed by the customary 19th-century apology: "He could scarcely recognise as his his
own thoughts, and repeated slowly to himself:—I am Stephen Dedalus. I am walking beside my father whose name is Simon Dedalus.
We are in Cork, in Ireland. Cork is a city. Our room is in the Victoria
Hotel. Victoria and Stephen and Simon. Simon and Stephen and
Victoria. Names" (p. 342). This reverie is set in relief to the passages of narrative preceding and following it. There is a concerted
effort to distinguish it stylistically from the other writing in the
chapter, which partially explains the reduction of this monologue
to its simplest terms. Stephen's mind, in this instance, is presented

far less complexly than in the first chapter, where the monologues flow more naturally into the narrative passages. The convention of the 19th-century novel of considering the monologue as a nonstructural aside which has to be dispatched artistically with as little pain as /217/ possible seems to be revived here for the last time. The associations, built on a pattern of self-identification, appear oversimplified. Only the final synthesis of the three names is convincing as inner monologue.

Although the style of the novel changes with the increasing maturity of Stephen Dedalus, to make for an interesting fusion between character and design, the method finally sinks into artifice. When the full rhythm of the chapters devoted to adolescence reaches a kind of crescendo in the opulent writing of the final pages of the fourth chapter, the technique seems a trifle forced. This "epiphany" scene, in which the pure fleshly beauty of the bathing girl arouses Stephen's sensuality, is marred by a kind of fin de siècle rhetoric, which seems far removed from the stream of consciousness writing of the opening chapter:

Her bosom was as a bird's, soft and slight, slight and soft as the breast of some darkplumaged dove. But her long fair hair was girlish: and girlish, and touched with the wonder of mortal beauty, her face.

She was alone and still, gazing out to sea; and when she felt his presence and the worship of his eyes her eyes turned to him in quiet sufferance of his gaze, without shame or wantonness. Long, long she suffered his gaze and then quietly withdrew her eyes from his and bent them towards the stream, gently stirring the water with her foot hither and thither. The first faint noise of gently moving water broke the silence, low and faint and whispering, faint as the bells of sleep; hither and thither, hither and thither: and a faint flame trembled on her cheek [p. 432].

The Joyce of *Ulysses* could have intended this passage only as pastiche. Indeed, it reminds one a bit of Gertie MacDowell's flirtation with Bloom, described in terms borrowed from an Ethel M. Dell novel.

The style is redeemed by the sober, almost austere writing of the fifth chapter. This last part is a credo rather than the final stages of the movement of a sensibility. It deserts the biographical framework of the rest of the book. The rigid dialectic of Stephen's aesthetic /218/ doctrine is the structural principle for the concluding section, which is appropriately set at that institution for which Cardinal Newman propounded his *Idea of a University*. This chapter is peculiarly bare of stream of consciousness writing, with the exception of the final pages, which are recorded as a diary. The notation

for April 14, in the purely stylistic sense, is an interior monologue:
"John Alphonsus Mulrennan has just returned from the west of
Ireland. European and Asiatic papers please copy. He told us he
met an old man there in a mountain cabin. Old man had red eyes
and short pipe. Old man spoke Irish. Mulrennan spoke Irish. Then
old man and Mulrennan spoke English. Mulrennan spoke to him
about universe and stars. Old man sat, listened, smoked, spat" (p.
524).

In the last three paragraphs the style changes once more, revert-
ing from the bare, notative kind to the romantic prose of Stephen's
adolescence. The passage is an incantation to Stephen's muse and
reads like a Biblical prophecy:

The spell of arms and voices: the white arms of roads, their promise of
close embraces and the black arms of tall ships that stand against the
moon, their tale of distant nations. They are held out to say: We are
alone—come. And the voices say with them: We are your kinsmen. And
the air is thick with their company as they call to me, their kinsman,
making ready to go, shaking the wings of their exultant and terrible youth.

April 26. Mother is putting my new secondhand clothes in order. She
prays now, she says, that I may learn in my own life and away from home
and friends what the heart is and what it feels. Amen. So be it. Welcome,
O life! I go to encounter for the millionth time the reality of experience
and forge in the smithy of my soul the uncreated conscience of my race.

April 27. Old father, old artificer, stand me now and ever in good
stead [p. 525].

The frequent stylistic changes in *A Portrait of the Artist,* from
the impressionism of infancy through the agonizing of adolescence
to the austere dialectic of young manhood and then back again, prepare for the varying internal rhythm of the episodes of *Ulysses.*
/219/

3. Symbol

[Image and Symbol in the "Portrait"]

WILLIAM YORK TINDALL

A Portrait of the Artist, at once the residence and the creation of
Stephen's nail-paring God, differs from most other novels of adolescence in detachment and method. At first glance, however, Joyce's
/76/ improvement upon the *Bildungsroman* seems simple enough
because the main burden is carried, as in ordinary novels of this
sort, by character and action. We have plainly before us the story
of a sensitive, gifted boy who is disappointed in his hope of communion with parents, country, and religion. Refusing the actual
world at last, as in the role of the Count of Monte Cristo he refuses
the muscatel grapes that Mercedes proffers, he constructs a better
world to replace it. "If you have form'd a circle to go into," says
cynical Blake, "go into it yourself, and see how you would do."

The theme of *A Portrait of the Artist* is normal enough. Joyce
differs from most of his predecessors, as Flaubert from his, in greater
dependence upon image, rhythm, juxtaposition, and tone to supplement the narrative and in giving attitudes and feelings body to support them. What Joyce in his notes for *Exiles* called "attendant
images" could be omitted without destroying the outline of his book,
but some of its quality and depth must be attributed to this accom-
paniment. At times, moreover, forgetting their capacity of attend-
ants, images and other devices become essential and assume the
principal burden as they were to do in *Ulysses*. Yielding place to

William York Tindall, *The Literary Symbol* (New York: Columbia University
Press, 1955), pp. 76-86.

other things at such times, the narrative grows "obscure," a word
which means that narrative has given way to suggestion and discourse to nondiscursive elements having more effect on feeling than
on mind. While still attendant, however, images may be too familiar
or obvious to attract notice. Even Tolstoi used them.

When Vronsky in *Anna Karenina* rides his mare to death at the
races, breaking her back by his awkwardness or zeal, his action, un-
necessary to the plot and far from realistic, embodies his relationship with Anna. But Tolstoi's image of the mare is so narrowly assigned and painfully deliberate that it does little more than discourse could. Joyce's images, though partly assigned, however deliberate, are sug- /77/ gestive, indefinite, and not altogether explicable.
Ambivalent, they reveal not only the quality of experience but its
complexity. Without attendant or essential images, *A Portrait of
the Artist* would be so much less immediate and less moving that
few would pick it up again.

Images play other parts in the great design. Embodying Stephen's
experience before he is entirely aware of it, and doing the same service for us, they prepare for moments of realization, which could not
occur without them. Operating below conscious notice, the images,
rhythms, and other forms project an unconscious process that comes
to light at last. This function is no more important, however, than
that of relating part to part and, composing a structure which, with
the dominant narrative it supplements and complicates, creates
what Stephen calls radiance or the meaning of the composite form.

The first two pages of *A Portrait of the Artist* present the images
that, when elaborated, are to compose the supplementary structure
and take their place in the form. We are confronted here with a
moocow coming down the road, with a rose (maybe green), with
wetting the bed, with a girl, and with an eagle that plucks out eyes—
not to mention a number of other things such as dancing to another's tune. Without much context as yet, these images, acquiring
fresh meanings from recurrence and relationship with others, carry
aspects of Stephen and his trouble. Never was opening so dense as
this or more important.

Take that road, long, narrow, and strictly bounded, along which
comes a moocow to meet the passive boy. Diction, rhythm, and the
opening phrase (the traditional beginning of an Irish "story") suggest the condition of childhood and its helplessness. Confined to the
road, the child cannot escape encounter with a creature traditionally associated with Irish legend and with everything maternal.
Later, /78/ Stephen delights to accompany the milkman in his
round of neighboring roads, although a little discouraged by the

foul green puddles of the cowyard. Cows, which have seemed so beautiful in the country on sunny days, now revolt him and he can look no longer at their milk. Yet as he pursues "the Rock Road," he thinks a milkman's life pleasant enough, and looks forward with equanimity to adopting it as his own. Innumerable connotations of word and phrase make it almost plain at last that the road suggests tradition, that the cow suggests church, country, and all maternal things, and that the milkman suggests the priest. The little episode, far from being a sign of these meanings, is no more than the embodiment of possibilities. What it implies awaits corroboration from later episodes, Stephen's rejection of the priesthood, for example, or his aesthetic query about the man hacking a cow by accident from a block of wood. It is certain that none of these connected images is casual. As for the road itself, it develops into the circular track round which Mike Flynn, the old trainer, makes Stephen run; into the track at Clongowes where Stephen, breaking his glasses, is almost blinded; into the dark road alongside which Davin meets his peasant woman; and, after many reappearances, all of which confirm and enlarge the initial idea and feeling of tradition, into its opposite, the road that promises freedom on the final page.

The images of rose, water, girl, and bird are so intricately involved with one another that it seems all but impossible to separate them for analysis. Take the rose, however, a symbol which, carrying traditional significance, becomes, after much recurrence, Stephen's image of woman and creativity. Lacking sufficient context at its first appearance to have certain meaning, the rose, made green by Stephen, is not altogether without possibilities. Green is the color of Ireland, of immaturity, and of vegetable creation; yet a green rose is un- /79/ natural. Art is unnatural too. Could the green rose anticipate Stephen's immature desire for Irish art? We cannot tell for sure. At school Stephen is champion of the white rose that loses to the red in an academic war of roses; and during his period of "resolute piety" his prayers ascend to heaven "like perfume streaming upwards from a heart of white rose." It is the red rose, however, that attends his creative ecstasies near the Bull Wall, after he resolves to follow mortal beauty, and in bed, after composing a poem. His soul, "swooning into some new world," shares Dante's penultimate vision: "A world, a glimmer, or a flower? Glimmering and trembling, trembling and unfolding, a breaking light, an opening flower, it spread in endless succession to itself, breaking in full crimson and unfolding and fading to palest rose, leaf by leaf and wave of light by wave of light, flooding all the heavens with its soft flushes, every flush deeper than other." This heavenly vision, which follows the hell of the

sermons and the purgatory of his repentance, anticipates his ultimate vision of Mrs. Bloom, the heavenly yet earthly rose of *Ulysses*.

Woman, associated with rose, embodies Stephen's aspiration and,
increasingly, his creative power. Eileen, the girl who appears at the
beginning of the book, unattainable because Protestant, is soon
identified with sex and the Tower of Ivory, symbol of the Blessed
Virgin. Mercedes, a dream who inhabits a garden of roses along the
milkman's road, suggests the Virgin by her name while adding overtones of remoteness, exile, and revenge. At Cork, however, Stephen's
"monstrous" adolescent thoughts injure her purity by desire. When
Emma, a teaser, replaces Mercedes as object of desire and becomes
in addition an image of his mother country and his church, Stephen
transfers his devotion to the Virgin herself, over whose sodality he
presides, and whose "office" becomes his formula. The wading girl
near the Bull Wall, who embodies mortal beauty, unites all previous sugges- /80/ tions. Associating her with Emma, the Virgin, the
rose, and the womb of the imagination, whose priest he becomes, he
finds her an image of his own capacity: "Heavenly God!" his soul
exclaims, its eye no doubt upon himself. His repeated "Yes" anticipates Mrs. Bloom's as the girl, stirring the waters "hither and
thither," anticipates the hither and thithering waters of Anna Livia
Plurabelle: "He would create."

Other women take their place in the great design. There is the
common girl, persisting in memory, who stops Stephen on the street
to offer flowers for which he cannot pay. Connected in his mind with
a kitchen girl who sings Irish songs over the dishes, she develops
near the end into the servant maid, who, singing "Rosie O'Grady"
in her kitchen, proffers the suggestion at least of Irish flowers, green
roses perhaps. Cranly's *"Mulier cantat"* unites her in Stephen's
mind with "the figure of woman as she appears in the liturgy of the
Church" and with all his symbolic women. Unprepared as yet to receive what she proffers in her song or unable to pay the price of acceptance, Stephen says, "I want to see Rosie first."

That Rosie, another anticipation of Mrs. Bloom, sings in a
kitchen is not unimportant. After each of his ecstasies, Stephen
comes back to the kitchen, which serves not only as an ironic device
for deflating him but as an image of the reality to which, if he is to
be an artist, he must return. It is notable that his acceptance of Mr.
Bloom and the communion with mankind that precedes the vision
of Mrs. Bloom takes place in a kitchen. Rosie in her kitchen, the last
great image of woman in *A Portrait of the Artist,* unites the ideal
with the actual. Neither the wading girl nor Mercedes, both ethe-
real, can present to Stephen the idea and feeling of a union which

someday he will understand. Far from seeing Rosie first, he sees her last, but by her aid, of which he is not fully aware as yet, he comes nearer his vision /81/ of above and below, of heavenly roses to be sure but of roses in kitchens.

Woman is not only rose but bird and sometimes bat. The bird, which makes its first appearance as the eagle who is to punish Stephen's guilt by making him blind as a bat, makes its next appearance as Heron, who, looking and acting like a bird of prey, tries to make Stephen conform. Bad at first, birds become good as Stephen approaches mortal beauty at the beach. He thinks of Daedalus, "a hawklike man flying sunward," and wants to utter cries of hawk or eagle, images no longer of oppression but, retaining authority, of creation. The wading girl is "a strange and beautiful seabird." "Her bosom was as a bird's, soft and slight, slight and soft as the breast of some dark-plumaged dove." As Stephen observes their flight, birds also become what he calls a "symbol of departure or loneliness." When, becoming birdlike Daedalus, he takes flight across the sea to exile, he unites all these meanings and confirms their association with water. Bats are anticipated by images of blinding, not only those of the eye-plucking eagle, of glasses broken on the track, and of dull red blinds that keep light from boys of Belvedere during their retreat but that of the woman into whose eye Mr. Casey spits: " 'Phth! says I to her.' 'O Jesus, Mary and Joseph!' says she . . . 'I'm blinded and drownded . . . I'm blinded entirely.' " When they appear at last, bats gather up these anticipatory associations with woman, custom, and country. Davin's peasant woman at her door along the dark lonely road seems to Stephen "a type of her race and of his own, a batlike soul waking to the consciousness of itself in darkness and secrecy and loneliness." Seeming almost a bird for a moment, Emma, revisited, becomes another bat, but its darkness, secrecy, and loneliness connect it with himself as artist about to try silence, exile, and cunning. Blind to reality as yet, he may improve. Like the images of /82/ bird and flower, the bat is ambivalent, not only bad but good. If bat suggests things as they are, and bird things as they ought to be, it is the artist's job to reconcile them. If all these women are aspects of woman, and if woman is an aspect of himself, the creative part, he too is presented by images of bird, bat, and, besides these, water.

Ambivalent from the first, water is either warm or cold, agreeable or frightening. The making of water at the beginning of the *Portrait* seems an image of creation that includes the artist's two realities. At school Stephen is shouldered into the "square ditch," square not because of shape but because it receives the flow of the urinal or "square." Plainly maternal by context, this image warns Stephen of the perils of regression, to which like one of those rats who enjoy the ditch, he is tempted by the discomforts of external reality. The "warm turf-coloured bogwater" of the bath adds something peculiarly Irish to his complex. Dirty water down the drain at the Wicklow Hotel and the watery sound of cricket bats (connected in his mind with pandybats and bats) confirm his fears. The concluding image of the first chapter, assigned only by previous associations, embodies his infantile career: "Pick, pack, pock, puck," go the cricket bats, "like drops of water in a fountain falling softly in the brimming bowl." If Stephen himself is suggested by this bowl and his development by an ablaut series, water is not altogether bad. This possibility is established toward the middle of the book, where changing character, water becomes good on the whole and unmistakably a symbol of creation. On his way to the beach, Stephen still finds the sea cold and "infra-human." The bathing boys repel him, but the sight of the wading girl gives water another aspect. Rolling up his trousers like J. Alfred Prufrock, he himself goes wading. From that moment of baptism and rebirth inaudible music and the sound of waters attend his creative ecstasies. It is true that, relapsing a little, /83/ Stephen fears water again in *Ulysses,* but Mr. Bloom, with whom he finally unites, is a water lover, and Anna Livia Plurabelle is the river Liffey.

These families of developing images that, supplementing the narrative, give it texture, immediacy, and more body are not the only symbolic devices Joyce commands. As we have noticed, large parallels, rhythms, shifts of tone, juxtaposition, and all else that Flaubert commended complicate the "significant form." But deferring these, I shall confine myself in this place to some of the relatively unassigned and unattached images that concentrate feeling at important points.

Consider, fot example, the opening of the second chapter. Uncle Charles, who is addicted to black twist, is deported to the outhouse, whence rising smoke and the brim of his tall hat appear as he sings old songs in tranquillity. Position gives this image an importance that import cannot justify. Hints of exile, creation, and piety, all relevant to the theme, may divert our understanding without satisfying it entirely. Few of Joyce's images are so mysterious as this and, while occupying our feelings, so resistant to discourse. The scenery at Cork appeals more readily to the understanding. While in that town with his father, Stephen finds in the word "Foetus," carved in the wood of a desk, what Eliot would call an objective correlative of the "den of monstrous images" within him. After this corroboration of inner disorder, he emerges from schoolroom into the sunny street where he sees cricketers and a maid watering plants; hears a German band and scale after scale from a girl's piano. In another book this urban noise and scenery might serve as setting alone. Here, more functional than that, it presents a vision of the normal, the orderly, and the quotidian from which the discovery of his monstrous interior has separated him. /84/

Characters are no less symbolic. The two dwarfish eccentrics that Stephen encounters, one on the street and the other in the library, seem caricatures of Stephen's possible future and of the soul of Ireland, but aside from that, they evade significance. By action, speech, and context, on the other hand, the figure of Cranly becomes more nearly definite. That last interview which drives Stephen to exile concentrates in Cranly the forces of admission, submission, confession, and retreat, and he becomes the embodiment of all that has plagued the imperfect hero. Cranly's preoccupation with a book called *Diseases of the Ox* adds to the picture. Since Stephen as "Bous Stephanoumenos" has been identified with the ox, Cranly's devotion to his book reveals him as Stephen's most reactionary critic, not, as we had supposed, his friend.

When Stephen turns seaward toward his great experience with the wading girl, an image which might escape casual notice not only suggests the finality of his action but adds to our understanding of his complexity: he crosses the bridge from Dollymount to the Bull. Readers of *Dubliners* may recall that crossing bridges in that work is as portentous as Caesar's crossing of the Rubicon; in *Ulysses* Stephen, a frustrated exile back from Paris, is "a disappointed bridge." In the *Portrait,* on the bridge which marks his passage from old custom to freedom and the waters of life, he meets a squad of uncouth, tall-hatted Christian Brothers, marching two by two, going the other way. Their direction, their appearance, and their regimentation are important, but what reveals Stephen's character is the contempt with which he regards those who are socially and intellectually inferior to Jesuits. The episode, therefore, includes both his escape from one tyranny and his submission to another, the greater tyranny of pride, which, until he understands the Blooms, will keep him from uniting the regions of reality by art. Stephen may think of charity or /85/ Joyce talk of pride, but this revealing episode contributes more than all that talk or thought to the portrait of an artist.

The writer of this kind of novel, says E. M. Forster, "is not necessarily going to 'say' anything about the universe; he proposes to sing." His song—and Forster has both Melville and Lawrence in mind—must "combine with the furniture of common sense." In *Aspects of the Novel*, where this reflection appears, Forster excludes Joyce from the great company to which he himself belongs. Rejecting symbolist as a term for it, he prefers prophetical. "A prophet does not reflect," he says. "That is why we exclude Joyce. Joyce has many qualities akin to prophecy and he has shown (especially in the *Portrait of the Artist*) an imaginative grasp of evil. But he undermines the universe in too workmanlike a manner, looking around for this tool or that: in spite of all his internal looseness he is too tight, he is never vague except after due deliberation; it is talk, talk, never song." As for *Ulysses,* it is "a dogged attempt to cover the universe with mud," an "epic of grubbiness and disillusion," and "a simplification of the human character in the interests of Hell." It seems a pity that one great symbolist cannot comprehend another, but the Irish Sea is wider than it looks and considerably deeper. /86/

4. Motif

[Motif in the "Portrait"]

Hugh Kenner, in his excellent article, "The Portrait in Perspective," points out that the motifs introduced on the first page or so of the book contain the germ of all that Joyce had to say in *A Portrait* and in each of his subsequent novels.[30] To trace one of these motifs in its various appearances through the book should demonstrate its value in cementing together the often discontinuous narrative blocks.

Joyce introduces the motif on page two:

When they were grown up he was going to marry Eileen.
He hid under the table. His mother said:
—O, Stephen will apologise.
Dante said:
—O, if not, the eagles will come and pull out his eyes.—

> Pull out his eyes,
> Apologise,
> Apologise,
> Pull out his eyes.[31]

Thus, even in early childhood, Stephen is revealed as guilty of an unspecified crime possibly related to sex (". . . he was going to marry Eileen") or to religion (Eileen is a Protestant) or simply to disobedience of constituted authority (his mother and his governess). Authority demands that he admit the alleged error of his way or suffer the painful consequences. In this first reference to the motif, as Kenner mentions, Prometheus is undoubtedly suggested: first, be-

Marvin Magalaner and Richard M. Kain, *Joyce: The Man, the Work, the Reputation* (New York: New York University Press, 1956), pp. 112-19, 325-26.

cause of his awful torment at the hands of the authority he had defied (Stephen's eyes are more vulnerable than his liver, so the Pro-
methean punishment undergoes alteration); second, because in
/112/ stealing fire from the gods, Prometheus performs literally
Stephen-Joyce's later act of taking creative inspiration from its mysterious source. So much for the initial statement of the motif.

Only two paragraphs later, a variation of the motif is presented.
Stephen, at Clongowes, is questioned by an older boy, Nasty Roche:

> What is your name?
> Stephen had answered: Stephen Dedalus.
> Then Nasty Roche had said:
> —What kind of a name is that?
> And when Stephen had not been able to answer Nasty Roche had asked:
> —What is your father?
> Stephen had answered:
> —A gentleman.
> Then Nasty Roche had asked:
> —Is he a magistrate?[32]

This sharp question and answer routine, suggesting in its definite-
ness a familiar catechism, reinforces the motif of apology for a hazy
guilt that outsiders feel Stephen ought to exhibit. Always troubled
by questions about his father in later boyhood, he is even at this
early period brought to the point at which he must remain silent or
confess that his father is not what he might be—a keenly felt reflection on the young boy himself. It is interesting, considering Joyce's
care in selecting names for his characters, that Roche ("rock," in
French) may well represent the church here putting the questions—
and a "Nasty" Roche at that.

Several pages further on, Stephen again feels a sense of sin and
guilt when questioned by Wells on whether he kisses his mother
every night before he goes to bed. The "other fellows" laugh when
he says that he does and redouble their laughter when, in confusion, he says that he does not. Once more, the little boy feels guilty
when society singles him out for questioning, scorn, and ridicule. He
"blushed under their eyes" and wondered, "What was the right answer to the question? He had given two and still Wells laughed." In
the climactic scene of Chapter 1, Stephen is questioned by Father
Dolan, here the actual representative of the Catholic Church, and
then punished for a crime of which he is innocent—a crime, to reinforce the motif, that involves punishment for having weak eyes.
/113/ When summoned from his seat in the classroom to be beaten
by Dolan, Stephen stumbles, "blinded" by fear and haste. At the
blow of the pandybat upon his hand, "A cry sprang to his lips, a

prayer to be let off. But . . . he held back the hot tears and the cry that scalded his throat." Stephen, the embryo artist and rebel, will not "Apologise" even when the world seeks to "Pull out his eyes." Stephen kneels on the floor, ironically out of fear and pain inflicted by the father rather than from adoration. He has not knuckled under to the pressures of his hostile environment.[33]

Numerous further instances of the pervasiveness of this motif might be adduced, but two or three additional examples should suffice. In high school at Belvedere, Stephen's schoolmates twit him about his ascetic ways, his father, and his girl friend. When he does not readily confess his latest love affair, he is playfully hit with Heron's cane until he jestingly recites the *Confiteor* to the reiterated beat of the admonition, "Admit." These same "friends" belabor him, more in seriousness than in jest, for refusing to allow, in a literary catechism, that "Byron was no good." Again he is tormented, like St. Stephen by the mob, for sticking to his beliefs. Again, the refrain is "Admit." To avoid an open clash, he is forced to confess his error in theology on an English composition, when questioned by Mr. Tate. Most dramatic, perhaps, is Stephen's confession to the old priest of his sins of the flesh—a terrified outburst occasioned by the long, dreadful sermon on Hell, which develops in macrocosm the motif of "Apologise/Pull out his eyes" enunciated in microcosm at the beginning of *A Portrait*.[34]

With powerful motifs such as this—or the theme of mother-lover-church or exile and flight or the religion of art and the dedication of the artist—running through the book to give it substance and form, there is little need for the step-by-step nursing that Galsworthy or Arnold Bennett so skillfully supplied for their readers. Relatively few in *A Portrait,* and comparatively simple, these themes increase and multiply, twine and intertwine, to form the narrative meshes of *Ulysses* and the *Wake*. The intellectually apprehended motifs of his *Portrait* become the elaborate musical and rhythmical and multi-leveled symbolic fabric of Joyce's maturer works.

Yet it is not too much to say that even in *A Portrait,* as in *Dubliners*—both preparatory exercises for the books to follow—the au-/114/ thor left little to chance. The marks of his consummate control are evident in every line. From the name of Betty Byrne (compounded of Elizabeth as mother of John the Baptist and of Byrne, real name of Cranly, who in *A Portrait* is identified as the precursor)[35] to the characterization of Simon Moonan as toady, no name or fact seems too unimportant to escape Joyce's obsession for total relevance. One case in point demonstrates how this compulsion may work toward the strengthening of a key motif.

Near the end of Chapter 2 of *A Portrait,* Joyce makes the offhand remark that with "the money of his [school] prizes," Stephen Dedalus "led a party of three or four to the theater to see . . . *The Lady of Lyons.*"[36] This is the first and last mention of Bulwer-Lytton's play in the book, although the name of the main character of the romance appears once, two pages farther on.[37] A synopsis of the plot of this casually mentioned play gives little hint of the use to which it is to be put by Joyce. Pauline Deschappelles, a proud beauty, scorns marriage for money or for the sake of acquiring a title. Her rejected suitors plot to humble her by tricking her into marriage with a social inferior, Claude Melnotte, the son of a gardener. Melnotte, just returned from Paris where his father's legacy has allowed hm to learn Latin, dancing, fencing, and the other arts, is the darling of the village. Though he wears fine clothes and looks like a prince, he hides his love for Pauline because he is conscious of his social handicap as a gardener's son. He watches his unattainable heroine from afar, sends her flowers anonymously, and finally dares to send her his poetry, which she rejects violently.

Insulted, Claude joins the conspiracy to force Pauline to wed beneath her station. She falls into the trap, but before the marriage his true love for her makes him unwilling to carry the plot to its end. His cohorts, the rejected suitors, insist, and the two are joined. Pauline discovers the fraud, spurns his attentions, and is allowed to retain her virtue. After several further turns of the plot, Claude goes off to battle to forget his part in the shameful affair. He returns rich and powerful several years later to find Pauline about to marry one of the suitors in order to save her father from bankruptcy. Having made his fortune in the wars, Claude is able to pay the debt, save his love from a fate worse than death, take revenge on the wicked suitors, and carry off the prize as the curtain comes down.
/115/

This is as unlikely a story with which to fortify a motif as one can find for an author who, above all, abhorred the sentimental and the banal. But just as Joyce found use in the Nausicaä episode of *Ulysses* for such a mood as a foil for the contrasting mood of Leopold Bloom, so in *A Portrait* Bulwer-Lytton's play has its appropriate place.[38]

Joyce had used the motif of the unworthy adolescent lover before in the "Araby" story of *Dubliners.*[39] There the boy narrator watches his beloved from afar, not daring to submit the ideality of his illusion to the soiled world of reality. In that story also there is the desire to bear gifts to his love—to seek adventure so that he may be worthy. In "Araby" Joyce hints at the ideal love of Dante for the ideal abstraction of Beatrice.

In *A Portrait,* the motif suggested by *The Lady of Lyons* is subordinate to, but on a plane parallel with, the theme of *The Count of Monte Cristo.* The latter serves as one of the unifying threads of the impressionist narrative. Its motif deserves separate treatment, which cannot be offered here except in brief allusion. Stephen is shown poring over a "ragged translation of *The Count of Monte Cristo,*"[40] which stamps firmly in his mind the "figure of that dark avenger" and of his secret lover, Mercedes, always pictured thereafter as standing in a garden. Stephen's adolescent identification with this avenging shadow, with this heroic lover-adventurer, leads to childish fantasies in which he sees himself a dignified and proud lover, able to refuse with haughtiness and restraint the tribute of Mercedes, "who had so many years before slighted his love." He revels in his imaginary response, "Madam, I never eat muscatel grapes."[41] The restlessness induced by the drab routine of growing up in Dublin sends him "wandering in the evening from garden to garden in search of Mercedes."[42]

The reinforcement of the Monte Cristo theme by *The Lady of Lyons* motif is clear. In both, and for all of Joyce's adolescent heroes, there is the unapproachable heroine against a background of gardens and flowers; the lover whose sense of inferiority prevents him from speaking out; the eventual acquiring of polish, of Continental culture and wealth (or the hope of such acquisition); the turning of the tables that gives the mature lover the opportunity to show his /116/ true worth by rescuing the now chastened heroine from difficulty and to "play the dark avenger" to his enemies.

It is obvious that Joyce expected such parallels as have been pointed out to be apparent to his readers. Both the play and the book enjoyed wide popularity among the middle classes in the nineteenth century. An indication of his being able to take this for granted is offered by the casual mention of Bulwer-Lytton's hero, Claude Melnotte, with no further reference to the source from which the hero was being drawn:

Only at times, in the pauses of his desire, when the luxury that was wasting him gave room to a softer languor, the image of Mercedes traversed the background of his memory. He saw again the . . . garden of rosebushes . . . and he remembered the sadly proud gesture of refusal which he was to make there, standing with her in the moonlit garden after years of estrangement and adventure. At those moments the soft speeches of Claude Melnotte rose to his lips and eased his unrest. A tender premonition touched him of the tryst he had then looked forward to and, in spite of the horrible reality which lay between his hope of then and now, of the holy encounter he had then imagined at which weakness and timidity and inexperience were to fall from him.[43]

It is also apparent how inextricably bound up are the two motifs in Joyce's own mind, so that Melnotte and Monte Cristo are interchangeable symbols of a state of feeling.

These "soft speeches" of Claude Melnotte offer considerable further reasons for Joyce's selection of *The Lady of Lyons* as the play to which Stephen, in *A Portrait,* should take his parents and friends. Claude's mother in the play, suspicious of her son's cultural acquisitions from the Continent and of his unorthodox artistic bent, nags him constantly to abandon the ways of the artist and return to honest, normal, lucrative pursuits:

> Leave glory to great folks. Ah! Claude, Claude! Castles in the air cost a vast deal to keep up! How is all this to end? What good does it do thee to learn Latin, and sing songs, and play on the guitar, and fence and dance, and paint pictures? All very fine; but what does it bring in?[44]

Though slightly more florid than the speeches of Stephen's mother, bidding him beware of dangerous authors like Ibsen and urging him to accept a job in Guinness' respectable brewery, these quoted /117/ remarks in the play must have carried a familiar note to mother and son. And Claude's "soft" answer is, though embroidered and dated, what we should have expected Stephen to say:

> Wealth! wealth, my mother!—wealth to the mind—wealth to the heart—high thoughts—bright dreams—the hope of fame—the ambition to be worthier to love Pauline.[45]

Melnotte's passion for Pauline follows the same pattern as Stephen's for his succession of dream lovers. First he wrestles with an inferiority complex: "Even from this low cell, poverty,—I lift my eyes to Pauline and forget my chains." Then follows the association of the loved one with flowers. "Thou knowest not that for the last six weeks I have sent every day the rarest flowers to Pauline; she wears them. I have seen them on her breast. . . ." Finally, emboldened by apparent success, Melnotte, like Stephen, composes poetry for the lady: "I have now grown more bold—I have poured my worship into poetry—I have sent my verses to Pauline—I have signed them with my own name."[46] Moreover, while Stephen ordinarily does not take overt action to achieve his aim in love, and therefore feels himself defeated, Melnotte, because he takes the step, is rejected utterly.

Yet, despite Joyce's deliberate emphasis on these superficial similarities, Stephen certainly is following a path basically different from the one traversed by such romantic heroes as Melnotte. The irony of the surface comparison, as Professor Charles Anderson has pointed out to the present writer, is underlined by the dissimilar character of their respective dream worlds. Melnotte can push his luck, can hope eventually to get the girl of his feverish dreams, the *ne plus ultra* of his worldly hopes. For Stephen the dream world is dissipated even as it takes form. The woman figure, whether Mercedes or another, is unattainable both as a flesh and blood person and as symbolic representation of the church, beckoning him to intimate communion through the sacramental "muscatel grapes," which he must refuse.

Melnotte, Dante, Stephen, Joyce, Monte Cristo—all these figures merge at times, at other times stand apart and operate separately to achieve the literary ends of the author. The story of Stephen's boyhood could have been told without the frequent iteration of /118/ parallel motifs. The recognition of such motifs, however, affords to the reader a control of the narrative, both intellectual and emotional, impossible in single-leveled fiction. Understanding this, Joyce strives to make every word count, both for itself and for the surrounding context. /119/

[30] In *Two Decades*, ed. Givens, p. 137. /325/

[31] Joyce, *A Portrait*, p. 2.

[32] *Ibid.*, p. 3.

[33] *Ibid.*, pp. 10, 52-54.

[34] *Ibid.*, pp. 85-91.

[35] This ingenious explanation is offered by Dr. Julian Kaye in an article to be published shortly in *Modern Language Notes*.

[36] Joyce, *A Portrait*, p. 110; Sir Edward Bulwer-Lytton, *The Lady of Lyons: or Love and Pride: A Play in Five Acts* (New York, 1846).

[37] Joyce, *A Portrait*, p. 112; I am indebted to Dr. Julian Kaye, who identified Claude Melnotte for me as the hero of the play.

[38] Joyce, *Ulysses*, pp. 340-76.

[39] Joyce, *Dubliners*, pp. 33-41.

[40] *A Portrait*, p. 68.

[41] *Ibid.*

[42] *Ibid.*, p. 73.

[43] *Ibid.*, pp. 111-12.

[44] Bulwer-Lytton, *The Lady of Lyons*, p. 16.

[45] *Ibid.*, pp. 16-17.

[46] *Ibid.*, p. 17. /326/

5. Language

James Joyce: A Study in Words

JOSEPH PRESCOTT

In the beginning was the Word . . .

The writings of Joyce show a progression from an early interest in words through a mature use of them to the excessive fondness of old age. In spite of variation from one work to another, the development is not always consistent and steady; sometimes there is a reversion to a former phase, sometimes an advance into a future phase. The direction, however, is unmistakable.

Joyce's writings give themselves readily to such analysis, because Stephen Dedalus, "the unnamed narrator of the first three studies in *Dubliners*,"[1] the chief character in *A Portrait of the Artist as a Young Man*,[2] and one of the chief characters in *Ulysses*,[3] is James Joyce recollected in tranquility. The danger of indiscriminately identifying even an autobiographical character with its creator is obvious. Usually the author and the character, although two aspects of the same personality, are still two aspects. In words, however, it is not only unwarrantable to distinguish the experiences of the two, it is impossible. Joyce has transformed his life into his art, and, since far and away the most revered thing in his life is the Word, he has put into his art not only his use of words but also his experiences with them and his speculations on these experiences.

In early childhood, when Stephen was being taught the law of the apology, words already formed patterns in his mind.

Joseph Prescott, "James Joyce: A Study in Words," *PMLA*, LIV (Mar., 1939), 304-07. One stylistic change affecting one sentence and one typographical correction have been made at Professor Prescott's request.

[1] Frank Budgen, *James Joyce and the Making of* ULYSSES (New York, 1934), p. 57.—Cf. *Dubliners* (New York, 1926), Introduction by Padraic Colum, pp. viii-ix.

[2] New York, 1928.

[3] New York, 1934.

His mother said:
—O, Stephen will apologise.
Dante said:
—O, if not, the eagles will come and pull out his eyes.—

> Pull out his eyes,
> Apologise,
> Apologise,
> Pull out his eyes.
>
> Apologise,
> Pull out his eyes,
> Pull out his eyes,
> Apologise.[4]

Stephen's reaction is primarily to sound. This is probably true for most of us. Words begin as sounds and end as symbols. While we are /304/ growing into articulation, gradually the representative quality of words supersedes in importance their significance as sound. We cease to trouble ourselves about their success as echoes, and speak, as Seán O'Faoláin says, "not so much in words as by means of words."[5] But this boy continued to be sensitive to their sound, to find in them experiences that shed light on their accepted, dictionary meaning, and to enrich their meaning with the color of his own personality.

At first they stir his memory: "That was a belt round his pocket. And belt was also to give a fellow a belt."[6] A boy at Clongowes is called the prefect's suck, and Stephen ponders:

Suck was a queer word . . . But the sound was ugly. Once he had washed his hands in the lavatory of the Wicklow Hotel and his father had pulled the stopper up by the chain after and the dirty water went down through the hole in the basin. And when it had all gone down slowly the hole in the basin had made a sound like that: suck. Only louder.[7]

And a little later, baffled by the equivocal attitude of his school-fellows to kissing one's mother, Stephen remembers: "His mother put her lips on his cheek; her lips were soft and they wetted his cheek; and they made a tiny little noise: kiss."[8]

The sounds of words fascinate the future artist before they breed in him emotions. The prefect of studies is called Dolan, and to Ste-

---

[4] *Portrait*, p. 2.
[5] Seán O'Faoláin, "The Cruelty and Beauty of Words," *Virginia Quarterly Review*, IV (April, 1928), 221.
[6] *Portrait*, p. 3.
[7] *Ibid.*, p. 6.
[8] *Ibid.*, p. 11.

phen, fresh from a "hot burning stinging tingling" encounter with him, "it was like the name of a woman who washed clothes."[8a]

As the boy grows older, words come to fill him with strange sensations. The age of the narrator in the first stories of *Dubliners* is not clear, so that one cannot correlate exactly his reactions there with those in the *Portrait*, but the same preoccupation is recorded:

Every night as I gazed up at the window I said softly to myself the word paralysis. It had always sounded strangely in my ears, like the word gnomon in the Euclid and the word simony in the Catechism.[9]

Similar thoughts and feelings move the boy throughout his adolescence. It is noteworthy, however, that his artistic yearnings are almost completely submerged during one phase of his religious experience. In all the section of the *Portrait* describing Stephen during the retreat, there is only a single remark on a single word,[10] and that comes so near the beginning of the retreat that it seems to be no more than an isolated instance of perseveration. The incubus of sin crushes every impulse of the artist, stifling, shrivelling. "His soul traversed a period of desolation /305/ in which the sacraments themselves seemed to have turned into dried up sources."[11] Only after the deflation of his emotional religiosity, induced in him by the retreat, does Stephen the "fearful jesuit,"[12] as he was later to be called, give way to Dedalus the artist. After a violent swing toward faith, there is an equally violent rebound in the direction of disbelief, and Stephen passes "beyond the challenge of the sentries who had stood as guardians of his boyhood and had sought to keep him among them that he might be subject to them and serve their ends."[13]

With his entry into the university Stephen gives full rein to his artistic inclinations. He plays on words as on the strings of a delicate instrument, he listens intently for all the overtones, he lives almost exclusively in a world of word-sensations.

He drew forth a phrase from his treasure and spoke it softly to himself:
—A day of dappled seaborne clouds.—
The phrase and the day and the scene harmonised in a chord. Words. Was it their colours? He allowed them to glow and fade, hue after hue: sunrise gold, the russet and green of apple orchards, azure of waves, the

[8a] *Ibid.*, p. 60.
[9] *Dubliners*, p. 7.
[10] *Portrait*, pp. 126-127.
[11] *Ibid.*, p. 176.
[12] *Ulysses*, p. 5.
[13] *Portrait*, p. 191.

greyfringed fleece of clouds. No, it was not their colours: it was the poise and balance of the period itself. Did he then love the rhythmic rise and fall of words better than their associations of legend and colour? Or was it that, being as weak of sight as he was shy of mind, he drew less pleasure from the reflection of the glowing sensible world through the prism of a language manycoloured and richly storied than from the contemplation of an inner world of individual emotions mirrored perfectly in a lucid supple periodic prose.[14]

The young artist is groping for the precise source of the power which words wield over him, but it eludes him. He can only fore-know as matter of fact that at various stages of his morning walks across the city the spirits of Hauptmann and Newman and Caval-canti and Ibsen will rise in his soul, each with emotions after its kind.

And now we come to a new phase in the development of Joyce. Gradually a mysterious unrest has seeped into his soul, poisoning his pleasure with disillusion. Words became "emptied of instantane-ous sense until every mean shop legend bound his mind like the words of a spell and his soul shrivelled up sighing with age as he walked on in a lane of dead language."[15] Slowly and vaguely the young Dedalus has become aware of an insufficiency in the language. He suffers the

> Blank misgivings of a Creature
> Moving about in worlds not realized.

Accepted forms of expression no longer represent life for him fully. And /306/ the feeling is heightened by the fact that Stephen's edu-cation in his most formative years had been steeped in a forgotten past.

... it wounded him to think he would never be but a shy guest at the feast of the world's culture and that the monkish learning in terms of which he was striving to forge out an esthetic philosophy, was held no higher by the age he lived in than the subtle and curious jargons of heraldry and falconry.[16]

Again the single word takes hold of him when he discusses with the English dean of studies the use of *tundish*. The young Irishman envies his instructor for having the tradition of English as a heritage while for himself it is only an acquisition. "His language, so familiar and so foreign," Stephen considers, "will always be for me an ac-

[14] *Ibid.*, pp. 193-194.
[15] *Ibid.*, pp. 207-208.
[16] *Ibid.*, p. 209.

quired speech. I have not made or accepted the words. My voice holds them at bay. My soul frets in the shadow of his language.—"[17]

Allowing for the adolescent tragedy with which the young man laments his fate, it is evident that Stephen, Joyce, did experience dissatisfaction with accepted forms of speech from an early period in his linguistic career. He himself probably never dreamt to what lengths that unrest would go. Nor could he have foreseen that he was himself to go through a process of growth in the language, of creation, and ultimately of dissolution. In the *Portrait* he is still moving in a world of conventional language. His interest in its words revolves chiefly about their onomatopoeic associations and their effect upon his spirit. He is now, too, pondering the notion of an esthetic. He is groping toward the "system" that is to inform his art with a rigidity which finally undoes it. Closely allied to his speculations about words, Joyce's theory of art dominates his use of them in his best work, *Ulysses*.

. . . and the Word was with God . . .

The *Portrait* describes Joyce's linguistic childhood, in which he is gathering strength for *Ulysses,* the production of his manhood. Now Joyce has got, created anew, the Word "with Jehovah" (and is beginning to raise Cain with the language). /307/

[17] *Ibid.*, p. 221.

6. The Sermons

Joyce's Hell-Fire Sermons

ELIZABETH F. BOYD

The central portion of Joyce's novel *A Portrait of the Artist as a Young Man* contains the story of the three-day retreat at the Jesuit school, Belvedere College, in Dublin. The main feature of the retreat is the four sermons on the Last Things delivered by Father Arnall, Stephen Dedalus's former master from the Clongowes Wood school. These sermons stand out, especially the latter two on hell and its pains, as brilliant compositions in a style distinctly different from the surrounding text. They seem like a verbatim report of actual sermons.

A comparison of these sermons, ostensibly composed by Joyce, with other versions in the long tradition of meditations based on S. Ignatius Loyola's *Spiritual Exercises,* reveals Joyce's debt to earlier writers and throws an interesting light on the novel. /**561**/

My search for a possible source or sources of the sermons in *A Portrait* began, naturally, with the "old neglected book written by Saint Alphonsus Liguori, with fading characters and sere foxpapered leaves," which Joyce mentions as in Stephen's possession after the retreat.[1] Liguori's *Visits to the Most Holy Sacrament,* prob-

Elizabeth F. Boyd, "Joyce's Hell-Fire Sermons," *Modern Language Notes,* LXXV (Nov., 1960), 561-71.

[1] James Joyce, *A Portrait of the Artist as a Young Man* (Modern Library ed.), p. 176. Kevin Sullivan, in *Joyce Among the Jesuits* (New York, 1958), pp. 138-141, suggests *The Sodality Manual* as a source of Father Arnall's sermons, as well as of the events of the retreat and its aftermath. The passages from the *Manual* which Sullivan parallels to the sermons indicate, as he points out, that this portion of the *Manual* belongs to the tradition of the *Spiritual Exercises* and is a cognate version, if not the primary source, of Joyce's work. It may well have been the first version that Joyce read, but I doubt that it was the last.

ably the work Joyce refers to, has appeared in many editions, and, as is customary with these devotional works, it is usually bound up with others by the same author. I have seen one edition which contains at the end Liguori's *Maxims of Eternity: or Mediations for Every Day in the Week*.[2] This is the eighteenth century Redemptorist Father's version of the traditional meditations; it covers, like Joyce's sermons, the prescribed outline of ideas and similar images and examples, but its style is gentle, polite, and abstract, quite unlike the brilliance and vigor of Joyce.

Liguori's sources, however, proved to be more rewarding. The traditional formula based on Loyola's work was brought to a peak of elaboration and refinement in the seventeenth century by several Italian Jesuit fathers noted for their eloquence as preachers. Giovanni Battista Manni (1606-1682) is the earliest in this series. His *Quattro Massime di Christiana Filosophia* (1643), many times reprinted, appeared in Latin in 1645 and in English, with the subtitle "Drawn from four Considerations of Eternitie," in 1675. Manni's *Four Maxims* was reprinted in Dublin in 1823 as a 55-page tract, and an Irish translation by James Scurry, published in 1820 (second edition in 1825), contained "An Introduction to the Irish Language for the use of Persons desirous of learning their Vernacular Tongue, without the aid of a Teacher." This is the kind of tract Joyce might have picked up in his efforts to learn Irish during his University period.[3] /562/

From Manni's pen, the tradition passed to Father Paul Segneri the Elder, Manni's coeval, who brought out in four volumes *La Manna dell' Anima (The Manna of the Soul)*, between 1673 and 1680, consisting of meditative exercises for every day in the year and some extras for special saints' days and "movable feasts"—an immensely long, repetitive work that nevertheless enjoyed some success. For a century or more it was republished at rather frequent intervals. However, the more popular works in the tradition were those quarried out of it by Father Paul Segneri the Younger (nephew of the author of *La Manna dell' Anima*) and by Father Giovanni Pietro Pinamonti, his faithful companion during twenty-six years of apostolical activity. Segneri the Younger's *Meditations*

---

[2] *Visits to the Most Holy Sacrament,* trans. from the Italian. . . . By a Catholic Clergyman (New York, n.d.). An edition that Joyce more probably knew is that by the Rev. Joseph Curr (Dublin, 1840), which does not contain the *Maxims of Eternity.*

[3] Another English translation of Manni's *Maxims* appeared in London in 1877, and besides there are versions in German, French, Dutch, Greek, Armenian, Spanish, Portuguese, Turkish, Polish, etc., and constant reprintings in Italian and Latin. I have read a Portuguese version in microfilm. /562/

for Each Day in a Week was naturally much more usable than his uncle's year-long meditations, and was frequently translated and re-edited up until the end of the eighteenth century. But Pinamonti's tracts, drawn from the same source, bear the prize for frequent re-printing and new editions. The most popular—his *True Wisdom,* his *Undeceiving Mirror,* and his *Hell Opened,* each containing meditations for a week—occupy pages and pages of bibliographical listing in the *Bibliothèque des écrivains de la Compagnie de Jésus* (1895, VI, 763-791).[4]

These constitute at least some of the vast tribe of devotional pamphlets and books from which the Redemptorist Father Liguori's *Maxims* inherited. What the relations are among all the versions of the Ignatian traditional formula it is beyond my power to say. But as between Manni, Father Segneri the Elder, Pinamonti, and Ligu-ori, the text of Pinamonti's *Hell Opened* is not only the most effec-tive rendering but much the closest version to Joyce's. The hell-fire sermons in *A Portrait* are so like it in outline, order, substance, ex-amples, and phrasing, that Pinamonti's little book appears to be Joyce's principal source. What Joyce seems to have done in his hell-fire sermons is to have condensed Pinamonti's pamphlet to about half its size by skipping elaborations and citations from Scripture and the Church Fathers and by mingling paraphrase with quota-tion. Since /563/ space does not permit a detailed comparison, a few typical extracts are reproduced below and commented upon.

From *L'Inferno aperto* . . . (1735), pp. 14-15:

E' vero, che sarà quivi il fuoco, ma vi sarà spogliato di luce. . . . con un miracolo tutto contrario a quello operato già nella Fornace di Babilonia; metre ivi dal comandamento di Dio fu tolto al fuoco l'ardore, e lasciato il lume; e nell'Inferno al fuoco sarà tolto il lume, e lasciata la vampa. Oltre a ciò essendo il medesimo fuoco acceso nel zolfo, avrà una luce pallida, e mesta; e questa stessa mescolata col fumo di quell'incendio, volgendosi, e rivolgendosi giù, e sù, empirà tutto il voto di quella Grotta, e formerà una procella di tenebre, conforme a cio, che sta scritto: *Hi sunt, quibus procella tenebrarum servata est in aeternum. Jude* 13. Finalmente la medesima moltitudine de' Corpi ammontati farà buona parte di quella

---

[4] Ten Italian editions of *L'Inferno aperto* (*Hell Opened*) are listed, after the first edition of 1688, up to 1842. The first English translation, of 1715, con-tains seven engravings by Van der Gucht, and was reprinted in London in 1845, and Derby, 1846. Other translations are listed in German, French, Latin, modern Greek, Dutch, Portuguese, and Basque, on through the nineteenth century. The editions I have used are: *L'Inferno aperto al Cristiano perchè non v'entri ovvero considerazione delle pene infernale,* dal P. Gian Pietro Pinamonti (Rome, 1735), and *Hell Opened to Christians* (London, 1845, and Indianapolis, 1886). /563/

notte orrenda; non rimanendo ivi quasi nulla d'aria, o d'altra cosa trasparente. . . . E se fra tutti i castighi dell' Egitto, alle tenebre sole si diede nome d'orribili . . . , che nome daremo noi a quelle tenebre, che non durano tre giorni soli, ma durano sempre?

From *Hell Opened* . . . (1845), pp. 8-9:

. . . there will be fire but deprived of light. . . . by a contrary miracle to what was wrought in the Babylonian furnace, for there, by the command of God, the heat was taken from the fire, but not the light or brightness; but in hell the *fire will lose its light, but not its heat.* Moreover, this same fire burning with brimstone will have a searching flame, which being mingled with the rolling smoke . . . will . . . raise a storm of darkness. . . . [This phrase, quoted from St. Jude, is a cliché of the formula.] The same mass of bodies heaped on one another . . . make up a part of that dreadful night; not a glimpse of transparent air. . . . Among all the plagues of Egypt, if darkness alone was called horrible; what name shall we give to that darkness, which is not to last for three days only, but for all eternity!

From Joyce, *A Portrait* . . . (Modern Library ed.), p. 137:

. . . For, remember, the fire of hell gives forth no light. As, at the command of God, the fire of the Babylonian furnace lost its heat but not its light so, at the command of God, the fire of hell, while retaining the intensity of its heat, burns eternally in darkness. It is a neverending storm of darkness, dark flames and dark smoke of burning brimstone, amid which the bodies are heaped one upon another without even a glimpse of air. Of all the plagues with which the land of the Pharaohs was smitten one plague alone, that of darkness, was called horrible. What name, then, shall we give to the darkness of hell which is to last not for three days alone but for all eternity?

In the above extract, on the fire of hell, Joyce's language uses active verbs in the first two sentences where the Italian, as is customary, uses passive ("sarà spogliato," "fu tolto . . . e lasciate," etc.), and Joyce /564/ repeats the phrase "at the command of God." Both changes tend to underline the personal responsibility of the Deity for this hellish torment. In Joyce's third sentence ("It is a neverending storm . . ."), besides shortening and simplifying, Joyce has tripled the idea of darkness; and with greater clarity and emphasis, he divides in two sentences the last idea, comparing hell with Egypt's night. In all, Joyce's shorter passage uses "darkness" four times and "dark" twice—a rhetorical emphasis that is absent from the Italian passage.

From *L'Inferno aperto* . . . (1735), pp. 83-87:

Considerazione VI. . . . Per l'Estensione delle pene. Considerate, che in questa vita se bene l'Uomo è capace di molti mali, non è però di tutti capace ad un tempo; perche quì un male corregge l'altro; e due Veleni compongono talora un Rimedio. Ma nell'Inferno sarà tutto il contrario, le pene si daranno ivi la mano. . . . e come di tutti i Sensi, e di tutte le Potenze si sono abusati per peccare, meritano in tutti i Sensi, e in tutte le Potenze d'esser puniti con tanti dolori. . . . Per tanto oltre a ciò, che s'è considerato sin'ora intorno a' Sensi esterni, le Potenze interiori come più perfette, così anche più capaci di duolo, saranno più tormentate. La Fantasia sarà sempre afflitta con immaginazioni spaventose. . . . L'appetito sensitivo ondeggerà come in un flusso, e riflusso, anzi come in un continuo naufragio di tedi, d'agonie, di rabbie, d'angustie. . . . L'intelletto loro sarà pieno d'orribili tenebre interiori, più che di tenebre esteriori n'è la loro Prigione. . . . La volontà sarà ostinata nella sua malizia, senza che mai in tutto lo spazio interminabile degli anni eterni abbia ad avere un minimo movimento verso l'onesto; anzi sempre aggiungendo peccati a peccati. . . . [Here Pinamonti takes two pages trying to express what Joyce sums up as scarcely to be realized.] Pp. 90-92: Per l'Intensione. . . . L'Inferno . . . è il Centro di tutti i mali. Per tanto come le cose, che stanno nel loro Centro, vi si ritrovano forti più, che mai altrove, e con tutte le loro qualità nell'ultimo grado, ed intensione; cosi i mali, che saranno nell'Inferno, vi saranno non solo senza numero molti, ma anche senza paragone intensi, e puri. Quivi primieramente le pene non averanno alcun contrario, che l'addolcisca, e le mitighi. . . . In oltre i beni stessi ivi si convertiranno in male; la compagnia, che altrove è sollievo de' Miseri, ivi sarà un sommo aggravio; la luce, che altrove è sì bella, ivi sarà più odiata delle medesime tenebre: la cognizione, che altrove tanto ricrea con la scienza, ivi sarà più tormentosa dell'ignoranza. . . . In questa vita presente i dolori o non son lunchi, o non son grandi; perchè la natura vi fa l'abito, e gli vinci, o cade sotto il peso, e rimane estinta. . . . Ma nell'Inferno sono regole al tutto opposte; mentre ivi i dolori saranno sempre in uno stato medesimo intollerabili per l'intensione, interminabili per la durazione, non alleggerendosi col tempo il patire, ne consumandosi dal tempo i Pazienti . . . mantenuti sempre non solo vivi ad un modo, ma vivaci, affinchè sentano la loro miseria, e non possano distorgliesene, nè pure un momento. . . . Così richiede la Maesta Divina oltraggiata da' Peccatori, così domanda il Sangue di Gesù Cristo calpestato; così vuole il Paradiso disprezzato, e posposto ad un fra /565/ cidume. La Divina Giustizia, che è nutrice, e riparatrice dell' onor divino, prende a vendicar questi torti, e a farsi conoscere quella, ch'ella è.

From *Hell Opened* . . . (1845), pp. 50-53:

Sixth Consideration . . . On Account of the Extension of the Pains of Hell. Consider, That man, in this life, though he be capable of many evils, he is not capable of them all at once; because here one evil corrects the other, and one poison oftentimes drives out another; but in hell it will be quite contrary; for pains there will lend each other a fresh sting. . . . Moreover, . . . as the internal powers are more perfect, so they are more capable of pain. . . . The fancy will always be afflicted with frightful imaginations . . . the sensitive appetite will . . . be . . . always sinking

into agonies, into rage and anguish. . . . Their understanding will be filled
with interior darkness, more terrible than the exterior, which fills their
prison. . . . Their will will be obstinate in malice, without being able,
during the whole endless space of eternal years, to have the least inclination to good, but continually adding malice to malice. . . .

Pp. 55-57: On Account of the Intenseness. . . . hell . . . is the centre of
all evils: and as all things are found to be much stronger in their centre
than elsewhere, . . . so the evils that are in hell, will not only be many
without number, but intense without comparison, and pure without mixture. Pains in this place will have no contraries to temper and soften
them. . . . Moreover, things that are otherwise good in themselves in this
place become bad. Company, which elsewhere is a comfort to the afflicted,
will here be their greatest trouble: the light which, in other places, is so
much coveted will be hated here more than darkness itself. Knowledge,
which in this world does so much delight, will be there more tormenting
than ignorance. . . . In this present life our sorrows are either not long
or not great: because nature either overcomes them by habits, or puts an
end to them by falling herself under their weight. . . . But in hell the
rules are quite contrary, for the pains there will always continue in the
same state; intolerable as to the intenseness, and endless as to duration.
. . . As there is nothing moderate in the torments, so there is no rest in the
tormented, who are continually kept, not barely alive, but in their full
senses, to have greater feeling of their misery, from which they cannot
so much as for one moment depart. . . . It is what the divine majesty,
injured by sinners, requires; it is what the blood of Christ, that is
trampled upon, demands; it is what heaven itself, despised and postponed
to filth and corruption, would have.

From Joyce, *A Portrait* . . . (Modern Library ed.), pp. 149-151:

The next spiritual pain to which the damned are subjected is the pain
of extension. Man, in this earthly life, though he be capable of many evils,
is not capable of them all at once inasmuch as one evil corrects and
counteracts another, just as one poison frequently corrects another. In
hell, on the contrary, one torment, instead of counteracting another, lends
it still greater force: and, moreover, as the internal faculties are more
perfect than the /566/ external senses, so are they more capable of suffering. Just as every sense is afflicted with a fitting torment so is every
spiritual faculty; the fancy with horrible images, the sensitive faculty with
alternate longing and rage, the mind and understanding with an interior
darkness more terrible even than the exterior darkness which reigns in
that dreadful prison. The malice, impotent though it be, which possesses
these demon souls is an evil of boundless extension, of limitless duration,
a frightful state of wickedness which we can scarcely realise unless we bear
in mind the enormity of sin and the hatred God bears to it.

Opposed to this pain of extension and yet co-existent with it we have
the pain of intensity. Hell is the centre of evils and, as you know, things
are more intense at their centres than at their remotest points. There are

no contraries or admixtures of any kind to temper or soften in the least the pains of hell. Nay, things which are good in themselves become evil in hell. Company, elsewhere a source of comfort to the afflicted, will be there a continual torment: knowledge, so much longed for as the chief good of the intellect, will there be hated worse than ignorance: light, so much coveted by all creatures from the lord of creation down to the humblest plant in the forest, will be loathed intensely. In this life our sorrows are either not very long or not very great because nature either overcomes them by habits or puts an end to them by sinking under their weight. But in hell the torments cannot be overcome by habit, for while they are of terrible intensity they are at the same time of continual variety, each pain, so to speak, taking fire from another and re-endowing that which has enkindled it with a still fiercer flame. Nor can nature escape from these intense and various tortures by succumbing to them for the soul is sustained and maintained in evil so that its suffering may be the greater. Boundless extension of torment, incredible intensity of suffering, unceasing variety of torture—this is what the divine majesty, so outraged by sinners, demands, this is what the holiness of heaven, slighted and set aside for the lustful and low pleasures of the corrupt flesh, requires, this is what the blood of the innocent Lamb of God, shed for the redemption of sinners, trampled upon by the vilest of the vile, insists upon.

Whether Joyce used the Italian original of Pinamonti or the English version, granting that he used either, is hard to determine. Maybe he used both, but it seems more probable that he translated and adapted directly from the Italian. For instance Joyce renders the idiom "si daranno ivi la mano" as "lends . . . still greater force," which is closer than the English version's "lend . . . a fresh sting." In the last sentence of the first paragraph of the above extract, Joyce evades the awkwardness of the literal English translation, "Their will will be obstinate," which he shifts in order to "The malice, impotent though it be." The sentence in the Italian beginning "e come di tutti i Sensi" is represented out of order in Joyce's text. This kind of minor transposition occurs rather frequently and, in my observation of cribbing, is a fairly customary trick. There is a good deal of trans- /567/ position in the second paragraph of the above passage, the paragraph on the intensity of hell's pains, though every item appears in Joyce that is in Pinamonti. The most striking changes are the order of "Company," "Knowledge," and "Light" in Joyce, as opposed to "Company," "Light," and "Knowledge" in Pinamonti; and, in the grand climax of the paragraph, the order runs in Joyce from "the divine majesty" and "the holiness of heaven" to "the blood of the innocent Lamb of God," a much more ironic arrangement and phrasing than Pinamonti's.

The following final set of extracts compares the less picturesque language of Manni's *Four Considerations on Eternity* (the sequel of his *Four Maxims*),[5] in a typical passage on the endlessness of eternity, with the vivid imagery on the same subject in Pinamonti and Joyce. Manni's extract may stand also for the phrasing of Fathers Paul Segneri the Elder and the Younger and Father Liguori, who all follow his version quite faithfully.

From Manni, IV. Eternity of Hell:

In thought sever from eternity a hundred thousand years, or a thousand million of ages—thinkest thou that one jot is taken from eternity? Take again thousands of millions—hast thou found the Alpha, not to say the Omega, of eternity? Take again as many millions of ages as there are stars in heaven, drops of water in the sea, and motes in the air, and particles of dust in the earth—dost thou suppose thou hast diminished one moment from eternity? It remains as entire, in height, length, depth, and breadth, as immeasurable, as interminable, as infinite as it was before, so much so that if God were to propose this offer to the Lost, that the whole space between earth and heaven should be nothing else than the finest sand, and that every hundred thousand million of ages an angel should come and take away a grain, and that when the last grain of sand should be taken away after the course of that unimaginable period of ages, then their pains should have no end, those unhappy souls would esteem themselves blessed at hearing this sentence, and scarce would feel that torment of intolerable pain.

From Pinamonti, *L'Inferno aperto* . . . (1735), p. 108:

Facciam dunque così: questo Monte sì smisurato si raddoppi tante volte, quante sono le arene del mare, le foglie degli alberi, le piume degle uccelli, le squamme de' pesci, i peli degli animali, gli atomi dell' aria, le gocciole /568/ dell'acqua, che son piovute, e pioveranno dal Cielo sino all' estremo. . . . E pure se io, e voi . . . passeremo tutti quest' anni essendo finiti . . . senza che si diminuisca per un' istante l'Eternità. . . . Voi dite che il pensare attentamente all' Eternità sarebbe perdere il cervello.

From Joyce, *A Portrait* . . . (Modern Library ed.), pp. 151-152:

Now imagine a mountain of that sand . . . multiplied as often as there are leaves in the forest, drops of water in the mighty ocean, feathers on birds, scales on fish, hairs on animals, atoms in the vast expanse of air: and imagine that at the end of every million years a little bird came to that mountain and carried away in its beak a tiny grain of that sand. . . .

---

[5] Contained in Pinamonti, *The Art of Knowing Ourselves: Or, the Looking-Glass which does not deceive*, trans. by the Author of St. Willibrord (London, 1877), pp. 77-97. A brief preface to Manni's part of the work states that "These four Considerations on Eternity, composed by Father John Baptist Manni, of the Society of Jesus, were first printed at Venice at the request of the Princess Mary Gonzaga of Mantua, to be distributed for the good of souls. They were afterwards reprinted at Rome, in 1673. . . ."

Yet at the end of that immense stretch of time not even one instant of eternity could be said to have ended . . . even then, at the end of such a period, after that eon of time the mere thought of which makes our brain reel dizzily, eternity would have scarcely begun.

If one reads the whole passage in Joyce, it is interesting to see that he has taken the hint of the Angel and the grain of sand, which appears in Manni and other versions but not in Pinamonti, and has transformed it into the "endless story" formula. But it is disappointing to discover that Pinamonti, and not Joyce, appears to be the originator of those exquisite additions to the frequently used formula of "leaves on trees, sands of the sea, atoms of air, and stars of the sky," namely, "feathers on birds, scales on fish, and hairs on animals." I had been treasuring this extension of the formula as evidence of Joyce's tongue-in-cheek relish for the naïveté of the physical description of eternity. But there they are—feathers, scales, and hairs—in Pinamonti, and in that order. It does not seem possible that coincidence or the accidents of inspiration can account for such faithful repetition.

Joyce does make some additions, either his own, or derived from some other versions of meditations on the four last things that I have not yet encountered. For instance, where Pinamonti simply advises considering the stench of hell owing to its "foul, confined air," and makes no elaboration, Joyce writes four emphatic sentences imagining it (pp. 137-138), beginning "Imagine some foul and putrid corpse. . . ."[6] A similar revolting addition in Joyce's sermons, though /569/ more brief, is appended to Pinamonti's physical description of the damned soul and body burning as a self-contained furnace —boiling blood, brains, heart, and bowels—to which Joyce adds "the tender eyes flaming like molten balls."[7] Usually, however, Joyce's

[6] Cf. Joyce's limerick, in a letter to Ezra Pound, April 9, 1917, in *Letters of James Joyce,* ed. Stuart Gilbert (New York, 1957), p. 102:

> There once was a lounger named Stephen
> Whose youth was most odd and uneven.
>   He throve on the smell
>   Of a horrible hell
> That a Hottentot wouldn't believe in.

[7] *A Portrait,* p. 139. Stanislaus Joyce, in *My Brother's Keeper* (New York, 1958), p. 82, recalls a sentence from "the Lenten sermons preached by Father Jeffcott," which is matched by a sentence in Joyce's sermons in *A Portrait,* p. 153, beginning "They reason thus because they are unable to comprehend. . . ." This sentence does not appear in Pinamonti, though the opening of Joyce's paragraph ("Yes, a just God! Men, reasoning always as men, are astonished that God should mete out an everlasting and infinite punishment in the fires of hell for a single grievous sin.") matches almost exactly the opening sentence of Pinamonti's: "E' Giusta. 3. Considerate che gli Uomini discorrendo sempre da Uomini, rimangono

brief additions are rhetorical, that is, sentences needed to keep the ideas clear and emphatic; he makes a practice of summarizing in a sentence or two at the end of a paragraph before passing on to the next point.

One of Joyce's material additions is suggestive. The phrase "time shall be no more," quoted from *Revelation,* ch. 10, is part of the formula in all versions, but Joyce lets it read: "Time is, time was, but time shall be no more!" Can this be a naughty allusion to the utterance of the brazen head in *Friar Bacon and Friar Bungay?* Joyce's vision of eternity in hell (pp. 152-153) in the paragraph following the passage quoted above, which he attributes to "a holy saint (one of our own fathers . . .),'' and in which eternity is likened to the ceaseless ticking of a clock repeating "ever, never," may have come from L. A. Muratori's edition of Paul Segneri the Younger's *Spiritual Exercises* or from Liguori's *Preparation for Death;* but the phrase—"ever, never,"—is the theme of Manni's *Four Maxims,* and has been often imitated. Only Pinamonti does not stress it.

These are the most striking deviations in Joyce's sermons on hell from the contents and order of Pinamonti's *L'Inferno aperto.* More typically, the differences simply consist of Joyce's omitting the prolixities of the Italian.

Since Joyce appears to have based his hell-fire sermons so closely on the seventeenth century Jesuit Father's meditations, there is some significance for interpreting *A Portrait of the Artist as a Young Man.* In the first place, there is no scandal of plagiarism involved. Pina- /570/ monti's pamphlet is not copyright material; it is one version of a long series of re-writings of the same material, and Joyce may well not only be excused for adding still another version without acknowledging his sources, but even be congratulated for having written the definitive, ultimate form.

In the second place, Joyce did not care a rap about technical plagiarism and probably would have welcomed identification of his source. Surely he would have expected someone to notice that he was relaying a seventeenth century text, especially since those little tracts had been so frequently reprinted in all the languages of Europe. He probably wanted his borrowing to be recognized, for it is a kind of

---

talora stupiti, che Dio ad una colpa sì breve di un peccatore, abbia stabilita una pena sempiterna nel fuoco. . . ." Pinamonti's paragraph rambles on in a legalistic proof of the infinite justice of God towards the infinite malice of sin which is the same in purport as Joyce's vehement sentence, but lacks its sting of absurdity. Louis Golding, in *James Joyce* (London, 1933), p. 57, among the few commentators on Joyce's hell-fire sermons, has noted the paradox of saying that the omnipotent God *could not* do something that the preacher did not wish Him to do.

silent comment on the unyielding traditions of the type of Catholicism he grew up with, toward which he maintained all his life the ambivalent attitude of admiration and rejection.

The third chapter of *A Portrait* is the story of young Stephen Dedalus's encounter with the full force of that Catholic tradition. It helps the emotional intensity and the logic of the story that the Church should present hell fire in this classic form. It is not some modern, lukewarm, parochial version that Stephen must face, but the great tradition of the Church in full armor at greatest intensity. This is what Stephen, the martyr of a heretical faith, and Dedalus, the crafty artist, must defeat with his own cunning and integrity. His evasion and defiance are made much more dramatic by enhancing the power of the tradition he is challenging.

The whole novel, *A Portrait of the Artist,* is a moulding of actualities into the form of art, and the Irish Jesuits are also to be represented here, faithfully, but idealized in art, by a transcript from their own traditional writings. In the surviving fragment of *Stephen Hero,* Stephen cries: "Can we not root this pest out of our minds and out of our society that men may be able to walk through the streets without meeting some old stale belief or hypocrisy at every street corner? I, at least, will try. . . ."[8] The retreat chapter in *A Portrait* constitutes an effective attack by Joyce, all the more so because he denies himself any ostentatious caricature, sneering, or facetiousness, maintaining instead a dignified solemnity, which is in keeping with Stephen's honest experience, and above all using an actual Jesuit document. /571/

[8] *Stephen Hero,* ed. Theodore Spencer (London, 1944), p. 209.

7. Christian Myth

Who Is Betty Byrne?

JULIAN B. KAYE

Joyce's autobiographical novel *A Portrait of the Artist as a Young Man* begins with a story which Simon Dedalus tells his infant son Stephen.

> Once upon a time and a very good time it was there was a moocow coming /93/ down along the road and this moocow that was down along the road met a nicens little boy named baby tuckoo. . . . [Spaced period are Joyce's.]
> His father told him that story: his father looked at him through a glass: he had a hairy face.
> He was baby tuckoo. The moocow came down the road where Betty Byrne lived: she sold lemon platt.[1]

The careful reader observes that Mr. Dedalus is telling the story as an answer to the child's question: "Where did I come from?" Moreover, he identifies the cow as Stephen's mother. The same careful reader, however, if he does not know that names are very important to Joyce, is likely to dismiss "the road where Betty Byrne lived" as just a detail improvised by Stephen's father to add verisimilitude to the tale. Nevertheless, this phrase is very important in that it adds a mythic dimension to the story and relates it to one of the most important themes in the novel.

In order to understand the significance of this phrase, the reader must possess a seemingly irrelevant piece of information—namely, that the original of the character Cranly in *A Portrait* is J. F. Byrne.

Julian B. Kaye, "Who Is Betty Byrne?" *Modern Language Notes*, LXXI (Feb. 1956), 93-95.

[1] P. 1. All citations of *A Portrait of the Artist as a Young Man* refer to the Modern Library edition (New York, 1928).

a college friend of Joyce's.[2] Then he must realize that Stephen conceives of himself as playing the role of Jesus to Cranly's John the Baptist.

Cranly is identified as the son of "Elizabeth and Zacchary. Then he is the precursor. Item: he eats chiefly belly bacon and dried figs. Read locusts and wild honey. Also, when thinking of him, saw always a stern severed head or death mask as if outlined on a grey curtain or veronica" (p. 293). Moreover, Stephen looks upon Cranly as a confessor, as someone with whom he can discuss his mission.

Stephen himself is marked as a sacrifice—as St. Stephen, the first Christian martyr, and as "Bous Stephanoumenos! Bous Stephaneforos!" (p. 195)—i.e., the sacrificial cow bearing the Divine Power and also bearing the crown of martyrdom. He refuses to acknowledge his putative father, Simon Dedalus, as his real father and instead invokes Dedalus the fabulous artificer—archetype of the artist—as his progenitor.[3] Moreover, Stephen records the following remarks in his notebook: "*March 24.* Began with a discussion with my mother [named Mary].[4] Subject: B. V. M. Handicapped by my /94/ sex and youth. To escape held up relations between Jesus and Papa against those between Mary and her son" (p. 294).

Stephen is comparing his relationship to his parents with that of Jesus to Mary and Joseph. In an argument with Cranly, Stephen likens his own refusal to make his mother happy by taking the Eucharist at Easter to Jesus' refusal to permit his mother to turn him from his duty.[5] Finally, in the course of expounding his esthetic theories to Lynch, Stephen compares the successful artist to God (p. 292).

But what is the relevance of all this to Betty Byrne? Betty Byrne's Christian name must be Elizabeth. She is therefore the mother of Cranly (J. F. Byrne) and of John the Baptist. Furthermore, as I said above, "the moocow" is Stephen's mother, whose name happens to be Mary. In other words, the first three paragraphs of *A Portrait,*

[2] See J. F. Byrne, *Silent Years* (New York, 1953).

[3] Pp. 294, 299 et al. See also *Ulysses.*

[4] It is true that James Joyce's mother was named Mary, but Joyce renamed, in *A Portrait* and *Ulysses*, almost all his friends and relatives. The fact that he retained his mother's Christian name unchanged seems to indicate that he found it suitable for the role he had assigned her.

[5] Pp. 285-6. The incident in the life of Jesus to which Stephen refers is described in Luke ii. 45-50 (all Biblical citations refer to the Authorized Version). In this passage there is "a discussion" between Mary and Jesus: ". . . and his mother said unto him, Son, why hast thou thus dealt with us? behold, thy father and I have sought thee sorrowing."

"And he said unto them, How is it that ye sought me? wist ye not that I must be about my Father's business?"

for all their baby talk, are, on one level of meaning, a recapitulation of Luke's story of the Annunciation and of the subsequent visit paid by Mary to her cousin Elizabeth. "And the angel departed from her. And Mary arose in those days, and went into the hill country with haste, into a city of Juda; and entered into the house of Zacharias ['where Betty Byrne lived'], and saluted Elisabeth" (Luke i. 38-40).

Thus Joyce makes the mythic identification of Stephen with Jesus and Cranly with John the Baptist part of Stephen's earliest memory—or, to be more exact, of what seemed to the adult Stephen to be his earliest memory.

One phrase remains unexplained. Why does Joyce say that Betty Byrne "sold lemon platt"? I can say only that I am looking forward to finding out. Meanwhile I console myself with the probably apocryphal remark attributed to Joyce: "I expect my readers to devote their lives to the study of my work." /95/

The Sacrificial Butter

C. G. ANDERSON

Between the writing of *Stephen Hero* and the conception of *A Portrait of the Artist as a Young Man* James Joyce epiphanized his esthetic. The *Stephen Hero* fragment contains most of the matter of Chapter V of the *Portrait,* and it contains most of the esthetic theory of the *Portrait* as a whole; what it lacks is the technique of arranging non-discursive symbols in such a way that they evoke directly feelings which cannot be expressed discursively. It is by means of this technique that Joyce presents the life of the young artist as a complete, harmonious, radiant image—as ". . . that thing which it is and no other thing."[1] (250)[2]

As we know from *Ulysses* and *Finnegans Wake* Joyce was fond of subtly explaining his own methods to the reader. In the *Portrait* he gives the key to the technique by pointing out that Cranly is John the Baptist: The exhausted loins are those of Elizabeth and Zachary. Then he is the precursor. Item: he eats chiefly belly bacon and dried figs. Read locusts and wild honey." (293)

But, as will be shown, it is clear from Joyce's handling of Cranly, who is not only John the Baptist but also Judas and Satan, that he did not intend to produce an allegory. In everything he wrote after *Stephen Hero* he treated his subject symbolically. The distinction is, /3/ as Yeats says in *Ideas of Good and Evil,* that while "a symbol is indeed the only possible expression of some invisible essence . . . allegory is one of many possible representations of an embodied thing, or familiar principle, and belongs to fancy and not to imagination: the one is a revelation, the other an amusement." Neverthe-

C. G. Anderson, "The Sacrificial Butter," *Accent,* XII (Winter, 1952), 3-13.

[1] Cf. *Stephen Hero,* pp. 211-213. St. Thomas' *claritas,* Hopkins' inscape, and Joyce's epiphany seem to be of a piece.

[2] Page references in parentheses are to *A Portrait of the Artist as a Young Man,* New York, The Modern Library, 1928.

less, on the reader's part some allegorizing is neccessary if he is to understand how a symbolic work achieves its effect.

Chapter V of the *Portrait* is controlled by three principal symbols: the Daedalus myth; the poet as God—creator, redeemer, and priest; and the betrayal-crucifixion. In addition to subsuming many lesser symbols, these three are themselves related. While Icarus in the Daedalus story is an analogue for the flight of the artist from home, nation, and church into exile, "old father, old artificer" Daedalus corresponds to God the Father and Creator. God the Father is united with Christ the Son, who as the Word joins in creation and as the first priest becomes a creator in Joyce's special sense. Christ the Creator as a young man, is betrayed and crucified in a way which corresponds to the betrayal of the artist as a young man by his family, his national society, and his church. Since the Daedalus element has been, in general, clear from the beginning, this article will examine only the second and third of these principal symbols.

1

Stephen's exposition of his esthetic to Lynch in Chapter V is the intellectual climax of the novel. Stephen is here an ordained priest of art proclaiming the gospel of art. As he says of himself, he is ". . . a priest of eternal imagination, transmuting the daily bread of experience into the radiant body of everliving life." (260) But to understand his priesthood, we must understand his conversion and baptism.

When, in Chapter IV, the director of University College suggests that Stephen consider becoming a Jesuit, Stephen decides that he will ". . . never swing the thurible before the altar as priest." (188) But later, as he walks along the beach, he hears ". . . the call of life to his soul not the dull gross voice of the world of duties and despair, not the inhuman voice that had called him to the pale service of the altar." (197) He is born again, and his soul arises from the ". . . grave of boyhood, spurning her graveclothes." (197) He feels that his calling and election are sure, and he immediately accepts his vocation: "Yes! Yes! Yes! He would create proudly out of the freedom and /4/ power of his soul . . . a living thing, new and soaring and beautiful, impalpable, imperishable." (197)

Stephen is baptized by wading in the sea, and he feels the regenerative power of the sacrament. He feels ". . . a new wild life . . singing in his veins" (197) and wonders, "Where was his boyhood now? Where was the soul that had hung back from her destiny to brood alone upon the shame of her wounds . . ?"[3] (197)

---

[3] During his baptism Stephen sees the wading figure of a girl—symbol of the fleshly beauty to which he has been converted, and symbol of Emma—on whom

At the opening of Chapter V Stephen already has passed from baptism through ordination, and is saying mass. Contrasting with the Shelleyan swoon of the baptism and its ecstatic aftermath in the final pages of Chapter IV, the first sentence of Chapter V is a rhetorical change of pace:

He drained his third cup of watery tea to the dregs and set to chewing the crusts of fried bread that were scattered near him, staring into the dark pool of the jar. (202)

Important as this deflation is to the stylistic structure of the novel, however, the sentence is at least as important because it introduces the symbol of the eucharist—specifically, as we shall see, of the eucharist in the Maundy Thursday Mass. The tea and bread are paralleled by the cocoa which Stephen drinks with Bloom in the cabmen's shelter and at 7 Eccles Street in the Eumaeus and Ithaca episodes of *Ulysses*. After Stephen has consumed his breakfast of bread and tea (read bread and wine), he takes up ". . . idly one after another the blue and white dockets. . . ." (202) of his pawn brokers. These represent the communion wafers. After he has fingered them, he puts them aside and gazes ". . . thoughtfully at the lid of the box [i.e., the tabernacle] speckled with louse marks." (202) Then his sister Maggie, representing the acolyte of the mass, prepares the water for the purification of his fingers, a ceremony which follows directly after the second ablution in the mass.

As is usual with Joyce, things are not so simple as they appear at second glance. Stephen's mother washes his neck. Because the reader already knows that Stephen has abhorred water since childhood and has lice (202, 275), he realizes at once that this is a rather singular endeavor; it is not an ordinary Ordinary of the mass, but one which /5/ no doubt has its Proper of the Season. What this Proper is, however, and what symbolic meaning it has, is discovered more gradually. Although Joyce knows very well what day it is, Stephen and the reader do not learn that it is Thursday until Stephen reads a newsagent's placard as he walks to school. (206) Thursday is the day which Stephen in his earlier Catholic fervor had dedicated to the Most Blessed Sacrament.[4] (170) And later, when Stephen refers to St. Thomas' *Pange lingua gloriosi*, he mentions to Lynch, who

---

". . . an emerald trail of sea-weed had fashioned itself as a sign upon the flesh." (199) Because she is baptized—chosen and marked with the sign—he sees her as a bird capable of flying with the "hawklike man," (264) although ultimately she becomes the "batlike soul" (259) who cannot soar with Icarus.

[4] It is also Bloomsday on June 16, 1904, and the day on which black masses are traditionally performed. There is no indication, however, that the mass in the *Portrait* is black.

knows the fact as well as he does, that it is "a hymn for Maundy Thursday." (246) The Maundy Thursday Communion Verse, which follows the Purification in the order of the mass liturgy, says that ". . . the Lord Jesus, after He had supped with His disciples, washed their feet." Stephen ". . . allowed his mother to scrub his neck and root into the folds of his ears and into the interstices at the wings of his nose," (203) and we are reminded that Peter, in the Maundy Thursday Gospel, when he consents to Christ's washing him at all, says, "Lord,, not my feet, but my hands also, and my head"[5]

After Stephen as priest has purified his fingers, his mother as server thrusts ". . . a damp overall into his hands, saying:—Dry yourself and hurry out for the love of goodness." (203) The overall, which represents the priest's napkin, is damp at the Purification because it has already been used in the Washing-of-the-Hands ceremony during the Offertory of the mass. The hurry and the return of Stephen's sister ". . . making signs to him to be quick and go out quietly by the back" (203) suggests the hustle of the final portion of the mass. Stephen gives the Benediction by ". . . smiling and kissing the tips of his fingers in adieu." (204) But at least two other meanings are compressed into this single ironic action. It is the priest wiping his lips and the priest kissing the altar before he pronounces the Benediction.[6]

As Stephen leaves the house he hears the mad nun in the nearby asylum screech, "Jesus! Jesus! Jesus!" (204) Her exclamation is in the correct mouth and in the correct ritualistic context to signify the thanksgiving of an individual madwoman for the mad sacrament /6/ of a mad service. But it also identifies Stephen with Christ, the first priest. That this identification is what Joyce is actually saying is borne out later in the chapter when the Maundy Thursday symbol is made more explicit by the consideration which Stephen and Lynch give to St. Thomas' *Pange lingua gloriosi* and to the *Vexilla Regis* of Venantius Fortunatus.

Between the ejaculation of the nun and the discussion of the

[5] That Stephen's mass does not begin at the beginning does not, perhaps, require explanation, but it is interesting that in former days the Holy Thursday Mass which is now in the Missal began at the Offertory, either because two other ceremonies preceded it or because the preliminary portion was not essential to the sacrifice.

[6] Skeat, whose *Etymological Dictionary* Joyce read "by the hour" (*Stephen Hero*, p. 26), translates *adieu* as "(I commit you) to God." The priest kisses the altar in the mass as representing Christ; but since Stephen, as we shall see, is not only priest but also Christ, it is perhaps inevitable that he should kiss himself.

hymns there are several symbols which carry in their complex of meanings and tones the meaning and tone of the mass. These, however, will be discussed in the second section of this article because they have more direct connections with the betrayal and crucifixion than with the Maundy Thursday ritual itself.

The two hymns are of primary importance in understanding Joyce's method of using liturgy as symbol. The first hymn is merely named and called the "highest glory of the hymnal." (246) But, Stephen says, ". . . there is no hymn that can be put beside that mournful and majestic processional song, the *Vexilla Regis*. . . ." (246) Lynch then sings a stanza of the second hymn from memory. In the liturgy the *Pange lingua gloriosi* is sung after the mass on Maundy Thursday, when the second Host, which has been consecrated to be reserved for the Good Friday Mass in which no consecration takes place, is carried in procession to the chapel or some other place. When the procession arrives at this place, the chalice containing the Host is incensed and placed in an urn or tabernacle. The procession then returns, and Vespers are sung in the choir. The *Vexilla Regis* is the hymn for Vespers during Passiontide.

The discussion of the hymns interrupts Stephen's expounding of the mysteries of art to Lynch, and they are by no means used merely to complete a parody or to give relief from what might have become an esthetically tedious exposition of an esthetic. The line *Pange lingua gloriosi* is translated in the Missal as "Now, my tongue the mystery telling"; and Lynch does not sing the first stanza of the *Vexilla Regis*, which begins in translation with "Behold the royal ensigns fly," but the second stanza, beginning "The mystery we now unfold." The hymns as symbol, therefore—and this is true of all Joyce's symbols—are not used as mere decoration, nor as extraneous allegorical signs; the meanings they add to the narrative are intimately important to the narrative, giving it depth of texture and expansiveness. It is important that we know that Stephen is expounding mysteries, but it is also important that we know he is expounding them in his symbolic office as Stephen-Christ, the first priest of art. /7/

When Lynch has finished singing, he and Stephen turn into Lower Mount Street. As we shall see this may be connected with Golgotha, for when they stop the crucifixion is re-enacted; but one of its other connections is the prophecy which Stephen made when he accepted the call to the religion of art in Chapter IV: ". . . dawn . . . [would] show him strange fields and hills and faces." (198) Here is the hill, and Donovan's bloated face appears.

Stephen and Lynch halt their procession; and although it is still

Thursday on the narrative level, the conversation with Donovan symbolically treats the Last Supper in retrospect. This is important because of the re-enactment of the crucifixion which is to take place shortly. Telling of a group of students (read disciples) who have passed their examinations successfully. Donovan says, "The Irish fellows in Clark's gave them a feed last night. They all ate curry."[7] (246) These students are apostles ready to go forth to all nations: "Halpin and O'Flynn are through the home civil. Moonan got fifth place in the Indian." (246)

Food continues to be the controlling image in their conversation. Stephen asks Donovan twice to bring him "a few turnips and onions" the next time he goes on a botany field trip so that he can "make a stew" (247); Donovan mentions that his sister is to make pancakes for supper; and Lynch expresses disgust that pancakeeating Donovan can get a good job while he has to smoke cheap cigarettes.[8]

Stephen ends the delineation of his esthetic with the now famous statement, "The artist, like the God of creation, remains within or behind or beyond or above his handiwork, invisible, refined out of existence, indifferent, paring his fingernails." (252) The artist is God; God is Jesus; Stephen is Jesus. As Jesus left the companionship of his disciples on Maundy Thursday for the exile of the cross and the grave, /8/ Stephen is leaving Lynch, his pope, and Emma, his Blessed Virgin, as well as his family, nation, and church for the exile of the artist and for Paris.

2

But the symbols examined above are from only a very small portion of the chapter. What happens symbolically between the tea and fried bread of Stephen's breakfast and the curry eaten at Clark's?

[7] Possibly it was curry of lamb with rice which they ate. Joyce, who knew the grail legends passed on by the medieval romancers, may have been consciously using the idea of the grail as the dish from which the disciples and Christ ate the Paschal Lamb on Maundy Thursday rather than as a chalice. Mallory uses it in this sense, and Joyce's favorite Skeat, in his *Etymological Dictionary*, traces the word to "Old French *graal, greal, grasal,* a flat dish." This definition plus the rice would connect it with ". . . the soup plate he had eaten the rice from for supper" (256), which Stephen finds on the table by his bed on the morning of what is narratively Friday. The rice, therefore, might also stand for the Host left over from Maundy Thursday, as explained above.

[8] Three comments. The cigarette-smoking business which is used all through the walk which Stephen and Lynch take together may be related to the use of incense during the mass procession on Maundy Thursday. Donovan's last field trip was on the preceding Saturday—to gather palms? Note that the basket used by Stephen to illustrate his esthetic theory to Lynch is a butcher's basket rather than a grocer's or chemist's.

Thousands of things. And after the curry other thousands. Some of these are clearly symbolic, and their symbolic content can be allegorized for purposes of analysis.

In the narrative Stephen walks to school. As he walks he thinks of himself as a doubting monk (205), meets a consumptive man (206), thinks of Cranly as a guilty priest (207), reflects on his interest in words (207), recalls the temptation of Davin by a country wife (209 ff.), is buttonholed by a woman selling flowers (213), thinks with something like compassion of Dublin (214), and thinks of Burnchapel Whaley, Buck Egan, and Buck Whaley. (214)

After witnessing Stephen's function as priest, it is clear to the reader why he should think of himself as a doubting monk.[9] But it may not be immediately apparent that the consumptive man is a type of Christ: and in him, as in the dwarf whom he, Cranly, and Dixon meet in the library (267), Stephen (as Christ) sees himself as he will be on Good Friday: ". . . an ugly little man who has taken into his body the sins of the world . . . a crooked ugly body for which neither God nor man have pity."[10] Joyce had attended the Tenebrae services of Holy Week and had taken notes on them. These notes were found with the *Stephen Hero* MS., and a photostatic copy is reproduced in *Stephen Hero*, facing page 116. He may have got the idea of the disfigured Christ from the Responsory of the second Nocturne of the Office of Holy Thursday: "Behold we have seen him disfigured and without beauty: his aspect is gone from him: he has borne our sins and suffered for us." To put it in a variety of theological language, the consumptive man and the dwarf are "types" of Christ (Stephen) /9/ as a scapegoat just as Noah or Jonah in the Bible are types of Christ.[11]

The time on the dairy clock is wrong because time is out of joint in the symbolic sequence of the chapter, and also because the dairy,

[9] The thought recurs, pp. 258 and 260. Skeat traces "monk" to several Anglo-Saxon Latin, and Greek words meaning "solitary" or "alone," meanings which have obvious significance in relation to Stephen.

[10] *Stephen Hero*, pp. 116 f.

[11] The Dwarf as a type of Christ is incestuous because he has taken into his body the sins of the world. Perhaps incest may be taken as incorporating all sins since it was the sin which Joyce found most terrifying to contemplate. Cf. the father's relation to his daughter in "A Flower Given to My Daughter" and "Simples" in *Pomes Penyeach*, and Earwicker's to Isabel in *Finnegans Wake*.

Joyce gives us many clues to a character's encountering his own image. In "An Encounter," for instance, "Stephen" encounters himself in the "queer" gentleman as he ". . . chewed one of those green stems on which girls tell fortunes." In *Ulysses*, p. 197, Stephen thinks, "His image, wandering, he met, I mine. I met a fool i' the forest." And later, p. 210, he says, "We walk through ourselves, meeting robbers, ghosts, giants, old men, young men, wives, widows, brothers-in-love. But always meeting ourselves."

which fuses as symbol with the temptation of Davin by the country wife, is connected with eternity before time—at least before that aspect of time called death.[12] Davin is Adam, who is tempted by this Irish Eve with a mug of milk for an apple. He is the person in the *Portrait* most closely related to "the broken lights of Irish myth" (210), and he is associated in Stephen's mind with primeval incest. (268 f.) Joyce links the country wife to the woman selling flowers (213 f.) and to temptresses in general (259), including Emma (259) and the Blessed Virgin (255), who is one of the lures of the fallen seraphim.[13] (255)

Cranly is thought of as a "guilty priest" (207) because he is, in one of his symbolic aspects, Judas. He betrays Stephen by stealing his best girl:

She passed out from the porch of the library and bowed across Stephen in reply to Cranly's greeting. He also? Was there not a slight flush on Cranly's face? (273)

In Stephen's own interpretation of Cranly as John the Baptist he was puzzled by St. John at the Latin Gate and sees him as the "precursor trying to pick the lock." (293) He writes in his diary, "Is he the shining /10/ light now? Well, I discovered him. I protest I did." (296)

The reader is as puzzled as Stephen unless he knows or takes the trouble to find out who St. John at the Latin Gate is. The feast of St. John before the Latin Gate, celebrated in the Church on May 6, marks the anniversary of the dedication of the Basilica of St. John Lateran outside the Gate of St. John in Rome during the time of Pope Adrian. The original church was dedicated to the Savior, but later, because it was served by a Benedictine monastery dedicated to St. John the Baptist and St. John the Evangelist, the church was dedicated to the two St. Johns as well. This later dedication has now superseded the original one in popular usage; or, in the framework of Joyce's symbolism, Christ has again been betrayed. Since the station for Maundy Thursday Mass is at St. John Lateran, Joyce's irony is apparent.[14]

[12] Shortly after looking at the dairy clock Stephen hears a clock strike eleven, and it is for him (as Christ) the eleventh hour. The time and the precision of the striking make him think of Mac Cann, dressed in ". . . a shooting jacket and breeches" (206), the precise symbol of the Roman (or British) state—in short, the Procurator of Judea. This will be treated below.

[13] In Catholic belief, of course, Eve is the woman by whom sin enters the world, and the Blessed Virgin is the woman by whom the means of salvation from sin enters the world. Mary is sometimes referred to in Catholic writing as the "celestial temptress" since she can tempt men to Christ.

[14] In "Tilly," the "extra measure" of *Pomes Penyeach*, Cranly is represented as "my torn bough." The poem is the "extra measure" as Judas became the

Stephen ponders "The soul of the gallant venal city" (214) of Dublin, which had ". . . shrunk with time to a faint mortal odour rising from the earth. . . ." (214) as Christ thinks of Jerusalem:

Jerusalem! Jerusalem! thou that killest the prophets, and stoneth them that are sent unto thee, how often would I have gathered together thy children, as the hen doth gather her chickens under her wings, and thou wouldest not.[15]

Several Irish prophets who have been killed by Irish men are mentioned in Chapter V, and all of these are connected with Stephen's own crucifixion. Yeats at the opening of the National Theatre is one of these: ". . . the catcalls and hisses and mocking cries ran in rude gusts around the hall." (266) And Stephen says to Davin: "No honorable and sincere man . . . has given up his life and his youth and his affection from the days of Tone to those of Parnell but you have sold him to the enemy or failed him in need or reviled him and left him for another." (237)

The Bucks Egan and Whaley and Burnchapel Whaley were infamous for many reasons. They performed, according to rumor, black /11/ masses while living in what was to become the University College building. Burnchapel also burns chapels, but it is Buck, his son, who is important for his connection with Cranly. Buck's second alias was "Jerusalem" Whaley because he won a bet, estimated to be between 10,000 and 15,000 pounds, for walking to Jerusalem and playing ball against the walls. This is the key to the mysterious grey handball which Cranly carries. (229, *etc.*) He and Davin play handball with it, "Cranly insisting his ball should be used," and in answer to its thud, he exclaims, "Your soul!" (238) In Stephen's ironic theology this supports the demonic character of Cranly as the betrayer, and it is made doubly ironic by Cranly's being the most "Roman" of Stephen's Catholic male friends.

The thoughts of the Bucks bring the narrative to Stephen's arrival at University College, where he enters the physics classroom to find the dean of studies lighting a fire in the fireplace. Stephen sees his actions as religious ritual:

Kneeling thus on the flagstone to kindle the fire . . . he seemed more than

---

"extra" disciple, and he is torn from Stephen (read Christ) as one of the branches of the true vine. He is also Satan (another betrayer) tempting Jesus to be a material Messias—Cranly was sidestepping the priesthood of art to open a porkstore in Wicklow; hence he drives cows in the poem. But since Stephen said, "Satan, really, is the romantic youth of Jesus reappearing for a moment" (*Stephen Hero*, p. 222), perhaps we can come full circle to John the Baptist as the romantic youth of Jesus.

[15] *Matthew* 33:37. Cf. the Tenebrae service for Maundy Thursday evening, the Office of Good Friday.

ever a humble server making ready the place of sacrifice in an empty temple, a levite of the Lord. (215)

But the position of this scene in relation to Buck Whaley, and the thoughts which Stephen has concerning the priest indicate that it is the ritual of the Catholic priest which is defective rather than the ritual of the priest of art. The dean's ". . . very soul had waxed old in that service without growing towards light and beauty" (216), ". . . in his eyes burned no spark of Ignatius' enthusiasm" (217), and ". . . it seemed as if he loved not at all the master." (217)

During the physics class Stephen considers offering himself as a "subject for electrocution." (225) And afterwards, as Stephen goes into the crowd of students in the entrance hall, "Cranly's dark eyes were watching him." (227) The crowd has gathered to watch his trial. He is tried by Mac Cann as Pilate for not submitting to Caesar in the form of the Tsar. Mac Cann, who is "ready to shed the last drop" (228) for the "universal peace" of the Tsar (or Augustus) even pronounces Pilate's *Ecce homo!* while clearing his throat, "Hom!" (229)

Stephen and Cranly cross the "weedy garden" (234) of Gethsemane together and find Lynch, the disciple to whom Stephen will confide the innermost mysteries of the religion of art, asleep; and the parallel with *Matthew* 26:40 and the Responsory to the eighth Lesson of the third /12/ Nocturne of the Holy Thursday Tenebrae is complete: "Could ye not watch one hour with me?"

Stephen and Lynch then set out on their peripatetic discussion of Stephen's esthetic, and Stephen symbolically reassures Lynch that he is not only God but "also an animal!" This may encourage the reader to recall Stephen's doubly ironic question of a few pages earlier, "Do you fancy I am going to pay in my own life and person for debts they made?" (237) And later, in the passage dealing with Stephen's lineage, the question "Did an angel speak?" (271) carries not only narrative and obscene levels but also refers directly to the means of conception between the Holy Ghost and the Blessed Virgin.

Although the crucifixion of Stephen is represented fully only by the book as a whole, it is symbolically re-enacted on the steps of the National Library at the end of Stephen's and Lynch's walk. As they approach the library, the sky is appropriately "veiled" and it begins to rain. Emma stands silently among her companions (the "other Marys" of the gospels) and Stephen watches her with "conscious bitterness" (253), thinking of her as a lure for him and Father Moran. She is specifically identified with the Virgin by the medical students' otherwise pointless talk of obstetrics, which the dying Stephen hears ". . . as if from a distance in interrupted pulsations." (254) As she prepares to go away with her companions, Stephen considers forgiving her.

The church year is continued in the burlesque Easter Mass which Stephen celebrates in the Circe episode of *Ulysses*, but the resurrection is foreshadowed in the *Portrait* by the sleep and waking which immediately follow Stephen's symbolic crucifixion:

A spirit filled him, pure as the purest water. . . . But how faintly it was inbreathed . . . as if the seraphim themselves were breathing upon him! (254)
The night had been enchanted. In a dream or vision he had known the ecstasy of seraphic life. (255)

This explication does not exhaust the meanings of even these few strands of symbols in a single chapter of the *Portrait*, a book which is a rich, closely woven fabric of symbol and narrative. But since all of the elements treated as symbols in the *Portrait* were either omitted or treated on a simple narrative level in *Stephen Hero*, the tracing of the few strands through a small part of the whole cloth may add to our understanding of the growth of Joyce as an artist. /13/

PART VII

AIDS AND SUGGESTIONS

Suggestions for Individual Interpretation, Class Discussions, and Themes

PART I

KAIN

1. Various critics have used the terms "mirror," "mirrors" and "mirroring" as metaphors for Joyce's technical achievement in the *Portrait*. Mr. Kain's "many-faceted prism" is certainly more suggestive; is it in any way a more accurate metaphor? Why? Why not?

2. Starting with the passage of the novel Mr. Kain refers to, in which Joyce has Stephen contrast "mirror" and "prism" as metaphors for "prose" and "language," and working from the novel proper (as well as from the critics), develop either or both of these metaphors as fully as the evidence allows.

3. From your reading of the novel and the various critical pieces, justify, elaborate, and document fully any one sentence in Mr. Kain's first paragraph.

ELLMANN

1. Match the events listed here with incidents within the novel. Is the correlation exact enough to make the *Portrait* an autobiography? (To answer this question as fully as the range of materials in this volume will allow, other selections should also be considered.)

2. Does the recognition of some correspondence between the artist's life and that of his hero aid or interfere with an understanding of his novel?

3. To what extent is some knowledge of Joyce's life necessary to a full understanding of the novel?

4. To what extent is knowledge of Joyce's life irrelevant to an understanding of his novel?

JONES

1. Is "the importance of childhood and early schooldays . . . in forming the artist" the only theme of Chapter I? Is it the most important one? Do any other themes begin to be developed?

2. Mr. Jones calls the style of Chapter I "mostly realistic," yet many readers experience considerable difficulty with this chapter, the opening pages in particular. How do you reconcile the "realism" with the difficulty?

3. Granted that Mr. Jones's purpose is to make Joyce available to the "common reader" upon whom many subtleties are presumably likely to be lost, he omits mention of the "Pull out his eyes,/Apologise" episode which other critics comment upon at length. As you read these other critics, determine for yourself the extent to which the episode is vital or irrelevant to an understanding of the novel.

4. Working along the lines suggested in the questions above, find what other incidents Mr. Jones has chosen to omit in his summary of the novel. Would it be possible to re-write the Jones selection using only the materials he omitted?

5. In what ways is the selection from *James Joyce and the Common Reader* a valuable starting point for an understanding of the novel?

6. Supposing a student who has read the novel went solely to Jones for assistance: in what ways would Mr. Jones's summary prove an impediment to an understanding of the book? (This same question ought, of course, to be asked about every critical article.)

7. Is Mr. Jones's *Portrait of the Artist* the same novel you read? That the other critics read?

PART II

GARNETT

["Publisher's reader" is the British equivalent of what in the United States we should call an editor, and Edward Garnett was a good one: he was continually on the lookout for new talent, and ever ready to encourage it whenever found. Among those writers whose careers he was instrumental in launching and fostering were Joseph Conrad, W. H. Hudson, D. H. Lawrence, and Edward Thomas. His strictures on Joyce's *Portrait*, then, are not to be taken lightly. Incidentally, it was through the translations of his wife, Constance Garnett, that the English-speaking world first became acquainted with such Russian giants as Dostoevsky, Chekhov, Tolstoy, and Turgenev.]

1. What is it in the novel that could have led Garnett to find the *Portrait* "too discursive, formless"? Define the "formlessness" of the *Portrait*.

2. What does Garnett mean by "the point of view will be voted 'a little sordid'"?

3. Explain what is "unconventional" about the *Portrait*.

4. What have other critics had to say about the ending of the *Portrait* that (a) supports or (b) contradicts Garnett's statement that "at the end of the book there is a complete falling to bits"? What do you think?

5. To what extent are Garnett's reservations about Joyce's novel justifiable?

6. On what points do you believe Garnett to be in error?

MAGALANER

1. Explain what there is in Joyce's novel that led to the early attacks upon it.

2. Write a short paper on the early praise accorded the *Portrait,* but do not merely paraphrase Professor Magalaner.

3. Defend the *Portrait* against some one (or all) of the early statements against it. See, particularly, the attack in *The Irish Times.*

4. What did W. N. P. Barbellion mean by Joyce's "verisimilitude"? Do later critics admire this property in the *Portrait?*

5. Discuss in detail the statement on Joyce's style that appeared in *The Scotsman.*

6. Has Mencken's prophesy that "a Joyce cult now threatens" come to pass? Do any of the selections published in this work smack of the "cult" or the "clique"?

PART III

LEVIN

1. Define *Bildungsroman* and *Künstlerroman.* How helpful are these terms for discussing novels?

2. Explain in detail Levin's assertion that "the narrative . . . has scarcely emerged from the lyrical stage." What other critical commentary supports this statement? denies it?

3. Is it true, as Levin maintains, that the *Portrait* is "based on a literal transcript of the first twenty years of Joyce's life"? How *literal* is the transcript? See, for instance, Kevin Sullivan on Clongowes Wood and Belvedere.

4. Compare Levin's conjectures on the *Ur-Portrait,* pages 46 and 47, with the *Ur-Portrait* (unknown to Professor Levin at the time of his writing) printed in *The Yale Review* (see Bibliography).

5. Accumulate what evidence there is that lends weight to Levin's comment, "Evasion and indirection were ingrained in Joyce's narrative technique."

6. Levin remarks upon the "oscillations of style" in the *Portrait* (page 49) and (page 50) comments on the tone of the novel. How does he support what he says, and what, in your words, does he say? Agree or disagree with him.

7. "Joyce is thinking in rhythms rather than metaphors," says Levin (page 52). To what extent is this statement applicable to the whole of the *Portrait?*

8. Can you defend Levin's statement, page 52, that conversation is the "most vital element in Joyce's writing"?

9. Compare and/or contrast Levin's discussion of the structure of the *Portrait* with that of some other critic (Dorothy Van Ghent or Grant Redford, for example).

10. Does Professor Levin consider the *Portrait* a romantic novel or a realistic one? What are the principal differences between the two? Do you agree with Levin?

KENNER

1. What did Joyce mean when he announced to Frank Budgen that Stephen "has a shape that can't be changed"? Is Stephen a static character? a flat one? Or was Joyce thinking of something beyond these technical denotations?

2. Kenner's statement that "the *Portrait* concentrates on stating themes, arranging apparently transparent words into configurations of the utmost symbolic density" is one upon which critics of the novel have taken various stands. Weigh the criticism that revolves about this concept, and then argue for or against Kenner's contention.

3. Explain what Professor Kenner means by "elaborate counterpoint."

4. Why does Kenner make a special point of Stephen's being a Dubliner?

5. What penalties, according to Kenner, is the careless reader apt to suffer? Can you think of others?

6. What does "lyric" mean when applied to a novel? When applied to the *Portrait?* How general is the agreement about the "lyricism" of the novel? Do the various critics who call the novel "lyric" agree upon the meaning of the term?

7. Explain Kenner's statement, "Unfortunately, the last chapter makes the book a peculiarly difficult one for the reader to focus, because Joyce had to close it on a suspended chord."

8. What, according to Kenner, is the organizing principle of the novel?

9. To what extent and for what reasons does Kenner find Joyce's vocabulary limited in the *Portrait?*

10. Do you agree with Kenner that Stephen is "priggish" and "humorless" in the last chapter?

11. The first two pages of the *Portrait,* according to Kenner, "enact the entire action in microcosm." Using Kenner and the other critics, develop this idea as far as you can carry it.

12. Compare Kenner on Joyce's use of hands with what Kevin Sullivan has to say about the same images. Are the interpretations mutually exclusive, or do they reinforce one another?

13. Is it true, as Kenner believes, that Stephen ends as a "being whose development was virtually ended"? If this is so, how does it affect an autobiographical interpretation of the novel? (Joyce, after all, did go on to write *Ulysses* and *Finnegans Wake.*)

14. Compare Kenner's reading of the Clongowes Wood and Belvedere episodes with that of Kevin Sullivan and those put forward by other critics. Do any of these interpretations cancel others out? Or is it possible that all are right?

15. Starting with Kenner's comments, examine in detail the image of womankind presented in the *Portrait.*

16. Compare Kenner's final section with the reading of Eugene Waith.

VAN GHENT

1. Mrs. Van Ghent says that the technique of stream of consciousness

or interior monologue, as used by Joyce, is a "formal aspect of the book" (page 267). What does she mean by the word *formal*?

2. Does Mrs. Van Ghent see a relationship between what Joyce is *saying* in the *Portrait* and the *form* of the novel? Explain. Do other critics develop such a relationship? Are their terms similar to Mrs. Van Ghent's?

3. Explain the comment on page 275 that the artist is "a midwife of epiphanies." What other critics would agree? Do you?

4. Does Mrs. Van Ghent think it is a flaw in the *Portrait* that the "ultimate epiphany is withheld" (page 276)? Is it really? What do other critics have to say?

5. Does Mrs. Van Ghent develop any lines of interpretation beyond those put forward by Levin and Kenner? What are they?

6. How much general agreement is there between the three critics read so far in this section? How much disagreement? Are the disagreements crucial?

7. Look up the word *impressionism* in your dictionary (or some glossary of literary terms), then decide whether or not the "portrait" of Stephen is impressionistic or not. Does Mrs. Van Ghent think that it is? Do other critics?

WAITH

1. Waith calls Stephen "difficult." What does he mean by the word?

2. Why and in what way or ways does Stephen "characteristically" observe himself observing the birds from the steps of the library? (See page 256.)

3. Waith disagrees with Hugh Kenner's essay, "The Portrait in Perspective." On what specific grounds? Which do you think is most nearly correct? Why? (It should be noted here that the selection from Kenner printed above differs considerably from the essay Waith has in mind.)

4. To what extent does the persuasiveness (if, indeed, you find it so) of Waith's examination of the images of flight and of flow modify earlier interpretations of the meaning of the novel (Levin, Kenner and Van Ghent; see Jones in Part I as well)?

5. Waith calls the description of Stephen's self-imposed religious regime which opens the fourth chapter "superbly comic." Do you agree with him? If so, wherein lies the comedy—in Joyce's attitude toward religion, or in his attitude toward Stephen?

6. Is it possible to make out a case for the "calling" of Stephen Dedalus which sounds a more positive note than that struck by Professor Waith?

KELLEHER

1. Considering your own experience with the book, is Professor Kelleher right in his assumption that the *Portrait* has a special appeal for youthful readers?

2. Kelleher writes that "when I first encountered Stephen Dedalus I was twenty and I wondered how Joyce could have known so much about

me." Have you wondered the same thing? Why? If not—if you made no identification—why not?

3. As an extension of the questions already raised, can a girl react to the *Portrait* in the same way that a boy can? Is the *Portrait*, that is, exclusively a young man's book? (Remember that some of the most sensitive readings of the novel have been products of critics who would probably not even themselves confess to being "young"—and that Mrs. Van Ghent and Miss Hendry [now Mrs. Chayes] have written sensitively and well on Joyce's novel.)

4. Does Kelleher consider the *Portrait* a realistic novel?

5. What does Kelleher mean by the novel's being "written backwards and forwards and sideways and in depth, all at once"?

6. If Kelleher is right in the above, if, as he says, there "aren't any separate parts" and the book is "all of a piece, one organic whole," how valid are the criticisms which consider it chapter by chapter? Or consider one chapter only, as does C. G. Anderson in Part VI?

7. Explain Kelleher's description, "deliberate and unobtrusive engineering" [of the *Portrait*].

8. Why and how is Joyce's symbolism more than "Just some more damned symbolism"?

9. With the use of Kelleher and other critics explain Joyce's use of the colors red and green.

10. What does Kelleher mean by "thus the *Portrait* functions well enough simply as a naturalistic novel"? Is this a usual opinion of the book?

11. What is Kelleher's opinion of what the moral commitment of the artist ought to be? What is yours? What, insofar as you can determine from the *Portrait*, was Joyce's?

PART IV

All of the selections reprinted in this part present essentially the same problem: to what extent did Joyce transcribe verifiable incidents of his own life into the pages of *A Portrait of the Artist as a Young Man?* Certainly what we find in the passages from Ellmann and Sullivan is the very stuff from which the novel was made, but is it the same stuff or has Joyce translated it into something different? If and where Joyce transcribes more or less accurately, what added dimensions does the thematic texture of the novel give to those incidents? If and where Joyce translates the material, altering it to a considerable extent, what thematic purposes do his alterations serve? Such questions lead inevitably to the central question, is the *Portrait* autobiography or is it art? What distinction do you draw between the two? Where is the line of demarcation between the two? Because the matters raised by the selections of Part IV are so much of a piece, and so self-evident, only a few leading questions on the separate selections are provided.

ELLMANN

1. Trace the thematic significance of Stephen's denial of his father in the *Portrait*.

2. How near to life is Dante drawn in the *Portrait?* In what respects is she changed in the novel? Why?

3. To what extent is the seemingly slight incident involving Eileen Vance expanded into symbol, motif and/or theme? See the first selection of Part V, and consider carefully what the critics have made of this.

4. How has Joyce crystallized the trip to Cork in the novel so that it becomes an integral part of the *Portrait?*

5. Why did Joyce make the Byron incident a part of the *Portrait?*

6. What are the purposes served by the artist's changes in the matter of the Sodality? What is the function of this passage in terms of the novel as a whole? How crucial did the actual events seem to be to Joyce? To Stephen? In what ways are their reactions different? What is gained by the differences?

7. How does the description of Stephen at University College differ from Ellmann's description of James Joyce there? What, in terms of the novel, are the significant differences, and why are they significant?

8. Are the motivations of Cranly in life and in the novel the same? What qualities does the Cranly of the *Portrait* represent? Why is Cranly necessary to the development of Joyce's themes?

9. Using Ellmann and the other commentators, devlop insofar as you can the relationship between *Stephen Hero* and the *Portrait*. What are their similarities? What are the crucial differences?

10. How satisfactory is Ellmann's account of Joyce's creative process? What evidence—or interpretation—do the other critics present that substantiates Ellmann's version? That contradicts it? Whose account do you accept? Why?

SULLIVAN

1. To what extent does Joyce use his career at Clongowes Wood for non-autobiographical and specifically artistic purposes?

2. Substitute Belvedere for Clongowes Wood in the question above.

3. Compare Sullivan's handling of the incidents which reappear within the *Portrait* with the versions presented by other critics. How complementary are the accounts and interpretations? Do any tend to cancel others out? Which? How?

4. Sullivan's book is called *Joyce among the Jesuits;* write an account of Stephen among the Jesuits.

JOYCE

Is Joyce's attitude toward Stephen, as expressed in the letter to Ezra Pound, similar to his attitude toward Stephen in the *Portrait?* In what way or ways does the limerick affect your own attitude toward what Joyce was doing with Stephen in the *Portrait*? How seriously should we take Joyce? How seriously should we take Stephen?

PART V

NOON

Chronologically, Father Noon's definition comes last among the selections reprinted which have to deal with the Joycean epiphany, but it is here printed first as a convenient starting point and check. As you read more about the epiphanies, modify and/or expand Father Noon's definition as you see need to; after considering all of the definitions, reword, if you can, this initial definition.

JOYCE

The first passage is an early version—if not the first version—of an incident that expands to form a vital part of the total texture of the novel. Joyce changed it somewhat in the *Portrait,* but for what purposes? Using only the single epiphany and Stephen's theorizing in the passage from *Stephen Hero,* work out your own definition of "epiphany." How does it differ from Father Noon's? Why did Joyce suppress the Eccles Street passage in the *Portrait?* Why did he gain—or lose—by doing so?

ASPECTS OF THE ESTHETIC THEORY

Because Joyce's esthetic theory embodied in and demonstrated by the *Portrait* is the common concern here, discussion of the other criticism represented in Part V is best suggested by grouping topics. Each critic has contributed, through his analysis of the esthetic theory, to the interpretation of the novel. Evaluation of each contribution will be profitable. So too can be syntheses of the meaning of Joyce's *integritas, consonantia,* and *claritas;* his *claritas* and *quidditas;* his categories of art: lyric, epic, dramatic; his *terror* and *pity;* his intellectual introversion and extroversion; his experience and dream; his classicism and romanticism. Thomism, Aristotelian theory, or Bergsonianism also offer valuable areas for analysis of Joyce's esthetics. More restricted discussion can center around Joyce's *élan vital,* "rhythm of beauty," and catharsis.

PART VI

REDFORD

1. Do you agree with Redford that there is "a relationship between artistic proposition and structure which has either been overlooked or too-little emphasized" (page 21)? If so, explain why this relationship was long overlooked or slighted. If not, contest Redford's statement.

2. Does Redford indicate, on page 21, that there is disagreement between his and Hugh Kenner's estimation of Stephen's effect on the reader?

Where and how do the two critics differ on Stephen? In what respects do they agree?

3. "Search and Rebellion," Redford says, are the themes of the *Portrait*. Is this acceptable to other critics of the book? Is it acceptable to you?

4. Redford offers, on page 22, the proposition which underlies the *Portrait*. Is this acceptable to the other critics?

5. Explain fully why the family Christmas dinner scene is presented by a method used nowhere else in the *Portrait*.

6. Is Redford at odds with Dorothy Van Ghent's essay on the *Portrait*? On what grounds? Are their readings basically different?

FRIEDMAN

1. Explain in detail what changes in Stephen's prose style take place in the *Portrait*, and the relationship of these changes to the theme of the novel.

2. Using Friedman's discussion of the *Portrait* as well as your reading of the novel and other critics of it, define "stream of consciousness" as used in the *Portrait*.

3. Friedman says, on page 218, that "the method finally sinks into artifice." What does he mean? Do you agree?

4. What is "fin de siècle rhetoric" (page 218)? Where would Stephen have come into contact with such style? Does Friedman think this style a flaw in the novel? Can you defend Joyce from the charge of bad writing labeled "fin de siècle rhetoric"?

TINDALL

1. What is the relevance of the quotation from William Blake (on page 77) to the *Portrait*?

2. Does Stephen construct a better world, as Tindall says? What is it better than? How is it better? What is the relationship between this "better world" and the theme of the novel?

3. Explain the term "attendant images" (page 77). In what way do they add to the quality and depth of the *Portrait*? Do other critics think the attendant images "could be omitted without destroying his book"? What do they say about the effect of these on the unity of Joyce's novel?

4. What does Tindall mean by "the composite form" of the *Portrait* (page 78)?

5. "Could the green rose anticipate Stephen's immature desire for Irish art?" (page 80). What is your answer to this question? What would other critics answer? Go further in your exploration of symbols of national art in the *Portrait* or in exploration of *green* and *rose* as symbols.

6. Do you agree with Tindall's statements on the use of women as symbols in the *Portrait*? Do the other critics?

7. Why does Tindall say "seems" in the statement, "The making of water at the beginning of the *Portrait* seems an image of creation that includes the artist's two realities" (page 83)? Is this symptomatic of a requirement this novel makes on criticism of it?

8. What do E. M. Forster's comments on the *Portrait* (quoted on page 86) indicate about the basic critical problem anyone examining this novel must face?

MAGALANER

1. Trace the motif of apology in the *Portrait,* using Kenner's, Magalaner's and Kain's and other examinations of it along with your own analysis of the novel.

2. Explain in detail Joyce's use of *The Count of Monte Cristo* in the *Portrait.* (Magalaner and Kain say it "serves as one of the unifying threads of the impressionist narrative.")

PRESCOTT

1. What does "Words begin as sounds and end as symbols" mean as applied to the *Portrait?*

2. In Prescott's statement, "The *Portrait* describes Joyce's linguistic childhood," explain the word *linguistic.*

BOYD

1. What is the significance of Miss Boyd's article?

2. What is the importance of Joyce's additions to his sermon sources?

3. What does Miss Boyd mean by "technical plagiarism" on page 571?

KAYE

1. Do you agree with Kaye's title question, "Who is Betty Byrne?" Are there flaws in Kaye's case for symbolic identification? If so, point them out; if not, how significant to interpretation of the novel is Kaye's article?

2. How does Kaye add to or modify the case for the *Portrait* as an autobiographical novel?

3. What does Kaye mean by "mythic dimension" (page 94)? What are the "mythic dimensions" of the *Portrait?*

4. "Why does Joyce say that Betty Byrne 'sold lemon platt'?"

ANDERSON

1. Explain Anderson's second sentence at length.

2. Trace the baptism motif through the novel, with Anderson and other critics as guides.

3. Explain the purpose of hymns, other songs, and poems in the *Portrait.*

4. Anderson speaks of food as a controlling image in the *Portrait* (page 8). Discuss this image in detail.

5. What does Anderson mean by "the crucifixion of Stephen is represented fully only by the book as a whole" (page 13)?

Some Suggested Research
Paper Topics

The following illustrate not the extent of possible topics to be drawn from the novel and the criticism but the kinds of topics that can be pursued. Other suggestions for papers are to be found in the questions on the individual authors.

1. Stephen Dedalus as Saint Stephen, proto-martyr
2. Stephen Dedalus as Daedalus, "fabulous artificer"
3. Stephen Dedalus as Christ
4. Joyce's family as the Dedalus family
5. The "form" of the *Portrait*
6. The structure of the *Portrait*
7. "Point of view" in the *Portrait*
8. The "genre" of the *Portrait*
9. Joyce's theory of the "epiphany": a definition and demonstration
10. Joyce's handling of the passage of time
11. Joyce's use of landscape in the *Portrait*
12. Joyce's use of atmosphere
13. Joyce's descriptive style in the *Portrait*
14. Dialogue in the *Portrait*
15. The evolution of Stephen's break with the Church
16. The evolution of Stephen's break with his family
17. The evolution of Stephen's break with his country
18. The role of sex in Stephen's development
19. Color imagery in the *Portrait*
20. Sense imagery in the *Portrait*
21. The significance of the Christmas dinner scene
22. The function of Stephen's friends (individually or collectively— Fleming, Lynch, Cranly, etc.)
23. The role of the Jesuits in the *Portrait*
24. The *Portrait* as a work of "psychological realism"
25. The *Portrait* as a work of symbolism
26. The *Portrait* as a stream-of-consciousness novel
27. The *Portrait* as confession
28. The obscurity of Joyce's *Portrait*

29. The *Portrait* as autobiography
30. "Art" vs. "Life" in Joyce's *Portrait*
31. Joyce's use of motifs
32. Joyce's use of "expressive form"
33. Joyce's use of "imitative form"
34. The *Portrait* as "lyric," "epic," or "dramatic"
35. The role of *Stephen Hero* in the development of the *Portrait*
36. Stephen's esthetic theory
37. The function of the sermons
38. Joyce's use of irony
39. The ending of the *Portrait*
40. Trends in the critical reception of the *Portrait*

The following topics are suggested for research outside this volume.

1. Trace Stephen's development in *Dubliners, Stephen Hero,* the *Portrait,* and *Ulysses.*

2. Make a study of the sources of the *Portrait* and/or influences on it

3. Discuss the *Portrait* as a Catholic novel.

4. Starting with this volume, compile a dictionary of literary terms for assessing the modern novel.

5. Discuss the *Portrait* as *Künstlerroman.*

6. Discuss the *Portrait* as atypical of novels contemporaneous with it.

7. Using *Dubliners,* the *Portrait,* and *Ulysses,* trace the development of Joyce's style.

8. Examine *Dubliners* and/or *Ulysses* from the standpoint of the esthetic theory as you find it expounded in the *Portrait* and in the critics

9. Discuss Joyce as technical innovator.

10. It is sometimes said that at the end of the *Portrait* Stephen is leaving Dublin to write *Ulysses.* What is the case for this, and what is the case against this?

A One-Hundred Item Checklist of Publications Relevant to the *Portrait*

Publications on *Stephen Hero* are included in this checklist, as are those items, essentially biographical, which have been excerpted in the text. The checklist proper derives in large measure from "Criticism of James Joyce" by Maurice Beebe and Walton Litz, *Modern Fiction Studies,* V (Spring, 1958), 71-99.

Anderson, C. G. "The Sacrificial Butter." *Accent,* XXI (Winter, 1952), 3-13.

Baker, James R. "James Joyce: Esthetic Freedom and Dramatic Art." *Western Humanities Review,* V (Winter, 1950-51), 29-40.

Beebe, Maurice. "James Joyce: Barnacle Goose and Lapwing." *PMLA,* LXXI (June, 1956), 306-08.

———. "Joyce and Aquinas: The Theory of Aesthetics." *Philological Quarterly,* XXXVI (Jan., 1957), 20-35.

Bernhardt-Kabisch, E. "A Portrait of the Artist as a Young Man." *Explicator,* XVIII (Jan., 1960), Item 24.

Block, Haskell M. "The Critical Theory of James Joyce." *Journal of Aesthetics and Art Criticism,* VIII (Mar., 1950), 172-84.

Boyd, Elizabeth F. "Joyce's Hell-Fire Sermons." *Modern Language Notes,* LXXV (Nov., 1960), 561-71.

Brumm, Ursula. "Symbolism and the Novel." *Partisan Review,* XXV (Summer, 1958), 329-42.

Burke, Kenneth. "Three Definitions." *Kenyon Review,* XIII (Spring, 1951), 181-86.

Connolly, Thomas E. "Joyce's Aesthetic Theory." *University of Kansas City Review,* XXIII (Oct., 1956), 47-50.

Daiches, David. "James Joyce: The Artist as Exile." In *Forms of Modern Fiction.* Edited by William Van O'Connor. Minneapolis: University of Minnesota Press, 1948, pp. 62-65.

———. *The Novel and the Modern World.* Chicago: University of Chicago Press, 1939, pp. 101-10.

Dougherty, Charles T. "Joyce and Ruskin." *Notes and Queries,* CXCVIII (Feb., 1953), 76-77.

Ellmann, Richard. "A Chronology of the Life of James Joyce." In *Letters of James Joyce.* Edited by Stuart Gilbert. New York: Viking Press, 1957, pp. 43-50.

———. "A Portrait of the Artist as Friend." *Kenyon Review,* XVIII (Winter, 1956), 53-67. Also in *Society and Self in the Novel: English Institute Essays 1955.* Edited by Mark Schorer. New York: Columbia University Press, 1956, pp. 60-77.

———. *James Joyce.* New York: Oxford University Press, 1959.

Farrell, James T. "Joyce's 'A Portrait of the Artist as a Young Man.' " In *James Joyce: Two Decades of Criticism.* Edited by Seon Givens. New York: Vanguard Press, 1948, pp. 175-90.

———. "Postscript on Stephen Hero." In *James Joyce: Two Decades of Criticism.* Edited by Seon Givens. New York: Vanguard Press, 1948, pp. 190-97.

Feehan, Joseph. Editor. *Dedalus on Crete: Essays on the Implications of Joyce's Portrait.* Los Angeles: Saint Thomas More Guild, Immaculate Heart College, 1957.

Fenichel, Robert R. "A Portrait of the Artist as a Young Orphan." *Literature and Psychology,* IX (Spring, 1960), 19-22.

Fleming, Rudd. "Dramatic Involution: Tate, Husserl, and Joyce." *Sewanee Review,* LX (Summer, 1952), 445-64.

———. "*Quidditas* in the Tragi-Comedy of Joyce." *University of Kansas City Review,* XV (Summer, 1949), 288-96.

Friedman, M. J. *Stream of Consciousness: A Study in Literary Method.* New Haven: Yale University Press, 1956, pp. 214-20.

Frierson, William C. *The English Novel in Transition.* Norman: University of Oklahoma Press, 1942, pp. 200-03.

Gilbert, Stuart. "James Joyce." In *James Joyce: Two Decades of Criticism.* Edited by Seon Givens. New York: Vanguard Press, 1948, pp. 458-61.

———. "The Latin Background of James Joyce's Art." *Horizon,* X (Sept., 1944), 178-88.

Goldberg, S. L. "Joyce and the Artist's Fingernails." *Review of English Literature,* II (Apr., 1961), 59-73.

Golding, Louis. *James Joyce.* London: Thornton Butterworth Ltd., 1933, pp. 34-68.

Gordon, Caroline. *How to Read a Novel.* New York: Viking Press, 1957, pp. 210-14.

———. "Some Readings and Misreadings." *Sewanee Review,* LXI (Summer, 1953), 388-93.

Gorman, Herbert. "Introduction." *A Portrait of the Artist as a Young Man.* By James Joyce. New York: Modern Library, 1928, pp. v-xii.

———. *James Joyce: His First Forty Years.* New York: B. W. Huebsch, 1924, pp. 65-100.

Guidi, Augusto. *Il Primo Joyce*. Rome: Edizioni di Storia e Letteratura, 1954, pp. 41-104.

Hackett, Francis. *Horizons: A Book of Criticism*. New York: B. W. Huebsch, 1919, pp. 163-68.

———. *On Judging Books*. New York: John Day, 1947, pp. 251-54.

Hendry, Irene. "Joyce's Epiphanies." *Sewanee Review*, LIV (July, 1946), 449-67. Also in *James Joyce: Two Decades of Criticism*. Edited by Seon Givens. New York: Vanguard Press, 1948, pp. 27-46.

Hennig, John. "Stephen Hero and Wilhelm Meister: A Study of Parallels." *German Life and Letters*, V (Oct., 1951), 22-29.

Honig, Edwin. "Hobgoblin or Apollo." *Kenyon Review*, X (Autumn, 1948), 664-81.

Hope, A. D. "The Esthetic Theory of James Joyce." *Australasian Journal of Psychology and Philosophy*, XXI (Dec., 1943), 93-114.

Jack, Jane H. "Art and *The Portrait of the Artist*." *Essays in Criticism*, V (Oct., 1955), 354-64.

Jones, William Powell. *James Joyce and the Common Reader*. Norman: University of Oklahoma Press, 1955, pp. 24-38.

Joyce, James. *Stephen Hero*. Edited by Theodore Spencer. Norfolk: New Directions, 1944.

———. *Stephen Hero*. Edited by John J. Slocum and Herbert Cahoon. New Edition. New York: New Directions, 1955.

———. *Letters of James Joyce*. Edited by Stuart Gilbert. New York: Viking Press, 1957.

Kain, Richard M., and Robert E. Scholes. "The First Version of Joyce's 'Portrait.'" *Yale Review*, XLIX (Mar., 1960), 355-69.

Karl, Frederick R., and Marvin Magalaner. *A Reader's Guide to Great Twentieth-Century English Novels*. New York: Noonday Press, 1959, pp. 209-21.

Kaye, Julian B. "Simony, the Three Simons, and Joycean Myth." In *A James Joyce Miscellany*. Edited by Marvin Magalaner. New York: James Joyce Society, 1957, pp. 24-30.

———. "Who Is Betty Byrne?" *Modern Language Notes*, LXXI (Feb., 1956), 93-95.

Kelleher, John V. "The Perceptions of James Joyce." *Atlantic Monthly*, CCI (Mar., 1959), 82 ff.

Kenner, Hugh. *Dublin's Joyce*. Bloomington: Indiana University Press, 1956, pp. 109-57.

———. "The Portrait in Perspective." In *James Joyce: Two Decades of Criticism*. Edited by Seon Givens. New York: Vanguard Press, 1948, pp. 132-74.

Kulemeyer, G. *Studien zur Psychologie im neuen englischen Roman*. Bottrop i. w., Postberg, 1933, pp. 12-15.

Kumar, Shiv K. "Bergson and Stephen Dedalus' Aesthetic Theory." *Journal of Aesthetics and Art Criticism*, XVI (Sept., 1957), 124-27.

Kunkel, Frank L. "Beauty in Aquinas and Joyce." *Thought Patterns,* II (1951), 61-69.

Levin, Harry. *James Joyce: A Critical Introduction.* Norfolk: New Directions, 1941, pp. 41-62 and *passim.*

Lind, Ilse Dusoir. "*The Way of All Flesh* and *A Portrait of the Artist as a Young Man:* A Comparison." *Victorian Newsletter,* No. 9 (Spring, 1956), 7-10.

Litz, Walton. "Early Vestiges of Joyce's *Ulysses.*" *PMLA,* LXXI (Mar., 1956), 51-60.

MacGregor, Geddes. "Artistic Theory in James Joyce." *Life and Letters,* LIV (July, 1947), 18-27.

McLuhan, Herbert M. "Joyce, Aquinas, and the Poetic Process." *Renascence,* IV (Autumn, 1951), 3-11.

Magalaner, Marvin. "James Mangan and Joyce's Dedalus Family." *Philological Quarterly,* XXXI (Oct., 1952), 363-71.

——, and Richard M. Kain. *Joyce: The Man, the Work, the Reputation.* New York: New York University Press, 1956, pp. 102-29.

——. *Time of Apprenticeship: The Fiction of Young James Joyce.* London: Abelard-Schuman, 1959, pp. 97-115 and *passim.*

Mason, Ellsworth. "Joyce's Categories." *Sewanee Review,* LXI (Summer, 1953), 427-32.

More, Paul Elmer. *On Being Human.* Princeton: Princeton University Press, 1936, pp. 70-74.

Morin, Edward. "Joyce as Thomist." *Renascence,* IX (Spring, 1957), 127-31.

Morse, J. Mitchell. "Art and Fortitude: Joyce and the Summa Theologica." *James Joyce Review,* I (Feb. 2, 1957), 19-30.

——. "Augustine's Theodicy and Joyce's Aesthetics." *ELH,* XXIV (Mar., 1957), 30-43.

——. *The Sympathetic Alien: James Joyce and Catholicism.* New York: New York University Press, 1959.

Moseley, Virginia D. "James Joyce's 'Graveyard of Boyhood.'" *Renascence,* XIII (Autumn, 1960), 10-20.

Noon, William T., S.J. "James Joyce: Unfacts, Fiction, and Facts." *PMLA,* LXXVI (June, 1961), 254-76.

——. *Joyce and Aquinas.* New Haven: Yale University Press, 1957, pp. 18-59 and *passim.*

O'Connor, Frank. *The Mirror in the Roadway: A Study of the Modern Novel.* New York: Alfred A. Knopf, 1956, pp. 301-08.

O'Faolain, Sean. "Introduction." *A Portrait of the Artist as a Young Man.* By James Joyce. New York: New American Library, 1954.

Pearce, Donald R. "'My Dead King!': The Dinner Quarrel in Joyce's Portrait of the Artist." *Modern Language Notes,* LXVI (Apr., 1951), 249-51.

Prescott, Joseph. "James Joyce: A Study in Words." *PMLA,* LIV (Mar., 1939), 304-07.

———. "James Joyce's Epiphanies." *Modern Language Notes*, LXIV (May, 1949), 346.

———. "James Joyce's *Stephen Hero*." *Journal of English and Germanic Philology*, LIII (Apr., 1954), 214-23. Revised and expanded in *Letteratura Moderne*, VI (Nov.-Dec., 1956), 679-88. This article has had several other printings as well, in a variety of languages.

Redford, Grant H. "The Role of Structure in Joyce's 'Portrait.'" *Modern Fiction Studies*, IV (Spring, 1958), 21-30.

Roberts, John H. "James Joyce: From Religion to Art." *New Humanist*, VII (May-June, 1934), 7-13.

Savage, D. S. *The Withered Branch: Six Studies in the Modern Novel*. London: Eyre & Spottiswoode, 1950, pp. 160-68.

Schorer, Mark. "Technique as Discovery." In *Critiques and Essays on Modern Fiction*. Edited by John Aldridge. New York: Ronald Press, 1952, pp. 75-77.

Schutte, William J. *Joyce and Shakespeare: A Study in the Meaning of Ulysses*. New Haven: Yale University Press, 1957, pp. 80-84.

Schwartz, Edward. "Joyce's Portrait." *Explicator*, XI (Feb., 1953), Item 27.

Seward, Barbara. "The Artist and the Rose." *University of Toronto Quarterly*, XXVI (Jan., 1957), 180-90.

Smidt, Kristian. *James Joyce and the Cultic Use of Fiction*. Oslo Studies in English No. 4. Oxford: Basil Blackwell, 1955, pp. 35-42, 53-61 and *passim*.

Stern, Richard G. "Proust and Joyce Underway: Jean Santeuil and Stephen Hero." *Kenyon Review*, XVIII (Summer, 1956), 486-96.

Stewart, J. I. M. *James Joyce*. Writers and Their Work Series No. 91. London: Longmans, 1957, pp. 15-22.

Strong, L. A. G. *The Sacred River: An Approach to James Joyce*. New York: Pellegrini and Cudahy, 1951, pp 23-27 and *passim*.

Sullivan, Kevin. *Joyce among the Jesuits*. New York: Columbia University Press, 1958.

Sypher, Wylie. "Portrait of the Artist as John Keats." *Virginia Quarterly Review*, XXV (Summer, 1949), 420-28.

Thrane, James R. "Joyce's Sermon on Hell: Its Source and Its Background." *Modern Philology*, LVII (Feb., 1960), 172-98.

Tindall, William York. *A Reader's Guide to James Joyce*. New York: Noonday Press, 1959, pp. 50-100.

———. *James Joyce: His Way of Interpreting the Modern World*. New York: Charles Scribner's Sons, 1950, pp. 16-22 and *passim*.

———. "The Symbolic Novel." *A.D.*, III (Winter, 1952), 56-68.

———. *The Literary Symbol*. New York: Columbia University Press, 1955, pp. 76-86, 239-46 and *passim*.

Van Ghent, Dorothy. *The English Novel: Form and Content*. New York: Rinehart, 1953, pp. 263-76, 463-73.

Waith, Eugene M. "The Calling of Stephen Dedalus." *College English*, XVIII (Feb., 1957), 256-61.

Wells, H. G. "James Joyce." In *New Review Anthology*. Edited by Groff Conklin. New York: Dodge, 1936, pp. 45-48.

Whalley, George. *Poetic Process*. London: Routledge and Kegan Paul, 1953, pp. 16-24.

Woodward, A. G. "Technique and Feeling in James Joyce's *A Portrait of the Artist as a Young Man*." *English Studies in Africa*, IV (Mar., 1961), 39-53.